ALSO BY RACHAEL RAY

Book of Burger

My Year in Meals

WEEK IN A DAY

5 DISHES > 1 DAY

RACHAEL RAY

PHOTOGRAPHS BY FRANCES JANISCH

ATRIA PAPERBACK

NEW YORK   LONDON   TORONTO   SYDNEY   NEW DELHI

ATRIA PAPERBACK
A Division of Simon & Schuster, Inc.
1230 Avenue of the Americas
New York, NY 10020

First Atria Paperback edition October 2013

ATRIA PAPERBACK and colophon are trademarks of Simon & Schuster, Inc.

FOOD NETWORK and associated logos are trademarks of Television Food Network, G.P., and are used under license.

For information about special discounts for bulk purchases, please contact Simon & Schuster Special Sales at 1-866-506-1949 or business@simonandschuster.com.

The Simon & Schuster Speakers Bureau can bring authors to your live event. For more information or to book an event, contact the Simon & Schuster Speakers Bureau at 1-866-248-3049 or visit our website at www.simonspeakers.com.

Designed by Jill Armus

Photographs by Frances Janisch
Food styling by Anne Disrude
Prop styling by Paige Hicks

Manufactured in the United States of America

10   9   8   7   6   5   4   3   2   1

Library of Congress Cataloging-in-Publication Data
Ray, Rachael.
   Week in a day / by Rachael Ray ; photographer, Frances Janisch.
      pages   cm
   1. Make-ahead cooking. 2. Cooking (Leftovers) I. Title.
   TX652.R345   2013
   641.5'52—dc23   2013019302

ISBN 978-1-4516-5975-7
ISBN 978-1-4516-5976-4 (ebook)

CONTENTS

Introduction	x
From a Taco to Morocco	1
The World in a Day	9
What's Cooking	17
You Learn Something New Every Day	24
Holi-Week	32
Thanksgiving Anytime	39
Something for Everyone	47
A Week of Comforts	55
One for All	63
Stick to Your Ribs	71
One-Pot Week	78
Hearty Classics	85
Stew on This	92
Mix & Match	99
Make a Double Batch!	107
Slow Ride	114
It's a Breeze	123
Bold Thinking	130
Multinational Make-Ahead	138
Fresh Start	146
Better Yet	153
Prepare Yourself	160
Meatlovers' Lane	168

Souperstar Suppers	175
Border Bonanza	183
Fall in Love with Fall	190
A Chicken in Every Pot	198
Back to the Grind	205
Double Take	212
Two for One	219
Season's Servings	226
Five Fiesta Favorites	234
Cold Weather Comforts	241
Wintry Mix	248
Noodle This	256
Get Saucy	263
Italian Comfort	270
Amazing Grains	279
Soupercharged	286
Tricks & Treats	293
Game On!	300
Count Your Chickens	307
Thanksgiving Before & After	314
Foundation Recipes	321
1 Grocery Bag, 3 Meals	325
Acknowledgments	343
Index	344

WEEK IN A DAY: AN ATRIA SMART BOOK

Inside *Week in a Day* with Rachael Ray.

You will find tags like the ones below throughout this book. You can scan them to access enhanced digital content. To do so, simply download the free Microsoft Tag app. Then hold your phone's camera a few inches away from the tag and enjoy what comes next. You can also visit pages.simonandschuster.com /weekinadaytags to access this content. If you access content through a mobile device, message and data rates may apply.

Join Rach on a personal tour of her *Week in a Day* set.
Rachael shows you around the *Week in a Day* show set.

Recipe for Creamy Mushrooms & Kale
(Page 72) View a bonus Side Dish recipe from Stick to Your Ribs.

Recipe for Pickled Red Onions
(Page 2) View a bonus Side Dish recipe from From a Taco to Morocco.

Rachael prepares Homemade Steak Sauce
(Page 75) Watch a how-to video from *Rachael Ray's Week in a Day.*

Rachael prepares Pickled Red Onions
(Page 2) Watch a how-to video from *Rachael Ray's Week in a Day.*

Rachael prepares Sausage, Pepper & Onion One-Pot
(Page 81) Watch a how-to video from *Rachael Ray's Week in a Day.*

Rachael prepares Golden Lemon-Olive Chicken
(Page 14) Watch a how-to video from *Rachael Ray's Week in a Day.*

Rachael prepares Nacho-Topped Chili Pot
(Page 84) Watch a how-to video from *Rachael Ray's Week in a Day.*

Recipe for Roasted Sliced Tomatoes
(Page 31) View a bonus Side Dish recipe from You Learn Something New Every Day.

Recipe for Mashed Potatoes with Herbs
(Page 88) View a bonus Side Dish recipe from Hearty Classics.

Recipe for Asparagus
(Page 31) View a bonus Side Dish recipe from You Learn Something New Every Day.

Recipe for Four-Cheese Polenta
(Page 133) View a bonus Side Dish recipe from Bold Thinking.

Recipe for Fruit & Nut Rice Pilaf
(Page 40) View a bonus Side Dish recipe from Thanksgiving Anytime.

Recipe for Cucumber Salad
(Page 133) View a bonus Side Dish recipe from Bold Thinking.

Recipe for Tuna-Stuffed Piquillo Peppers
(Page 149) View a bonus Side Dish recipe from Fresh Start.

Recipe for Thai Cucumbers
(Page 155) View a bonus Side Dish recipe from Better Yet.

Recipe for Puttanesca-Style Panzanella
(Page 159) View a bonus Side Dish recipe from Better Yet.

Recipe for Apple-Cabbage Slaw
(Page 185) View a bonus Side Dish recipe from Border Bonanza.

Recipe for Mashed Sweet Potatoes
(Page 195) View a bonus Side Dish recipe from Fall in Love with Fall.

Recipe for Quick Pickled Onions
(Page 236) View a bonus Side Dish recipe from Five Fiesta Favorites.

Recipe for Chile-Cinnamon Brittle with Mixed Nuts
(Page 298) View a bonus Treat recipe from Tricks & Treats.

Getting ready for your *Week in a Day*
(Page 321) Rachael shares timing and organizational tips for getting the most out of *Week in a Day.*

1 Grocery Bag, 3 Meals: List #1
(Page 326) Scan to view the shopping list for Grocery Bag #1 on your mobile device.

1 Grocery Bag, 3 Meals: List #2
(Page 328) Scan to view the shopping list for Grocery Bag #2 on your mobile device.

1 Grocery Bag, 3 Meals: List #3
(Page 331) Scan to view the shopping list for Grocery Bag #3 on your mobile device.

1 Grocery Bag, 3 Meals: List #4
(Page 333) Scan to view the shopping list for Grocery Bag #4 on your mobile device.

1 Grocery Bag, 3 Meals: List #5
(Page 334) Scan to view the shopping list for Grocery Bag #5 on your mobile device.

1 Grocery Bag, 3 Meals: List #6
(Page 337) Scan to view the shopping list for Grocery Bag #6 on your mobile device.

1 Grocery Bag, 3 Meals: List #7
(Page 338) Scan to view the shopping list for Grocery Bag #7 on your mobile device.

1 Grocery Bag, 3 Meals: List #8
(Page 341) Scan to view the shopping list for Grocery Bag #8 on your mobile device.

Scan here for even more *Week in a Day* recipes!
(Page 358) View Rachael's exclusive bonus recipes not featured in the book.

INTRODUCTION

Week in a Day is a concept for busy foodies with impossible schedules. Like most of my friends and family, I have one day off a week—if I'm lucky. I shop early in the day and then I go home, get organized, separate ingredients, put on some comfy jeans or jammies, open some wine, and then I cook. Sometimes I'll spend five or six hours straight chopping, roasting, and stirring simmering pots. But when I'm done, we have enough food for as many as five nights—a whole workweek—right in the fridge and freezer. When the day is especially long or you're feeling extra exhausted, imagine how comforting it is to know that dinner—your own homemade delicious food—is waiting for you as soon as you walk in. Pop a pot on the stove or throw that casserole into the oven, and by the time you have changed your clothes and checked your e-mails, dinner is served.

Whether you cook two meals or five, the idea of Week in a Day is that you get a leg up on the long week ahead so any night you don't feel like cooking, you already have!

In addition, I have created a special section that makes another fun promise for busy foodies: 1 Grocery Bag, 3 Meals. With a basic pantry and one bag of groceries, you can cook up three delicious, simple suppers. Also, check out the QR codes and bring this book to life with additional content, recipes, tips, and tricks from me to you.

Rach

READ ME FIRST!

Getting home-cooked meals on the table on weeknights can be a real challenge, even with *30 Minute Meals* on your side. This book is about a different strategy, the strategy of make-ahead.

Every recipe in this book was chosen specifically for its make-ahead-ability. Soups, stews, casseroles, pasta sauces—all dishes that not only keep well but often improve when made ahead. As I like to say, "The longer it sets, the better it gets."

Here's how you make this work:

- **Pick the recipes you want to make.** You can choose all of the recipes in one of my suggested menus, or you can choose just a couple of them. Or you can even put together your own set of meals by looking through all the menus in the book.
- **Make a shopping list.** Check the pantry first, then make a list of all the things you still need to get for the recipes.
- **Do the big shop on the day before you cook.**
- **Cook Day:** This is the day when you get it all done. If you follow one of my menus, you'll see that I often start you with a long-cooking dish that can be baking or braising for several hours while you work on the rest of the recipes. Sometimes, I even suggest that the long-cooking dish you start off with be your reward at the end of your Cook Day.
- **Foundation Recipes:** One of my favorite strategies for make-ahead meals is to make a big batch of something that I can use in multiple recipes on my Cook Day. Making a big pot of Basic Poached Chicken (page 322), for example, can yield a whole bunch of recipes, like salads, stews, casseroles, and more.
- **Make-ahead:** Each recipe has instructions for when to stop cooking a dish and how to store it.
- **Night of:** These instructions guide you on how to finish cooking the dish that you've either refrigerated or frozen earlier in the week.

But here's an important note:

If you want to cook any one of the recipes in this book straight through, without stopping to store it as a make-ahead, just ignore the **Make-ahead/Night of** sections and keep on cooking!

WEEK 01

FROM A TACO TO MOROCCO

GLOBE-SPANNING COMFORT
FOOD, ALL MADE AT HOME,
AND IN JUST ONE DAY

DISH
1
BRAISED
PORK
TACOS
PAGE 2

DISH
2
CRAB CAKE
MAC 'N'
CHEESE
PAGE 4

DISH
3
MOROCCAN
MEAT LOAF WITH
LEMON-HONEY
GRAVY
PAGE 5

DISH
4
RATATOUILLE
WITH POACHED
EGGS & GARLIC
CROUTONS
PAGE 6

DISH
5
PORK
RAGU
PAGE 8

Braised Pork Tacos

Although you could have this as a make-ahead dish because it takes 3 hours to cook, you might want to have it as your reward on **Cook Day** instead. The pork shoulder that gets braised here is also used to make a Pork Ragu (page 8). SERVES 4

1 (4- to 5-pound) boneless **pork shoulder** (pork butt)
Salt and **pepper**
2 tablespoons **vegetable oil**
2 tablespoons **EVOO**
2 **onions**, cut into wedges, root end attached
4 large cloves **garlic**, smashed
1½ teaspoons chopped **oregano** leaves
1 **fresh red chile**, thinly sliced
2 fresh **bay leaves**
1 (12-ounce) bottle Mexican **beer**
2 cups **chicken stock**
Juice of 4 **oranges** (about 2 cups)
Pickled Red Onions (see QR code below)
1 **chipotle chile in adobo**, seeded and finely chopped, plus 1 tablespoon adobo sauce
Juice of 2 **limes**
16 **flour** or **corn tortillas**
1 cup drained **pickled jalapeño** slices or **banana pepper** rings
¼ head **red cabbage**, shredded
1 cup crumbled **queso fresco** or 2 cups shredded **Monterey Jack cheese**

Preheat the oven to 325°F. Season the pork generously with salt and pepper and let sit at room temperature for 30 minutes.

Pat the pork dry with a paper towel. In a large Dutch oven or heavy-bottomed pot, heat the vegetable oil (2 turns of the pan) over high heat. Put the pork in the pot and evenly brown the meat all over, 10 to 12 minutes. Transfer the pork to a plate.

Turn the heat down to medium-high and add the EVOO (2 turns of the pan) to the Dutch oven. Add the onions, garlic, oregano, red chile, bay leaves, and salt and pepper and cook for 7 to 8 minutes. Deglaze with the beer. Stir in the chicken stock and orange juice. Return the pork to the pot (the liquid should come about two-thirds of the way up the meat) and bring to a simmer. Cover and put the pork in the oven. Cook until the meat is very tender, 2½ to 3 hours, turning the meat halfway through cooking.

While the pork is cooking, prepare the pickled red onions.

Transfer the pork to a cutting board and tent with foil to keep warm. When cool enough to handle, pull the meat apart with 2 forks. Set aside one-third of the shredded pork for the Pork Ragu (page 8).

Simmer the braising liquid over medium heat until reduced by half. Remove the bay leaves. Add the chipotle, adobo sauce, and lime juice. Stir in the shredded pork.

[**Make-ahead:** Let cool and refrigerate.]

[**Night of:** Return to room temp before reheating gently over medium-low heat.]

When ready to serve, char the tortillas over an open flame and keep warm in a tortilla warmer or covered with a towel.

To serve, put the pork on a platter and garnish with pickled onions and pickled jalapeño slices. Serve with the shredded cabbage, crumbled cheese, and charred tortillas for wrapping.

Recipe for Pickled Red Onions
View a bonus Side Dish recipe.

Watch Rachael prepare Pickled Red Onions.

Crab Cake Mac 'n' Cheese

A smashup of two great comfort foods: spicy crab cakes marry mac 'n' cheese. I like to use a crazy corkscrew hollow pasta called cavatappi for this. SERVES 4 TO 6

Salt and pepper

1 pound cavatappi, conchiglie, or elbow macaroni

2 tablespoons EVOO

6 tablespoons (¾ stick) butter

3 ribs celery with leafy tops, finely chopped

1 medium onion, finely chopped

½ small red bell pepper, finely chopped

3 or 4 cloves garlic, finely chopped

1 fresh bay leaf

2 tablespoons chopped fresh thyme leaves

1 tablespoon grated lemon zest

12 ounces fresh lump crabmeat, picked through for bits of shell and flaked

1 tablespoon Rachael Ray Seafood Seasoning or Old Bay seasoning

3 tablespoons flour

2½ cups milk

Freshly grated nutmeg

1 tablespoon Dijon mustard

5 ounces (about 1 rounded cup) grated sharp white cheddar cheese

5 ounces (about 1 rounded cup) shredded Gruyère or Swiss cheese

3 tablespoons hot sauce (I like Frank's RedHot)

1 cup panko bread crumbs

A generous handful of flat-leaf parsley, finely chopped

½ cup grated Parmigiano-Reggiano cheese

Bring a large pot of water to a boil over medium heat. Salt the water and cook the pasta for 3 to 4 minutes (it will be undercooked). Drain well, let cool, and transfer to a large bowl.

Meanwhile, in a medium saucepan, heat the EVOO (2 turns of the pan) and 1 tablespoon of the butter over medium to medium-high heat. Add the celery, onion, bell pepper, garlic, bay leaf, thyme, lemon zest, and salt and pepper. Cook until the vegetables are tender, 6 to 8 minutes. Add the crabmeat and season liberally with the seafood seasoning. Stir to combine, then remove from the heat. Discard the bay leaf.

In a medium saucepan, melt 3 tablespoons of the butter over low heat. Whisk in the flour. Cook for 1 minute, then whisk in the milk and bring to a bubble. Season the sauce with salt, pepper, and nutmeg and cook for a few minutes, until the mixture coats the back of a spoon. Add the mustard, cheddar, and Gruyère and stir in a figure-8 until melted.

Add the cheese sauce and vegetable-crab mixture to the pasta and transfer the mixture to individual baking crocks or a large casserole.

[Make-ahead: Cover and refrigerate.]

[Night of: You can bake the casserole straight from the fridge.] Preheat the oven to 375°F.

In a small skillet, melt the remaining 2 tablespoons butter over low heat and add the hot sauce. Warm through, then add the panko and toss to evenly coat the crumbs in the sauce. Let cool, then toss in the parsley and Parm.

Place the crocks or casserole on a baking sheet to catch any drips. If making on Cook Day, top the mac 'n' cheese with the spicy crumb mixture and bake until browned and heated through, about 10 minutes. If this is a make-ahead, bake the casserole for 30 to 35 minutes to heat through, then top with the crumbs and bake for 10 minutes longer to brown them.

Moroccan Meat Loaf with Lemon-Honey Gravy

I like to shake it up when it comes to classic dishes, like good ol' meat loaf. So we're going to add a lot of exotic flavors to it. **Suggested side:** Zucchini Couscous (recipe follows). SERVES 4

1½ pounds **ground lamb** or **chicken**
1 small **onion**, peeled
2 cloves **garlic**, finely chopped
⅔ cup **panko bread crumbs**
2 tablespoons **EVOO**
1 large **egg**
Grated zest and juice of 2 **lemons**
¼ cup finely chopped **green olives**
1 tablespoon ground **cumin**
1 teaspoon ground **turmeric** (only if using ground chicken)
2 pinches of ground **cinnamon**
Leaves from a handful of **flat-leaf parsley**, finely chopped
A handful of fresh **mint** leaves, finely chopped
2 tablespoons **butter**
2 tablespoons **flour**
1 cup **chicken stock**
1 tablespoon **Worcestershire sauce**
¼ cup **honey**
Salt and **pepper**

Preheat the oven to 325°F. Line a rimmed baking sheet with parchment paper.

Place the meat in a medium bowl. Using a box grater or handheld flat grater, grate the onion directly over the meat. Add the garlic, panko, EVOO, egg, half the lemon zest, and half the lemon juice. Mix to combine. Add the olives, cumin, turmeric (only if using chicken), cinnamon, parsley, and mint. Combine well. Form the mixture into 4 oval loaves and place on the baking sheet. Bake until golden brown, 35 to 40 minutes.

[**Make-ahead:** Let the meat loaves cool and refrigerate.]
[**Night of:** Return the meat loaves to room temp.]

In a deep skillet, melt the butter over medium to medium-high heat. Whisk in the flour, then add the chicken stock, Worcestershire, honey, and salt and pepper. Slide the meat loaves into the sauce. Cover and bring to a bubble, then reduce the heat to low and reheat the meat loaves. Transfer the meat loaves to a serving plate. Return the pan to the heat, stir in the remaining lemon juice and zest, and increase the heat to high. As soon as the sauce becomes syrupy, 1 to 2 minutes, drizzle it over the meat loaves.

Zucchini Couscous SERVES 4

2 tablespoons **butter**
2 cloves **garlic**, finely chopped
½ pound **zucchini**, cut into small cubes
Salt and **pepper**
1½ cups **chicken stock**
1½ cups **couscous**
A handful of fresh **mint** leaves, finely chopped

In a medium saucepan, melt the butter over medium heat. Add the garlic and stir to combine. Stir in the zucchini, season with salt and pepper, and cook for 5 minutes. Add the stock and bring to a bubble. Add the couscous and mint. Turn off the heat and cover the pan. Let stand for 5 minutes, then fluff with a fork.

Ratatouille with Poached Eggs & Garlic Croutons

If you want a slightly sweeter stew, go for the San Marzano tomatoes, but for a slightly smokier flavor, choose the fire-roasted tomatoes. SERVES 4

4 tablespoons (½ stick) **butter**

4 cloves **garlic**: 2 cloves finely chopped, 2 thinly sliced

8 slices (1 inch thick) **baguette**

2 teaspoons dried **herbes de Provence** or **dried thyme**

½ cup shredded or grated **Parmigiano-Reggiano cheese**

Salt and **pepper**

1 **eggplant** (1½ pounds), cut into ½-inch cubes

2 **red bell peppers**

2 tablespoons **EVOO**

1 pound small **zucchini**, cut into ½-inch cubes

2 medium **onions**, cut into ½-inch cubes

Leaves from 2 sprigs fresh **rosemary**, finely chopped

1 (28- or 32-ounce) can whole **San Marzano tomatoes** or **fire-roasted diced tomatoes**

1 tablespoon aged **balsamic vinegar**

4 extra-large or jumbo **eggs**

A handful of fresh **basil** leaves, torn

Preheat the oven to 375°F. Line a baking sheet with parchment paper.

In a small saucepan, melt the butter over low heat. Add the chopped garlic and let it bubble for 2 minutes.

In a medium bowl, combine the bread, 1 teaspoon of the herbes de Provence, and the Parm. Drizzle the garlic butter over the bread and toss to coat. Arrange the croutons on the baking sheet and bake until golden and evenly browned, about 20 minutes. Remove from the oven and let cool.

[**Make-ahead:** Store the croutons in an airtight container in a cool place.]

Salt the eggplant and drain it in a colander for 30 minutes.

Meanwhile, char the bell peppers all over on the stovetop over a gas flame or under the broiler with the oven door ajar to let steam escape. Place the blackened peppers in a bowl and cover tightly. When cool enough to handle, rub off the skins with a paper towel, then halve, seed, and dice the peppers.

In a Dutch oven, heat the EVOO (2 turns of the pan) over medium-high heat. Add the eggplant, zucchini, onions, sliced garlic, rosemary, the remaining 1 teaspoon herbes de Provence, and salt and pepper. Cover the pot and cook to soften the vegetables, about 15 minutes, stirring occasionally. Add the tomatoes (if using whole tomatoes, break them up with a potato masher) and half a tomato can of water. Stir in the roasted peppers and bring to a boil over medium heat. Reduce the heat and simmer for 15 minutes to concentrate the flavors.

[**Make-ahead:** Let cool and refrigerate.]

[**Night of:** Return the ratatouille to room temp before reheating gently over medium heat, covered.]

Stir in the balsamic vinegar. Make 4 nests or wells in the ratatouille and crack an egg into each nest. Cover and cook the eggs to the desired doneness, 2 to 5 minutes. Scoop the ratatouille and eggs into shallow bowls and top with croutons and torn basil.

Pork Ragu

Suggested side: Serve the ragu over 1 pound pappardelle pasta cooked al dente, or 1 cup quick-cooking polenta, cooked according to package directions. SERVES 4

3 tablespoons **EVOO**

1 **carrot**, finely chopped

2 ribs **celery** from the heart with leafy tops, finely chopped

1 **onion**, finely chopped

3 or 4 cloves **garlic**, finely chopped

1 fresh **bay leaf**

Salt and **pepper**

¼ cup **tomato paste**

1 cup dry **white** or medium-bodied **red wine**

2 cups **chicken stock**

¾ to 1 pound **cooked shredded pork shoulder** (from Braised Pork Tacos, page 2)

Pinch of ground **cloves**

⅔ cup **milk**

Shredded **Parmigiano-Reggiano**, or, for more tang, grated **Pecorino Romano cheese**

A handful of finely chopped **parsley** leaves

Heat a Dutch oven or large heavy-bottomed pot over medium-high heat. Add the EVOO (3 turns of the pan), then the carrot, celery, onion, and garlic. Stir in the bay leaf and season with salt and pepper. Cook the vegetables until softened, 5 to 6 minutes. Add the tomato paste and stir for 1 minute. Add the wine and cook for another minute. Stir in the stock and bring the sauce to a simmer. Add the pork and cloves. When the sauce returns to a simmer, add the milk and reduce the heat to low to thicken the sauce a bit.

[**Make-ahead:** Let the sauce cool and refrigerate.]

[**Night of:** Return the sauce to room temp, then reheat over medium-low heat. Add a splash of stock or water to thin it if necessary.]

Let the sauce mellow while you cook the pasta or polenta. Remove the bay leaf before serving the sauce tossed with pasta ribbons or atop bowls of creamy polenta. Garnish with lots of cheese and parsley.

WEEK 02

THE WORLD IN A DAY

GOOD OLD-FASHIONED AMERICAN
DISHES SHARE THE STAGE WITH SOME
INTERNATIONAL FAVORITES.

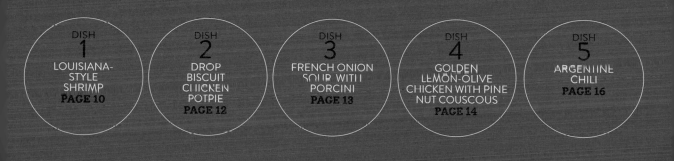

DISH
1
LOUISIANA-
STYLE
SHRIMP
PAGE 10

DISH
2
DROP
BISCUIT
CHICKEN
POTPIE
PAGE 12

DISH
3
FRENCH ONION
SOUP WITH
PORCINI
PAGE 13

DISH
4
GOLDEN
LEMON-OLIVE
CHICKEN WITH PINE
NUT COUSCOUS
PAGE 14

DISH
5
ARGENTINE
CHILI
PAGE 16

Louisiana-Style Shrimp

The sauce base for this dish gets made ahead, but you should buy the shrimp no earlier than the day before you're going to serve this. **Suggested side:** Brown or white long-grain rice cooked according to package directions, but use chicken stock for the liquid and stir in some chopped scallions. SERVES 4

2 tablespoons **EVOO**

½ pound **andouille sausage**, diced or crumbled

3 tablespoons **butter**

1 **green bell pepper**, chopped

1 **onion**, chopped

3 or 4 small ribs **celery**, chopped

4 cloves **garlic**, chopped

1 **fresh red chile**, seeded and finely chopped

2 tablespoons finely chopped fresh **thyme**

2 fresh **bay leaves**

1 tablespoon **sweet paprika** (smoked or regular)

2 tablespoons **flour**

1 (12-ounce) bottle **beer** (I used Abita from Louisiana)

1 cup **chicken** or **seafood stock**

1 tablespoon **Worcestershire sauce**

Hot sauce

1½ pounds medium-large **shrimp**, peeled and deveined

Sliced **scallions**, for garnish (optional)

In a Dutch oven or deep skillet, heat 1 tablespoon of the EVOO (1 turn of the pan) over medium-high heat. Add the sausage and cook until browned. Remove the sausage from the pan and drain on paper towels. Add the remaining 1 tablespoon EVOO (1 turn of the pan) and the butter to the pan and let the butter melt into the oil. Stir in the bell pepper, onion, celery, garlic, chile, thyme, and bay leaves and cook until tender, 7 to 8 minutes. Sprinkle in the paprika and stir. Add the flour and stir for 1 minute more. Stir in the beer and cook down for 2 minutes. Stir in the stock and Worcestershire, reduce the heat to low, and simmer for about 3 minutes to combine the flavors. Stir in hot sauce to taste. Add the reserved browned sausage.

[**Make-ahead:** Let cool and refrigerate.]

[**Night of:** Return the sauce to room temp before reheating gently over medium heat.]

Bring the sauce to a low boil over medium heat, then stir in the shrimp. Cover and cook until the shrimp are pink and firm, 3 to 5 minutes. Remove the bay leaves and transfer the shrimp mixture to a serving bowl. Garnish with scallions, if desired.

Drop Biscuit Chicken Potpie

Store-bought biscuit mix is definitely a go-to ingredient for me. I often add fresh herbs to the mix and sometimes coarsely ground black pepper. SERVES 4 TO 6

2 tablespoons **EVOO**
16 **button mushrooms**, sliced or quartered
2 medium **carrots**, diced
1 starchy **potato**, peeled and chopped
3 or 4 small ribs **celery**, chopped
1 medium **onion**, chopped
Salt and **pepper**
4 tablespoons (½ stick) **butter**
3 tablespoons **flour**
4 cups **chicken stock**, homemade (page 322) or store-bought
Leaves from 3 or 4 sprigs fresh **tarragon**, chopped
1 rounded tablespoon **Dijon mustard**
1½ pounds diced or shredded **Poached Chicken** (page 322); see Note
1 cup frozen **green peas**
1 (8-ounce) box **buttermilk biscuit mix** (I use Jiffy)
Finely chopped fresh **dill**, **chives**, or **parsley**, for the biscuits

In a deep skillet, heat the EVOO (2 turns of the pan) over medium heat. Add the mushrooms and cook until tender but not brown, stirring frequently, about 8 minutes. Add the carrots, potato, celery, onion, and salt and pepper. Cover the pan and cook for 10 minutes more, stirring occasionally.

Meanwhile, in a saucepan, melt the butter over medium heat. Whisk in the flour and cook for 1 minute. Whisk in the stock and cook until thick enough to lightly coat the back of a spoon. Stir in the tarragon and Dijon mustard.

Stir the sauce into the vegetables. Add the chicken and peas and transfer the mixture to a deep 3-quart casserole.

[**Make-ahead:** Let cool and refrigerate.]

[**Night of:** Let the casserole come to room temp while you preheat the oven.]

Preheat the oven to 375°F.

Mix up the biscuit dough for drop biscuits (not rolled biscuits) and stir in some herbs for flavor.

If making on **Cook Day**, top the chicken with the biscuit dough and place the casserole on a baking sheet. Bake until the biscuits are lightly golden and crispy at the edges, about 10 minutes. If this is a make-ahead, bake the chicken for 20 minutes to heat through, then top with the biscuit dough and bake for 10 minutes longer, until the biscuits are golden.

Note: Make the following changes to the Basic Poached Chicken (page 322): Use a 5- to 6-pound chicken; increase the celery to 4 and onion to 2. Let the chicken cool in the broth. Strain the broth, return to the pot, and reduce over low heat until you have 2 quarts of strongly flavored stock, about 1 hour (depending on how much you started with). Skin and pull the chicken meat as described in the basic recipe.

French Onion Soup with Porcini

For a more dramatic presentation, you can ladle the soup into individual ovenproof soup crocks (like traditional French onion soup crocks), top them with the (not-yet-melted) cheese toasts, and place them in the oven to melt the cheese. SERVES 4

8 tablespoons (1 stick) **butter**
4 large **onions**, very thinly sliced
1 teaspoon dried **thyme**
Salt and **pepper**
1 ounce **dried porcini mushrooms**
¼ to ⅓ cup **dry sherry**
1 cup **white wine**
Small herb bundle: **flat-leaf parsley**, a few sprigs fresh **sage**, and fresh **bay leaves**, tied together with kitchen twine
8 cups **beef stock**
8 thick slices (½ inch) **baguette**
1 large clove **garlic**, peeled and halved
1½ cups grated **Gruyère cheese**
½ cup grated **Parmigiano-Reggiano cheese**

In a large Dutch oven, melt 6 tablespoons of the butter over medium heat. Add the onions, thyme, and salt and pepper. Cook, stirring occasionally, until the onions caramelize, 40 to 45 minutes.

Meanwhile, in a small saucepan, combine the mushrooms and water to cover. Bring to a boil over high heat, reduce to a simmer, and cook to soften, 10 to 15 minutes.

Deglaze the Dutch oven with the sherry. Stir in the wine.

Transfer the mushrooms with a slotted spoon to a cutting board and coarsely chop. Add the porcini to the onions. Carefully pour in the mushroom liquid, leaving the last few spoonfuls in the pan as grit may have settled there.

Add the herb bundle and beef stock to the soup and simmer for 30 to 45 minutes.

[Make-ahead: Let cool and refrigerate.]

[Night of: Return the soup to room temp before reheating gently over medium heat while you prepare the croutons.]

Preheat the oven to 425°F. Place a cooling rack over a baking sheet.

Spread out the bread on the rack and bake until deep golden brown. Butter the toasts using the remaining 2 tablespoons butter and liberally rub them with the cut garlic. Top with the cheeses and return them to the oven until the cheese is melted and bubbling.

Ladle the soup into serving bowls and serve with the cheese toasts.

Golden Lemon-Olive Chicken with Pine Nut Couscous

Moroccan dishes (like this one) are filled with spices that are usually balanced with both citrus and something sweet, like dried fruit or honey. I combined those two ideas by using Meyer lemons, which are sweeter than traditional lemons. SERVES 4

2 tablespoons **EVOO**

3 medium **onions**, peeled, each cut into 6 wedges, root end intact

4 fresh **bay leaves**

4 large cloves **garlic**, smashed

Salt and **pepper**

1 cup good-quality large **green olives**, pitted

5 tablespoons **butter**

4 **Meyer lemons** or **organic lemons**: 2 thinly sliced, 1 zested on a rasp-style grater and juiced, 1 juiced

A generous pinch of **saffron threads**

3 tablespoons **flour**

4 cups **chicken stock**, homemade (page 322) or store-bought

1½ teaspoons ground **turmeric**

1½ teaspoons ground **cumin**

A pinch of ground **cinnamon**

1½ to 2 pounds diced or shredded **Poached Chicken** (see Note, page 12)

¼ cup **pine nuts**

1½ cups **couscous**

¼ cup finely chopped fresh **mint**

¼ cup finely chopped fresh **flat-leaf parsley**

In a Dutch oven or deep skillet, heat the EVOO (2 turns of the pan) over medium-high heat. Add the onions, bay leaves, garlic, and salt and pepper. Stir for 3 to 4 minutes, then cover the pan and sweat the onions for 3 to 4 minutes more. Uncover the pot and stir in the olives.

Meanwhile, in a deep medium skillet, heat 1 tablespoon of the butter over medium to medium-high heat. Working in 2 batches, add the sliced lemons and gently brown. As they brown, add them to the onions and olives.

Add 3 tablespoons of the butter to the skillet and let it melt. Add the saffron and lemon zest and stir for 1 minute. Whisk in the flour and cook for a minute more. Whisk in 2½ cups of the chicken stock, the turmeric, cumin, and cinnamon and let thicken for a couple of minutes. Stir in the lemon juice and reduce the heat to low.

Add the sauce to the onions, then add the chicken and gently stir to combine.

[Make-ahead: Let cool and refrigerate.]

[Night of: Return the chicken to room temp before reheating gently over medium heat.]

In a medium saucepan, melt the remaining 1 tablespoon butter over medium heat. Add the pine nuts and gently toast them to light golden brown. Stir in the remaining 1½ cups chicken stock and bring to a boil. Stir in the couscous, turn off the heat, cover, and let stand for 5 minutes. Add the mint and parsley and fluff the couscous with a fork. Spoon the couscous into a serving bowl.

Transfer the chicken mixture to a serving bowl or platter, remove the bay leaves, and serve with the couscous.

Watch Rachael prepare Golden Lemon-Olive Chicken.

Argentine Chili

I went to Argentina once, and those guys are meat *obsessed*. They're also obsessed with chimichurri, that great herby, vinegary condiment. It's on restaurant tables in that country the same way we have bottles of ketchup. So this is my bow to those two Argentinean passions. **Suggested side:** Warm, crusty bread. SERVES 4

1 tablespoon **EVOO**
2 pounds lean **ground sirloin**
4 to 5 ounces **Spanish chorizo**, casings removed, chopped
1 **onion**, finely chopped
4 large cloves **garlic**, very thinly sliced
2 small **fresh red chiles**, very thinly sliced
Salt and **pepper**
Leaves from 1 sprig fresh **oregano**, chopped, or 1 teaspoon dried
1 rounded tablespoon **smoked sweet paprika**
1 rounded tablespoon ground **arbol** or **ancho chile powder**
2 tablespoons **tomato paste**
2 cups **beef stock**
Chimichurri (recipe follows)
Finely chopped **tomatoes**, for garnish (optional)

Heat a Dutch oven or large heavy-bottomed pot over high heat. Add the EVOO (1 turn of the pan). Pat the beef dry, add to the pan, and cook until crispy, breaking it up into crumbles as it browns, 8 to 10 minutes. Add the chorizo and render the fat a bit. Add the onion, garlic, and chiles. Season with salt and lots of pepper. Cook until the onion is softened, 5 to 6 minutes. Add the oregano, paprika, and chile powder. Add the tomato paste and stir for 1 minute. Stir in the stock, reduce the heat, and simmer for a few minutes to combine the flavors.

[Make-ahead: Let cool and refrigerate or freeze.]

[Night of: Return the chili to room temp before reheating gently over medium-low heat with a little extra stock or water to loosen it up.]

Transfer the hot chili to serving bowls and top with chimichurri sauce and tomatoes (if desired).

Chimichurri MAKES ABOUT 1½ CUPS

1 cup packed chopped mixed fresh herbs: **parsley**, **thyme**, **rosemary**, **oregano**, **basil**, and/or **cilantro**
2 large **shallots** or 1 small **onion**, chopped
1 large clove **garlic**, grated or finely chopped
3 tablespoons **red wine vinegar**
¼ to ⅓ cup **EVOO**
Salt and **pepper**

In a food processor, combine the herbs, shallots, garlic, vinegar, and EVOO. Season with salt and pepper. Pulse-process until finely chopped but still a loose sauce. Can be made fresh or refrigerated for a few days in an airtight container.

WEEK 03

WHAT'S COOKING

FIVE MEALS THAT WILL FILL YOUR
KITCHEN WITH THE KIND OF
ENTICING AROMAS THAT
MAKE PEOPLE ASK, "MMMMM,
WHAT ARE YOU COOKING??"

DISH
1
ROAST CHICKEN
DINNER WITH
ROASTED
GARLIC
PAGE 18

DISH
2
PORTOBELLO-
PORCINI
CACCIATORE
PAGE 19

DISH
3
ROAST CHICKEN
ENCHILADAS SUIZAS
STACKED
CASSEROLE
PAGE 20

DISH
4
SAUSAGE &
BROCCOLI
RABE STOUP
PAGE 22

DISH
5
RICE PILAF &
CHORIZO
CASSEROLE
PAGE 23

Roast Chicken Dinner with Roasted Garlic

Plan to have this meal on **Cook Day.** Two chickens get roasted, one for this dish and a second for Roast Chicken Enchiladas Suizas Stacked Casserole (page 20). **Suggested side:** Crusty, warm bread for mopping. SERVES 4

2 whole **chickens** (4 to 5 pounds each)

4 tablespoons chopped fresh **thyme**

Salt and **pepper**

8 tablespoons (1 stick) **butter,** softened

12 small **potatoes,** halved

4 small **onions,** peeled and quartered, root end intact

EVOO, for liberal drizzling

2 heads **garlic,** tops cut off to expose the cloves, plus 4 cloves garlic, smashed

Leaves from 6 sprigs fresh **rosemary,** finely chopped

1 tablespoon **fennel seeds** or **fennel pollen**

1 **lemon,** halved

2 **limes,** halved

1 (9-ounce) box frozen **artichoke hearts,** thawed, drained well, and halved

Preheat the oven to 475°F.

Season the chickens inside and out with the thyme and liberal amounts of salt and pepper. Rub the outside of each bird with 4 tablespoons of the butter. You're now going to set up 2 separate roasting pans with different ingredients and flavors. The birds will be roasted at more or less the same time, though one goes a little longer because of the vegetables involved.

Chicken #1: Put the potatoes and onions in a roasting pan and liberally drizzle with EVOO and salt and pepper. Dress the heads of garlic with EVOO and season with salt and pepper. Press the cut sides of the garlic heads into the rosemary so that some adheres to the garlic. Sprinkle the remainder of the rosemary over the potatoes and onions, and toss everything gently to coat. Place the chicken over the vegetables. Sprinkle the chicken with fennel seeds or pollen. Squeeze the juice of the lemon over the chicken, then put the lemon halves in the cavity of the bird along with 2 smashed cloves garlic. Tie the legs together with kitchen twine. Add the dressed garlic heads to the pan.

Chicken #2: Put the second chicken in a roasting pan and squeeze the lime juice over it, then stuff the lime halves into the bird along with the remaining 2 smashed cloves garlic. Tie the legs.

Roast both birds for 15 minutes. Baste with pan juices, reduce the temperature to 375°F, and roast for 45 minutes. Remove Chicken #2 and set it aside. Add the artichokes to Chicken #1, mixing them in with the potatoes, and continue roasting 15 to 30 minutes.

Meanwhile, when Chicken #2 is cool enough, pull the meat into small pieces. Discard the skin and bones. Set the chicken and juices aside for Roast Chicken Enchiladas Suizas (page 20).

Let Chicken #1 rest for 10 minutes before carving. Arrange on a serving platter with the vegetables. Pour the pan juices over the chicken and vegetables (de-fat the juices, if you'd like). When ready to serve, divide the roasted garlic among the plates.

Heads-up: When you're using kitchen twine at the same time as you're handling raw chicken, always precut the pieces you'll need so you don't touch the ball of twine with chicken-y hands.

Portobello-Porcini Cacciatore

I wanted to make this a meat-free meal, so I needed to bump up the portobellos to give it a really meaty flavor. When you're cooking mushrooms: Don't salt the mushrooms until after you've browned them, because the salt pulls the liquid out of the mushrooms and makes it hard to brown them. SERVES 4 TO 6

1 ounce **dried porcini mushrooms**
¼ cup **EVOO**
6 **portobello mushroom caps**, gills scraped, sliced
2 tablespoons chopped fresh **thyme**
1 **fresh red chile**, thinly sliced
4 large cloves **garlic**, very thinly sliced
2 **cubanelle peppers**, very thinly sliced
1 medium **red** or **yellow onion**, quartered and thinly sliced
Salt and **pepper**
1 cup dry **white wine**
1 (28- or 32-ounce) can **San Marzano tomatoes** (look for DOP on the label)
A few leaves fresh **basil**, torn, plus more shredded, for garnish
1 pound **whole wheat penne** or **rigatoni**
2 tablespoons **butter**
Grated **Pecorino Romano cheese**, for topping and serving

In a small saucepan, combine the porcini and water to cover. Bring to a boil over medium heat, reduce to a simmer, and cook to soften, 10 to 15 minutes. Scoop out the mushrooms and chop. Reserve the soaking liquid.

Meanwhile, in a Dutch oven, heat the EVOO (4 turns of the pan) over medium-high heat. Add the portobellos and cook, stirring occasionally, until dark and tender, 12 to 15 minutes. Add the thyme, chile, garlic, cubanelles, onion, and salt and pepper. Cook to soften the onion, 8 to 10 minutes. Deglaze the pan with the wine.

Add the porcini, then carefully pour in the soaking liquid, leaving the last few spoonfuls in the pan as grit may have settled there. Stir in the tomatoes, breaking them up with a potato masher, then add the basil. Simmer for 20 minutes to thicken up.

[**Make-ahead:** Let cool and refrigerate.]

[**Night of:** Return the sauce to room temp before reheating gently over medium heat, stirring occasionally, while you cook the pasta.]

Bring a large pot of water to a boil. Salt the water and cook the pasta al dente. Drain the pasta and return it to the pot. Add the butter and half the sauce, tossing with tongs 1 or 2 minutes for the flavors to absorb.

Serve in shallow bowls with more mushroom cacciatore on top. Garnish with lots of grated cheese and some shredded basil. Pass more cheese at the table.

Roast Chicken Enchiladas Suizas Stacked Casserole

In Mexico, if a dish is labeled *suiza* (which means Swiss), then there's got to be some cream involved. In this case it's tangy Mexican *crema*, but you could sub in crème fraîche or sour cream. SERVES 4

4 medium **poblano chiles**
2 tablespoons **EVOO**
1 fresh **jalapeño chile**, chopped
2 medium **onions**, chopped
4 cloves **garlic**, finely chopped
12 medium-large **tomatillos**, husked, rinsed, and quartered
2 small handfuls of fresh **cilantro** leaves
1 teaspoon ground **cumin**
2 teaspoons **honey**
4 cups **chicken stock**
Salt and **pepper**
Juice of 1 **lime**
12 (6-inch) **flour tortillas** or 16 (5-inch) **corn tortillas**, softened over a flame or in a dry skillet
2 pounds pulled or shredded **roast chicken** (page 18)
1 cup **Mexican crema**
1½ cups shredded **Swiss cheese**
1½ cups shredded **Monterey Jack cheese**
Red onion rings, for garnish (optional)

Preheat the broiler to high. Arrange the poblanos on a baking sheet and broil to char the skin an all sides, 10 to 12 minutes, with the oven door ajar to let steam escape. They can also be easily charred on the stovetop over an open flame if you have gas burners. Put the poblanos in a bowl and cover tightly. When cool enough to handle, rub off the skins with a paper towel, then seed and coarsely chop the poblanos.

In a deep skillet, heat the EVOO (2 turns of the pan) over medium-high heat. Add the jalapeño, onions, and garlic and cook until the onions soften, about 5 minutes.

Put the tomatillos, chopped poblanos, and half of the cilantro in a food processor. Process until an almost smooth sauce forms, about 1 minute. Pour the sauce into the skillet and stir to combine. Stir in the cumin, honey, stock, and salt and pepper. Reduce the heat and simmer about 20 minutes to concentrate the flavors. Add the lime juice and turn off the heat.

Pour a thin layer of sauce into the bottom of a 9 by 13-inch baking dish. Layer in 3 flour tortillas or 4 corn tortillas, then top with some chicken, dot with sauce and small spoonfuls of crema, and sprinkle with a little Swiss and Jack cheeses. Repeat for 2 more layers.

[**Make-ahead:** Let cool, cover, and refrigerate.]

[**Night of:** Return the casserole to room temp while you preheat the oven.]

Preheat the oven to 375°F.

Put the baking dish on a baking sheet and bake, uncovered, until heated through and bubbling on top, 40 to 50 minutes.

Serve the casserole garnished with red onion rings, if desired.

Sausage & Broccoli Rabe Stoup

This stoup (thicker than soup, thinner than stew) is a real comfort food combo for my family: sausage + broccoli rabe. **Suggested side:** Crusty bread, such as ciabatta, for mopping. SERVES 4

Salt
1 large bunch **broccoli rabe** (1¼ to 1½ pounds), cut into 1½- to 2-inch lengths
1 tablespoon **EVOO**
1¼ to 1½ pounds bulk **Italian sweet** or **hot sausage**, or links, casings removed
1 **onion**, chopped
3 or 4 cloves **garlic**, finely chopped or very thinly sliced
1 **fresh red chile**, very thinly sliced
2 tablespoons chopped fresh **thyme**
1 tablespoon grated **lemon** zest
Freshly grated **nutmeg**
6 cups **chicken stock**
¾ cup **orecchiette pasta**
Grated **pecorino** or **Parmigiano-Reggiano cheese**, for serving

In a medium pot, bring a few inches of water to a boil over medium heat. Salt the water. Add the broccoli rabe and cook for 4 to 5 minutes to reduce the bitterness. Cold-shock in ice water. Drain very well.

In a soup pot or Dutch oven, heat the EVOO (1 turn of the pan) over medium-high heat. Add the sausage and cook, breaking it into crumbles as it browns, 7 to 8 minutes. Add the onion, garlic, and chile and cook a few minutes more. Stir in the thyme and lemon zest. Add the broccoli rabe and season with a few grates of nutmeg. Stir in the stock and 2 cups water and bring to a boil. Simmer a few minutes to combine the flavors.

[**Make-ahead:** Let cool and refrigerate.]

[**Night of:** Return the stoup to room temp before reheating gently over medium-low heat; add a little extra water or stock if necessary to loosen it up and give the pasta something to cook into.]

Bring the stoup to a low boil. Add the pasta and cook al dente, about 10 minutes.

Ladle the stoup into shallow bowls and garnish with grated cheese.

Rice Pilaf & Chorizo Casserole

Piquillos are mild Spanish peppers that are roasted and peeled and then packed in cans or jars. You can use Italian roasted peppers or pimientos if you can't find piquillos. SERVES 4

A generous pinch of **saffron threads**
2 cups **chicken stock**
EVOO, for drizzling
1¼ to 1½ pounds **Spanish chorizo**, casings removed, cut on an angle into ¾-inch slices
1 large **Spanish onion**, chopped
Salt and **pepper**
¼ cup chopped **piquillo peppers** or **pimientos**, drained
1 cup frozen **green peas**, thawed
⅓ cup **dry sherry** or ½ cup **dry white wine**
3 tablespoons **butter**, softened
½ cup broken **thin spaghetti** (1- to 1½-inch pieces)
1 cup **long-grain white rice**
1½ cups grated **Manchego cheese**
½ cup chopped fresh **flat-leaf parsley**

Put the saffron in a small pot with 1½ cups of the stock and 1 cup water. Bring to a boil over medium heat, then reduce to low and let steep for a few minutes while you prepare the chorizo and onions.

Heat a deep skillet with a tight-fitting lid over medium-high heat. Add a drizzle of EVOO to the hot skillet, then the chorizo. Brown the chorizo evenly on both sides, 4 to 5 minutes total. Transfer the chorizo to a plate. Add another drizzle of EVOO to the skillet. Add the onion. Season with salt and pepper and cook until softened, about 5 minutes. Add the piquillos and peas and stir to heat through. Deglaze the pan with the sherry and stir 1 to 2 minutes. Scrape the onions and peas onto a plate.

Return the skillet to medium heat and melt 2 tablespoons of the butter. Add the pasta and stir until deeply golden brown, 3 to 4 minutes. Stir in the rice and saffron stock and bring to a boil. Reduce the heat to low, cover, and cook until the rice is tender, about 18 minutes. Fluff with a fork. Scrape in the vegetables and about one-third of the Manchego and toss gently to combine.

Grease a 9 by 13-inch baking dish with the remaining 1 tablespoon butter. Spread the rice mixture into the dish and sprinkle with the remaining Manchego. Nestle the chorizo into the rice so it's just poking up a little.

[**Make-ahead:** Let cool and refrigerate.]

[**Night of:** Return the casserole to room temp while you preheat the oven.]

Preheat the oven to 375°F.

Douse the casserole with the remaining ½ cup chicken stock. Loosely cover and bake for 20 minutes. Uncover and bake until heated through and barely crispy at the edges, about 10 minutes.

Serve topped with parsley.

WEEK 04

YOU LEARN SOMETHING NEW EVERY DAY

HERE'S A WEEK'S WORTH OF FANTASTIC MAKE-AHEADS. THE CENTERPIECE—AND THE REWARD FOR COOKING ALL DAY—IS A GREAT, NEW (TO ME) METHOD OF ROASTING A LEG OF LAMB.

DISH
1
SLOW-ROASTED PARCHMENT-WRAPPED LEG OF LAMB WITH GARLIC & HERBS
PAGE 25

DISH
2
PORTUGUESE FISH SUPPER
PAGE 26

DISH
3
CHIPOTLE CHICKEN THIGHS
PAGE 28

DISH
4
PEAS & POTATO SOUP WITH TARRAGON PESTO
PAGE 30

DISH
5
STUFFED PEPPERS WITH LAMB & EGGPLANT
PAGE 31

Slow-Roasted Parchment-Wrapped Leg of Lamb with Garlic & Herbs

This slow-cooking lamb is your payoff for a whole day of cooking, so have it on **Cook Day**. It makes enough lamb for this meal as well as Stuffed Peppers with Lamb & Eggplant (page 31). **Suggested sides:** Roasted Sliced Tomatoes and Asparagus (see QR codes on page 31). SERVES 4 TO 6

1 bone-in **leg of lamb** (7 to 8 pounds), trimmed of fat
8 large cloves **garlic**, sliced
6 sprigs fresh **rosemary**, broken into 2-inch pieces
⅓ cup **EVOO**
Juice of 2 **lemons**
Salt and **pepper**
½ cup chopped mixed fresh herbs: **thyme** and **flat-leaf parsley**
Mint & Shallot Sauce (recipe follows)

Arrange a couple of large sheets of parchment paper on a work surface. Set the leg of lamb on top of the parchment and cut small slits all over. Nestle the garlic and rosemary into the slits, letting the rosemary stick out a bit. In a small bowl, whisk together the EVOO and lemon juice. Rub all over the lamb. Season liberally with salt and pepper. Rub with the herb mixture. Cover the leg with another sheet of parchment paper. Roll the bottom and top pieces of parchment together, rolling them toward the lamb, to form a packet. Secure with kitchen twine and marinate in the refrigerator for 3 to 4 hours.

Preheat the oven to 300°F.

Put the lamb, still in its parchment package, in a roasting pan and rest the leg bone on one corner of the pan to settle juices under the leg as it roasts. Roast the lamb for 3 hours. Remove it from the oven and let it rest for 30 minutes. Unwrap and carve one-third of the meat into ½-inch slices and set aside for the Stuffed Peppers with Lamb & Eggplant (page 31). Slice the rest of the lamb, arrange on a serving platter, and spoon the pan juices over the slices. Serve with Mint & Shallot Sauce.

Mint & Shallot Sauce MAKES 1½ CUPS

1 cup **white balsamic vinegar**
⅓ cup **sugar**
1 tablespoon **coarse sea salt**
3 large **shallots**, coarsely chopped
1 cup loosely packed fresh **mint** leaves
½ cup fresh **flat-leaf parsley** leaves

In a small saucepan, combine the vinegar, ½ cup water, and the sugar and bring to a boil over medium heat. Add the salt and stir until the sugar and the salt are dissolved. Reduce the heat to low.

In a food processor, pulse-chop the shallots, mint, and parsley until finely chopped. Transfer the mixture to a small storage container and pour the hot brine over it. Cover the container and refrigerate, or let stand at room temperature until ready to serve.

Portuguese Fish Supper

The sauce gets made ahead, but buy the fish no earlier than 48 hours before you plan on serving this meal. **Suggested side:** Crusty bread or rolls or Portuguese rolls, for mopping. SERVES 4

1 tablespoon **EVOO**
5 ounces **Spanish chorizo**, casings removed, diced or crumbled
1 medium **onion**, chopped
2 large cloves **garlic**, chopped
1 small bunch **lacinato kale** (also called black, Tuscan, or dinosaur kale), thinly sliced
Salt and **pepper**
Freshly grated **nutmeg**
1 cup **chicken stock**
1 (8-ounce) can **tomato sauce**
1 (14.5-ounce) can **diced tomatoes** or **fire-roasted diced tomatoes**
1 (15-ounce) can **chickpeas**, rinsed and drained
Leaves from 1 or 2 sprigs fresh **thyme**, chopped
4 thick (6- to 8-ounce) pieces **cod** or **haddock** fillet
Rachael Ray Seafood Seasoning, **Old Bay seasoning**, or **sweet paprika**
Chopped fresh **flat-leaf parsley**, for garnish

In a Dutch oven or deep skillet, heat the EVOO (1 turn of the pan) over medium-high heat. Add the chorizo and render for a couple of minutes. Add the onion and cook until softened, about 5 minutes. Stir in the garlic and cook for 1 to 2 minutes. Wilt in the kale and season with salt and pepper and a few grates of nutmeg. Stir in the stock, tomato sauce, diced tomatoes, chickpeas, and thyme. Bring to a simmer and cook over low heat for 10 minutes.

[Make-ahead: Let cool and refrigerate.]

[**Night of:** Return the sauce to room temp before reheating gently over medium heat, stirring occasionally.]

Bring the sauce to a bubble. Season the fish with seafood seasoning and salt and pepper. Add the fish to the sauce and cover. Cook until the fish is opaque and cooked through, 5 to 7 minutes.

Ladle into shallow bowls and garnish with parsley.

Chipotle Chicken Thighs

Years ago, if I wrote "chipotle chile in adobo" in a recipe, I'd have to stop and have a whole separate explanation of what that is. Now I think everybody knows it's a smoked pepper and it's put down into a blend of spices and vinegar. **Suggested side:** Tortillas (charred) or bread (heated in the oven), for mopping. SERVES 4

8 bone-in, skin-on **chicken thighs**
Sweet paprika (smoked or regular)
Salt and **pepper**
2 tablespoons **EVOO**
1 (4- to 5-ounce) chunk **Spanish chorizo**, casing removed, crumbled or chopped
1 large **carrot**, peeled and chopped
1 **onion**, chopped
2 cloves **garlic**, chopped
2 tablespoons fresh **thyme** leaves, chopped
1 **chipotle chile in adobo**, seeded and finely chopped, plus 1 tablespoon adobo sauce
1 (15-ounce) can crushed **tomatoes**
1 cup **chicken stock**, for reheating the chicken
Chunky Guacamole (recipe follows)

Season the chicken with paprika, salt, and pepper. In a Dutch oven or deep, large skillet with a lid, heat the EVOO (2 turns of the pan) over medium to medium-high heat. Add the chicken and brown on all sides. Transfer the chicken to a plate and spoon off the excess fat. Add the chorizo and brown a couple of minutes, then transfer to a plate. Stir in the carrot, onion, garlic, thyme, and chipotle, and cover the pot. Reduce the heat a bit and cook, stirring occasionally, to soften the carrot, 7 to 8 minutes. Add the tomatoes and bring to a bubble, then return the chicken and chorizo to the pot and simmer until cooked through, 7 to 8 minutes.

[Make-ahead: Let cool and refrigerate.]

[Night of: Return the chicken to room temp. Add 1 cup chicken stock to the pan and reheat, covered, over medium heat. Uncover and simmer 10 minutes.]

Arrange the chicken in shallow bowls topped with lots of sauce and a mound Chunky Guacamole.

Chunky Guacamole SERVES 4

2 slightly underripe **avocados**
Juice of 2 **limes** or 1 large **lemon**
1 small fresh **red Fresno chile**, seeded and very thinly sliced
1 clove **garlic**, grated
1 vine-ripened **tomato**, seeded and coarsely chopped
¼ cup coarsely chopped fresh **cilantro** or **flat-leaf parsley**
½ small **red onion**, chopped or thinly sliced
Salt

Scoop the avocado flesh into a bowl. Douse with the lime juice. Add the chile, garlic, tomato, cilantro, and onion. Season with salt and lightly mash (keep it on the chunky side).

WEEK 05

HOLI-WEEK

WHAT'S THE ONE THING NO ONE
WANTS FOR THE HOLIDAY? HOLIDAY
COOKING STRESS. SO MORE THAN EVER, YOU NEED
NO-FUSS FOOD TO HELP YOU GET
THROUGH THE HOLIDAY SEASON IN ONE PIECE.

DISH
1
PORTOBELLO
CREAM SAUCE WITH
WHOLE WHEAT
LINGUINE
PAGE 33

DISH
2
ITALIAN
POT ROAST
PAGE 34

DISH
3
STUFFED
EGGPLANT WITH
VEAL &
SPINACH
PAGE 36

DISH
4
FLEURI'S
CURRY LENTIL
SOUP
PAGE 37

DISH
5
ITALIAN
BARBECUED
BEEF
SANDWICHES
PAGE 38

Portobello Cream Sauce
with Whole Wheat Linguine

There are three tricks to getting perfectly browned mushrooms: Don't clean them by running under cold water; make sure the pan is really hot when you add the mushrooms; and don't add any salt to the mushrooms until *after* they're browned.

SERVES 4

1 tablespoon **EVOO**

2 tablespoons **butter**

4 large **portobello mushroom caps**, gills scraped, thinly sliced

1 teaspoon ground **thyme**

1 large **shallot**, finely chopped

2 cloves **garlic**, sliced

Salt and **pepper**

⅓ cup **Marsala** or **port**

½ cup **chicken stock**

1½ cups **heavy cream**

Freshly grated **nutmeg**

1 pound **whole wheat linguine**

Grated **Parmigiano-Reggiano cheese**, for serving

1 cup coarsely chopped **walnuts**, toasted, for serving

1 large bunch **watercress** or **upland cress**, stemmed and chopped

In a Dutch oven or deep skillet, heat the EVOO (1 turn of the pan) and butter over medium to medium-high heat. Add the mushrooms and cook until browned, about 10 minutes. Stir in the thyme, shallot, garlic, and salt and pepper and cook for 2 to 3 minutes more. Deglaze the pan with the Marsala. Add the stock, cream, and a few grates of nutmeg. Reduce the heat and simmer until it is just thick enough to coat the back of a spoon, about 10 minutes.

[**Make-ahead:** Let cool and refrigerate.]

[**Night of:** Return the sauce to room temp before reheating gently over medium-low heat.]

Bring a large pot of water to a boil. Salt the water and cook the pasta al dente. Ladle out about a cup of the starchy cooking water. Drain the pasta and return it to the pot; add a little of the starchy water. Add the sauce, tossing with tongs for 1 or 2 minutes for the flavors to absorb.

Serve the pasta topped with Parm, walnuts, and watercress.

Italian Pot Roast

Make this dish to have on **Cook Day.** It cooks slowly for a good part of the day, and fills the house with fantastic aromas. When you're done with the other dishes, all you have to do to get this dinner on the table is cook up some pasta. This also makes beef that will be used in the Italian Barbecued Beef Sandwiches (page 38). SERVES 4

1 **rump roast** (4½ to 5 pounds), trimmed and tied
1 head **garlic**, cloves separated and peeled
Salt and **pepper**
¼ cup **EVOO**
4 medium **onions**, red or yellow, peeled, each cut into 8 wedges, root end intact
2 fresh **bay leaves**
6 medium **carrots**, cut into thick pieces on an angle
4 ribs **celery** from the heart with leafy tops, cut into thick pieces
Leaves from 4 sprigs fresh **rosemary**, finely chopped
¼ cup **tomato paste**
2 cups **dry white wine**
2 cups **chicken stock**
1 pound **egg pasta** (such as tagliatelle)
8 tablespoons (1 stick) **butter**
Leaves from 4 sprigs fresh **sage**, chopped

Poke holes all over the roast. Slice 4 large cloves of garlic. Stick the garlic into the holes. Liberally season the meat all over with salt and pepper. In a large Dutch oven, heat the EVOO (4 turns of the pan) over medium-high heat. When the oil smokes, add the meat and brown on all sides. Transfer the meat to a plate. Smash the remaining garlic and add it to the pot along with the onions, bay leaves, carrots, celery, rosemary, and salt and pepper. Cover the pot with a lid and sweat the vegetables for 7 to 8 minutes, stirring occasionally. Add the tomato paste and stir for 1 minute. Deglaze the pan with the wine and let reduce for 1 to 2 minutes. Stir in the stock. Return the meat to the pot, cover, reduce the heat to a simmer, and cook for 2½ hours.

Bring a large pot of water for the pasta to a boil over medium heat.

Transfer the meat to a cutting board and let rest for 15 minutes. Slice the roast and arrange half the meat on a platter. Remove the vegetables with a slotted spoon and arrange them alongside the meat. Discard the bay leaves. Spoon some sauce over the meat and vegetables. Set aside the remaining meat for Italian Barbecued Beef Sandwiches (page 38).

Salt the boiling water and cook the pasta al dente. Meanwhile, in a medium skillet, melt the butter over low heat. Add the sage leaves and cook until the foam subsides.

Drain the pasta and return it to the pot. Toss it with the sage butter and season with salt. Pour into a serving bowl. Ladle the remainder of the juices from the Dutch oven over the pasta.

Serve the meat and veggies with pasta alongside.

Stuffed Eggplant with Veal & Spinach

Little stuffed eggplants are so adorable, especially when you can get small, young ones. Those shapely little eggplants are just so darn cute. SERVES 4

4 small (5- to 6-inch) **eggplants** (about 1¾ pounds total)

Salt and **pepper**

1 (9- or 10-ounce) box frozen **chopped spinach**, thawed and wrung dry in a kitchen towel

1 tablespoon **EVOO**, plus more for drizzling

1 pound **ground veal**

1 teaspoon ground or rubbed **sage**

2 cloves **garlic**, minced

5 tablespoons **butter**

3 slightly rounded tablespoons **flour**

2 cups **milk**

Freshly grated **nutmeg**

1 large **egg**

¾ cup grated **Parmigiano-Reggiano cheese**

3 slices good-quality **crusty white bread**, crusts trimmed

Leaves from 2 or 3 sprigs fresh **flat-leaf parsley**

Halve the eggplants lengthwise. Scoop out the flesh, leaving a ⅛-inch-thick shell (if you score the flesh deeply in a diamond pattern first, it's easier to get out). Salt the shells and invert over paper towels to drain for 30 minutes. Salt the flesh and drain it in a strainer.

Put the spinach in a bowl, pulling it into shreds as you do. Preheat the oven to 350°F.

In a large skillet, heat the EVOO (1 turn of the pan) over medium-high heat. Pat the meat dry and add to the pan. Add the sage and salt and pepper. Lightly brown the meat, breaking it into crumbles as it cooks. Stir in the garlic and cook for 30 seconds. Add the meat mixture to the spinach.

In a saucepan, melt 4 tablespoons of the butter over medium heat. Whisk in the flour and cook for 1 minute. Whisk in the milk; season with salt, pepper, and a little nutmeg. Cook the sauce until thick enough to coat the back of a spoon. Let cool slightly, then add to the veal and spinach.

Pat the salted flesh of the eggplant dry and finely chop. Stir it into the meat mixture along with the egg and ½ cup of the Parm.

Tear the bread and combine it in a food processor with the parsley. Pulse-grind into crumbs. Stir in the remaining ¼ cup Parm.

Pat the eggplant shells dry. Drizzle EVOO into a baking dish that will comfortably hold all the eggplant. Arrange the eggplant shells in the dish and mound the filling into them. Top with the bread crumbs. Dot the remaining 1 tablespoon butter over the eggplant.

Bake the eggplant until the filling is lightly golden, about 30 minutes.

[**Make-ahead:** Let cool and refrigerate.]

[**Night of:** Return the eggplant to room temp while you preheat the oven to 350°F. To reheat, put the eggplant in the oven, loosely covered, for 20 minutes. Uncover and bake until deeply golden, 10 to 15 minutes.]

Fleuri's Curry Lentil Soup

Fleuri is a friend of mine who is a master baker but doesn't do a ton of cooking because she happens to be married to a world-class chef. However, she could not wait to tell me about her super-easy recipe for soup. She proudly described it to me, and then her husband busted her and explained that he had taught her how to make it. Either way, it's delicious, and I gave her the credit. **Suggested side:** Naan bread, heated on a griddle with a few drops of water until crisp and hot on each side, then brushed liberally with melted butter. SERVES 4

¼ cup **EVOO**

5 or 6 cloves **garlic**, finely chopped or grated

1 small **carrot**, finely chopped

1 small **fresh chile**, seeded and finely chopped

1 large **shallot**, finely chopped

1½ cups **yellow**, **red**, or **green lentils**

2 tablespoons **curry powder** blend or **ras el hanout** (see my Ras el Hanout recipe, page 95)

Salt

4 cups **chicken** or **vegetable stock**

1 bunch **"farm spinach"** (see Heads-up), stemmed, washed, dried, and coarsely chopped

In a soup pot, heat the EVOO (4 turns of the pan) over medium-high heat. Add the garlic, carrot, chile, and shallot and cook until the mixture softens, 2 to 3 minutes. Stir in the lentils and toss to coat in the oil. Add the curry powder and salt. Add the stock and 2 to 3 cups water and bring to a boil over medium heat. Reduce the heat and simmer until the lentils are tender, about 40 minutes.

Puree with an immersion blender into a smooth soup. Adjust the seasonings.

[**Make-ahead:** Let cool and refrigerate.]

[**Night of:** Return the soup to room temp before reheating gently over medium heat.]

Return the soup to a bubble and stir in the spinach until wilted.

Heads-up: "Farm spinach" is what I call the spinach that comes with stems on, bundled together—as opposed to the stemmed and prewashed leaves that come in bags.

Italian Barbecued Beef Sandwiches

These sandwiches use the beef that was made for the Italian Pot Roast (page 34), but if you're not making that dish, you can use thick-sliced deli roast beef instead.

SERVES 4

BALSAMIC BBQ SAUCE

1 cup good-quality **ketchup**
2 large cloves **garlic**, finely chopped
2 tablespoons **dark brown sugar**
2 tablespoons dark amber **maple syrup**
2 tablespoons **Worcestershire sauce**
3 tablespoons aged **balsamic vinegar**
1 teaspoon **smoked sweet paprika**
1 teaspoon coarsely ground **pepper**

SANDWICHES

1 cup **beef** or **chicken stock**
1½ to 2 pounds **roast beef** (from Italian Pot Roast, page 34), sliced
4 crusty **Italian sub rolls** or chunks of **ciabatta bread**
1 cup **giardiniera** (Italian hot pickled vegetables), drained and chopped
Hot & Sweet Caprese Salad (recipe follows)

Make the barbecue sauce: In a small saucepan, combine the ketchup, garlic, brown sugar, maple syrup, Worcestershire, vinegar, paprika, and pepper. Bring to a boil over medium heat. Reduce the heat to low and cook until thickened, about 30 minutes.

[**Make-ahead:** Let cool and refrigerate.]

[**Night of:** Return the barbecue sauce to room temp before reheating gently over medium heat. Take the beef out of the fridge.]

Make the sandwiches: In a skillet, bring the stock to a boil over medium heat, then reduce to a simmer. Add the beef and warm the meat through. When the liquid has just about evaporated, pour the barbecue sauce over the meat and stir gently to combine.

Lightly toast or warm the bread. Pile the barbecue meat into the sub rolls and top with pickled chopped vegetables. Serve the salad on the side.

Hot & Sweet Caprese Salad SERVES 4

2 cups **arugula** or **watercress** leaves, chopped
4 balls **bocconcini**, quartered
16 **cherry tomatoes**, halved
½ cup fresh **basil** leaves, torn or chopped
EVOO, for drizzling
Salt and **pepper**

In a salad bowl, combine the arugula, bocconcini, tomatoes, and basil. Drizzle with EVOO and season with salt and pepper. Toss to combine.

WEEK 06

THANKSGIVING ANYTIME

IF YOU WISHED THAT TURKEY
DAY COULD COME MORE THAN
ONCE A YEAR, THEN HERE IS A RECIPE
FOR ANYTIME-OF-YEAR TURKEY PLUS 4
SATISFYING DISHES THAT COULD BE
ENTRÉES OR THANKSGIVING SIDES.

DISH
1
ROASTED
BRINED TURKEY
BREAST
PAGE 40

DISH
2
BROCCOLI &
CAULIFLOWER
GRATIN MAC 'N'
CHEESE
PAGE 42

DISH
3
PARSNIP,
POTATO & SPINACH
CASSEROLE
WITH ROASTED
MUSHROOMS
PAGE 43

DISH
4
GINGER-SOY
CARROT
SOUP
PAGE 44

DISH
5
TURKEY & CREAMY
MUSHROOM-
TOMATO "GRAVY"
WITH GNOCCHI
PAGE 46

Recipe for Fruit & Nut Rice Pilaf
View a bonus Side Dish recipe.

Roasted Brined Turkey Breast

This is the meal you'll be making to serve on **Cook Day** (it also makes extra turkey for Turkey & Creamy Mushroom-Tomato "Gravy" with Gnocchi, page 46). **Suggested side:** Fruit & Nut Rice Pilaf (see QR code above). SERVES 4 TO 6

Jumbo-size (3- to 5-gallon) plastic food storage bags

1 gallon water (preferably bottled **spring water**)
1 cup kosher **salt**
½ cup **superfine sugar**
6 fresh **bay leaves**
2 large **shallots**, quartered lengthwise, roots intact
1 tablespoon **coriander seeds**
1 tablespoon **black peppercorns**
1 tablespoon **paprika**
1½ teaspoons **allspice berries**
1 tablespoon **Rachael Ray Perfect Poultry Seasoning** or other **poultry seasoning**
6 cloves **garlic**, coarsely chopped
1 full bone-in, skin-on **turkey breast** (6 to 7 pounds)
Salt and **pepper**
EVOO, for drizzling
Maple-Worcestershire Gravy (recipe follows)

Open a jumbo plastic food storage bag in the sink and add the water, 1 cup kosher salt, sugar, bay leaves, shallots, coriander, peppercorns, paprika, allspice, poultry seasoning, and garlic and swish around to combine. Add the turkey breast and seal the bag. Refrigerate for 24 hours.

Preheat the oven to 400°F.

Pat the turkey breast dry (discard the brine), season with salt and pepper, drizzle all over with EVOO, and put it in a roasting pan. Roast for 30 minutes. Baste with the pan juices, reduce the oven temperature to 325°F, and roast until the turkey reaches 160°F when an instant-read thermometer is inserted in the thickest part, about 40 minutes.

Transfer the turkey to a cutting board. Cover with foil and let rest for 15 minutes. While the turkey is resting, make the gravy.

Carve the breast and set aside 1 pound of the meat for Turkey & Creamy Mushroom-Tomato "Gravy" with Gnocchi (page 46). Arrange the remaining turkey on a serving platter. Serve with the gravy.

Heads-up: The turkey has to be brined the day before your **Cook Day**.

Maple-Worcestershire Gravy SERVES 4 TO 6

4 tablespoons (½ stick) **butter**
1 **shallot**, finely chopped
Leaves from 2 sprigs fresh **thyme**, finely chopped
3 tablespoons **flour**
2 cups **chicken stock**
¼ cup **Worcestershire sauce**
⅓ cup dark amber **maple syrup**
Lots of coarsely ground **pepper**

In a medium saucepan, melt the butter over medium to medium-high heat. Add the shallot and thyme and cook for 2 minutes. Whisk in the flour and cook for 1 minute. Whisk in the stock, Worcestershire, maple syrup, and lots of pepper. Cook until thick enough to coat the back of a spoon, 10 to 12 minutes.

Broccoli & Cauliflower Gratin Mac 'n' Cheese

I almost always make a white sauce (what I call a "béchamel") to melt cheese into to make mac 'n' cheese, but I stumbled across this method where you just throw everything into a baking dish and stick it in the oven. So here it is. Give it a try. It's a pretty fun change-up. SERVES 6

Salt and **pepper**

1 small bunch **broccoli**, trimmed into florets

1 small or ½ large head **cauliflower**, trimmed and cut into florets

1 pound **whole wheat macaroni**, **penne**, or other **short-cut pasta**

2 cups **sour cream** (reduced-fat or regular)

1 tablespoon **Dijon mustard**

⅓ cup finely chopped **chives**

2 cloves **garlic**, grated or pasted

A few drops of **hot sauce**

2½ cups grated **extra-sharp cheddar cheese**

Bring a large pot of water to a boil over medium heat. Salt the water and add the broccoli and cauliflower. Boil for 5 minutes, then remove them with a slotted spoon or strainer and drain. Bring the water back to a boil, add the pasta, and cook until 2 minutes shy of al dente. Drain.

Meanwhile, in a large bowl, combine the sour cream, mustard, chives, garlic, hot sauce, and salt and pepper. Add the pasta and cauliflower and two-thirds of the cheese. Stir to combine, then transfer it to a 9 by 13-inch baking dish or a shallow 2- to 3-quart casserole and cover with the remaining cheese.

[Make-ahead: Let cool and refrigerate.]

[Night of: Return the casserole to room temp while you preheat the oven to 375°F.]

Put the baking dish on a baking sheet and bake it in the middle of the oven until deeply golden and bubbling, 40 to 45 minutes.

Parsnip, Potato & Spinach Casserole with Roasted Mushrooms

This is a really hearty vegetarian main course, or a great option for a side dish on Thanksgiving. SERVES 4 TO 6

CASSEROLE

4 large **starchy potatoes** (such as russets), peeled and cut into chunks
4 medium **parsnips**, peeled and cut into chunks
Salt and **pepper**
1 small **onion**, peeled
1 (9- or 10-ounce) box frozen **chopped spinach**, thawed and wrung dry in a kitchen towel
2 tablespoons **butter**
½ cup **heavy cream**
½ cup **milk**
Freshly grated **nutmeg**
2 large **eggs**, beaten
1 cup grated **Gruyère** or **Parmigiano-Reggiano cheese**
Paprika

ROASTED MUSHROOMS

2½ pounds mixed **mushrooms**
8 to 10 cloves **garlic**, smashed
Leaves from 2 or 3 sprigs fresh **thyme**
½ cup **EVOO**
Juice of 1 **lemon**
Salt and **pepper**

Make the casserole: In a large pot, combine the potatoes and parsnips with water to cover. Bring to a boil over medium heat, salt the water, and cook until tender, 12 to 15 minutes. Drain and return to the hot pot. Grate in 3 to 4 tablespoons of onion, then add the spinach (pull it into shreds as you add it), butter, cream, and ¼ cup of the milk. Season with salt, pepper, and a few grates of nutmeg. Mash the mixture together and taste to adjust the seasonings. Add the extra ¼ cup milk if the mash is too tight. Cool to room temperature. Stir in the eggs and transfer to a 9 by 13-inch-baking dish or a shallow 2- to 3-quart casserole. Cover with the cheese and sprinkle with paprika.

[Make-ahead: Let cool and refrigerate.]

[Night of: Return the casserole to room temp while you preheat the oven.]

Meanwhile, prepare the mushrooms: Preheat the oven to 400°F. Wipe the mushrooms, stem them, and slice. If you have portobellos, scrape their gills. Buttons may be halved; coarsely chop shiitakes, oysters, and other wild mushrooms.

In a rimmed baking sheet, toss the mushrooms with the garlic, thyme, and EVOO. Roast until dark and tender, about 30 minutes.

At the same time, put the casserole on a baking sheet and put it in the lower third of the oven. Bake until hot and golden, 35 to 40 minutes.

Douse the mushrooms with the lemon juice and season with salt and pepper.

Serve the casserole and top with the mushrooms (see Heads-up).

Heads-up: If you have any roasted mushrooms left over, save them to stir into the mushroom-tomato "gravy" in Dish 5, page 46.

Ginger-Soy Carrot Soup

A really elegant starter soup for Thanksgiving, but also a great meatless entrée. For the entrée, a fried egg up on top adds some good protein, but if you or your guests don't eat eggs, then just leave them out. **Suggested side:** Toasted sesame rolls, for dunking. SERVES 4

2 tablespoons **EVOO** or **vegetable oil**

1 large **onion**, chopped

3 or 4 cloves **garlic**, chopped

1-inch piece fresh **ginger**, grated or finely chopped

1 **fresh chile**, seeded and chopped

2 pounds **carrots**, sliced or chopped

¼ cup **tamari**

4 cups **chicken** or **vegetable stock**

Salt and **pepper**

4 large **eggs**, fried (optional)

Finely chopped **chives** or **scallions**, for garnish

Dark sesame oil, for garnish

In a soup pot or large Dutch oven, heat the EVOO (2 turns of the pan) over medium-high heat. Add the onion, garlic, ginger, and chile and sweat them for a few minutes. Stir in the carrots and tamari, cover, and cook to soften, 7 to 8 minutes. Add the stock and 1 cup water and bring to a boil. Reduce the heat and simmer the soup until the carrots are tender. Puree with an immersion blender (or in batches in a food processor or blender) to as smooth or chunky as you like. Season with salt and pepper.

[Make-ahead: Let cool and refrigerate.]

[Night of: Return the soup to room temp before reheating gently over medium heat.]

Serve the soup in shallow bowls with a fried egg on top, if you'd like. Garnish each serving with chives or scallions and a drizzle of sesame oil.

Turkey & Creamy Mushroom-Tomato "Gravy" with Gnocchi

This recipe uses leftover turkey from the Roasted Brined Turkey Breast (page 40).

SERVES 4 TO 6

2 tablespoons **EVOO**

3 tablespoons **butter**

½ pound **white button mushrooms**, sliced

Leaves from 2 sprigs fresh **rosemary**, finely chopped

Leaves from 1 or 2 sprigs fresh **thyme**, chopped

1 fresh **bay leaf**

1 medium **onion**, finely chopped

2 cloves **garlic**, finely chopped or grated

Salt and **pepper**

¼ cup **tomato paste**

1 tablespoon **Worcestershire sauce**

2 cups **chicken stock**

1 pound chopped **cooked turkey** (from Roasted Brined Turkey Breast, page 40)

½ cup **heavy cream**

1½ pounds fresh **gnocchi**

Freshly grated **nutmeg**

Grated **Parmigiano-Reggiano** or **Gruyère cheese**, for serving

In a Dutch oven, heat the EVOO (2 turns of the pan) and 2 tablespoons of the butter over medium heat. Add the mushrooms, rosemary, thyme, and bay leaf and cook until the mushrooms are lightly brown, 7 to 8 minutes. Stir in the onion, garlic, and salt and pepper. Increase the heat a bit and cook to soften the onion, about 5 minutes. Stir in the tomato paste, Worcestershire, and stock. Bring to a boil, then reduce the heat to a simmer. Add the turkey and heat until the mixture bubbles.

[Make-ahead: Let cool and refrigerate.]

[Night of: Return the turkey sauce to room temp before reheating, covered, over medium heat.]

When the turkey sauce is hot, uncover, remove the bay leaf, and stir in the cream. Keep warm over low heat. (If you have any mushrooms left over from the Roasted Mushrooms from Dish 3, page 43, stir them in now.)

Bring a large pot of water to a boil. Salt the water and add the gnocchi. Cook until they float, 1 to 2 minutes. Drain the gnocchi and return to the pot. Stir in the remaining 1 tablespoon butter and season with a few grates of nutmeg. Serve in shallow bowls topped with lots of sauce and some cheese.

WEEK 07

SOMETHING FOR
EVERYONE

IF YOUR FAMILY COMPLAINS THAT
YOU'RE MAKING THE SAME COUPLE OF
MEALS WEEK AFTER WEEK, HERE ARE 5
COMPLETELY DIFFERENT MEALS
TO SATISFY EVERY APPETITE
IN THE HOUSE.

DISH
1
SPINACH-STUFFED
BRACIOLE IN
SUNDAY SAUCE
WITH
PAPPARDELLE
PAGE 48

DISH
2
SPANISH
CHICKEN &
RICE SOUP
PAGE 51

DISH
3
SPINACH &
ARTICHOKE
BAKED WHOLE-
GRAIN PASTA
PAGE 52

DISH
4
MEATY
MEATLESS
CHILI
PAGE 53

DISH
5
OPEN-FACED
SAUSAGE,
3-PEPPER &
MUSHROOM
SANDWICHES
PAGE 54

Spinach-Stuffed Braciole in Sunday Sauce with Pappardelle

Here's the meal you should plan to have on **Cook Day.** At the same time as you're setting up this meal for the end of the day, you're also setting up another meal for later in the week. When you make the Sunday Sauce here, you'll be cooking the sausages for Open-Faced Sausage, 3-Pepper & Mushroom Sandwiches with Provolone (page 54). SERVES 4

BRACIOLE
1 (9- or 10-ounce) box frozen **chopped spinach**, thawed and wrung dry in a kitchen towel
Salt and **pepper**
Freshly grated **nutmeg**
2 large hard-boiled **eggs**, peeled and finely chopped
2 tablespoons dried **currants** or chopped **raisins**
2 to 3 tablespoons toasted **pine nuts**
2 large cloves **garlic**, finely chopped
¼ cup shredded **Parmigiano-Reggiano cheese**
4 (8-ounce) pieces thin-cut **top round veal** or **beef** pounded very thin (about ⅛ inch)
2 tablespoons **EVOO**

SUNDAY SAUCE
1 tablespoon **EVOO**
1 **carrot**, finely chopped
1 **onion**, finely chopped
4 cloves **garlic**, thinly sliced
1 large fresh **bay leaf**
Salt and **pepper**
Leaves from 2 or 3 sprigs fresh **rosemary**, finely chopped
Leaves from 2 or 3 sprigs fresh **sage**, thinly sliced
¼ cup **tomato paste**
1 cup **dry white wine**
2 cups **chicken stock**
1 (28- or 32-ounce) can **San Marzano tomatoes** (look for DOP on the label)

1 tablespoon **EVOO**
8 **Italian sausage** links (hot, sweet, or a combination)
8 ounces **pappardelle** or 12 ounces **egg tagliatelle**
1 tablespoon **butter**
A small handful of fresh **flat-leaf parsley**, finely chopped
A generous handful of fresh **basil** leaves, torn or shredded
Shaved **Parmigiano-Reggiano cheese**, for serving

Make the braciole: Pull the spinach into shreds as you put it in a large bowl. Season with salt, pepper, and a few grates of nutmeg. Add the eggs, currants, pine nuts, garlic, and Parm and gently combine.

Season the meat with salt and pepper and arrange each slice with one narrow end near you. Divide the filling evenly among the slices, scattering the filling and leaving a ½-inch border at the sides. Fold the edges over the filling and tuck them in as you roll each braciole to secure the filling. Wrap and roll each braciole and secure the ends and middle with kitchen twine in both directions (like wrapping a package).

In a large Dutch oven, heat the 2 tablespoons EVOO (2 turns of the pan) over medium-high heat. Add the braciole and cook to evenly brown all over, 6 to 8 minutes. Transfer to a plate.

(continued)

Spinach & Artichoke Baked Whole-Grain Pasta

Just by switching up and using a whole-grain or whole wheat pasta, you're getting a ton of fiber and protein. So you really add a lot to the nutritional value of your meal when you use it. SERVES 4

2 tablespoons **EVOO**

1 large **shallot**, chopped

4 cloves **garlic**, finely chopped or grated

1 (9-ounce) box frozen **artichoke hearts**, thawed, halved, and patted dry

½ cup **dry white wine**

4 tablespoons (½ stick) **butter**

3 slightly rounded tablespoons **flour**

2 cups **milk**

Salt and **pepper**

Freshly grated **nutmeg**

5 ounces **Gruyère cheese**, shredded (about 1½ cups)

1 pound **whole wheat** or **whole-grain penne**, **macaroni**, or other **short-cut pasta**

2 (9- or 10-ounce) boxes frozen **chopped spinach**, thawed and wrung dry in a kitchen towel

1 cup shredded **Parmigiano-Reggiano cheese**

Bring a large pot of water to a boil.

Meanwhile, in a medium skillet, heat the EVOO (2 turns of the pan) over medium to medium-high heat. Add the shallot and garlic and cook for 2 to 3 minutes. Add the artichokes and cook until they are lightly brown. Deglaze the pan with the wine.

In a saucepan, melt the butter over medium heat. Whisk in the flour and cook for 1 minute. Whisk in the milk; season with salt and pepper and a little nutmeg. Cook the sauce until thick enough to coat the back of a spoon. Adjust the seasonings and stir in the Gruyère, stirring in a figure-8 until melted.

Salt the boiling water and cook the pasta al dente. Drain and return to the pot. Add the cheese sauce, spinach (pulling it into shreds as you add it), and artichoke mixture. Transfer to a shallow 3-quart baking dish and cover with the Parm.

[**Make-ahead:** Let cool and refrigerate.]

[**Night of:** Return the casserole to room temp while you preheat the oven.]

Preheat the oven to 375°F with a rack in the center.

Bake the casserole on a baking sheet until browned and bubbling on top, 45 minutes.

Meaty Meatless Chili

Anchos are dried poblano chiles and they taste (to me) like spicy raisins. SERVES 4

3 dried **ancho chiles**, stemmed and seeded

4 cups **vegetable** or **chicken stock**

¼ cup **EVOO**

8 **portobello mushroom caps**, gills scraped, chopped

4 large cloves **garlic**, thinly sliced

1 large **onion**, chopped

1 **fresh green** or **red chile**, thinly sliced

Salt and **pepper**

1 scant tablespoon **smoked sweet paprika**

1 scant tablespoon ground **cumin**

1 scant tablespoon ground **coriander**

Pinch of ground **cinnamon**

2 (15-ounce) cans **black beans**, drained

1 (14- to 15-ounce) can **fire-roasted diced** or **crushed tomatoes**

1 **avocado**

1 cup **sour cream**

Juice of 1 **lime**

A handful of fresh **cilantro** or **flat-leaf parsley** leaves

Toasted hulled **pumpkin seeds** (pepitas) or **sunflower seeds**, for garnish (optional)

A couple of handfuls of **tortilla chips** (optional)

Toast the anchos in a dry saucepan over medium-high heat until fragrant but not burned. Add the stock and bring to a simmer. Cook until softened, about 10 minutes. Transfer to a blender or food processor and puree.

In a Dutch oven, heat the EVOO (4 turns of the pan) over medium-high heat. Add the mushrooms and cook until well browned, 12 to 15 minutes. Add the garlic, onion, fresh chile, and salt and pepper and cook to soften the onion, 5 to 6 minutes. Add the paprika, cumin, coriander, and cinnamon. Add the chile puree, beans, and tomatoes and cook for 15 minutes, until thickened.

[**Make-ahead:** Let cool and refrigerate.]

[**Night of:** Return the chili to room temp before reheating gently over medium heat, stirring frequently. Once the chili is reheated, uncover and simmer until ready to serve.]

Scoop the avocado into a food processor. Add the sour cream, lime juice, and cilantro and process into a smooth avocado–sour cream sauce. Season with salt and process again.

Serve the chili in shallow bowls and garnish with the avocado sauce and pepitas and tortilla chips (if using).

Open-Faced Sausage, 3-Pepper & Mushroom Sandwiches with Provolone

If you are preparing this dish for later in the week and have already bought the bread, place it in the freezer in an airtight bag. Unwrap to thaw at room temperature, and then heat until crusty in a warm oven. SERVES 4

8 cooked **Italian sausages** (from Spinach-Stuffed Braciole, page 48), plus half the sauce from the recipe

2 tablespoons **EVOO**

4 **portobello mushroom caps**, gills scraped, sliced

1 **onion**, halved and sliced

2 **cubanelle peppers**, seeded and sliced

1 **fresh red chile**, thinly sliced

2 large cloves **garlic**, sliced

Chicken stock or water, for reheating

Salt and **pepper**

1 large loaf **ciabatta bread**

12 ounces **sharp provolone cheese**, shredded

A small handful of fresh **flat-leaf parsley**, for garnish

[**Make ahead:** Combine the sausages and the sauce and refrigerate.]

In a large skillet, heat the EVOO (2 turns of the pan) over medium-high heat. Add the mushrooms and cook to soften, about 5 minutes. Add the onion, cubanelles, chile, and garlic (see Heads-up) and cook the cubanelles to tender-crisp, another 5 minutes. [**Make-ahead:** Let cool and refrigerate.]

[**Night of:** Return the sausages and sauce to room temp. Return the mushrooms to room temp, then reheat with a splash of stock or water over medium heat. Season with salt and pepper.]

Preheat the oven to 375°F. Arrange cooling racks over 2 baking sheets.

Reheat the sausages in the sauce over medium heat. Remove them from the pot and halve them lengthwise (this way, if you have a combo of hot and sweet sausages, people can have both if they want). Stir some of the sauce into the mushroom mixture.

Split the bread horizontally, then halve crosswise for 4 open-faced "sandwiches." Arrange the bread cut side up on the cooling racks. Dot the top with some of the sauce. Top with the sausages, cut side down, then the mushroom-pepper mixture. Top with the cheese. Bake until the cheese is melted and browned at the edges, 12 to 15 minutes. Garnish with parsley and serve.

Heads-up: Do not salt the mushrooms and peppers, as salt will draw more liquid out, and we are undercooking a bit for a make-ahead meal.

WEEK 08

A WEEK OF
COMFORTS

FIVE COMFORT FOOD CLASSICS,
INCLUDING THE GRANDDADDY
OF ALL COMFORT FOODS:
SPAGHETTI AND MEATBALLS

DISH
1
THE ULTIMATE
LINGUINE
WITH CLAM
SAUCE
PAGE 56

DISH
2
KNOCKS &
BEANS
SUPREME
PAGE 58

DISH
3
BAKED ZITI
WITH SPINACH &
VEAL
PAGE 59

DISH
4
VEGETABLE &
DUMPLING SOUP
PAGE 60

DISH
5
ON TOP OF OL'
SMOKY, ALL COVERED
WITH CHEESE:
SPAGHETTI &
MEATBALLS
PAGE 62

The Ultimate Linguine with Clam Sauce

I love to make this with a long-cut pasta that has flavor infused right into it, like pepperoncini spaghetti or lemon linguine. You can make the clam sauce either white or red (with tomatoes). If you choose a red sauce, then the first thing you have to do is blanch and peel the tomatoes (see Heads-up). **SERVES 4**

CLAMS

4 pounds **cherrystone clams**, scrubbed

1 cup **dry white wine** or crisp, light-bodied **beer**

1 (8-ounce) bottle **clam juice**

FRESH SEAFOOD SEASONING PASTE

1 small **red onion**, coarsely chopped

1 **fresh red chile**, coarsely chopped

Grated zest of 1 **lemon**

3 or 4 large cloves **garlic**, peeled

1 tablespoon fresh **thyme** leaves

¼ cup packed fresh **flat-leaf parsley** leaves

2 fresh **bay leaves**

¼ cup **EVOO**

5 or 6 **anchovy fillets**

4 red heirloom or vine-ripened **tomatoes** (optional), peeled and diced (see Heads-up)

1 pound **linguine** or **spaghetti**

Cook the clams: Place the clams, wine, and clam juice in a large pot. Bring to a boil, cover, and reduce the heat to a simmer. Cook until the clams open, 8 to 10 minutes. Scoop out the clams and shuck them. (Discard any clams that have not opened.) Strain the broth and set aside; wipe out the pot and return to the stove.

[Make-ahead: Place the shucked cooked clams in a food storage container, let cool completely, and refrigerate.]

Make the seafood paste: In a food processor, combine the red onion, chile, lemon zest, garlic, thyme, parsley, and bay leaves and pulse-chop into a thick, finely chopped, speckled paste.

In the cleaned-out clam pot, heat the EVOO (4 turns of the pan) over medium to medium-high heat. Add the anchovies, cover the pot with a splatter screen or lid, and shake until the anchovies begin to break up. Reduce the heat a bit, uncover, and stir until the anchovies melt into the oil. Add the seasoning paste and stir for 2 minutes. Stir in the reserved clam broth. Add the tomatoes (if using) and simmer for 5 minutes.

[Make-ahead: Let cool and refrigerate.]

[Night of: Get the clams out of the fridge. Return the sauce to room temp before reheating gently over medium heat.]

Bring a large pot of water to a boil. Salt the water and cook the pasta al dente. Once the pasta is cooking, stir the clams into the sauce and simmer a few minutes. Ladle out about a cup of the starchy cooking water and add to the sauce. Drain the pasta and return it to the pot. Add the sauce, tossing with tongs for 1 or 2 minutes for the flavors to absorb.

Heads-up: If you're using tomatoes in the sauce, score the skin on the bottom of each tomato with a large X, being careful not to cut deeper than the skin. Bring a large pot of water to a rolling boil. Add the tomatoes and cook for 30 seconds. Remove with a slotted spoon or tongs and plunge into an ice water bath to cool. Peel, halve, and dice the tomatoes into small pieces.

Knocks & Beans Supreme

This is a version of a classic American comfort-food dish, franks and beans. But I use knockwurst, because they're much more impressive. SERVES 4

EVOO, for drizzling

6 **knockwurst sausages**

8 slices good-quality **smoky bacon**, cut crosswise into ½-inch pieces

2 (16- to 22-ounce) cans good-quality **baked beans** (I like Bush's Grillin' Beans)

2 large cloves **garlic**, finely chopped

1 large **shallot**, finely chopped

Coarsely ground **pepper**

¼ cup **steak sauce** (I like Lea & Perrins Thick Classic Worcestershire Sauce)

2 **fresh red chiles**, chopped

A small bunch thin **scallions**, thinly sliced on an angle

Leaves from 1 or 2 small sprigs fresh **thyme** and/or fresh **marjoram**, finely chopped

1 (16-ounce) can **brown bread**, plain or with raisins

2 tablespoons **butter**

[If making this to serve on **Cook Day**, preheat the oven to 375°F. If making this for later in the week, you'll preheat the oven on the night of.]

In a deep skillet, simmer the sausages in about an inch of water to heat them through. Drain. When the knocks are cool enough to handle, slice them crosswise at an angle into 3 or 4 pieces, about 2 inches long.

Wipe out the skillet and return to the stove. Add a drizzle of EVOO to the pan and heat over medium-high heat. Add the knocks to the skillet and sear at the edges. Transfer the sausages to a plate. Cook the bacon until almost crisp but not quite. Transfer the bacon to paper towels to drain. Reserve the bacon drippings in the pan.

In a 9 by 13-inch baking dish or a shallow 2- to 3-quart casserole, stir together the beans, garlic, shallot, and lots of pepper. Nestle the chunks of knocks into the beans, arranging them all around the casserole and allowing them to peek up and out a bit. Dot the beans with steak sauce. Scatter the chiles, scallions, and herbs over the top. Scatter the bacon on top. Using a pastry brush, dot the exposed areas with some of the bacon drippings still in the skillet.

[**Make-ahead:** Let cool and refrigerate.]

[**Night of:** Return the beans to room temp while you preheat the oven to 375°F.]

Place the casserole on a baking sheet and bake until the top is crispy in spots and bubbling all over, 20 to 25 minutes.

Meanwhile, heat a griddle or cast-iron skillet. Cut the bread into ¾-inch-thick slices. Melt the butter on the griddle and toast the bread until slightly browned and crispy on one side. Flip and brown the second side.

Baked Ziti with Spinach & Veal

This dish is actually just a quick take on cannelloni, which are giant tubes of pasta that you stuff with a filling (often of spinach and veal) and then bake under a béchamel. So this dish will hit all the same flavor notes, but with a lot less effort.

SERVES 4 TO 6

Salt and **pepper**

1 pound **whole wheat** or **whole-grain ziti**

2 tablespoons **EVOO**

1 pound **ground veal**

1 small **carrot**, finely chopped

2 large **shallots** or 1 medium **onion**, finely chopped

3 or 4 large cloves **garlic**, finely chopped

2 tablespoons very thinly sliced fresh **sage**

1 cup **dry white wine** or **chicken stock**

4 tablespoons (½ stick) **butter**

3 rounded tablespoons **flour**

2½ cups **milk**

Freshly grated **nutmeg**

2 bunches **"farm spinach,"** stemmed, washed, dried, and chopped (see Heads up, page 37)

1½ cups grated **Italian Fontina** (such as Fontina Val d'Aosta) or **Gruyère cheese**

¾ cup grated **Parmigiano-Reggiano cheese**

[If making this to serve on **Cook Day**, preheat the oven to 375°F. If making this for later in the week, you'll preheat the oven on the night of.]

Bring a large pot of water to boil. Salt the water and cook the pasta until 2 minutes shy of al dente. Drain and return to the pot.

In a skillet, heat the EVOO (2 turns of the pan) over medium to medium-high heat. Add the veal and cook, breaking it into crumbles as it browns. Add the carrot, shallots, garlic, sage, and salt and pepper and cook to soften the shallots, about 5 minutes. Deglaze the pan with the wine. Reduce the heat to a simmer.

In a saucepan, melt the butter over medium heat. Whisk in the flour and cook for 1 minute. Whisk in the milk; season with salt, pepper, and a little nutmeg. Cook the sauce until thick enough to coat the back of a spoon. Adjust the seasoning.

Wilt the spinach into the veal and stir to combine. Add with the sauce to the drained pasta and toss together. Transfer to a 9 by 13-inch baking dish or a shallow 2- to 3-quart casserole and top with the cheeses.

[**Make-ahead:** Let cool and refrigerate.]

[**Night of:** Return the casserole to room temp while you preheat the oven to 375°F.]

Place the casserole on a baking sheet to catch the drips and bake until browned and bubbling, 15 to 20 minutes if still hot from preparation; 35 to 45 minutes if reheating.

Vegetable & Dumpling Soup

When I have a bunch of chopped vegetables that I'm cooking together for something like a soup, I like to do what I call "chop and drop." As you chop a vegetable, drop it into the pot. Then move on to the next vegetable and do the same, until all your veggies are in the pan. This keeps your cutting board clear. SERVES 4

¼ cup **EVOO**

1 bulb **fennel**, finely diced, ¼ cup (or more) minced fronds reserved

4 ribs **celery** from the heart with leafy tops, diced

2 **parsnips**, peeled and diced

2 **carrots**, diced

2 all-purpose **potatoes**, peeled and diced

1 large **onion**, diced

4 cloves **garlic**, chopped (optional)

2 large fresh **bay leaves**

2 tablespoons fresh **thyme** leaves, chopped

Salt and **pepper**

1 cup **dry white wine**

4 cups **vegetable** or **chicken stock**

3 tablespoons **butter**

2 tablespoons **flour**

1 (8-ounce) box **buttermilk biscuit mix** (I use Jiffy)

A handful of fresh **flat-leaf parsley**, finely chopped

1 cup frozen **green peas**, thawed

¼ cup finely chopped fresh **dill**, plus more for garnish

In a large Dutch oven, heat the EVOO (4 turns of the pan) over medium-high heat. Add the fennel, celery, parsnips, carrots, potatoes, onion, garlic (if using), bay leaves, thyme, and liberal amounts of salt and pepper. Cover and sweat the vegetables, stirring fairly frequently, 8 to 10 minutes. Deglaze the pan with the wine. Stir in the stock and 2 cups water and bring to a boil.

In a small skillet, melt the butter over medium heat. Whisk in the flour and cook for 1 minute. Stir the roux into the soup. Simmer the soup a few minutes to combine the flavors.

[Make-ahead: Let cool and refrigerate.]

[**Night of:** Return the soup to room temp before reheating gently over medium heat, stirring occasionally.]

Mix up the biscuit dough for drop biscuits, adding the parsley. Bring the soup to a boil. Add the peas, dill, and ¼ cup reserved fennel fronds. Using 2 spoons, shape 8 small egg-shaped dumplings of biscuit dough and drop into the soup. Cover and simmer over medium-low heat for 10 minutes. Discard the bay leaves.

Serve the soup in shallow bowls. Garnish with dill or more fennel fronds, or both.

On Top of Ol' Smoky, All Covered with Cheese: Spaghetti & Meatballs

I make meatballs so often that I like to play around with the mixtures. This one is a real winner! SERVES 4

12 ounces **ground pork**

12 ounces **ground beef sirloin**

Salt and **pepper**

3 slices good-quality **bread** (such as peasant bread or boule), crusts trimmed

1 cup **milk**

Freshly grated **nutmeg**

1 large or extra-large **egg yolk**, beaten

A generous handful of fresh **flat-leaf parsley** tops, finely chopped

6 cloves **garlic**: 2 finely chopped, 4 thinly sliced

4 ounces **mortadella** or **prosciutto cotto**, coarsely chopped

½ cup grated **pecorino cheese**, plus a hunk to shave at the table

3 tablespoons **EVOO**, plus more for liberal drizzling

1 tablespoon **fennel seeds**

1 **fresh red chile**, seeded and finely chopped

1 **onion**, finely chopped

Leaves from 1 sprig fresh **marjoram** or **oregano**, finely chopped, or 1 teaspoon dried

¼ cup **tomato paste**

1 cup **white wine**

1 cup **chicken stock**

1 (28- or 32-ounce) can **San Marzano tomatoes** (look for DOP on the label)

½ cup fresh **basil** leaves

1 pound **spaghetti**

2 tablespoons **butter**

Preheat the oven to 375°F. Place a cooling rack over a baking sheet or cover a baking sheet with parchment paper.

Place the pork and beef in a bowl and season liberally with salt and pepper. In a food processor, pulse-chop the bread into crumbs. Scrape into a small bowl and add the milk. Soak just until moistened. Squeeze most of the milk from the bread and add the bread to the meat, rubbing it into small pieces as you add it. Season with a few grates of nutmeg. Add the egg yolk, half the parsley (1 or 2 tablespoons), and the chopped garlic.

In the food processor, pulse-chop the mortadella until very finely chopped. Add to the meats along with the grated pecorino. Drizzle liberally with EVOO and mix everything together gently. Roll into walnut-size meatballs and place on the cooling rack. Roast to light brown but not cooked through, 12 to 15 minutes.

Meanwhile, in a large Dutch oven, heat the 3 tablespoons EVOO (3 turns of the pan) over medium to medium-high heat. Add the fennel seeds, chile, onion, sliced garlic, marjoram, and salt and pepper and cook to soften the onion, 4 to 5 minutes. Add the tomato paste and stir 30 seconds. Deglaze the pan with the wine. Add the stock and tomatoes, breaking them up with a potato masher. Bring to a boil, then reduce to a simmer and add a few torn basil leaves, reserving some for garnish. Add the remaining parsley and gently slide in the meatballs. Simmer for 15 to 20 minutes to combine the flavors and finish cooking the meatballs.

[Make-ahead: Let cool and refrigerate.]

[Night of: Return to room temp before reheating to a bubble over medium heat. Uncover and simmer while you cook the pasta.]

Bring a large pot of water to a boil. Salt the water and cook the pasta al dente. Ladle out about a cup of the starchy cooking water. Drain the pasta and return it to the pot. Add the butter, a few ladles of sauce, and the starchy water, tossing with tongs for 1 or 2 minutes for the butter to melt and the flavors to absorb.

Serve in bowls with lots of sauce and meatballs on top, lots of shaved cheese, and a few leaves of torn basil.

WEEK 09

ONE
FOR ALL

HOW TO TAKE 2 FOUNDATION
RECIPES AND USE THEM TO BUILD
5 MEALS FOR THE WEEK

DISH
1
HEARTY &
HEALTHY 3-BEAN
MINESTRONE
PAGE 64

DISH
2
SMOKY
SPANISH
HUNTER'S
CHICKEN
PAGE 65

DISH
3
SPICY ROASTED
TOMATO MARINARA
WITH SPAGHETTI
SQUASH
PAGE 66

DISH
4
MEXICAN-STYLE
PESTO WITH
WHOLE-GRAIN
PASTA
PAGE 68

DISH
5
EGGPLANT
PARM
STACKS
PAGE 70

Hearty & Healthy 3-Bean Minestrone

Most of my life, anytime I wanted heat in a dish I would just throw in some crushed red pepper flakes. But with the wide availability of little fresh chiles, I find that I've switched almost entirely to using the fresh. I especially enjoy the flavor of Fresno chiles, because they're not too hot and they're a little bit fruity. **Suggested side:** Hot crusty bread for mopping. SERVES 4

2 tablespoons **EVOO**, plus more for drizzling
1 slice (⅛ inch thick) **prosciutto di Parma**, about ¼ pound, chopped (optional)
1 **onion**, chopped
2 or 3 ribs **celery**, finely chopped
2 **carrots**, finely chopped
1 pound small **potatoes**, chopped (see Heads-up)
4 cloves **roasted garlic** (from Roasted Tomatoes, page 323)
1 fresh **red Fresno** or **Holland finger chile**, finely chopped or thinly sliced
Salt and **pepper**
1 (15-ounce) can **cannellini beans**, drained
1 (15- to 15.5-ounce) can **chickpeas**, drained
8 cups **Parmigiano-Herb Stock** (page 323)
4 **Roasted Tomatoes** (page 323), chopped
5 ounces thin **green beans** (haricots verts), cut into thirds
1 small head **escarole** or small bunch **chard**, shredded
A little grated **lemon** zest
Shredded **Parmigiano-Reggiano cheese**, for serving

In a soup pot or large Dutch oven, heat the EVOO (2 turns of the pan) over medium to medium-high heat. Add the prosciutto (if using) and stir a couple of minutes. Add the onion, celery, carrots, potatoes, garlic, chile, and salt and pepper. Cover the pan and sweat the vegetables for 10 minutes, stirring occasionally. Add the cannellini beans, chickpeas, stock, and tomatoes. Bring to a boil and add the green beans. Bring the soup back to a bubble to cook the beans, then turn off the heat.

[**Make-ahead:** Let cool and refrigerate.]

[**Night of:** Return the soup to room temp before reheating over medium-high heat.]

Return the soup to a boil and wilt in the escarole. Stir in some lemon zest.

Serve the soup in shallow bowls and top with Parm and a drizzle of EVOO.

Heads-up: Instead of potatoes, you could make the minestrone with 1 cup small pasta. In a pot of salted boiling water cook the pasta al dente.

[**Make-ahead:** Let the pasta cool and drizzle with a touch of EVOO. Cover and store separately from the soup.]

[**Night of:** After you bring the soup to a bubble, stir the pasta into it.]

Smoky Spanish Hunter's Chicken

Ingredients like paprika, sherry, and saffron give a cacciatore a little bit of a Spanish makeover . . . not to mention the Manchego cheese in the polenta. SERVES 4

2 large **red bell peppers**

2 pounds boneless, skinless **chicken thighs**, trimmed of all fat (8 to 10 pieces)

Salt and **pepper**

3 tablespoons **EVOO**

½ pound **cremini mushrooms** or 3 medium **portobello mushroom caps**, gills scraped, thinly sliced

2 medium **sweet onions**, thinly sliced

3 or 4 cloves **garlic**, chopped or sliced

¼ cup **dry sherry** or ½ cup **dry white** or **red wine**

6 **Roasted Tomatoes** (page 323)

1½ teaspoons **smoked sweet paprika**

3 cups **Parmigiano-Herb Stock** (page 323)

A couple of pinches of **saffron threads**

1 cup quick-cooking **polenta**

A handful of grated **Manchego cheese**

A handful of fresh **flat-leaf parsley** tops, chopped

Char the bell peppers all over on the stovetop over a gas flame or under the broiler with the oven door ajar to let steam escape. Place the peppers in a bowl and cover tightly. When cool enough to handle, rub off the skins with a paper towel, then halve and seed the peppers and thinly slice.

Season the chicken liberally with salt and pepper. In a Dutch oven, heat 1 tablespoon EVOO (1 turn of the pan) over medium-high heat. Add the chicken and brown a few minutes on each side, then transfer to a plate. Add the remaining 2 tablespoons EVOO (2 turns of the pan) and the mushrooms and cook until well browned, 10 to 12 minutes. Add the onions, garlic, and salt and pepper and cook, stirring occasionally, to soften the onions and garlic, 8 to 10 minutes. Deglaze the pan with the sherry. Stir in the tomatoes, roasted peppers, and paprika. Cook for 10 minutes. Add the chicken and simmer 10 minutes more.

[**Make-ahead:** Let cool and refrigerate.]

[**Night of:** Return the chicken to room temp before reheating gently over medium heat, covered. Uncover and simmer while you make the polenta.]

In a saucepan, combine the stock and saffron and bring to a boil. Whisk in the polenta and keep whisking until it thickens, 2 to 3 minutes. Season with salt and stir in the Manchego.

Serve the polenta in shallow bowls and top with the chicken and sauce. Garnish with parsley.

Spicy Roasted-Tomato Marinara with Spaghetti Squash

If you're making this meal to serve on **Cook Day**, you can roast the spaghetti squash while you're making the marinara. SERVES 4

3 tablespoons **EVOO**, plus more for drizzling

5 or 6 flat **anchovy fillets**

1 **sweet onion**, thinly sliced or chopped

1 fresh **red Fresno** or **Holland finger chile**, sliced or chopped

3 or 4 cloves **garlic**, sliced or chopped

Leaves from 1 or 2 small sprigs fresh **marjoram** or **oregano**, finely chopped

2 tablespoons **tomato paste**

½ cup **dry red** or **white wine**

1 cup **Parmigiano-Herb Stock** (page 323)

8 **Roasted Tomatoes** (page 323)

A handful of fresh **flat-leaf parsley**, finely chopped

A few fresh **basil** leaves, torn

2 medium **spaghetti squash**

Salt and **pepper**

Shredded **Parmigiano-Reggiano cheese**, for serving

In a Dutch oven, heat the 3 tablespoons EVOO (3 turns of the pan) over medium heat. Add the anchovies, cover the pan with a splatter screen or lid, and shake until the anchovies begin to break up. Reduce the heat a bit, uncover, and stir until the anchovies melt. Add the onion, chile, garlic, and marjoram. Cover and cook until the onion is very sweet and soft, 10 to 15 minutes. Add the tomato paste and stir 1 minute. Deglaze the pan with the wine. Add the stock, roasted tomatoes, parsley, and basil and simmer over medium heat for 10 to 15 minutes to combine flavors.

[**Make-ahead:** Let cool and refrigerate.]

[**Night of:** Return the marinara to room temp while you begin roasting the spaghetti squash. When the squash has been in the oven for 30 minutes, bring the sauce to a bubble over medium heat, then reduce to low to keep it warm.]

Preheat the oven to 450°F. Line 1 or 2 baking sheets with foil (whatever you need to fit 4 squash halves).

Halve the squash lengthwise and scoop out the seeds. Season the squash with salt and pepper and place cut side down on the baking sheet. Roast until very tender, 45 minutes to 1 hour.

Holding each squash half with a potholder, use a fork to scrape the "spaghetti" strands into a bowl. Save the shells. Drizzle the hot "spaghetti" with a little EVOO, adjust the seasoning, and toss well.

Spoon the "spaghetti" back into the shells and top with lots of marinara and Parm.

Mexican-Style Pesto with Whole-Grain Pasta

You can make this with a whole wheat or a multigrain spaghetti. Or you might want to try one of those gluten-free pastas made with brown rice flour. SERVES 4

3 fresh **red Fresno chiles**

¼ cup **pistachios** or sliced **almonds**

1 cup packed fresh **cilantro** leaves or **flat-leaf parsley**

1 cup packed **arugula** or other spicy greens

Leaves from 1 or 2 sprigs fresh **marjoram** or **oregano**

2 cloves **garlic**, grated or finely chopped

1 teaspoon ground **cumin**

Juice of 1 **lime**

About ⅓ cup **Parmigiano-Herb Stock** (page 323)

¼ cup **EVOO**

Salt and **pepper**

1 pound **whole-grain spaghetti**

Grated **Manchego cheese**, for serving

Char the chiles all over on the stovetop over a gas flame or under the broiler with the oven door ajar to let steam escape. Place the chiles in a bowl and cover tightly. When cool enough to handle, rub off the skins with a paper towel, then halve and seed the chiles and put them in a food processor.

Meanwhile, lightly toast the nuts in a dry skillet.

Add the toasted nuts, cilantro, arugula, marjoram, garlic, cumin, lime juice, stock, EVOO, and salt and pepper to the chiles. Pulse-chop to form a pesto.

[**Make-ahead:** Place in a container, cover, and refrigerate.]

[**Night of:** Remove the pesto from the fridge.]

Scrape the pesto into a large serving bowl.

Bring a large pot of water to a boil. Salt the water and cook the pasta al dente. Ladle out about a cup of the starchy cooking water and stir into the pesto. Drain the pasta and add to the sauce, tossing with tongs for 1 or 2 minutes for the flavors to absorb.

Serve immediately with Manchego on top.

Eggplant Parm Stacks

This is the meal that you make *last* on **Cook Day**, because it's what you're going to have for dinner. SERVES 4 TO 6

Salt and **pepper**

2 medium **eggplants** (1 pound each), cut crosswise into ½-inch-thick rounds

3 tablespoons **EVOO**

2 medium **onions**, thinly sliced

5 cloves **garlic**, finely chopped

1 small **fresh chile**, seeded and finely chopped (optional)

Leaves from 1 sprig fresh **marjoram** or **oregano**, finely chopped

6 **Roasted Tomatoes** (page 323), chopped, with their juices

1 cup **flour**

4 large **eggs**

1½ cups **panko bread crumbs**

1 cup grated **Parmigiano-Reggiano cheese**

½ cup yellow **cornmeal**

2 teaspoons **fennel pollen** or **ground fennel** (optional)

Vegetable oil, for shallow-frying

1 bunch **green** or **red chard**, washed, stemmed, and shredded

Freshly grated **nutmeg**

1 cup fresh **basil** leaves

1 pound **fresh mozzarella cheese**, thinly sliced

Salt the eggplant slices and drain in a colander for 30 minutes.

In a large skillet with a lid, heat 2 tablespoons EVOO (2 turns of the pan) over medium-high heat. Add the onions, 4 cloves of the garlic, the chile (if using), marjoram, and salt and pepper. Cover the pan and sweat until the onions are very soft and sweet, 10 to 15 minutes. Stir in the tomatoes. Reduce the heat to medium and cook uncovered for 15 minutes to thicken the sauce (it should be quite thick).

Preheat the oven to 400°F. Place a cooling rack over a baking sheet.

When the eggplant is ready, line up 3 shallow bowls on the counter: Spread the flour out in one, beat the eggs in the second, and mix together the panko, Parm, cornmeal, and fennel pollen (if using) in the third. Coat each eggplant slice in the flour, then in egg, and finally in the panko mix, pressing to make sure the coating sticks.

In a large heavy-bottomed skillet, heat ¼ inch of vegetable oil over medium to medium-high heat. Working in batches, cook the eggplant slices 3 to 4 minutes on each side. Drain on the cooling rack. Sprinkle the hot eggplant with a little salt.

When all of the eggplant has been fried, carefully wipe the skillet clean and heat the remaining 1 tablespoon EVOO (1 turn of the pan) over medium heat. Add the remaining 1 clove garlic and stir 1 minute. Add the chard and wilt it; season with salt, pepper, and a few grates of nutmeg. Turn off the heat.

Build the stacks on the cooling rack in this order: eggplant, chard, tomato-onions, basil leaves, mozzarella, and eggplant. Bake for 5 minutes to melt the mozzarella. Serve immediately.

WEEK 10

STICK
TO YOUR
RIBS

FIVE WELL-BALANCED,
STICK-TO-YOUR-RIBS SUPPERS

DISH
1
ROAST
PORK &
POTATOES
PAGE 72

DISH
2
CORN &
CRAB CHOWDER
POTPIES
PAGE 73

DISH
3
MINUTE STEAK
HOAGIES WITH
HOMEMADE
STEAK SAUCE
PAGE 75

DISH
4
CALABRESE
CHICKEN
ONE-POT
PAGE 76

DISH
5
PORK &
POBLANO
GREEN CHILI
POT
PAGE 77

Roast Pork & Potatoes

You're roasting 2 loins of pork for this recipe, one to be served for dinner on **Cook Day,** and the other to be used to make Pork & Poblano Green Chili Pot (page 77). In order to have the pork ready close to dinnertime, season the pork (step 1) and let the loins hang out for a couple of hours at room temp. Then roast them 2 hours before dinnertime, which still gives you time to assemble the chili. **Suggested side:** Creamy Mushrooms & Kale (see QR code below). SERVES 6

2 boneless **pork loins** (2½ to 3 pounds each)

EVOO, for liberal drizzling

Sea salt and coarsely ground **pepper**

2 medium **onions**, very finely chopped

4 cloves **garlic**, thinly sliced or finely chopped

1 fresh **red Fresno chile**, seeded and finely chopped

Leaves from 3 or 4 sprigs fresh **rosemary**, finely chopped

2 tablespoons fresh **thyme** leaves, chopped

2 pounds small **potatoes**, halved

1½ teaspoons **fennel seeds** or **fennel pollen**

1 cup **white wine** or **chicken stock**

Preheat the oven to 400°F.

Rub the loins with EVOO and lots of salt and pepper. In a bowl, combine the onions, garlic, chile, rosemary, thyme, and salt and pepper. Drizzle with EVOO and toss. Arrange a bed of potatoes in a roasting pan. Place the pork loins over the potatoes. Sprinkle the fennel on the loin being served on **Cook Day**. Pile the onion mixture evenly over both pork loins.

Roast for 45 minutes. Pour the wine evenly around the pan, then shake the pan to loosen the potatoes (or use a spoon to mix them around a bit). Roast until the meat reaches 145°F on an instant-read thermometer, another 15 minutes or so. Set one pork loin aside for Pork & Poblano Green Chili Pot (page 77). Let the other loin rest at least 10 minutes before carving.

Serve the pork with the potatoes and pan drippings.

Recipe for Creamy Mushrooms & Kale
View a bonus Side Dish recipe.

Corn & Crab Chowder Potpies

Puff pastry is a fabulous thing to have in the freezer at all times. With just about no effort on your part, you can really dress up a weeknight dinner like this one. SERVES 4

1 tablespoon **EVOO**

3 or 4 slices **speck** or **bacon**, chopped or thinly sliced crosswise

5 or 6 **baby potatoes**, chopped

3 or 4 small ribs **celery**, chopped

1 **onion**, finely chopped

2 large cloves **garlic**, chopped or thinly sliced

1 fresh **red Fresno chile**, finely chopped

2 tablespoons fresh **thyme** leaves, chopped

1 tablespoon **crab-boil seasoning** (such as Old Bay)

Salt and **pepper**

3 cups **chicken stock**

3 cups **milk**

4 tablespoons (½ stick) **butter**

3 rounded tablespoons **flour**, plus more for unfolding the puff pastry

1 rounded tablespoon **Dijon mustard**

2 cups **corn kernels**, fresh (from 3 to 4 ears) or thawed frozen

1 sheet frozen **puff pastry**, thawed but chilled well

1 **egg**, beaten with a splash of water

1 (6- to 8-ounce) tub fresh **lump crabmeat**, picked through for bits of shell

A few drops of **hot sauce**

In a Dutch oven, heat the EVOO (1 turn of the pan) over medium to medium-high heat. Add the speck and render a couple of minutes. Add the potatoes, celery, onion, garlic, chile, thyme, crab seasoning, and salt and pepper. Cover and cook for 10 minutes, stirring occasionally. Add the stock and milk and bring to a boil while you make a roux.

In a small skillet, melt the butter over medium heat. Whisk in the 3 tablespoons flour and cook the roux for 1 minute. Stir in the mustard. Transfer the roux to the chowder and stir well. When the roux has incorporated, stir in the corn and bring to a bubble. Reduce the heat and cook to slightly thicken.

[**Make-ahead:** Let cool and refrigerate.]

[**Night of:** Return the chowder to room temp before reheating gently, covered, over medium heat while you bake the pastry tops.]

Preheat the oven to 425°F.

Unfold the puff pastry onto a lightly floured work surface. Choose four 3-cup bowls or ramekins to serve the potpies in. Invert them onto the dough and trace around them with a knife to cut pieces to fit the tops. Arrange the pastry on a nonstick baking sheet or parchment paper–lined baking sheet and brush with the egg wash. Bake until golden, 10 to 12 minutes.

Uncover the chowder and bring up to a simmer. Sprinkle the crab with hot sauce and stir into the chowder to heat through.

Ladle the chowder into the individual dishes and top with the pastry.

Minute Steak Hoagies with Homemade Steak Sauce

While you're up, might as well make a double or triple batch of the sauce. It's a great thing to have on hand. SERVES 4

STEAK SAUCE
1 large **shallot**, coarsely chopped
1 **fresh red chile** (such as long red or Fresno), sliced
2 large **cloves** garlic
2 large fresh **bay leaves**
1 teaspoon **mustard seeds** or **dry mustard**
¼ cup **dry sherry**
¼ cup **Worcestershire sauce**
1 tablespoon **black peppercorns**
1 cup high-quality **ketchup** (preferably low-sugar)
2 tablespoons **soy sauce** or **tamari**
1 cup **beef stock**

4 **hoagie rolls**
1¼ pounds **flank steak** (see Heads-up)
1 tablespoon high-temperature **cooking oil** (such as canola or peanut)
1 big bunch **watercress** (stemmed), **upland cress**, or **baby arugula**

Make the steak sauce: In a food processor, combine the shallot, chile, garlic, bay leaves, mustard, sherry, Worcestershire, and peppercorns and process into a smooth paste. Scrape the flavor paste into a small saucepan and stir in the ketchup, soy sauce, and stock. Bring to a boil, reduce the heat to a simmer, and cook for 30 minutes.

[**Make-ahead:** Let cool and refrigerate.]

[**Night of:** Return the sauce to room temp before reheating gently over medium heat.]

Preheat the oven to 325°F and warm up the rolls (don't split them open yet; this is just to crisp the outsides a bit).

Very thinly slice the flank steak against the grain. In a large skillet, heat the oil over high heat until it smokes. Add the meat and toss for 2 minutes. Turn off the heat and combine the steak with the warm steak sauce.

Cut open the rolls and stuff the hoagies with spicy greens and hot and saucy steak.

Heads-up: If you put the flank steak in the freezer for 10 minutes or so, it will firm up and be much easier to very thinly slice.

Watch Rachael prepare Homemade Steak Sauce.

Calabrese Chicken One-Pot

I fine-chopped the Calabrese salami (a spicy-hot salami from southern Italy) in the food processor because it's easier than chasing it around with a knife. I very coarsely chopped it first, though, to give the processor blades something to work with. **Suggested side:** Ciabatta bread, crusted up in the oven, for mopping. SERVES 4

4 bone-in, skin-on **chicken breast** halves

Salt and **pepper**

1 tablespoon **EVOO**, plus more for drizzling

¼ pound **Calabrese salami**, very finely chopped

1 **onion**, chopped or thinly sliced

2 small ribs **celery**, chopped

1 **cubanelle pepper**, chopped or thinly sliced

3 or 4 cloves **garlic**, chopped or thinly sliced

1½ teaspoons **smoked sweet paprika**

1 teaspoon **fennel seeds**

1 cup **dry red wine**

1 (28-ounce) can **stewed tomatoes**

1 (15-ounce) can **tomato sauce**

A handful of fresh **flat-leaf parsley** tops, finely chopped

Season the chicken breasts with salt and pepper. In a Dutch oven, heat the 1 tablespoon EVOO (1 turn of the pan) over medium-high heat until very hot. Add the chicken and brown on both sides. Transfer the chicken to a plate.

Add the salami to the pan and stir for 1 minute. Add the onion, celery, cubanelle, and garlic and cook to soften the onion, about 5 minutes. Add the paprika and fennel seeds. Deglaze the pan with the wine. Add the tomatoes, tomato sauce, parsley, and the chicken. Bring to a boil, reduce to a simmer, cover, and cook until the chicken is cooked through, 10 to 12 minutes.

[**Make-ahead:** Let cool and refrigerate.]

[**Night of:** Return the chicken and sauce to room temp before reheating gently over medium heat. Add a splash of water or stock to the pan to start out, just to loosen things up.]

Serve with an extra drizzle of EVOO.

Pork & Poblano Green Chili Pot

The pork for this dish comes from Roast Pork & Potatoes (page 72). **Suggested side:** Instead of the tortilla chips, you could serve the chili with either charred tortillas or Cheesy Polenta (recipe follows). SERVES 4

4 large **poblano chiles**
2 fresh **jalapeño chiles**
2 tablespoons **EVOO**
2 **onions**, chopped
3 or 4 cloves **garlic**, chopped or
    sliced
12 **tomatillos**, husked, rinsed,
    and chopped
Salt and pepper
A handful of fresh **cilantro** leaves
1½ teaspoons ground **cumin**
1 tablespoon **honey**
2 cups **chicken stock**
1½ pounds **cooked pork** (from
    Roast Pork & Potatoes, page
    72), diced
2 **limes**: 1 juiced, 1 cut into
    wedges
Tortilla chips, for serving

Char the poblanos and jalapeños all over on the stovetop over a gas flame or under the broiler with the oven door ajar to let steam escape. Place the chiles in a bowl and cover tightly. When cool enough to handle, rub off the skins with a paper towel, then halve, seed, and chop the chiles.

Meanwhile, in a Dutch oven, heat the EVOO (2 turns of the pan) over medium heat. Add the onions and sweat them for 10 minutes. Add the garlic and tomatillos and cook 10 minutes more; season with salt and pepper. Scrape the mixture into a food processor. Add the cilantro, cumin, and honey and puree. Return the puree to the Dutch oven.

Stir the chopped chiles and stock into the puree and bring to a boil. Reduce the heat to low and simmer to combine the flavors. Stir the pork into the chili and let it return to a bubble, then remove from the heat.

[Make-ahead: Let cool and refrigerate.]

[**Night of:** Return the chili to room temp before reheating gently over medium heat.]

When the chili is back up to a bubble, stir in the lime juice. Coarsely break up some tortilla chips and put in the bottom of a serving bowl. Ladle the chili over the chips. Serve with lime wedges for squeezing.

Cheesy Polenta SERVES 4

2 cups **chicken stock**
1 cup **milk**
1 cup quick-cooking **polenta**
1 cup shredded **Manchego**
    cheese

In a medium saucepan, combine the stock and milk and bring to a boil. Whisk in the polenta and keep whisking until it thickens, 2 to 3 minutes. Stir in the Manchego and serve warm.

WEEK 11

ONE-POT
WEEK

IF YOU'RE FACING ONE OF
YOUR BUSIEST WEEKS EVER, HERE
ARE 5 STRAIGHT ONE-POT DISHES
THAT WILL TAKE YOU THROUGH
THE ENTIRE WORKWEEK WITH EASE.

DISH
1
CREAMY CHICKEN &
MUSHROOM
ONE-POT WITH
POTPIE TOPPERS
PAGE 79

DISH
2
SAUSAGE,
PEPPER &
ONION
ONE-POT
PAGE 81

DISH
3
CAULIFLOWER
MAC 'N'
CHEESE
PAGE 82

DISH
4
MINESTRA
WITH BEEF &
PORK
POLPETTE
PAGE 83

DISH
5
NACHO-
TOPPED
CHILI POT
PAGE 84

Creamy Chicken & Mushroom One-Pot with Potpie Toppers

If you want, you could serve the chicken and mushroom filling as a thick soup with crusty, warm baguette for dipping instead of baking the puff pastry toppers. SERVES 4

3 large boneless, skinless **chicken breast** halves

3 **onions**: 1 quartered (root end intact) and 2 chopped

2 fresh **bay leaves**

2 tablespoons **EVOO**

8 ounces **button mushrooms**, sliced or quartered

4 **baby potatoes**, diced

2 **parsnips**, peeled and cut into ½-inch cubes

2 small ribs **celery**, chopped

Leaves from 2 or 3 sprigs fresh **sage**, very thinly sliced

Salt and **pepper**

3 tablespoons **butter**

3 tablespoons **flour**, plus more for unfolding the puff pastry

¼ to ½ cup **white wine**

1 rounded tablespoon **Dijon mustard**

2 cups **chicken stock**

½ cup **heavy cream**

1 sheet frozen **puff pastry**, thawed but chilled well

1 **egg**, beaten with a splash of water

In a Dutch oven or deep skillet, combine the chicken, onion quarters, and 1 bay leaf. Add water to come to the top of the chicken. Bring to a low boil, reduce the heat to a simmer, and poach the chicken for 12 to 15 minutes. Remove the chicken and when cool enough to handle, dice or shred with forks. Strain the poaching liquid and reserve. Dry the pan.

In the same pan, heat the EVOO (2 turns of the pan) over medium-high heat. Add the mushrooms and brown lightly. Add the chopped onions, potatoes, parsnips, celery, sage, the remaining bay leaf, and salt and pepper. Cover the pot and sweat the vegetables for 10 minutes, stirring occasionally. Remove the bay leaf. Melt in the butter, sprinkle in the 3 tablespoons flour, and stir to make a light roux. Deglaze the pan with the wine. Add 2 cups of the reserved poaching liquid. Whisk in the mustard and 2 cups chicken stock. Stir in the cream and simmer to thicken to a light gravy consistency. Adjust the salt and pepper and add the chicken.

[**Make-ahead:** Let cool and refrigerate.]

[**Night of:** Return the chicken to room temp before reheating gently over medium heat.]

Preheat the oven to 425°F.

Unfold the puff pastry onto a lightly floured work surface. Choose four 3-cup bowls to serve the potpies in. Invert them onto the dough and trace around them with a knife to cut pieces to fit the tops. Arrange the pastry on a nonstick baking sheet or parchment paper–lined baking sheet and brush with the egg wash. Bake until golden, 10 to 12 minutes.

Ladle the chicken and mushroom filling into the bowls and top with the potpie toppers.

Sausage, Pepper & Onion One-Pot

Suggested side: Ciabatta bread, crisped up in the oven, for mopping. I love ciabatta bread because it's all crust. We used to fight over the crust in my family; the prizes were the heels (and elbows) of the loaves, because they were the crunchiest. SERVES 4

2 pounds **Italian hot** and/or **sweet sausages**
3 tablespoons **EVOO**
1½ teaspoons **fennel seeds**
1 **fresh red chile**, thinly sliced
2 **cubanelle peppers**, thinly sliced
1 **red bell pepper**, thinly sliced
2 large **red** or **yellow onions**, thinly sliced
4 cloves **garlic**, thinly sliced
Salt and **pepper**
2 tablespoons **tomato paste**
½ cup **dry white wine**
1 cup **chicken stock**
1 (15-ounce) can **tomato sauce** or **stewed tomatoes**
A generous handful of **flat-leaf parsley** tops, finely chopped

In a Dutch oven or deep skillet, combine the sausages, 1 inch of water, and 1 tablespoon EVOO (1 turn of the pan). Bring to a boil, then reduce the heat a bit and allow the water to boil away. The sausages will gently cook through in the water, then the oil will crisp the casings to a deep brown. Transfer the sausages to a plate.

In the same pan, heat the remaining 2 tablespoons EVOO (2 turns of the pan) over medium-high heat. Stir in the fennel seeds and chile and cook until fragrant. Add all the sliced peppers, the onions, garlic, and salt and pepper and cook to soften the peppers, about 15 minutes. Add the tomato paste and stir for 1 minute. Deglaze the pan with the wine. Add the stock and tomato sauce and let simmer and thicken up a bit while you cut up the sausages.

Thickly slice the sausages on an angle (3 or 4 slices per sausage) and add to the sauce.

[**Make-ahead:** Let cool and refrigerate.]

[**Night of:** Return the sausage mixture to room temp before reheating gently over medium heat or in a 350°F oven.]

Just before serving, stir in the parsley.

Watch Rachael prepare
Sausage, Pepper & Onion
One-Pot.

Cauliflower Mac 'n' Cheese

The pots in the recipes for this week all do double duty so that the recipes can live up to the promise of "one-pot" cooking. Even though the mac 'n' cheese ends up in a baking dish, all the stovetop cooking is done in one pot: the pasta, the cauliflower, and the cheese sauce. SERVES 6

Salt and pepper
1 pound **whole wheat** or **whole-grain short-cut pasta** (such as macaroni, ziti, or penne rigate)
1 tablespoon **EVOO**
1 large head **cauliflower**
1 cup **chicken stock**
3 tablespoons **butter**
1 **onion**, finely chopped
4 cloves **garlic**, finely chopped
3 tablespoons **flour**
2½ cups **milk**
Leaves from 3 to 4 sprigs fresh **sage**, very thinly sliced
Freshly grated **nutmeg**
1 cup shredded **sharp white cheddar cheese**
1 cup shredded **Gruyère cheese**
1 cup shredded **Parmigiano-Reggiano cheese**
2 tablespoons **Dijon mustard**
1 small bunch **watercress**, washed and chopped

[If making this to serve on **Cook Day**, preheat the oven to 400°F. If making this for later in the week, you'll preheat the oven on the night of.]

Fill a soup pot or Dutch oven with water and bring to a boil. Salt the water and cook the pasta until 2 minutes shy of al dente. Drain. Dry the pot and return it to the stove.

In the same pot, heat the EVOO (1 turn of the pan) over medium to medium-high heat. Cut the core out of the cauliflower (the head stays intact) and set the head in the pot. Add the stock, cover, and steam until tender, 12 to 15 minutes. Transfer to a plate. Discard the cooking liquid and wipe out the pot. When cool enough to handle, separate the cauliflower into florets.

Meanwhile, return the pot to medium heat and melt the butter. Add the onion and garlic and cook to soften, 3 to 4 minutes. Sprinkle with the flour and stir for 1 minute. Whisk in the milk and add the sage; season with salt, pepper, and a few grates of nutmeg. Cook until thickened. In a bowl, combine all 3 cheeses. Stir the mustard into the sauce, then stir in two-thirds of the combined cheeses until melted.

Add the pasta and cauliflower to the sauce. Transfer to a deep 9 by 13-inch baking dish and top with the remaining cheese.

[**Make-ahead:** Let cool and refrigerate.]

[**Night of:** Return the casserole to room temp while you preheat the oven to 400°F.]

Place the casserole on a baking sheet and bake until heated through and browned, 40 to 45 minutes.

Serve in bowls topped with chopped spicy watercress.

Minestra with Beef & Pork Polpette

You can replace the potatoes with ¾ cup small soup pasta (like ditalini or pennette), but then cook it on the night you're going to serve the minestra and add it to the reheating soup. **Suggested side:** Ciabatta bread, crusted up in the oven, for mopping. SERVES 4

SOUP
2 tablespoons **EVOO**
4 ounces thickly sliced (⅛ inch) **pancetta** or **speck**, coarsely chopped
2 medium **onions**, chopped
4 cloves **garlic**: 3 thinly sliced, 1 smashed but whole
1 **starchy potato** (such as russet), peeled and diced
1 fresh **bay leaf**
Salt and **pepper**
2 heads **escarole**, chopped
Freshly grated **nutmeg**

1 (15- to 19-ounce) can **cannellini beans**, drained
6 cups **chicken stock**

MEATBALLS
3 slices **white bread** or **peasant bread**, crusts trimmed
Milk, for soaking the bread
8 ounces **ground beef**
8 ounces **ground pork**
1 teaspoon **fennel seeds**, **fennel pollen**, or **ground fennel**
1 teaspoon **sweet paprika** (smoked or regular)

1 teaspoon crushed **red pepper flakes** (optional)
Salt and **pepper**
A generous handful of grated **Parmigiano-Reggiano cheese**
A handful of fresh **flat-leaf parsley** tops, finely chopped
1 **egg** yolk
EVOO, for drizzling

EVOO and grated **Parmigiano-Reggiano cheese**, for serving

Make the soup: In a soup pot or Dutch oven, heat the EVOO (2 turns of the pan) over medium-high heat. Add the pancetta and render a couple of minutes. Add the onions, sliced garlic, potato, bay leaf, and salt and pepper and cook to soften the onions, about 5 minutes. Add the escarole and season with salt, pepper, and a few grates of nutmeg. Cover to wilt. Stir in the beans, stock, and 2 cups water. Bring to a boil, then reduce to a rolling simmer while you make the meatballs.

Make the meatballs: Douse the bread with milk to soften. Place the ground meats in a bowl. Season the meat with fennel, paprika, red pepper flakes (if using), and salt and pepper. Add the cheese, parsley, and egg yolk. Squeeze the milk out of the bread and pull it into little crumbs as you add it to the meat. Drizzle with EVOO and roll the meat into walnut-size balls.

Remove the bay leaf from the soup. Add the meatballs and poach until cooked through.

[**Make-ahead:** Let cool and refrigerate.]

[**Night of:** Return the soup to room temp before reheating gently over medium heat.]

Serve the soup in shallow bowls with shredded Parm on top and an extra drizzle of EVOO.

Nacho-Topped Chili Pot

When I make a big pot of chili, especially as a make-ahead, I like a nice, lean ground sirloin because when you pull that out of the fridge, you really don't want to be looking at a layer of congealed fat that you can't skim off because the chili is all chunky and bumpy. SERVES 4 TO 6

4 **poblano chiles**
2 large fresh **jalapeño chiles**
2 tablespoons **EVOO**
2 pounds **ground sirloin**
1 large **onion**, finely chopped
4 cloves **garlic**, finely chopped
1 tablespoon ground **cumin**
1 tablespoon ground **coriander**
1 tablespoon **smoked sweet paprika**
2 tablespoons **chili powder** blend (I use Gebhardt's)
Salt and **pepper**
¼ cup **tomato paste**
1 (12-ounce) bottle **beer** (I use Negra Modelo), at room temperature
2 cups **beef stock**
1 (16-ounce) can spicy **vegetarian refried beans**
Good-quality **tortilla chips** (I use Xochitl)
2 cups shredded soft **Mexican melting cheese, Monterey Jack, yellow cheddar**, or a combo
1 fresh **red Fresno chile**, thinly sliced
Sliced **pickled jalapeños**

Char the poblanos and fresh jalapeños all over on the stovetop over a gas flame or under the broiler with the oven door ajar to let steam escape. Place the chiles in a bowl and cover tightly. When cool enough to handle, rub off the skins with a paper towel, then halve and seed the chiles and coarsely puree in a food processor.

In a deep skillet, heat the EVOO (2 turns of the pan) over medium-high heat. Add the meat and cook, breaking it into crumbles as it browns. Add the onion, garlic, cumin, coriander, paprika, chili powder, and salt and pepper. Cook to soften the onion, about 5 minutes. Add the tomato paste and stir for 1 minute. Deglaze the pan with the beer. Add the stock and heat through. Stir in the chile puree and simmer a few minutes for the flavors to combine.

[**Make-ahead:** Let cool and refrigerate.]

[**Night of:** Return the chili to room temp before reheating gently over medium heat, stirring occasionally.]

Preheat the broiler with a rack in the center of the oven.

In a glass bowl, combine the refried beans with a splash of water. Reheat in the microwave.

Uncover the chili and top with tortilla chips. Drizzle the refried beans over the chips and cover the entire top with the cheese. Place under the broiler until lightly browned and the cheese has melted.

Serve the chili topped with the fresh chile and pickled jalapeños.

Watch Rachael prepare Nacho-Topped Chili Pot.

WEEK 12

HEARTY CLASSICS

CLASSIC, HEARTY,
DELICIOUS . . . AND MADE AHEAD.
WHAT'S NOT TO LOVE?

DISH
1
ZINFULLY
DELICIOUS
SHORT RIBS
PAGE 86

DISH
2
TURKEY
STUFFING
MEAT LOAVES
PAGE 88

DISH
3
PORTOBELLO &
SPINACH
BOLOGNESE
PAGE 89

DISH
4
SHORT RIB
RAGU WITH
DRUNKEN
PAPPARDELLE
PAGE 90

DISH
5
GREEN
PASTITSIO
PAGE 91

Zinfully Delicious Short Ribs

It's best to serve these ribs the day *after* you make them (or later in the week), because they need at least a day to sit so that you can skim off the fat and let the flavors fully develop. This dish makes 4 extra ribs for Short Rib Ragu with Drunken Pappardelle (page 90). SERVES 4 (2 RIBS PER PERSON)

12 meaty bone-in **beef short ribs**, all of similar weight and size

1 teaspoon ground **allspice** or a couple of pinches of ground **cloves**

1 scant tablespoon **smoked sweet paprika**

Salt and **pepper**

4 tablespoons **vegetable** or **olive oil**

4 large cloves **garlic**, peeled

1 fresh **red Fresno chile**, coarsely chopped

4 fresh **bay leaves**

1 cup packed fresh **flat-leaf parsley** tops

Leaves from 2 or 3 sprigs fresh **rosemary**

2 medium **onions**, cut into wedges, with root end intact

3 large **carrots**, sliced on an angle or chopped into bite-size pieces

2 small ribs **celery** with leafy tops, sliced

1 (750 ml) bottle **red zinfandel wine**

4 cups **beef stock**

4 tablespoons (½ stick) **butter**

4 tablespoons **flour**

A couple of handfuls of baby **arugula**, for serving

Preheat the oven to 350°F.

Pat the ribs dry and season with the allspice, paprika, and liberal amounts of salt and pepper.

In a large Dutch oven, heat 2 tablespoons of the oil (2 turns of the pan) over high heat. In two batches, brown the ribs, turning frequently. (Pour off some of the fat between batches.) Transfer the ribs to a plate. Pour off the fat.

Meanwhile, in a food processor, combine the garlic, chile, bay leaves, parsley, and rosemary and pulse-chop to a fine paste.

Heat the remaining 2 tablespoons oil (2 turns of the pan) in the Dutch oven over medium-high heat. Add the onions, carrots, celery, and salt and pepper and cook, stirring, to soften the onions, 5 to 10 minutes. With a slotted spoon transfer the vegetables to a plate. Add the flavor paste to the oil and stir 5 minutes. Deglaze the pan with the wine and simmer to reduce by two-thirds, about 15 minutes. Return the ribs to the pot and add the stock. Bring to a boil, cover, and put in the oven. Bake for 2½ hours. Return the onions and carrots to the pot for the last 20 to 30 minutes.

Set aside 4 of the ribs and 1 cup of the braising liquid for Short Rib Ragu with Drunken Pappardelle (page 90).

[**Make-ahead:** Let the remaining 8 ribs and vegetables cool, then refrigerate.]

[**Night of:** While it's still cold from the fridge, pull any congealed fat off the top of the braising liquid and from around the beef. Reheat uncovered, over medium heat, for 20 minutes or so, just to heat through.]

Remove the ribs from the pan and cover to keep warm.

In a medium skillet, melt the butter. Whisk in the flour and cook to make a light brown roux, about 5 minutes. Add 1 cup of the braising liquid to the roux, then stir the mixture back into the Dutch oven. Cook the sauce until thickened, about 20 minutes.

Serve 2 ribs per person and top with the sauce and vegetables. Put some arugula on the plate.

WEEK 13

STEW
ON THIS

'STEW GOOD TO BE TRUE:
5 NIGHTS OF FANTASTIC,
MOUTHWATERING FOOD.

DISH
1
RED
PORK
POSOLE
PAGE 93

DISH
2
MOROCCAN
MEATBALLS
WITH EGGS
PAGE 94

DISH
3
SMOKY
CHICKEN &
CIDER
PAGE 96

DISH
4
COWBOY
CHILI & BAKED
BEAN POT
PAGE 97

DISH
5
PAPPARDELLE
WITH
PULLED PORK
PAGE 98

Red Pork Posole

This pork and hominy stew is made with half of the pulled pork from the foundation recipe (page 324). If you're having the Pickled Red Onions & Chiles (below), you can make them ahead, too. SERVES 4

4 **dried ancho chiles**, stemmed and seeded
2 cups **chicken stock**, plus more for the stew (optional)
2 tablespoons **EVOO**
1 large **onion**, chopped
4 cloves **garlic**, chopped
1 tablespoon **smoked sweet paprika**

1 tablespoon **chili powder** blend
1½ teaspoons ground **cumin**
Kosher salt and **pepper**
2 (14-ounce) cans **hominy**, rinsed and drained (about 3 cups)
A handful of fresh **cilantro** tops, chopped
1 generous tablespoon **agave syrup** or **honey**

2 **limes**: 1 juiced, 1 cut into wedges
1 portion (1 to 1½ pounds) **Pulled Pork** (page 324)
Shredded **queso fresco** or other mild cheese, for serving
Pickled Red Onions & Chiles (recipe follows)
Charred **flour** or **corn tortillas**, for serving

Toast the chiles in a dry saucepan over medium-high heat until fragrant but not burned. Add the stock and water to cover, if necessary, and bring to a simmer. Cook until softened, about 10 minutes. Transfer to a food processor and puree.

Meanwhile, in a skillet, heat the EVOO (2 turns of the pan) over medium heat. Add the onion, garlic, paprika, chili powder, cumin, and salt and pepper. Cook until the vegetables are very soft, 10 to 12 minutes. Stir in the chile puree, hominy, cilantro, agave syrup, lime juice, and pulled pork. Add just enough water (or stock) to form a stew as loose or thick as you like, 1 to 2 cups additional liquid.

[**Make-ahead:** Let cool and refrigerate.]

[**Night of:** Return the posole to room temp before reheating gently over medium heat.]

Spoon the hot posole into shallow bowls and top with queso fresco and pickled onions and chiles. Serve with warm charred tortillas for dipping and wrapping.

Pickled Red Onions & Chiles SERVES 4

1 cup **cider vinegar**
¼ cup **sugar**
1 teaspoon **kosher salt**
1 teaspoon **coriander seeds**
2 **red onions**, cut into ¼-inch-thick rings
1 fresh **jalapeño chile**, sliced
2 fresh **red Fresno chiles**, sliced

In a saucepan, combine the vinegar, ½ cup water, the sugar, salt, and coriander seeds. Bring to a boil over medium-high heat, stirring until the sugar is dissolved. Arrange the onion rings and chile rings in a small container with a tight-fitting lid and pour the brine over the top. Cool, cover, and store in the fridge for a minimum of several hours and up to several days.

Moroccan Meatballs with Eggs

This dish was my husband John's favorite by far on our trip to Morocco. You may omit the eggs but it is traditionally served with soft-poached eggs for mixing in as you eat. **Suggested side:** Flatbread warmed and then brushed with melted butter.

SERVES 4

MEATBALLS

1 pound **ground lamb** or **beef**
2 slices stale good-quality **bread**, crusts trimmed, processed into fresh bread crumbs
1 **egg**
¼ **onion** (use the rest of the onion in the sauce)
2 large cloves **garlic**, minced or pasted
A small handful of fresh **mint** leaves, finely chopped
Pinch of ground **cinnamon**
Freshly grated **nutmeg**
Kosher salt and **pepper**
EVOO, for liberal drizzling

SAUCE

1 tablespoon **EVOO**
¾ medium **onion**, chopped
2 large cloves **garlic**, sliced
1 small **zucchini**, sliced on an angle or chopped
1 (28-ounce) can **diced tomatoes**
1 (8-ounce) can **tomato sauce**
1 tablespoon **honey**
1 tablespoon **ras el hanout**, store-bought or homemade (recipe follows)
1 (15-ounce) can **chickpeas**, drained

4 large **eggs**
Chopped fresh **cilantro**, for garnish

Preheat the oven to 350°F. Set a cooling rack over a large baking sheet.

Make the meatballs: In the large bowl, combine the meat, bread crumbs, egg, 2 to 3 tablespoons grated onion (grate it right into the bowl to catch the juice), garlic, mint, cinnamon, a few grates of nutmeg, salt and pepper, and a liberal drizzle of EVOO (about 2 tablespoons). With dampened hands (use a bowl of warm water) roll the meat into walnut-size balls and arrange on the cooling rack. Bake until cooked through, 20 to 25 minutes.

Meanwhile, make the sauce: In a Dutch oven, heat the EVOO (1 turn of the pan) over medium to medium-high heat. Add the onion, garlic, and zucchini and cook to soften the onion, 7 to 8 minutes. Add the tomatoes, tomato sauce, honey, and ras el hanout and bring to a bubble. Stir in the chickpeas. Remove the meatballs from the oven and slide into the sauce.

[**Make-ahead:** Let cool and refrigerate.]
[**Night of:** Return the meatballs to room temp before reheating gently over medium heat, adding about 1 cup water to loosen the sauce, if necessary.]

Uncover the pot and make 4 wells in the sauce. Crack in the eggs, cover the pot, and simmer to poach to desired doneness.

Scoop the stew and meatballs into shallow bowls, carefully lifting out one egg per person. Garnish with cilantro.

Ras el Hanout (Head of the Shop) Spice Blend

This is a spice mix that can be found online and in many larger markets. It can contain as many as 100 spices and as few as 10. I make a basic blend from spices I have on hand in my own pantry.

1 tablespoon ground **coriander**
1 tablespoon ground **cumin**
1 tablespoon **sweet paprika**
1 tablespoon ground **turmeric**
1½ teaspoons freshly grated
  nutmeg
1 teaspoon ground **allspice**
1 teaspoon ground **cardamom**
1 teaspoon **cayenne pepper**
1 teaspoon ground **cinnamon**
½ teaspoon ground **cloves**

Combine all the ingredients in a small bowl. Store in an airtight container away from heat. It will last up to several months.

Smoky Chicken & Cider

I'm from upstate New York and we're apple-picking people. This sweet-tart one-pot has apples three ways: apple cider vinegar, apple cider, and apples. Be sure to use "cloudy" organic apple cider for this. SERVES 4

EVOO, for drizzling

8 ounces good-quality **smoky bacon**, chopped

8 to 10 pieces bone-in, skin-on **chicken** (a combo of breasts, drumsticks, and thighs)

Kosher salt and **pepper**

2 **onions**, sliced

4 **carrots**, cut on an angle into ½-inch-thick slices

2 tablespoons fresh **thyme** leaves, chopped

2 or 3 large fresh **bay leaves**

3 tablespoons **flour**

2 cups cloudy **apple cider**

⅓ cup dark amber **maple syrup**

¼ cup **cider vinegar**

1 to 2 cups **chicken stock**

1 pound small **Yukon Gold potatoes**, quartered

2 **Golden Delicious apples**, quartered and sliced

In a large Dutch oven, heat a drizzle of EVOO over medium-high heat. Add the bacon and brown. Remove with a slotted spoon and drain on paper towels.

Season the chicken pieces liberally with salt and pepper. Working in batches, add to the hot fat and brown well on all sides. Transfer to a plate. Add the onions, carrots, thyme, bay leaves, and salt and pepper. Cover the pan and sweat the vegetables, stirring occasionally, until the onion is softened, 5 to 6 minutes. Add the flour and stir for 1 to 2 minutes. Add the cider, maple syrup, vinegar, and 1 cup stock, stirring after each addition. Slide in the potatoes and apples; sprinkle the bacon over the top. Nestle in the chicken and add more stock until the liquid comes up the sides of the chicken but does not cover it. Cover the pan, reduce the heat, and simmer to cook the chicken through, about 15 minutes.

[**Make-ahead:** Let cool and refrigerate.]

[**Night of:** Return the chicken to room temp before reheating gently over medium heat or in a 325°F oven.]

Transfer the cooked chicken to a serving platter or shallow bowls. If you want a thicker sauce, continue to cook it on the stovetop to reduce a bit. Then spoon the apples, vegetables, and sauce over and around the chicken.

Cowboy Chili & Baked Bean Pot

Chili is one of those dishes—sort of like burgers, fried chicken, and Buffalo anything—
you just can't get enough of, and people will always want another recipe for it.

SERVES 4 TO 6

1 tablespoon **vegetable oil**

6 slices **smoky bacon**, chopped
(optional)

1½ pounds **coarse-ground sirloin**

2 **starchy potatoes** (such as
russets), peeled and chopped

1 large **onion**, chopped

2 fresh **red Fresno chiles**, sliced

1 **carrot**, chopped

4 cloves **garlic**, chopped

2 tablespoons **chili powder** blend

1 large fresh **bay leaf**

Kosher salt and **pepper**

1 (12-ounce) bottle **beer**, at room
temperature

4 cups **beef stock**

¼ cup **steak sauce** (such as
Lea & Perrins Thick Classic
Worcestershire Sauce)

1 (16-ounce) can **baked beans**

1 (14.5-ounce) can **diced
tomatoes** or **fire-roasted diced
tomatoes**

Scallions, thinly sliced on an
angle, for serving

In a large Dutch oven, heat the oil (1 turn of the pan) over medium-
high heat. Add the bacon (if using) and cook until browned.
With a slotted spoon, transfer the bacon to paper towels. Pat
the beef dry. Add to the oil and cook, breaking it into crumbles
as it browns. Add the potatoes, onion, chiles, carrot, garlic, chili
powder, and bay leaf. Season liberally with salt and pepper, and
cook for 10 minutes, stirring frequently.

Deglaze the pan with the beer and stir until the beer cooks out
almost completely. Stir in the stock, steak sauce, baked beans,
and tomatoes and simmer until thickened to desired consistency,
20 minutes for loose and 45 minutes for super-thick chili.

[**Make**-ahead: Let cool and refrigerate.]

[**Night of:** Return the chili to room temp before reheating gently
over medium heat. Add a little water if necessary to loosen up the
chili, especially if you cooked it to super-thick. Remove the bay
leaf.]

Serve in shallow bowls, topped with scallions.

Pappardelle with Pulled Pork

This dish uses half of the pulled pork from the foundation recipe (page 324). It's also a good dish to serve at the end of your **Cook Day**—it's easy and comforting. This easy dish is based on a pork and torn fresh pasta dish served at Danny Meyer's Maialino (loose translation: little pig) restaurant in New York City. My husband and I turn into little piggies when we eat this dish at home, too. SERVES 4

1 portion (1 to 1½ pounds)
  Pulled Pork (page 324) in its
  braising liquid
Kosher salt and **pepper**
1 pound **pappardelle** or other
  wide ribbon pasta
3 tablespoons **butter**, cut into
  pats
Juice of 1 **lemon**
Large bunch **arugula, watercress**,
  or **spinach**, washed and
  trimmed
Freshly grated **nutmeg**
Grated **Parmigiano-Reggiano
  cheese**, for garnish
Chopped fresh **flat-leaf parsley** or
  celery leaves, for garnish

[**Make-ahead:** Store the pulled pork in the braising liquid, refrigerated.]

[**Night of:** Return the pork and liquid (if refrigerated) to room temp. Reheat over medium heat while you cook the pasta.]

Bring a large pot of water to a boil. Salt the water and cook the pasta al dente. Ladle out about a cup of the starchy cooking water. Drain the pasta and return it to the pot. Add the butter, lemon juice, pulled pork, 2 cups of the braising liquid, and some starchy water if needed to produce enough sauce to coat the pasta and give the pappardelle movement. Wilt the arugula greens into the pasta and season with salt, pepper, and nutmeg. Toss with tongs for 1 or 2 minutes for the flavors to absorb.

Serve in shallow dishes and top with Parm and parsley.

WEEK 14

MIX & MATCH

IF YOUR CRAVINGS CHANGE
FROM NIGHT TO NIGHT,
THEN THIS WEEK OF MEALS
HAS GOT YOU COVERED.

DISH
1
SOUPED-UP
TRADITIONAL
CHICKEN NOODLE
SOUP
PAGE 100

DISH
2
SPICY ZUCCHINI,
PEPPER &
POTATO SOUP
PAGE 101

DISH
3
BUFFALO BBQ
PULLED CHICKEN
WITH BLUE CHEESE
CORN BREAD
TOPPER
PAGE 102

DISH
4
EGGPLANT &
SQUASH
CURRY
PAGE 104

DISH
5
LAZY LASAGNA
WITH LAMB RAGU,
SPINACH &
RICOTTA
PAGE 106

Buffalo BBQ Pulled Chicken with Blue Cheese Corn Bread Topper

If you are serving this on **Cook Day,** you can bake the dish right in the same skillet you cooked the pulled chicken in. But if this is a make-ahead, you can reheat the mixture in a baking dish and then add the corn bread topper. SERVES 4 TO 6

2 tablespoons **EVOO**

3 or 4 small ribs **celery**, chopped

2 large **carrots**, chopped

1 **onion**, chopped

4 cloves **garlic**, chopped or grated

1 fresh **red Fresno** or **long red chile**, seeded and finely chopped

2 tablespoons fresh **thyme** leaves

Salt and **pepper**

1 (12-ounce) bottle **lager beer** or 1½ cups **chicken stock**

2 tablespoons **light brown sugar**

1 (15-ounce) can **tomato sauce**

¼ to ⅓ cup **hot sauce** (to taste)

2 tablespoons **Worcestershire sauce**

2 tablespoons **cider vinegar**

Chopped or pulled meat from 4 pieces **Poached Chicken** (see Note, page 100)

2 (8.5-ounce) boxes **corn muffin mix** (see Heads-up)

1 cup crumbled **blue cheese**

4 **scallions**, whites and greens, finely chopped

[If making this to serve on **Cook Day,** preheat the oven to 425°F. It making this for later in the week, you'll preheat the oven on the night of.]

In a large ovenproof skillet, heat the EVOO (2 turns of the pan) over medium-high heat. Add the celery, carrots, onion, garlic, chile, thyme, and salt and pepper and cook to soften the carrots, 10 to 12 minutes. Deglaze the pan with the beer.

In a bowl, stir together the brown sugar, tomato sauce, hot sauce, Worcestershire, and vinegar. Pour into the skillet and stir to combine. Mix in the chicken, using tongs.

[Make-ahead: Let cool and refrigerate.]

[Night of: Return the chicken mixture to room temp before reheating gently over medium heat while you preheat the oven to 425°F. You can bake the casserole in either an ovenproof skillet or a baking dish.]

Make the corn bread batter according to package directions, then stir in the blue cheese and scallions. Pour the batter over the chicken filling in an even layer and bake to golden brown and firm to the touch, 12 to 15 minutes.

Heads-up: I use Jiffy brand mix for this. You'll need 2 eggs and ⅔ cup milk to make both boxes of mix.

Eggplant & Squash Curry

I like to make this with kuri squash just so I can say I'm making kuri curry. I use a West Indian curry blend here. It is primarily cumin, coriander, and turmeric, and bright yellow-orange in color—a nice match-up to the color of the squash. SERVES 4 TO 6

1 to 1¼ pounds peeled **kuri**, **pumpkin**, or **butternut squash**, cut into bite-size pieces

2 tablespoons **EVOO**, plus more for drizzling

Salt and **pepper**

Freshly grated **nutmeg**

3 mild **red frying peppers** or 2 small **red bell peppers**, quartered lengthwise and thinly sliced crosswise

2 small **onions** or 1 large, quartered and thinly sliced

4 cloves **garlic**, sliced

1-inch piece fresh **ginger**, grated

1 **eggplant** (1 to 1¼ pounds), cut into bite-size pieces

2 tablespoons **West Indian curry powder**

1 tablespoon **chili powder** blend

1 teaspoon ground **cardamom**

3 or 4 **plum tomatoes** (see Heads-up) or 1 (14.5-ounce) can **diced** or **stewed tomatoes**

½ cup **mango chutney**, plus more for serving

2 cups **chicken stock**, homemade (page 322) or store-bought

Raw **Bhutanese red rice** or **brown rice** (enough for 4 to 6 servings)

Grated zest and juice of 1 **lime**

1 bunch **scallions**, sliced on an angle

Preheat the oven to 425°F.

Toss the squash with a drizzle of EVOO and season with salt, pepper, and nutmeg. Arrange the squash on a baking sheet and roast until tender and brown at the edges, 25 to 30 minutes.

In a Dutch oven or deep skillet, heat 2 tablespoons EVOO (2 turns of the pan) over medium to medium-high heat. Add the frying peppers, onions, garlic, ginger, and salt and pepper and sweat the vegetables for a few minutes. Add the eggplant, curry powder, chili powder, and cardamom. Stir to combine, then cover the pot and cook, stirring occasionally, until the eggplant is tender, 12 to 15 minutes. Stir in the roasted squash, tomatoes, chutney, and stock.

[Make-ahead: Let cool and refrigerate.]

[Night of: Return the curry to room temp before reheating gently over medium heat while you cook the rice.]

Cook the rice according to package directions, adding the lime zest to the water for the rice. When the rice is cooked, stir in the lime juice and scallions, then fluff with a fork.

Serve the curry on a bed of rice, with extra chutney for mixing in.

Heads-up: If using fresh tomatoes, you need to peel them. With a sharp knife, score an X in the skin on the bottom of each tomato, being careful not to cut deeper than the skin. Place the tomatoes in boiling water for 30 seconds, remove with a slotted spoon or tongs, and plunge into an ice water bath to cool. Peel, halve, and chop the tomatoes (save the juices).

Lazy Lasagna with Lamb Ragu, Spinach & Ricotta

This ragu is the lamb version of a classic bolognese sauce. SERVES 6

LAMB RAGU
2 tablespoons **EVOO**
1½ pounds **ground lamb**
Leaves from 1 or 2 sprigs fresh **rosemary**, finely chopped
1 tablespoon chopped fresh **oregano** or **marjoram**, or 1 teaspoon dried
½ teaspoon ground **cloves**
Salt and **pepper**
1 **onion**, finely chopped
1 **carrot**, finely chopped or grated
4 large cloves **garlic**, grated or finely chopped
¼ cup **tomato paste**
2 cups **chicken stock**, homemade (page 322) or store-bought
1 cup **dry white wine**

LASAGNA
Salt
1 pound wavy-edge **lasagna noodles**, broken into large, irregular pieces
2 (9- or 10-ounce) boxes frozen **chopped spinach**, thawed and wrung dry in a kitchen towel
3 tablespoons **butter**
2 rounded tablespoons **flour**
2½ cups **milk**
Pepper
Freshly grated **nutmeg**
2 cups fresh **ricotta cheese**
¼ to ⅓ cup chopped fresh **mint** and/or **parsley**
1 cup shredded or grated **Parmigiano-Reggiano cheese**

Make the ragu: In a Dutch oven, heat the EVOO (2 turns of the pan) over medium-high heat. Pat the lamb dry, add to the oil, and cook, breaking it into crumbles as it browns. Add the rosemary, oregano, cloves, and salt and pepper. Once the meat has browned, add the onion, carrot, and garlic and cook, stirring frequently, to soften the carrot, about 10 minutes. Add the tomato paste and stir for 1 minute. Stir in the stock and wine, reduce to a gentle simmer, and let it hang out while you cook the pasta.

[If making this to serve on **Cook Day**, preheat the oven to 425°F. If making this for later in the week, you'll preheat the oven on the night of.]

Make the lasagna: Bring a large pot of water to a boil. Salt the water and cook the lasagna noodles 2 minutes shy of al dente. Ladle out about a cup of the starchy cooking water. Drain the pasta and return it to the pot. Toss the pasta with the lamb ragu and some of the starchy water to loosen. Pull the spinach into shreds as you add it to the pasta. Toss to combine. Pour the pasta into a 9 by 13-inch baking dish or lasagna pan.

Meanwhile, in a saucepan, melt the butter over medium heat. Whisk in the flour and cook for 1 minute. Whisk in the milk; season with salt and pepper and a little nutmeg. Cook until the sauce is thick enough to coat the back of a spoon.

In a bowl, combine the ricotta with the mint. Dot the pasta evenly with ricotta. Pour the sauce in an even layer around the casserole and top with the Parm.

[Make-ahead: Let cool and refrigerate.]

[**Night of:** Return the lasagna to room temp while you preheat the oven to 350°F. Reheat the lasagna, covered, for 30 minutes, then increase the oven temperature to 425°F.]

Bake, uncovered, until browned and bubbling, 15 to 20 minutes.

WEEK 15

MAKE A DOUBLE BATCH!

SOMETIMES YOU WANT TO EXPERIMENT IN THE KITCHEN, AND SOMETIMES YOU JUST WANT TO GO FOR SURE THINGS. HERE ARE 5 SURE THINGS TO ADD TO YOUR ARSENAL.

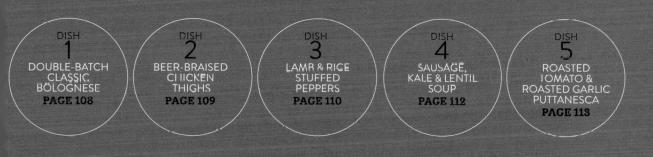

DISH 1
DOUBLE-BATCH CLASSIC BOLOGNESE
PAGE 108

DISH 2
BEER-BRAISED CHICKEN THIGHS
PAGE 109

DISH 3
LAMB & RICE STUFFED PEPPERS
PAGE 110

DISH 4
SAUSAGE, KALE & LENTIL SOUP
PAGE 112

DISH 5
ROASTED TOMATO & ROASTED GARLIC PUTTANESCA
PAGE 113

Double-Batch Classic Bolognese

You know you love it, and you know you make it your own special way if you've ever made it before. Here is my take on the classic. It's a great pasta sauce to "double-batch," especially in the winter months when you want something hearty. **Suggested side:** Simple green salad. SERVES 4

2 cups **milk**

¼ cup **EVOO**

¼ pound **pancetta**, finely diced

4 ounces trimmed **chicken livers**, finely diced (optional, but recommended)

2 small **onions**, finely chopped

2 small ribs **celery** with leafy tops, finely chopped, plus more chopped celery leaves for serving

1 large **carrot**, finely chopped

6 cloves **garlic**, chopped

Leaves from 2 small sprigs fresh **rosemary**, finely chopped

2 fresh **bay leaves**

2½ pounds **ground beef** (chuck or sirloin) and **veal** mix

2 pinches of ground **cloves**

Kosher salt and **pepper**

Freshly grated **nutmeg**

1½ cups **dry white wine**

2 cups **beef stock**

2 cups **chicken** or **vegetable stock**

2 (28-ounce) cans Italian **tomato puree**

1 pound **egg tagliatelle** or **bucatini pasta**

3 tablespoons **butter**

Grated **Parmigiano-Reggiano cheese**

In a small saucepan, warm the milk over lowest heat.

In a large Dutch oven, heat the EVOO (4 turns of the pan) over medium to medium-high heat. Add the pancetta and cook until lightly browned. Add the livers (if using) and cook until still slightly pink. Add the onions, celery, carrot, garlic, rosemary, and bay leaves and cook the carrot to tender, about 10 minutes.

Add the ground meat and cook, breaking it into crumbles, but do not brown. Sprinkle with the cloves and season with salt, pepper, and nutmeg. Stir in the wine and allow it to cook into the meat, 2 to 3 minutes. Add the warm milk and allow it to absorb for 1 minute. Stir in the beef stock, chicken stock, and tomato puree. Bring to a bubble, then reduce the heat and simmer over low heat for 2 hours, stirring occasionally.

[**Make-ahead:** Let cool. Divide the sauce in half. Freeze one half and refrigerate the other for later in the week.]

[**Night of:** Return the sauce to room temp before reheating gently over medium heat while you cook the pasta.]

Bring a large pot of water to a boil. Salt the water and cook the pasta al dente. Ladle out about a cup of the starchy cooking water. Drain the pasta, return it to the pot, and toss with the butter. Add the sauce and some of the starchy water, tossing with tongs for 1 or 2 minutes for the flavors to absorb.

Serve the pasta in shallow bowls topped with grated Parm and celery leaves.

Beer-Braised Chicken Thighs

You can't get more "budget" than chicken thighs. Plus, they're great for make-ahead meals because they stay nice and moist, even after reheating. **Suggested side:** Warm baguette, for mopping. SERVES 4

8 bone-in, skin-on **chicken thighs**
Kosher salt and **pepper**
1 tablespoon **EVOO**
1 link **andouille sausage**, casing removed, chopped, or 4 slices **bacon**, chopped
1 **onion**, chopped
2 ribs **celery**, chopped
1 **green bell pepper**, chopped
2 or 3 cloves **garlic**, chopped
2 tablespoons chopped fresh **thyme**
1 rounded tablespoon **flour**
1 (12-ounce) bottle **lager beer**, at room temperature
1 (14.5-ounce) can **diced tomatoes with chiles** or **stewed tomatoes**
1 cup **chicken stock**
2 tablespoons **hot sauce**
Scallions, thinly sliced, for garnish

Pat the chicken dry and season with salt and pepper. In a Dutch oven, heat the EVOO (1 turn of the pan) over medium-high heat. Working in batches, brown the chicken well on both sides, 3 to 4 minutes per side. Transfer the chicken to a plate. Discard half of the drippings. Add the andouille sausage and brown for 2 minutes. Reduce the heat to medium and add the onion, celery, bell pepper, garlic, and thyme. Cook to soften the vegetables, about 10 minutes.

Add the flour and stir for 1 to 2 minutes. Pour in the beer and let the foam subside. Stir in the tomatoes, stock, and hot sauce. Let the sauce thicken a bit, and then slide in the chicken, cover, and simmer to cook through, about 10 minutes.

[**Make-ahead:** Let cool and refrigerate.]

[**Night of:** Return the chicken to room temp before reheating gently over medium heat.]

Serve in shallow bowls, garnished with the scallions.

Lamb & Rice Stuffed Peppers

Stuffed peppers are a terrific make-ahead meal, just like stuffed cabbage—or stuffed anything, really. SERVES 4

4 large **red bell peppers**
1 tablespoon **unsalted butter**
¼ cup **orzo pasta**
3 or 4 cloves **garlic**, chopped
1 cup **long-grain white rice**
¾ pound **ground lamb**
Leaves from 2 small sprigs fresh **rosemary**, finely chopped
¼ cup chopped fresh **flat-leaf parsley**
Leaves from 2 sprigs fresh **marjoram** or **oregano**, chopped, or 1½ teaspoons dried
Kosher salt and **pepper**
6 tablespoons **EVOO**
1 **onion**, chopped
2 **cubanelle peppers**, chopped
1 (15-ounce) can **tomato sauce**
1 cup crumbled **feta cheese** or **goat cheese**

Preheat the oven to 375°F.

Cut off the tops of the bell peppers and scoop out the seeds and ribs. Carefully trim the bottoms if necessary to make the peppers stand straight when upright. In a large stockpot place a steamer rack over a few inches of boiling water, or set a colander over a couple of inches of boiling water. Steam the peppers for 10 minutes.

In a saucepan, melt the butter over medium heat. Add the orzo and stir to brown lightly. Stir in half of the garlic. Stir in the rice to coat, then add 2 cups water. Bring to a boil, reduce to a simmer, cover, and cook for 15 minutes. Spread the rice mixture on a baking sheet to cool.

Combine the ground lamb with the cooled pilaf, rosemary, parsley, and half of the marjoram; season with salt and pepper. Overstuff the peppers with the filling. Arrange the peppers in a baking dish. Drizzle about 1 tablespoon EVOO over each pepper and roast until crispy at the edges and cooked through, 50 minutes to 1 hour.

[**Make-ahead:** Let cool and refrigerate.]

Meanwhile, in a saucepan, heat the remaining 2 tablespoons EVOO (2 turns of the pan) over medium-high heat. Add the onion, cubanelles, and the remaining garlic and marjoram, and cook to soften the onion, about 5 minutes. Add the tomato sauce and season with salt and pepper.

[**Make-ahead:** Let cool and refrigerate.]

[**Night of:** Return the peppers to room temp while you preheat the oven to 375°F. Add ½ cup water to the baking dish with the peppers. Cover and bake until heated through, about 30 minutes. Uncover, let the water evaporate, and crisp the top, 20 minutes more. Reheat the sauce over medium-low heat to heat through.]

Serve the peppers hot with sauce over the top of the peppers or in a puddle underneath. Top with crumbled feta.

WEEK 15

DISH

4

Sausage, Kale & Lentil Soup

One of the most satisfying greens for soups and stews is kale. It really stands up to cooking—*and* reheating—without breaking down and losing its great texture. I tend to favor the flat-leaf lacinato kale because it's a lot quicker to pull out the stems, but regular curly kale would be fine, too. SERVES 4

1 tablespoon **EVOO**

1 pound bulk **Italian hot sausage** or links, casings removed

1 **onion**, chopped

2 ribs **celery**, chopped, leafy tops reserved

1 large **carrot**, chopped

1 large **starchy potato** (such as russet), peeled and finely diced

1 fresh **red Fresno** or **long red chile**, thinly sliced or finely chopped

2 large cloves **garlic**, chopped or sliced

Leaves from 2 sprigs fresh **rosemary**, finely chopped

1½ teaspoons ground **cumin**

Kosher salt and **pepper**

1 bunch **lacinato kale** (also called black, Tuscan, or dinosaur kale), stemmed and very thinly sliced

Freshly grated **nutmeg**

¼ cup **tomato paste**

1 cup **white wine**

1¾ cups **brown lentils**

4 cups **chicken stock**

In a soup pot or large Dutch oven, heat the EVOO (1 turn of the pan) over medium to medium-high heat. Add the sausage and cook, breaking it into crumbles as it browns. Add the onion, celery, carrot, potato, chile, garlic, rosemary, cumin, and salt and pepper and cook to soften the onion, 8 to 10 minutes.

Wilt in the kale and season with a few grates of nutmeg. Add the tomato paste and stir for 30 seconds. Deglaze the pan with the wine and cook to reduce by half. Stir in the lentils, stock, and 2 cups water. Bring to a boil, reduce to a simmer, and cook until the lentils are tender, about 35 minutes.

[**Make-ahead:** Let cool and refrigerate.]

[**Night of:** Return the soup to room temp before reheating gently over medium heat.]

Serve with chopped celery leaves to garnish.

Roasted Tomato & Roasted Garlic Puttanesca

A puttanesca sauce is by definition fast. But I've given the classic a twist by slowing it down and making the sauce with slow-roasted garlic and tomatoes. SERVES 4

1 head **garlic**, top cut off to expose the cloves

¼ cup **EVOO**, plus more for drizzling

Kosher salt and **pepper**

12 to 14 large **plum tomatoes**

2 sprigs fresh **marjoram** or **oregano**, leaves picked and chopped, or 1 teaspoon dried

6 flat **anchovy fillets**

1 small fresh **red Fresno chile** or **Italian cherry pepper**, seeded and coarsely chopped

3 tablespoons **capote capers** (see Heads-up) or stemmed **caperberries**, coarsely chopped

½ cup loosely packed pitted **oil-cured olives**, coarsely chopped

1 pound **penne** or **bucatini pasta**

½ cup chopped **fresh flat-leaf parsley**

Preheat the oven to 375°F. Line a baking sheet with parchment paper or foil. Arrange a cooling rack over the baking sheet.

Drizzle the garlic with some EVOO and season with salt and pepper. Wrap in foil.

Halve the tomatoes lengthwise and place in a bowl. Toss with a drizzle of EVOO, the marjoram, and salt and pepper. Arrange on the baking sheet cut side down. Bake 20 to 25 minutes, then flip and roast 20 minutes more. Roast the garlic 45 to 50 minutes alongside the tomatoes.

Transfer about two thirds of the tomatoes to a food processor. Coarsely chop the remainder and set aside. Squeeze the garlic out of its skins into the food processor. Pulse until smooth.

In a large skillet, heat the ¼ cup EVOO (4 turns of the pan) over medium to medium-high heat. Add the anchovies, cover the pan, and shake until the anchovies begin to break up. Reduce the heat a bit, uncover, and stir until the anchovies melt. Add the chile and cook for 1 or 2 minutes to infuse the oil. Add the tomato-garlic puree and stir to combine. Stir in the capers and olives.

[**Make-ahead:** Let cool and refrigerate. Store the chopped tomatoes separately.]

[**Night of:** Remove the chopped tomatoes from the fridge. Return the sauce to room temp before reheating gently over medium heat while you cook the pasta.]

Bring a large pot of water to a boil. Salt the water and cook the pasta al dente. Ladle out about a cup of the starchy cooking water and add to the sauce. Drain the pasta and return it to the pot. Add the sauce and reserved tomatoes, tossing with tongs for 1 or 2 minutes for the flavors to absorb.

Serve in shallow bowls, topped with the parsley and drizzled with more EVOO.

Heads-up: Capers are graded by size. The very smallest capers are called nonpareils. Capotes are longer (over ⅓ inch across), and the very biggest are called grusas.

WEEK 16

SLOW RIDE

A SUREFIRE WAY TO GET A WEEK'S
WORTH OF FOOD IN ONE DAY:
START WITH ONE SLOW-COOKED
(AND IRRESISTIBLE DISH), AND WHILE
THAT'S COOKING, WHIP UP 4 MORE
JAW-DROPPING COMFORT-FOOD MEALS.

DISH
1
GRANDPA'S
BRAISED BEEF
PAGE 115

DISH
2
ALL-DAY
ROAST PORK
PAGE 116

DISH
3
BRAISED
CHICKEN WITH
MUSHROOMS
PAGE 119

DISH
4
CECI
SAUCE
WITH PENNE
PAGE 120

DISH
5
ANCHO-
CHIPOTLE
TURKEY CHILI
PAGE 122

Grandpa's Braised Beef

This is a recipe that dates back to my grandfather Emmanuel. He was my mom's dad, and one of her fondest memories of her childhood—she was one of ten children—was dinnertime. The kids would get so excited at dinner, because my grandfather was such an amazing cook (even though he was a stonemason by trade). **Suggested side:** Ciabatta bread for mopping. SERVES 4 TO 6

EVOO
4 **onions**, very thinly sliced
6 cloves **garlic**, very thinly sliced
3 pounds **beef chuck, bottom round**, or **top sirloin steak**, in one piece
Sea salt and **pepper**
4 or 5 **starchy potatoes** (such as russets)
1 (28- or 32-ounce) can **San Marzano tomatoes** (look for DOP on the label)
2 tablespoons chopped fresh **thyme**
Leaves from 2 sprigs fresh **rosemary**, finely chopped
A few handfuls of grated **Parmigiano-Reggiano cheese**
A few leaves of fresh **basil**, torn

Preheat the oven to 325°F.

In a large skillet, heat a thin layer of EVOO over medium heat. Add the onions and garlic and cook them until very soft and very light caramel, 20 to 30 minutes. Turn off the heat and set aside.

Heat a large Dutch oven (preferably oval) or heavy-bottomed roasting pan over medium-high heat. Pour in a thin layer of EVOO. Pat the meat dry and season very liberally with salt and pepper. Brown the meat to a deep brown all over, 12 to 15 minutes.

Peel the potatoes and very thinly slice them lengthwise into planks. Working over the can to catch the juices, slice the tomatoes with a paring knife and set aside.

Arrange half the onions over the meat, sprinkle with 1 tablespoon of the thyme, and season with salt and pepper. Arrange half the potatoes over the onions and dress with a liberal drizzle of EVOO, half the rosemary, a handful of Parm, and salt and pepper. Top the potatoes with half the tomatoes and their juices, and season with salt and pepper. Scatter all the basil over the tomatoes. Repeat the layers, but do not add basil to the top layer of tomatoes.

Cover the pan and bake the meat until very tender, about 4 hours.

[**Make-ahead:** Let cool and refrigerate.]

[**Night of:** Return the beef to room temp while you preheat the oven to 325°F. Reheat, covered, until warmed through, 45 minutes to 1 hour.]

Switch the oven to broil. Uncover the beef, drizzle the top with EVOO, sprinkle with some Parm, and broil to lightly crust the top.

To serve, cut down through the layers of the potatoes, tomatoes, and onions to portion the meat. Spoon into shallow bowls with the pan juices.

All-Day Roast Pork

This takes pretty much all day to cook, so make this your reward at the end of **Cook Day.** The pork is served with Spicy Apple Chutney, Mashed Citrus Sweet Potatoes, and Sautéed Chard (recipes follow). Make the chutney early in the day, because it can sit. Then make the sweet potatoes and chard a short time before you're ready to sit down. Use the leftovers from the pork to make sandwiches on ciabatta bread with extra-sharp white cheddar cheese and leftover chutney. SERVES 4 (WITH LEFTOVERS)

5 pounds bone-in **pork shoulder** (butt)
2 tablespoons chopped fresh **thyme**
2 teaspoons **fennel seeds**
Sea salt and **pepper**
2 medium **onions**, sliced
1 head **garlic**, cloves peeled and sliced
2 medium **carrots**, sliced
2 ribs **celery**, sliced
5 or 6 fresh **bay leaves**
2 cups **chicken stock**
1 cup **white wine**

Preheat the oven to 450°F.

Score the fat on the top of the roast in a crosshatch pattern with the scores about ¾ inch apart. Rub with the thyme, fennel seeds, and salt and pepper. Set in a roasting pan. Roast until crispy on top, about 30 minutes.

Reduce the oven temperature to 325°F, cover tightly with foil, and roast for 4 hours.

Remove the pork from the pan and set on a cutting board. Spoon off most of the fat from the pan and add the onions, garlic, carrots, celery, bay leaves, and salt and pepper, stirring to combine with the drippings. Set the roast on top of the vegetables, cover again with foil, and roast until tender, 1 to 1½ hours more.

Transfer the roast to a cutting board and cover loosely with the roasting foil. Skim off the fat again and place the roasting pan over medium-high heat on the stovetop. Deglaze the pan with the stock and wine and stir for a few minutes with a wooden spoon to scrape up all drippings. Strain the sauce and pour it into a serving bowl or gravy boat.

Slice the pork.

Spicy Apple Chutney MAKES A LOT

Store whatever isn't used on **Cook Day** in the fridge.

1 tablespoon **EVOO**
2 medium **onions**, chopped
2 fresh **red Fresno chiles**, seeded and finely chopped
1-inch piece fresh **ginger**, grated or minced

6 medium **Braeburn** or **Gala apples**, peeled and chopped
2 tablespoons **dark brown sugar**
1 tablespoon chopped fresh **thyme**
¼ cup dark amber **maple syrup**

¼ cup **cider vinegar**
1 tablespoon fresh **lemon** juice
Kosher salt
Freshly grated **nutmeg**

In a saucepan, heat the EVOO (1 turn of the pan) over medium to medium-high heat. Add the onions, chiles, and ginger and cook to soften the ginger, 10 to 12 minutes. Stir in the apples, brown sugar, thyme, maple syrup, vinegar, lemon juice, and a little salt and nutmeg. Cover and cook, stirring occasionally, until a thick sauce forms, 15 to 20 minutes. Adjust the seasoning and transfer to a serving dish.

Mashed Citrus Sweet Potatoes SERVES 4

4 large **sweet potatoes**, peeled and cut into ¼-inch slices
1 tablespoon grated **orange** zest
1 cup **chicken stock**
Juice of 1 **lemon**
Kosher salt and **pepper**

In a saucepan, cover the sweet potatoes with water. Bring to a boil over medium-high heat and cook until tender, 10 to 15 minutes. Drain and return to the hot pot. Mash with the zest, stock, lemon juice, and salt and pepper. Keep warm until ready to serve.

Sautéed Chard SERVES 4

2 tablespoons **EVOO**
1 very large bunch **red chard**, stemmed and shredded
Kosher salt and **pepper**
Freshly grated **nutmeg**

In a large skillet, heat the EVOO (2 turns of the pan) over medium heat. Add the chard and season with salt, pepper, and nutmeg. Cook until just tender, about 5 minutes. Keep warm until ready to serve.

Braised Chicken with Mushrooms

Suggested side: Quick-cooking polenta made according to package directions (pop into the freezer if storing for more than one night). SERVES 4

2 cups **chicken stock**
1 ounce **dried porcini mushrooms**
2 tablespoons **EVOO**
4 bone-in, skin-on **chicken legs** (drumstick with thigh attached)
Kosher salt and **pepper**
1 pound **cremini mushrooms**, thinly sliced
2 **onions**, sliced
2 **carrots**, finely chopped
2 ribs **celery**, finely chopped
5 or 6 cloves **garlic**, thinly sliced
Leaves from a few sprigs fresh **thyme**, finely chopped
2 large fresh **bay leaves**
½ to ¾ cup **Marsala** or **dry sherry**
½ cup **celery leaves** or fresh **flat-leaf parsley**, chopped

In a small saucepan, heat the stock and porcini to soften the mushrooms, 10 to 15 minutes. Reserving the soaking liquid, scoop out the mushrooms and chop.

In a large Dutch oven, heat the EVOO (2 turns of the pan) over medium-high heat. Pat the chicken dry and season liberally with salt and pepper. Working in two batches if necessary, brown the chicken skin side down for 5 minutes, then flip and brown the second side, 3 to 4 minutes more. Transfer to a plate.

Add the cremini to the drippings in the pan and cook until browned, 10 to 15 minutes. Add the onions, carrots, celery, garlic, thyme, bay leaves, and salt and pepper and cook to soften the onions, about 10 minutes.

Deglaze the pan with the Marsala. Push the vegetables to the edges. Put the chicken back in the pot and arrange the vegetables on top. Add the chopped porcini. Carefully pour in the soaking liquid, leaving the last few spoonfuls in the pan as grit may have settled there.

Cover and simmer for 30 minutes over low heat.

[**Make-ahead:** Let cool and refrigerate.]

[**Night of:** Return the chicken to room temp before reheating gently over medium heat or in a 325°F oven for 20 to 30 minutes. Remove the bay leaves.]

Serve garnished with the celery leaves.

Ceci Sauce with Penne

Compared with the other dishes for this week, this is a really Easy Ride, not a Slow Ride. You can make this in minutes any night of the year, but it's also a great make-ahead. *Ceci* is Italian for chickpeas. SERVES 4

3 tablespoons **EVOO**, plus more for serving

1 **onion**, finely chopped

4 cloves **garlic**, finely chopped

1 fresh **red Fresno** or **long red chile**, finely chopped

Leaves from 2 sprigs fresh **rosemary**, finely chopped

1 fresh **bay leaf**

Salt and **pepper**

1 (29-ounce) can **chickpeas**, rinsed and drained

1½ cups **chicken stock**

1 (28-ounce) can whole or crushed **San Marzano tomatoes** (look for DOP on the label)

1 pound **whole wheat** or **multigrain penne**

Freshly grated **pecorino cheese**, for serving

Finely chopped fresh **flat-leaf parsley**, for serving

In a Dutch oven or deep skillet, heat the EVOO (3 turns of the pan) over medium to medium-high heat. Add the onion, garlic, chile, rosemary, bay leaf, and salt and pepper and cook to soften the onion, 7 to 8 minutes.

Meanwhile, in a food processor, quick-pulse about two-thirds of the chickpeas to fine bits. Add the chopped chickpeas and the remaining whole chickpeas to the onion and heat through. Stir in the stock and tomatoes, breaking them up with a potato masher. Simmer the sauce to thicken a little.

[**Make-ahead:** Let cool and refrigerate.]

[**Night of:** Return the sauce to room temp before reheating gently over medium heat, stirring occasionally, while you cook the pasta.]

Bring a large pot of water to a boil. Salt the water and cook the pasta al dente. Ladle out about a cup of the starchy pasta cooking water. Drain the pasta and return it to the pot. Add the sauce and some starchy water if needed to make everything work together. Toss with tongs for 1 or 2 minutes for the flavors to absorb.

Serve the pasta in shallow bowls topped with a drizzle of EVOO and a sprinkle of pecorino and parsley.

Ancho-Chipotle Turkey Chili

This chili is all about smoky flavor. There's smoked bacon, chipotles (which are smoked jalapeños), smoked paprika, and the "smoky" flavors of cumin and ancho chiles. SERVES 6

4 or 5 **dried ancho chiles**, stemmed and seeded
4 cups **chicken stock**
1 tablespoon **EVOO**
4 ounces **applewood-smoked bacon**, chopped
2 pounds **ground turkey** (light and dark meat)
Kosher salt and **pepper**
1 **onion**, chopped
4 cloves **garlic**, chopped
2 tablespoons finely chopped seeded **chipotle chiles in adobo**

1 rounded tablespoon **smoked sweet paprika**
1 scant tablespoon ground **cumin**
1 scant tablespoon ground **coriander**
2 teaspoons **unsweetened cocoa powder**
2 pinches of ground **cinnamon**
¼ cup **tomato paste**
1 (12-ounce) bottle **Mexican beer** (such as Negra Modelo), at room temperature

GARNISHES
Chopped **onions**
Chopped **scallions**
Cilantro leaves
Lime wedges
Tortilla chips
Shredded **extra-sharp cheddar cheese**
Sour cream
Toasted **pumpkin seeds**
Diced **avocado** dressed with **lime** or **lemon** juice

Toast the anchos in a dry saucepan over medium-high heat until fragrant but not burned. Add the stock and bring to a simmer. Cook until softened, about 10 minutes. Transfer to a food processor and puree.

In a large Dutch oven or deep skillet, heat the EVOO (1 turn of the pan) over medium-high heat. Add the bacon and brown a few minutes, and then transfer the bacon to a plate with a slotted spoon.

Add the ground turkey to the oil and cook, breaking it into crumbles as it browns. Season with salt and pepper. Add the onion, garlic, chipotle, paprika, cumin, coriander, cocoa, and cinnamon. Stir and cook until the onion is softened, about 10 minutes. Add the tomato paste and stir for 1 minute. Deglaze the pan with the beer.

Add the ancho puree and the reserved bacon. Simmer over low heat to thicken, 20 to 30 minutes.

[Make-ahead: Let cool and refrigerate.]

[Night of: Return the chili to room temp before reheating gently over medium heat, stirring occasionally.]

Serve with the garnishes of your choice.

WEEK 17

IT'S A BREEZE

FIVE LOW-MAINTENANCE
MEALS THAT APPEAL TO THE
LAZY PERSON WHO LIVES INSIDE
EACH AND EVERY ONE OF US

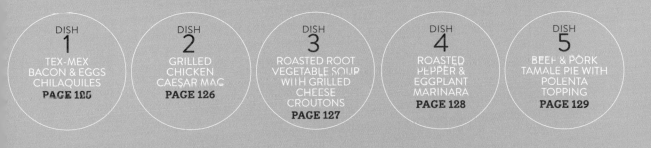

DISH
1
TEX-MEX
BACON & EGGS
CHILAQUILES
PAGE 125

DISH
2
GRILLED
CHICKEN
CAESAR MAC
PAGE 126

DISH
3
ROASTED ROOT
VEGETABLE SOUP
WITH GRILLED
CHEESE
CROUTONS
PAGE 127

DISH
4
ROASTED
PEPPER &
EGGPLANT
MARINARA
PAGE 128

DISH
5
BEEF & PORK
TAMALE PIE WITH
POLENTA
TOPPING
PAGE 129

Tex-Mex Bacon & Eggs Chilaquiles

Chilaquiles—in addition to being a fun word to say—are ripped up, toasted tortillas with toppings. Like a gigantic dinner nacho. SERVES 4

12 **corn** or **flour tortillas**, cut into strips
Vegetable oil cooking spray
1 tablespoon **vegetable oil**
8 slices thick-cut **smoky bacon**, cut crosswise into ½-inch pieces
1 **red onion**, quartered and sliced
2 fresh **red Fresno** or **jalapeño chiles**, sliced
4 cloves **garlic**, chopped
1 (29-ounce) can **black beans**, rinsed and drained
1 tablespoon ground **cumin**
1 rounded tablespoon **chili powder** blend
Salt and **pepper**
1 cup **dark beer** (such as Negra Modelo), at room temperature
1 (14.5-ounce) can **fire-roasted diced tomatoes**
A small handful of fresh **cilantro** leaves, chopped
1½ to 2 cups shredded **hot pepper cheddar cheese** or **pepper jack cheese**
4 **eggs**
1 **avocado**, diced
1 **lime**, cut into wedges

Preheat the oven to 425°F. Place a cooling rack over a baking sheet.

Place the tortilla strips on the cooling rack and coat with cooking spray. Bake until crisp, 12 to 15 minutes. Arrange in a 9 by 13-inch baking dish or a shallow 2- to 3-quart casserole.

[If making this dish to serve on **Cook Day**, leave the oven on. If making this for later in the week, you'll bake the casserole on the night of.]

In a skillet, heat the oil over medium-high heat. Add the bacon and brown, then transfer to a plate with a slotted spoon. To the drippings in the skillet, add the onion, chiles, and garlic and cook for a few minutes. Add the beans, cumin, chili powder, and salt and pepper. Stir in the beer and tomatoes and cook for 1 minute to thicken. Stir in the cilantro. Adjust the seasonings, then pour over the tortillas. Scatter the bacon bits and cheese on top.

[**Make-ahead:** Let cool and refrigerate.]

[**Night of:** Return the casserole to room temp while you preheat the oven to 425°F.]

Bake until bubbling and hot.

Meanwhile, cook the eggs sunny-side up or over easy—however your family members like their eggs.

Serve the hot chilaquiles topped with an egg and diced avocado, with a lime wedge for squeezing.

Grilled Chicken Caesar Mac

I'm using whole wheat penne here, because I want a pasta hearty enough to stand up to the strength of the Caesar-style sauce. **Suggested side:** A salad of shredded escarole or romaine dressed with lemon juice and EVOO. SERVES 4 TO 6

1 pound boneless, skinless **chicken breast**

EVOO, for liberal drizzling

Salt and coarsely ground **pepper**

6 tablespoons (¾ stick) **butter**

1 cup **panko bread crumbs**

1½ cups shredded **pecorino cheese**

2 large cloves **garlic**, finely chopped

1 tablespoon **anchovy paste**

3 rounded tablespoons **flour**

1 cup **chicken stock**

2 cups **milk**

1 tablespoon **Worcestershire sauce**

1 pound **penne pasta** or **whole wheat penne**

[If making this to serve on **Cook Day**, preheat the oven to 425°F. If making this for later in the week, you'll preheat the oven on the night of.]

Heat a grill pan over high heat. Coat the chicken in EVOO and season with salt and pepper. Grill until cooked through, about 6 minutes per side. Transfer to a plate.

Bring a large pot of water to a boil.

In a saucepan, melt the butter. Place the panko in a bowl, spoon 3 tablespoons of the butter over them, and toss to moisten. Add ¾ cup of the pecorino, toss, and set aside.

To the butter remaining in the pan, add the garlic, anchovy paste, and lots of pepper and stir for 2 minutes. Whisk in the flour and cook for 1 minute. Whisk in the stock, milk, and Worcestershire. Cook until thick enough to coat the back of a spoon, then stir in the remaining ¾ cup pecorino.

Salt the boiling water and cook the pasta until 1 minute shy of al dente. Drain and return it to the pot. Add the sauce, tossing with tongs for 1 or 2 minutes for the flavors to absorb. Halve the chicken breasts lengthwise, then thinly slice. Add to the pasta. Transfer to a 9 by 13-inch baking dish or a shallow 2- to 3-quart casserole and top with the panko.

[**Make-ahead:** Let cool and refrigerate.]

[**Night of:** Return the casserole to room temp while you preheat the oven to 425°F.]

Bake the casserole, covered, until warmed through, about 20 minutes. Uncover and bake to brown the top.

Roasted Root Vegetable Soup with Grilled Cheese Croutons

Any vegetable tastes better when you roast it, if you ask me. SERVES 4

SOUP

3 medium **sweet potatoes**, peeled and cut into 2-inch cubes
2 large **carrots**, cut into large chunks
2 **parsnips**, peeled and cut into large chunks
1 medium **celery root**, peeled and cut into chunks
EVOO, for drizzling
Salt and **pepper**
Freshly grated **nutmeg**
1 head **Roasted Garlic** (recipe follows)
4 to 6 cups **chicken** or **vegetable stock**
A drizzle of **honey**
Hot sauce

CROUTONS

4 thick-cut slices good-quality **white bread**
4 thick-cut slices **sharp yellow cheddar cheese**
Olive oil cooking spray

Preheat the oven to 425°F. (You may already have the oven on for roasting the garlic, in which case just pop the vegetables in at the same time.)

Make the soup: In a roasting pan, toss the sweet potatoes, carrots, parsnips, and celery root in just enough EVOO to coat. Season with salt, pepper, and nutmeg. Roast the vegetables until tender and caramelized at the edges, 40 to 45 minutes.

Squeeze the roasted garlic into the food processor. Add the vegetables and stock to the processor (work in batches if necessary) and puree until mostly smooth. Season the soup with honey and hot sauce to taste. Add more stock, if needed, to get the consistency you want.

[**Make-ahead:** Let cool and refrigerate.]
[**Night of:** Return the soup to room temp.]
Reheat the soup gently, covered, over low heat.

Make the croutons: Preheat the oven to 425°F. Set a cooling rack over a baking sheet. Assemble 2 sandwiches using 2 bread slices and 2 slices cheese per sandwich. Cut each sandwich into 9 squares and place on the rack with space between them. Coat the sides and tops of each mini sandwich with olive oil cooking spray. Bake until golden and the cheese melts.

Serve the soup with a few grilled cheese croutons floating in the bowl.

Roasted Garlic

EVOO, for drizzling
2 heads **garlic**, tops cut off to expose the cloves
Salt and **pepper**
Leaves from 1 sprig fresh **rosemary**, finely chopped

Preheat the oven to 425°F.

Drizzle EVOO over the heads of garlic and season with salt and pepper. Press the cut side of one of the heads of the garlic into the rosemary (this is for the marinara, page 128). Wrap the garlic heads individually in foil and roast until soft but still moist, 40 to 45 minutes.

Roasted Pepper & Eggplant Marinara

When you have the oven going for roasting the garlic and/or roasting the vegetables for the Roasted Root Vegetable Soup (page 127), see if you have room to roast the eggplant, too. SERVES 4

2 large **red bell peppers**
1 large fresh **red Fresno** or **long red chile**
1 medium-large **eggplant**
EVOO
Salt and **pepper**
1 large head **Roasted Garlic** with rosemary (page 127)
2 cups **chicken stock**
1 (28- or 32-ounce) can **San Marzano tomatoes** (look for DOP on the label)
2 fresh **basil** leaves, torn
Leaves from 1 sprig fresh **oregano**, finely chopped
1 pound **long fusilli pasta**
Grated **pecorino cheese**, for serving
Chopped fresh **flat-leaf parsley**, for serving

Char the bell peppers and chile all over on the stovetop over a gas flame or under the broiler with the oven ajar to let the steam escape. Place the peppers and chiles in a bowl and cover tightly. When cool enough to handle, rub off the skins with a paper towel, then halve and seed. Set aside.

Preheat the oven to 425°F.

Halve the eggplant lengthwise and brush with EVOO. Season with salt and pepper and place cut side down on a baking sheet. Roast to very tender, 30 to 40 minutes.

Let the eggplant cool until easy to handle, then scoop the flesh into a food processor. Squeeze in the roasted garlic and add the roasted peppers and chiles, then puree.

In a saucepan, heat the stock and tomatoes, breaking the tomatoes up a bit with a potato masher. Stir in the eggplant-pepper puree, basil, oregano, and salt and pepper. Simmer the sauce to combine the flavors.

[**Make-ahead:** Let cool and refrigerate.]

[**Night of:** Return the sauce to room temp before reheating gently over medium heat while you cook the pasta.]

Bring a large pot of water to a boil. Salt the water and cook the pasta al dente. Drain the pasta and return it to the pot. Add the sauce, tossing with tongs for 1 or 2 minutes for the flavors to absorb.

Serve topped with pecorino and a sprinkle of parsley.

Beef & Pork Tamale Pie with Polenta Topping

I sneak a little bit of unsweetened cocoa and a pinch of cinnamon into almost every Mexican dish that I do. Just a little something in the background that makes people go, "What *is* that??" SERVES 6

1 tablespoon **vegetable oil**
1 pound **ground pork**
1½ pounds **ground beef sirloin**
1 **onion**, finely chopped
4 cloves **garlic**, finely chopped
2 tablespoons pureed **chipotle chiles in adobo** (see Heads-up, page 182)
1 tablespoon ground **coriander**
1 tablespoon ground **cumin**
2 teaspoons **unsweetened cocoa powder**
¼ teaspoon ground **cinnamon**
Salt and **pepper**
¼ cup **tomato paste**
1 (12-ounce) bottle **Mexican beer** (such as Negra Modelo), at room temperature
1 cup **beef stock**

POLENTA TOPPING

1½ cups **chicken stock** or water
1½ cups **milk**
1 cup quick-cooking **polenta**
2 tablespoons **butter**
1 generous tablespoon **honey**
Salt and **pepper**
1½ cups shredded **cheddar** or **smoked cheddar cheese**

In a large skillet, heat the oil (1 turn of the pan) over high heat. Add the pork and sirloin and cook, breaking them into crumbles as they brown. Add the onion, garlic, chipotle puree, coriander, cumin, cocoa, cinnamon, and salt and pepper. Cook to soften the onion, about 5 minutes. Stir in the tomato paste and cook for 1 minute. Deglaze the pan with the beer. Add the beef stock and heat through to combine the flavors.

[**Make-ahead:** Let cool and refrigerate.]

[**Night of:** Transfer the meat mixture to an ovenproof skillet and return to room temp before reheating gently over medium heat.]

Preheat the broiler.

Make the polenta topping: In a saucepan, bring the chicken stock and milk to a boil. Whisk in the polenta and keep whisking until very thick, about 3 minutes. Stir in the butter and honey and season with salt and pepper.

Spread the polenta in an even layer over the meat. Top with the cheddar and brown under the broiler.

WEEK 18

BOLD THINKING

BIG, BOLD,
IN-YOUR-FACE
FLAVORS

DISH
1
SOUTHERN
ITALIAN-STYLE
SHORT RIBS
PAGE 131

DISH
2
VEAL OR
LAMB
PAPRIKASH
PAGE 133

DISH
3
DECONSTRUCTED
ARRABBIATA
PAGE 134

DISH
4
TURMERIC & CUMIN
CHICKEN WITH
ORANGES, OLIVES &
CHICKPEA
COUSCOUS
PAGE 136

DISH
5
BEEF &
BROCCOLI
PAGE 137

Southern Italian–Style Short Ribs

Four extra ribs are cooked in this dish to use in Beef & Broccoli (page 137). SERVES 4

10 bone-in **beef short ribs**, trimmed of excess fat

Salt and **pepper**

2 tablespoons **EVOO**, plus more for drizzling

3 or 4 **anchovy fillets**

4 cloves **garlic**, sliced

2 fresh **bay leaves**

2 **onions**, cut into wedges, with root end attached

1 large or 2 medium bulbs **fennel**, cut into wedges, plus ½ cup chopped fennel fronds

¼ cup **tomato paste**

2 tablespoons chopped **golden raisins**

A pinch of ground **cloves**

1 (750 ml) bottle **Nero d'Avola** or other **spicy red wine**

½ cup fresh **flat-leaf parsley** leaves, coarsely chopped

Grated **orange** or **lemon** zest (or both), for garnish

Shaved **pecorino cheese**, for garnish

Preheat the oven to 500°F. Meanwhile, bring the short ribs to room temperature.

Pat the ribs dry, then sprinkle liberally with salt and pepper and drizzle with EVOO. Arrange the ribs on a broiler pan and roast until well browned, 12 to 15 minutes. (Leave the oven on but reduce the temperature to 350°F.)

Meanwhile, in a large Dutch oven, heat the 2 tablespoons EVOO (2 turns of the pan) over medium-high heat. Add the anchovies, cover the pan with a splatter screen or lid, and shake until the anchovies begin to break up. Reduce the heat a bit, uncover, and stir until the anchovies melt. Add the garlic, bay leaves, onions, and fennel, and season with pepper. Stir for a few minutes for the fennel and onions to begin to brown and soften slightly. Add the tomato paste, raisins, and cloves and stir for 1 to 2 minutes more. Add the wine and cook until reduced by half, about 10 minutes.

Add the short ribs and stir to coat with the sauce. Cover and bake until the ribs are very tender, 2½ to 2¾ hours; turn them in the sauce about halfway through.

Transfer the ribs to a platter and cover with foil. Return the pan to the stovetop and cook for 10 to 15 minutes to reduce the sauce.

Set aside 4 of the short ribs for Beef & Broccoli (page 137). Add the remaining ribs (on or off the bone) to the reduced sauce.

[Make-ahead: Let cool and refrigerate.]

[**Night of:** Return the beef to room temp before reheating gently over low heat or in a 325°F oven. Remove the bay leaves.]

Put the ribs on a serving platter and top with the parsley, fennel fronds, a sprinkle of zest, and some pecorino.

Veal or Lamb Paprikash

I have a Hungarian friend who is a brilliant cook. Her specialty is paprikash, and I always have my fingers crossed when we go to her house, wishing that this is what she will be serving. My paprikash is based on her recipe. Any leftover stew is great for lunch or with poached eggs. **Suggested sides:** Four-Cheese Polenta and Cucumber Salad (see QR codes below). SERVES 4 (WITH LEFTOVERS)

2½ pounds **veal shoulder** or boned **shank meat**, cut into bite-size cubes, or 2½ pounds **lamb shoulder** or boned **leg meat**, cut into bite-size cubes

Salt and **pepper**

Flour, for dredging

EVOO, for drizzling

6 tablespoons (¾ stick) **butter**, cut into pieces

3 **onions**, chopped

3 tablespoons plus 1 teaspoon good-quality **sweet paprika**

1½ teaspoons ground **cumin**

2 or 3 large cloves **garlic**, smashed

2 large fresh **bay leaves**

1 **green bell pepper**, coarsely chopped

1 **red bell pepper**, coarsely chopped

1 large **tomato** or **heirloom tomato**, chopped

1½ cups **chicken stock** (if using veal) or **beef stock** (if using lamb)

1½ cups **dry white wine** (if using veal) or **dry red wine** (if using lamb)

1½ cups **crème fraîche**

½ cup drained **caperberries**, for garnish (optional)

Preheat the oven to 350°F. Bring the meat to room temperature.

Pat the meat dry with paper towels, then sprinkle liberally with salt and pepper and dredge in flour. In a large Dutch oven, heat a drizzle of EVOO over medium-high heat. Working in batches, brown the meat all over. Transfer to a plate.

Add another drizzle of EVOO to the pan and reduce the heat to medium. Add the butter and let it melt. Add the onions and cook until very tender, 15 to 20 minutes. Add 3 tablespoons of the paprika, the cumin, garlic, bay leaves, bell peppers, and tomato, and stir to combine and heat through, 1 to 2 minutes. Add the stock and wine, then return the meat to the pan. Cover, transfer to the oven, and bake until the meat is tender, about 2 hours.

Transfer the meat to a platter and cover with foil. Discard the bay leaves. Using an immersion blender, puree the sauce in the pan. Stir in 1 cup of the crème fraîche and cook until the sauce is reduced, 20 to 30 minutes. Return the meat to the pan.

[**Make-ahead:** Let cool and refrigerate.]

[**Night of:** Return the stew to room temp before reheating over medium heat or in a 325°F oven.]

Just before serving, stir in the remaining 1 teaspoon paprika to brighten the flavor. In a small skillet, fry the caperberries (if using) in a little EVOO until crisp. Top the stew with a few dollops of crème fraîche and some fried caperberries.

Recipe for Four-Cheese Polenta
View a bonus Side Dish recipe.

Recipe for Cucumber Salad
View a bonus Side Dish recipe.

Deconstructed Arrabbiata

Three make-ahead sauces, combined with starchy cooking water, hot spaghetti, and cheese at the table, add up to a mind-blowingly different pasta all' arrabbiata. SERVES 4

TOMATO SAUCE
1 (28- or 32-ounce) can **San Marzano tomatoes** (look for DOP on the label)
½ **onion**
Pinch of **sugar**
3 or 4 fresh **basil** leaves, torn
2 cloves **garlic**, grated or pasted
EVOO, for drizzling
Sea salt and **pepper**

CHILE PASTE
2 or 3 **Italian cherry peppers** or **red Fresno chiles**
Sea salt
1 clove **garlic**, very finely chopped
¼ cup **harissa**

PARSLEY AND BASIL PESTO
¼ cup **pine nuts**
1 cup fresh **basil** leaves
1 cup fresh **flat-leaf parsley** leaves
⅓ cup grated **Parmigiano-Reggiano cheese**
1 clove **garlic**, finely grated or pasted
Salt and **pepper**
Freshly grated **nutmeg**
EVOO

Salt
1 pound **spaghetti**
Shaved or grated **Parmigiano-Reggiano cheese**
EVOO, for drizzling

Make the tomato sauce: Put the tomatoes and their juice in a food processor. Grate 3 to 4 tablespoons of the onion directly into the food processor so the juice falls in. Add the sugar, basil, garlic, and a liberal drizzle of EVOO (about 1 tablespoon), and season with salt and pepper. Whiz the mixture up until it's pureed. Transfer it to a small pot. Bring to a simmer over medium-low heat and cook 20 to 30 minutes.

[Make-ahead: Let cool and refrigerate. It also freezes well if you want to make a double or triple batch.]

Make the chile paste: Finely chop the chiles (remove the seeds if you want to curb their heat a little). Sprinkle some salt over the chiles on the cutting board, then mash in the garlic to form a paste. Mix with the harissa in a small container.

[Make-ahead: Measure out one-third of the chile paste for the Beef & Broccoli, page 137. Cover and refrigerate the remainder.]

Make the pesto: In a small skillet, lightly toast the pine nuts. Let cool completely, then transfer to a food processor. Add the basil, parsley, Parm, garlic, salt, pepper, and a few grates of nutmeg. Pulse until well blended. With the machine running, drizzle in the EVOO to the count of 6; it will be somewhere between ⅓ cup and ½ cup, just enough to bring the pesto together. Transfer to a small container.

[Make-ahead: Cover and refrigerate. The pesto freezes well, so double or triple the batch if you like.]

[Night of: Return the chile paste and pesto to room temp. Reheat the tomato sauce over medium-low heat.]

Bring a large pot of water to a boil. Salt the water and cook the spaghetti al dente. Ladle out about a cup of the starchy cooking water and place in a large serving bowl. Drain the pasta. Add the tomato sauce, half of the pesto, and a little bit of the chile paste (you can add more later to adjust the level of heat) to the cooking water. Add the pasta, tossing with tongs for 1 or 2 minutes for the flavors to absorb. Add more chile paste if desired and toss again.

Top with lots of Parm and a drizzle of EVOO. Serve more chile paste and pesto on the side for people to add if they'd like.

WEEK 18

DISH 4

Turmeric & Cumin Chicken with Oranges, Olives & Chickpea Couscous

Whenever I cook with a whole chicken, as in this Moroccan-style dish, I put the wings in a saucepan with about a quart of water to make a poaching liquid for the dish as well as for the couscous that goes with it. Of course you could use store-bought stock. SERVES 4

1 whole **chicken** (4 to 5 pounds), cut up
Kosher salt
Juice of 1 **lime**
2 **oranges**: 1 juiced, 1 sliced (but not peeled)
6 cloves **garlic**: 3 finely chopped, 3 thinly sliced
3 tablespoons **EVOO**
1 rounded tablespoon ground **turmeric**
1½ teaspoons **cumin seeds**
4 small fresh **bay leaves**
2 (3-inch) **cinnamon sticks**
2 fresh **serrano** or **jalapeño chiles**, halved lengthwise
1 cup cracked **green olives** or **olive mix**
2 tablespoons **butter**
1 (15-ounce) can **chickpeas**, rinsed and drained
A handful of fresh **cilantro** or **parsley** leaves, finely chopped, plus a few sprigs for garnish
1½ cups **couscous**

Pull off and discard the skin from the thighs, drumsticks, and breasts. Put the wings in a small pot, cover with water, and sprinkle with salt. Simmer gently for 30 minutes. Discard the wings and reserve the poaching liquid.

Meanwhile, combine the remaining chicken pieces with the lime juice, orange juice, and chopped garlic. Sprinkle liberally with salt and toss to coat. Cover and marinate at room temperature for at least 45 minutes and up to 1 hour.

In a large, deep skillet, heat the EVOO (3 turns of the pan) over medium-high heat. Add the sliced garlic, turmeric, and cumin seeds and stir for a minute to toast the spices. Add the bay leaves, cinnamon sticks, and chiles and cook for 1 or 2 minutes. Add the chicken and turn to coat it in the oil, then cook until the chicken is lightly browned, about 10 minutes.

Add the orange slices and olives. Cook until heated through. Add 1 cup of the poaching liquid. Partially cover and simmer for 20 minutes. Remove the cinnamon sticks (see Heads-up).

[Make-ahead: Let the chicken cool, then refrigerate. Store the leftover poaching liquid separately.]

[Night of: Return the chicken to room temp, then reheat gently over medium heat. Discard the bay leaves. Return the poaching liquid to room temp for cooking the couscous.]

In a large saucepan, combine 1½ cups of the poaching liquid, the butter, chickpeas, and cilantro. Bring to a boil, then stir in the couscous. Turn off the heat, cover, and let stand for 5 minutes. Fluff with a fork.

Serve the chicken, orange slices, and olives on a bed of couscous. Garnish with cilantro sprigs.

Heads-up: Don't leave the cinnamon sticks in the dish when you store it for a make-ahead, because cinnamon ends up overpowering the other flavors.

Beef & Broccoli

The short ribs for this dish were cooked in the Southern Italian–Style Short Ribs recipe (page 131) and the chile paste is from Deconstructed Arrabbiata (page 134).

SERVES 4

Sea salt
1 large bunch **broccoli rabe**, trimmed and cut into 2-inch pieces
2 tablespoons high-temperature **cooking oil** (such as peanut)
1 **onion**, quartered lengthwise and sliced
1 small **red bell pepper**, quartered and sliced
Chile Paste from Deconstructed Arrabbiata (page 134)
4 cloves **garlic**, sliced
1 (2-inch) piece fresh **ginger**, peeled and grated
½ cup **dry sherry**
1 tablespoon **cornstarch**
1 cup **beef stock**
3 tablespoons **hoisin sauce**
2 tablespoons **soy sauce** (reduced-sodium or tamari)
4 **beef short ribs**, shredded, from Southern Italian–Style Short Ribs (page 131)
1 cup **long-grain white**, **jasmine**, or **brown rice**
Grated zest of 1 **lime**, plus lime wedges for serving
Shredded **scallions** and chopped fresh **cilantro** or **parsley**, for garnish

In a saucepan, bring a couple of inches of salted water to a boil. Add the broccoli rabe and cook for 5 to 6 minutes. Cold-shock the broccoli rabe in a large bowl of ice water. Drain well and squeeze dry.

In a large, deep skillet, heat the cooking oil (2 turns of the pan) over high heat. Add the onion and bell pepper and stir-fry for 2 to 3 minutes. Add 1 teaspoon chile paste, the garlic, and ginger, and stir-fry for 2 minutes. Add the sherry. Dissolve the cornstarch in a small amount of the stock, then add it with the remaining stock. Stir a minute to thicken, then add the hoisin sauce, soy sauce, broccoli rabe, and short ribs. Heat through.

[Make-ahead: Let cool and refrigerate.]

[Night of: Return the stir-fry to room temp before reheating over medium heat with a splash of water to loosen it up.]

Cook the rice according to the package instructions. Stir in the lime zest.

Serve the beef stir-fry over the rice, with lime wedges on the side. Garnish with scallions and cilantro.

WEEK 19

MULTINATIONAL
MAKE-AHEAD

A WEEK'S WORTH OF MAKE-AHEAD DISHES FROM ALL OVER THE WORLD

DISH
1
SAVORY & SWEET PORK STEW WITH ANCHO CHILES
PAGE 139

DISH
2
SALSA-MARINATED CHICKEN WITH MEXICAN RICE
PAGE 141

DISH
3
ESCAROLE SOUP WITH CAESAR CROUTONS
PAGE 142

DISH
4
ASPARAGUS & PISTACHIO PESTO PASTA
PAGE 143

DISH
5
VINDALOO OF CHICKEN
PAGE 144

Savory & Sweet Pork Stew with Ancho Chiles

This Mexican stew is seriously deep with flavor, with an ancho chile sauce thickened with rich toasted almonds and peanuts. SERVES 4 TO 6

1 medium **red onion**, sliced into rings
Juice of 2 **limes**
Salt and **pepper**
5 or 6 **dried ancho chiles**, stemmed and seeded
4 cups **chicken stock**
½ cup **blanched almonds**
½ cup unsalted **raw peanuts**
1 tablespoon **unsweetened cocoa powder**
½ teaspoon ground **cloves**
3 or 4 cloves **garlic**, grated or pasted
1 small **yellow onion**, chopped
A handful of **raisins**
Vegetable or **peanut oil**
2 pounds **pork shoulder** (butt), cut into bite-size cubes
2 large fresh **bay leaves**
1 **cinnamon stick**
12 **flour** or **corn tortillas**
Queso fresco or **Cotija cheese**, crumbled

Separate the red onion into rings and place in a small plastic container. Dress with the lime juice and season with salt and pepper.

[**Make-ahead:** Refrigerate.]

In a saucepan, combine the ancho chiles and stock. Bring to a low boil over medium heat. Reduce the heat to a simmer and cook until softened, about 10 minutes.

Meanwhile, in a large Dutch oven, toast the almonds and peanuts over medium heat until browned. Transfer the nuts to a food processor. Add the ancho chiles and stock, the cocoa, cloves, garlic, yellow onion, and raisins. Season with salt and pepper. Puree until smooth. (You may need to do this in two batches.)

In the same Dutch oven, heat a thin layer of oil (about 2 tablespoons) over medium-high heat. Pat the pork dry and sprinkle with salt and pepper. Working in batches, brown the pork, adding more oil between batches as needed. Return all the pork to the pot and pour the ancho sauce over it. Bring to a boil and add the bay leaves and cinnamon stick. Reduce the heat to a simmer and cook until the pork is very tender, 1¼ to 1½ hours (depending on how large you cubed the meat).

[**Make-ahead:** Let cool and refrigerate. Remove the cinnamon stick before storing.]

[**Night of:** Return the stew to room temp before reheating gently over medium heat. Remove the bay leaves.]

Warm or char the tortillas. Serve the stew with the lime-pickled onions, crumbled cheese, and the tortillas.

Salsa-Marinated Chicken with Mexican Rice

Everyone knows that salsa is terrific with chips, but you've got to think outside the box. It's also good in Mexican rice and it makes a fabulous marinade. This dish is best baked on **Cook Day** or on the following day. **Suggested side:** Canned black beans heated up with a little cumin, salt, and pepper; or spicy vegetarian refried beans, seasoned with a little cumin and heated with a little water to loosen them up.

SERVES 4

4 large **plum tomatoes**
1 small **yellow** or **red onion**
2 or 3 cloves **garlic**, grated or pasted
1 fresh **red Fresno chile**, thinly sliced
1 fresh **jalapeño chile**, finely chopped
Generous handful of fresh **cilantro** leaves, chopped
Salt and **pepper**
⅓ cup **EVOO**
2 pounds boneless, skinless **chicken breasts** or **thighs**
2 tablespoons **butter**
1 cup **long-grain white rice**
2 cups **chicken stock**
1 **lime**

On the large holes of a box grater, grate the tomatoes and onion into a large bowl. Add the garlic, chiles, and cilantro and stir to combine. Measure out half of the salsa and transfer to a storage container, season with a little salt, and refrigerate. Add the EVOO to the remaining salsa. Sprinkle the chicken liberally with salt and pepper, add to the salsa, and stir to coat. Cover and marinate in the refrigerator for at least 30 minutes, or 2 hours if you're serving this on **Cook Day.**

[**Make-ahead:** Transfer to a plastic freezer bag, seal, then put in another bag. Store on the lowest shelf of the refrigerator.]

[**Night of:** Return the chicken to room temp while you cook the rice.]

Heat a grill, a grill pan, or a griddle to medium-high.

In a medium saucepan, melt the butter over medium heat. Add the rice and cook, stirring, until golden brown, 3 to 4 minutes. Add the reserved salsa and the chicken stock and bring to a boil. Reduce the heat to a simmer, cover, and cook for 20 minutes. Five minutes in, cook the chicken, turning occasionally, until cooked through, 12 to 15 minutes.

Cut the lime into wedges and douse the chicken with lime juice when it comes off the grill. Serve the chicken with the rice.

Escarole Soup with Caesar Croutons

I usually start this style of Italian soup (a *minestra*) with some chopped pancetta, but John and I like to have one night a week when we eat meat free. I still make the soup with chicken stock, though, because I just like the flavor better. But you could make this even more vegetarian by using vegetable stock. And we definitely don't worry about the anchovies in the Caesar croutons; they just wouldn't be the same without them. SERVES 4

CAESAR CROUTONS

½ loaf **white Pullman** or **brioche bread**
⅓ cup **EVOO**
4 **anchovy fillets** or 2 teaspoons **anchovy paste**
1 tablespoon **Worcestershire sauce**
2 cloves **garlic**, finely chopped
Juice of ½ **lemon**
1 cup shredded **pecorino cheese**
Cracked **pepper**

SOUP

2 tablespoons **EVOO**
2 or 3 cloves **garlic**, finely chopped
1 medium **onion**, chopped
Salt and **pepper**
2 heads **escarole**, coarsely chopped
Freshly grated **nutmeg**
6 cups **chicken stock**
2 (15-ounce) cans **cannellini beans**
Grated zest of 1 **lemon**

Preheat the oven to 350°F.

Make the Caesar croutons: Place a cooling rack over a baking sheet. Trim the crust from the bread, then cut the bread into ¾- to 1-inch cubes. Spread the bread cubes on the rack and bake until light golden, 12 to 15 minutes. (Leave the oven on.)

Meanwhile, in a small saucepan, heat the EVOO and anchovies or anchovy paste over medium-low heat. Cover the pan with a splatter screen or lid and shake until the anchovies begin to break up. Uncover and stir until the anchovies or paste melt into the oil. Stir in the Worcestershire, garlic, and lemon juice, then remove from the heat.

Place the croutons in a bowl, pour on the dressing, and toss to coat. Sprinkle with the cheese and season liberally with pepper. Spread the croutons directly on the baking sheet (no rack) and return to the oven until they are deep golden, 7 to 10 minutes.

[**Make-ahead:** Let cool and store in foil in a cool, dry place.]

Make the soup: In a soup pot, heat the EVOO (2 turns of the pan) over medium heat. Add the garlic and onion and season with salt and pepper. Cook until softened, 5 to 6 minutes. Wilt in the escarole, then season with salt, pepper, and a few grates of nutmeg. Add the chicken stock, beans, and lemon zest. Simmer until the greens are tender and no longer bitter.

[**Make-ahead:** Let cool and refrigerate.]

[**Night of:** Return the soup to room temp before reheating gently over medium heat. Take care not to overcook, because you don't want to lose all the flavor and color in the greens. Serve the croutons at room temp or reheat them in a low oven if you want to serve them warm.]

Serve the soup in shallow bowls topped with lots of Caesar croutons.

Asparagus & Pistachio Pesto Pasta

Pesto is perfect, perfect, perfect for make-ahead cooking. Make extra every time you make it and store it in the freezer. SERVES 4

1 pound thin **asparagus**
¼ cup fresh **mint** leaves
¼ cup fresh **flat-leaf parsley** leaves
¼ cup fresh **tarragon** leaves or ½ cup fresh **basil** leaves
¼ cup grated **Parmigiano-Reggiano cheese**
3 to 4 tablespoons toasted **pistachios**
1 clove **garlic**, grated or pasted
Juice of 1 **lime** or ½ **lemon**
⅓ to ½ cup **EVOO**
Salt and **pepper**
1 pound **penne pasta**
1 cup shelled fresh **green peas** or thawed frozen peas
Shaved **Parmigiano-Reggiano cheese**, for garnish

Trim the tough ends from the asparagus. Store half the spears upright in a glass filled halfway with water to keep them fresh until ready to serve. Chop the remaining asparagus and place in a food processor. Add the mint, parsley, tarragon, Parm, pistachios, garlic, and lime juice. Add the EVOO, pouring to a count of 6 (see Heads-up). Season with salt and pepper. Pulse until the pesto comes together.

[**Make-ahead:** Place in a small container and refrigerate for up to 5 days.]

[**Night of:** Return the pesto to room temp.]

Bring a large pot of water to a boil.

Place the pesto in a large serving bowl.

Slice the asparagus spears on an angle into 1½-inch pieces.

Salt the boiling water and cook the pasta for 5 minutes. Add the peas and sliced asparagus and cook for 2 to 3 minutes more. Ladle out about a cup of the starchy cooking water and add it to the pesto. Drain the pasta and vegetables and add to the pesto, tossing with tongs for 1 or 2 minutes for the flavors to absorb.

Season with salt and pepper and garnish with shaved cheese.

Heads-up: When I make pesto, or other similar sauces, I don't measure the EVOO in a measuring cup. Instead, I pour in the oil to a certain count. In this case, it's to a count of 6, which ends up being somewhere between ⅓ and ½ cup.

Vindaloo of Chicken

This Indian dish sounds like a party, doesn't it? I like to make my own curry blend whenever I'm making Indian food so I can go a little heavier on one spice or a little lighter on another. Sort of customizing to suit my mood and the food. SERVES 4 TO 6

HOT CURRY SPICE BLEND
1 rounded tablespoon ground **turmeric**
2 teaspoons ground **coriander**
2 teaspoons ground **cumin**
2 teaspoons **hot paprika**
1 teaspoon **dry mustard**
¼ teaspoon ground **cardamom**
¼ teaspoon ground **cinnamon**

CHICKEN
1 whole **chicken** (4 to 5 pounds), cut up into thighs, drumsticks, wings, and 2 breast pieces
Salt and **pepper**

2 or 3 large cloves **garlic**, finely chopped
Juice of 2 **limes**

VINDALOO
2 tablespoons **vegetable** or **peanut oil**
4 large cloves **garlic**, finely chopped
2 fresh **bay leaves**
1 fresh **red Fresno** or other moderate-heat **red chile pepper**, seeded and finely chopped

1 (2-inch) piece fresh **ginger**, peeled and grated or minced
1 **onion**, chopped
Salt
1 (14.5-ounce) can **diced tomatoes**

1½ cups **jasmine rice**
Naan bread
Melted **butter**
Garnishes: chopped toasted **peanuts** or **almonds**, chopped **fresh mint**, chopped fresh **cilantro**

Make the curry spice blend: Stir together all the spices.

Prepare the chicken: Place the chicken wings in a small pot, cover with water, and season with salt. Bring to a boil, then reduce the heat to a low simmer and poach for 30 minutes.

Discard the skin from the remaining chicken. Place the chicken in a shallow dish and dress with half the spice blend, the garlic, lime juice, and some salt and pepper. Cover and marinate for 1 hour.

Make the vindaloo: In a Dutch oven or deep skillet, heat the oil over medium-high heat. Add the garlic, bay leaves, chile, ginger, onion, and the remaining spice blend. Season with salt. Cook, stirring frequently, until the onion is softened, 7 to 8 minutes. Add the tomatoes and about 1 cup of the poaching liquid and bring to a boil. Slide in the chicken and partially cover the pan. Reduce the heat to a simmer and cook the chicken until cooked through, about 30 minutes.

[**Make-ahead:** Let cool and refrigerate. Refrigerate the remaining poaching liquid separately.]

[**Night of:** Return the poaching liquid to room temp. Return the vindaloo to room temp before gently reheating over medium heat while you cook the rice.]

In a saucepan, prepare the rice according to the package directions, using the reserved poaching liquid (supplement with store-bought chicken stock if necessary).

Meanwhile, heat a griddle or large skillet over medium-high heat. Splash with water and heat the naan bread. When the naan comes off the griddle, brush with a little melted butter.

Spoon the chicken and sauce over the rice. Top with garnishes. Serve the naan on the side.

WEEK 20

FRESH START

FIVE MEALS LOADED
WITH FARM-FRESH
INGREDIENTS

DISH
1
SPRING
CHICKEN WITH
CARROTS &
PEAS
PAGE 147

DISH
2
SPICY CLAM &
CORN CHOWDER
WITH
CROUTONS
PAGE 148

DISH
3
YELLOW TOMATO
GAZPACHO WITH
TOASTED ALMOND
BREAD CRUMBS
PAGE 149

DISH
4
GARDEN-STYLE
STRAW &
HAY PASTA WITH
BAGNA CAUDA
PAGE 151

DISH
5
RISOTTO-
STUFFED
PEPPERS &
ZUCCHINI
PAGE 152

Spring Chicken with Carrots & Peas

You can use store-bought chicken stock instead of the poaching liquid if you want to skip that step. **Suggested side:** Baguette, crisped up in the oven and spread with some butter. SERVES 4 TO 6

1 whole **chicken** (4 to 5 pounds), cut into 8 pieces
2 or 3 slices **lemon**
2 fresh **bay leaves**
Salt and **pepper**
1 tablespoon **EVOO**
6 large **shallots**, sliced
1 teaspoon **sugar**
1 cup **dry white wine**
3 cups shelled fresh **green peas** or thawed frozen peas
1 large bunch **spring carrots** (¾ to 1 pound), thinly sliced on an angle
A handful of fresh **dill**, chopped
A handful of fresh **flat-leaf parsley**, finely chopped
3 tablespoons **butter**

Place the chicken wings in a small saucepan and cover with water. Add the lemon and bay leaves and season with salt. Bring to a boil, then reduce the heat and simmer for 20 to 30 minutes. Strain the poaching liquid (save the wings for a treat for your pet, if you have one).

Meanwhile, pat the chicken pieces dry and sprinkle liberally with salt and pepper on both sides. In a Dutch oven or deep skillet, heat the EVOO (1 turn of the pan) over medium-high heat. Add the chicken, skin side down, and cook until crisp, 15 to 18 minutes. Flip the pieces and cook, partially covered with a lid or foil, until cooked through, 8 to 10 minutes. Transfer the chicken to a plate.

Reduce the heat a bit and add the shallots and sugar; season with salt and pepper. Cook until tender, about 10 minutes. Deglaze the pan with the wine and cook until reduced by half, 2 to 3 minutes. Add 1 cup of the poaching liquid. Add the peas, carrots, dill, and parsley.

[**Make-ahead:** Arrange the chicken on top of the stew, let cool, and refrigerate.]

[**Night of:** Return the stew to room temp before reheating gently over medium heat. You can reheat the chicken right in the pot, or if you'd prefer, you can briefly broil the chicken separately to recrisp the skin.]

Stir the butter into the stew and season with a little more salt and pepper. Continue simmering until the peas and carrots are tender, 6 to 7 minutes.

Place the chicken on plates or in shallow bowls and ladle the stew alongside and on top.

Spicy Clam & Corn Chowder with Croutons

Buy the clams within 48 hours of serving and cook them just before you're ready to serve. SERVES 4

CHOWDER BASE
1 tablespoon **EVOO**
⅓ pound lean **bacon**, chopped
4 large **ears corn**, kernels cut off and cobs scraped
2 tablespoons fresh **thyme** leaves, finely chopped
2 tablespoons **Rachael Ray Seafood Seasoning** or **Old Bay seasoning**
4 cloves **garlic**, chopped
3 or 4 small ribs **celery** with leafy tops, chopped
2 fresh **bay leaves**
2 fresh **jalapeño** or **red Fresno chiles**, chopped or thinly sliced
1 **red onion**, chopped
4 cups **chicken stock**
3 or 4 **heirloom tomatoes**, chopped

CROUTONS
3 **English muffins**, chopped into bite-size cubes
4 tablespoons (½ stick) **butter**
2 tablespoons **hot sauce**
2 tablespoons finely chopped fresh **flat-leaf parsley**
1 teaspoon **Rachael Ray Seafood Seasoning** or **Old Bay seasoning**

4 pounds **littleneck clams**, scrubbed
1 (12-ounce) bottle **lager beer**
Sea salt and **pepper**
Hot sauce, for serving

Preheat the oven to 350°F.

Make the chowder base: In a soup pot or Dutch oven, heat the EVOO (1 turn of the pan) over medium-high heat. Add the bacon and cook until crisp, about 5 minutes. Add the corn and cook until the kernels are lightly browned at the edges, 6 to 8 minutes. Add the thyme, seafood seasoning, garlic, celery, bay leaves, chiles, and onion, and cook until the onion and celery are softened, 6 to 8 minutes. Stir in the chicken stock and tomatoes. Bring to a simmer, then turn off the heat.

[Make-ahead: Let cool and refrigerate.]

Make the croutons: Arrange the English muffin cubes on a wire rack set over a baking sheet. Toast in the oven until light golden. In a small saucepan, melt the butter with the hot sauce. Place the croutons in a bowl and toss with the parsley, seafood seasoning, and butter mixture. Return to the rack and bake until deeply golden. Let cool.

[Make-ahead: Store the croutons in an airtight container or in a foil pouch until ready to use.]

[Night of: Return the chowder to room temp before reheating gently over medium-low heat.]

Place the clams and beer in a large pot with a tight-fitting lid and season with sea salt and pepper. Cover and bring to a boil, then cook at a rapid simmer until the clams open, 3 to 5 minutes. Discard any unopened clams.

Divide the clams and their cooking liquid among 4 shallow bowls. Ladle the chowder over them and garnish with croutons. Serve with hot sauce.

Yellow Tomato Gazpacho with Toasted Almond Bread Crumbs

This gazpacho is great all by itself, but if you really want to have a Spanish-style make-ahead meal for a hot summer night, serve it with Tuna-Stuffed Piquillo Peppers (see QR code below). SERVES 4

GAZPACHO
Salt and **pepper**
8 **yellow tomatoes**
2 ribs **celery** with leafy tops, coarsely chopped
2 slices (½ inch thick) stale **white** or **peasant bread**, crusts trimmed
1 or 2 cloves **garlic**, grated or pasted
1 fresh **serrano chile**, seeded and chopped
1 small **red onion**, grated on the large holes of a box grater
½ **seedless cucumber**, peeled and chopped
A small handful of fresh **cilantro**
Juice of 1 **lime**
EVOO, for drizzling

BREAD CRUMBS
3 cups torn stale **white** or **peasant bread**
A couple of handfuls of salted oil-roasted **Marcona almonds**

Preheat the oven to 350°F.

Make the gazpacho: Bring a pot of water to a boil and season with salt. Fill a large bowl with ice water. Cut an X in the bottom of each tomato, then drop into the boiling water and cook for 30 seconds. Transfer the tomatoes to the ice water bath to cool for 30 seconds, then peel, seed, and chop.

Working in two batches, puree the tomatoes, celery, bread, garlic, chile, onion, cucumber, cilantro, lime juice, and a drizzle of EVOO in a blender or food processor. Add a splash of water if necessary. Season with salt and pepper. Combine both batches in a pitcher. Adjust the seasonings.

[Make-ahead: Refrigerate.]

Make the bread crumbs: Spread the bread on a baking sheet and toast in the oven until golden. Let cool, then put in a food processor with the almonds. Process until crumbs form.

[Make-ahead: Store in an airtight container at room temperature.]

[Night of: Dig in.]

Ladle the gazpacho into bowls and serve topped with the bread crumbs.

Recipe for Tuna-Stuffed Piquillo Peppers
View a bonus Side Dish recipe.

Garden-Style Straw & Hay Pasta with Bagna Cauda

Bagna cauda is a great make-ahead, either as a pasta topper or as a party dip with crudités. SERVES 4 TO 6

2 heads **hardneck garlic** (about 24 cloves), cloves separated, skin left on

Sea salt

1½ to 2 pounds assorted farm-fresh **vegetables**, a couple of handfuls of each (see Heads-up)

¼ cup **EVOO**

2 (2-ounce) tins or 1 (4-ounce) jar good quality flat **anchovy fillets**, drained

2 cups **heavy cream** or **half-and-half**

4 tablespoons (½ stick) **butter**

Pepper

8 ounces **egg pasta** (such as tagliatelle)

8 ounces **spinach pasta** (such as tagliatelle)

¼ cup fresh **flat-leaf parsley** leaves, finely chopped

Bring a small pot of water to a low boil, add the garlic, and simmer for 20 minutes. Let cool, drain, peel, and mash into a paste. Season with sea salt.

Bring a few inches of water to a boil in a large pot and season with salt. Fill a large bowl with ice water. Cut the vegetables into similar shapes and sizes but keep them separate. Blanch the vegetables, one kind at a time, until tender-crisp. Delicate vegetables like thin beans will take 1 to 2 minutes; firmer vegetables like squash will take 3 minutes. After each batch, use a slotted spoon or strainer to transfer them to the ice water bath to cool. Drain well.

[Make-ahead: Store the vegetables in the fridge.]

In a small saucepan, heat the EVOO (4 turns of the pan) over medium heat. Add the anchovies, cover the pan with a splatter screen or lid, and shake until the anchovies begin to break up. Reduce the heat a bit, uncover, and stir until the anchovies melt. Add the heavy cream, butter, and garlic paste and season with salt and pepper. Cook, stirring, until the bagna cauda is thickened.

[Make-ahead: Let cool and refrigerate.]

[Night of: Return the vegetables to room temp. Reheat the bagna cauda very gently over medium-low heat. Adjust the seasonings.]

Bring a large pot of water to a boil. Salt the water and cook the pasta al dente, adding the vegetables in the last 2 minutes of cooking to reheat them. Ladle out about a cup of the starchy cooking water. Drain the pasta and vegetables and return them to the pot. Add the sauce, tossing with tongs for 1 or 2 minutes for the flavors to absorb, and adding some of the starchy water if needed to loosen it up.

Serve garnished with the parsley.

Heads-up: Baby vegetables and very colorful vegetables are a good bet here. Think baby golden beets, baby carrots, baby zucchini, asparagus, purple cauliflower, romesco cauliflower, sugar snap peas, haricots verts, baby zucchini, or pattypan squash.

Risotto-Stuffed Peppers & Zucchini

The risotto is delicious stuffed into either peppers or zucchini, so keep that in mind if one looks better than the other at the market. Or you can use small firm yellow squash with the zucchini rather than peppers. SERVES 4

4 cups **chicken stock**
1 teaspoon grated **orange** zest
1 teaspoon grated **lemon** zest
Generous pinch of **saffron threads**
2 medium **zucchini**
2 **red bell peppers**, halved lengthwise
4 tablespoons **EVOO**, plus more for drizzling
Salt and **pepper**
4 cloves **garlic**, finely chopped
1 medium **onion**, finely chopped
1½ cups **arborio rice**
½ cup **dry white wine**
1 cup grated **Parmigiano-Reggiano cheese**
2 tablespoons **butter**
Juice of ½ **lemon**
Juice of ½ **orange**
½ cup **panko bread crumbs** or **homemade dry bread crumbs**
½ cup finely chopped fresh **flat-leaf parsley**, or a combination of **parsley** and fresh **mint**

In a saucepan, combine the chicken stock, 2 cups water, the orange and lemon zests, and saffron and bring to a low simmer.

Halve the zucchini lengthwise and gently scrape out the center flesh and seeds. Chop the flesh and seeds and reserve. Halve each zucchini again crosswise. Arrange the zucchini and bell peppers cut side up in a baking dish. Drizzle with EVOO and season with salt and pepper.

In a round-bottomed risotto pot or saucepan, heat 2 tablespoons EVOO (2 turns of the pan) over medium to medium-high heat. Add the garlic and onion and cook, stirring, until softened, 2 to 3 minutes. Add the chopped zucchini and season with salt and pepper. Cook, stirring often, until lightly browned, 2 to 3 minutes more. Stir in the rice, then add the wine and cook until the wine is absorbed, about 1 minute. Add the stock a few ladles at a time, stirring vigorously after each addition and allowing the liquid to mostly disappear before adding more. The rice will take about 18 minutes to cook al dente. In the last minute or so of cooking, stir in ½ cup of the Parm, the butter, and the lemon and orange juices.

Scoop the risotto into the vegetables.

[Make-ahead: Let cool, cover with foil, and refrigerate.]

[Night of: Return the stuffed vegetables to room temp while you preheat the oven.]

Preheat the oven to 425°F.

Combine the remaining 2 tablespoons EVOO and ½ cup Parm with the bread crumbs. Sprinkle over the stuffed vegetables. Re-cover with foil and bake for 35 minutes. Uncover and bake until the tops are browned, 10 to 15 minutes more. Garnish with the parsley.

WEEK 21

BETTER YET

EXPENSIVE BOTTLED SAUCES?
ROTISSERIE CHICKEN? YOU CAN DO BETTER
THAN THAT WITH HOMEMADE DISHES
THAT ARE BETTER TASTING, BETTER FOR YOU,
AND SOMETIMES EVEN CHEAPER THAN
THOSE "GOURMET" SUPERMARKET ITEMS.

DISH
1
THAI
RIBS &
DRUMSTICKS
PAGE 154

DISH
2
CHERRY
TOMATO FRA
DIAVOLO SAUCE
WITH SEAFOOD &
PASTA
PAGE 156

DISH
3
ROASTED CHICKEN
DINNER WITH
POTATOES &
ARTICHOKES
PAGE 157

DISH
4
LENTIL
STOUP WITH
MUSHROOMS
PAGE 158

DISH
5
EASY-BRINE
CHICKEN BREASTS
WITH SICILIAN
GLAZE
PAGE 159

Thai Ribs & Drumsticks

I like to make both ribs and chicken drumsticks with my Thai marinade. The pork is for my husband, who could eat pork 24/7, and the chicken is for me. **Suggested sides:** Jasmine rice, cooked according to package directions, and Thai Cucumbers (see QR code on page 155). SERVES 4

1 cup fresh **cilantro** leaves and tender stems

½ cup packed **light brown sugar**

¼ cup **honey**

¼ cup reduced-sodium **soy sauce**

2 tablespoons **Asian fish sauce**

4 cloves **garlic**, smashed

2 fresh **serrano chiles**, seeded and chopped

1 fresh **red Fresno chile**, sliced

1 (2-inch) piece fresh **ginger**, peeled and grated

1 stalk **lemongrass**, white part chopped, tops reserved

2 pounds **baby back pork ribs**, cut into single ribs

8 **chicken drumsticks**, skinned

1 **lime**, sliced

Sweet & Sour Chili Sauce (recipe follows)

½ cup unsalted **roasted cashews** or **peanuts**, finely chopped

1 bunch **scallion** greens, thinly sliced

In a blender or food processor, combine the cilantro, brown sugar, honey, soy sauce, fish sauce, garlic, chiles, ginger, and the white part of the lemongrass and puree until a fairly smooth, thick sauce forms.

Put the ribs and drumsticks in a large resealable plastic bag or shallow plastic storage container. Add the marinade, lime slices, and lemongrass tops to the bag. Squish the bag to get the marinade all over the meat. Get as much air as possible out of the bag and seal. If you're making this to serve on **Cook Day**, marinate in the fridge for at least 1 hour and ideally 4 hours.

[**Make-ahead:** Store in the lowest part of the refrigerator.]

[**Night of:** Let the ribs and chicken sit at room temperature while you preheat the oven.]

Preheat the oven to 350°F.

Arrange the ribs in an even layer in a baking dish and add the marinade and lime slices. Cover tightly with foil and bake for 1 hour. Remove from the oven and add the drumsticks. Cover and bake for 30 minutes more.

Increase the oven temperature to 425°F. Uncover the baking dish and bake until the ribs and drumsticks are deeply browned, 20 to 25 minutes.

Transfer the ribs and drumsticks to a serving platter and drizzle with about half of the Sweet & Sour Chili Sauce. Top with the nuts and scallion greens. Pass the remaining sauce at the table.

Sweet & Sour Chili Sauce MAKES ABOUT 1¼ CUPS

⅓ cup **superfine sugar**

1 (1-inch) piece fresh **ginger**, thinly sliced

3 tablespoons **rice vinegar**

2 tablespoons chopped fresh **cilantro**

2 tablespoons chopped fresh **mint**

2 tablespoons **sriracha sauce**

1 tablespoon **Asian fish sauce**

1 fresh **red Fresno chile**, finely chopped

Juice of 1 **lime**

In a small saucepan, combine ½ cup water, the sugar, and the ginger. Bring to a simmer and cook for a couple of minutes to infuse the syrup. Pour the syrup into a small bowl and let cool. Discard the ginger. Stir in the vinegar, cilantro, mint, sriracha, fish sauce, chile, and lime juice.

[**Make-ahead:** Store in the refrigerator.]

Recipe for Thai Cucumbers

View a bonus Side Dish recipe.

Lentil Stoup with Mushrooms

Stoup = mash-up of soup and stew. **Suggested side:** Warmed naan or pita bread, or pita chips. SERVES 4

2 tablespoons **EVOO**

3 tablespoons **butter**, plus more for brushing

1 pound **cremini mushrooms**, quartered

4 **shallots**, chopped

2 large cloves **garlic**, grated

1 fresh **bay leaf**

Salt and **pepper**

½ cup **dry sherry**

4 cups **chicken stock**

1½ cups small **green (Puy) lentils**

1 bunch **"farm spinach"** (see Heads-up), washed and stemmed

Grated **lemon** zest

Freshly grated **nutmeg**

Greek yogurt, crème fraîche, or **sour cream**, for serving (optional)

In a soup pot or Dutch oven, heat the EVOO (2 turns of the pan) over medium-high heat. Melt in the 3 tablespoons butter. Add the mushrooms and cook until deeply browned, 12 to 15 minutes. Add the shallots, garlic, and bay leaf and season with salt and pepper. Deglaze the pan with the sherry and cook for a few more minutes. Stir in the chicken stock, lentils, and 3 cups water. Bring to a boil, reduce to a simmer, and cook for 20 minutes.

[**Make-ahead:** Let cool and refrigerate.]

[**Night of:** Return the soup to room temp before gently reheating over medium heat.]

Remove the bay leaf. Stir the spinach into the hot soup to wilt it. Season with lemon zest, nutmeg, and salt and pepper to taste.

Ladle the soup into bowls and top with a dollop of Greek yogurt, if desired.

Heads-up: "Farm spinach" is what I call spinach that does not come prewashed and in a plastic bag. It has stems and generally needs lots of washing.

Easy-Brine Chicken Breasts with Sicilian Glaze

While you're at it, just throw in a couple of extra chicken breasts and you'll have extra meat to slice for sandwiches or chicken salad the next day. Because this chicken will be sitting in the brine for a couple of days, I use half the salt I would normally use so that the chicken doesn't get too salty. **Suggested side:** Puttanesca-Style Panzanella (see QR code below). SERVES 4

GLAZE

2 tablespoons **EVOO**
4 cloves **garlic**, finely chopped
Leaves from 2 or 3 sprigs fresh
  rosemary, finely chopped
1 fresh **red Fresno chile** or **Italian**
  cherry pepper, finely chopped
½ cup **Marsala**, **dry sherry**, or
  spicy red wine
1 **blood orange** or **navel orange**
½ cup **chicken stock**
⅓ cup **honey**

CHICKEN

3 to 4 tablespoons grated **red**
  onion
2 tablespoons **kosher** or **fine sea**
  salt
4 cloves **garlic**, chopped
Leaves from a few sprigs fresh
  rosemary
1 **lemon**, sliced
4 boneless, skinless **chicken**
  breast halves (about 2 pounds)
EVOO, for brushing

Make the glaze: In a small saucepan, heat the EVOO (2 turns of the pan) over medium to medium-high heat. Add the garlic, rosemary, and chile and stir for a few minutes. Add the wine and cook until reduced to 3 to 4 tablespoons, about 2 minutes. Peel the zest from the orange in strips and add to the pot. Stir in the chicken stock and honey, then cook at a low simmer until reduced to about ½ cup, about 20 minutes. Let cool.

[**Make-ahead:** Let cool and refrigerate.]

Brine the chicken: Put the onion, salt, garlic, rosemary, lemon slices, and 4 cups water in a large resealable plastic bag. Add the chicken, squeeze out the air, seal, and place on a plate (in case the bag leaks).

[**Make-ahead:** Marinate for at least 2 days. Store in the lowest part of the refrigerator.]

[**Night of:** Return the chicken to room temp. Gently reheat the glaze.]

Heat a grill pan, griddle, or cast-iron skillet over medium-high heat. Drain the chicken and pat dry. Brush the chicken with EVOO. Cook, turning occasionally, until the chicken is cooked through, 12 to 15 minutes. Baste the chicken with the warmed glaze during the last 5 minutes of cooking.

Recipe for Puttanesca-Style Panzanella
View a bonus Side Dish recipe.

WEEK 22

PREPARE
YOURSELF

THERE'S MORE THAN ONE WAY
TO GET DINNER DONE AHEAD OF TIME.
HERE ARE 5 COMPLETELY
DIFFERENT MAKE-AHEAD MEALS.

DISH
1
STUFFED
CHICKEN
SALTIMBOCCA
PAGE 161

DISH
2
MAKE-AHEAD
PAELLA-
STYLE
CASSEROLE
PAGE 162

DISH
3
ROASTED RED
PEPPER
MINESTRONE
PAGE 164

DISH
4
ROASTED
SQUASH
CHILI MAC
PAGE 165

DISH
5
MIDDLE
EASTERN
GARLIC-ROASTED
CHICKEN
PAGE 166

Stuffed Chicken Saltimbocca

The chicken can be prepped ahead and frozen or refrigerated. If refrigerated, it should be baked within 2 days, so if you're cooking on a Sunday, you should plan this for Tuesday's dinner. **Suggested side:** Arugula & Tomatoes with Garlic Bread Crumbs (recipe follows). SERVES 4

1 cup fresh **sheep** or **cow's milk ricotta**
8 to 10 leaves fresh **sage**, very thinly sliced
Splash of **milk** or **half-and-half**
¼ cup grated **Parmigiano-Reggiano cheese**
Kosher salt and **pepper**
4 boneless, skinless **chicken breast** halves
8 slices **prosciutto di Parma**
EVOO, for drizzling

Mix together the ricotta, sage, milk, and Parm. Season with salt and pepper.

Split and butterfly the chicken. Starting on a fat side of the chicken breast, cut horizontally across the breast but not all the way through. Open it like a book. Pound the chicken to ⅛ to ¼ inch thick. Season the chicken with salt and pepper. Divide the ricotta filling evenly among the chicken pieces, and fold over each breast, sealing the cheese inside. Wrap each chicken breast with 2 overlapping slices of prosciutto.

[Make-ahead: Individually wrap and refrigerate for up to 2 days or freeze.]

[**Night of:** Unwrap the chicken and return to room temp.]
Preheat the oven to 400°F.

Dress the chicken with enough EVOO to lightly coat. Bake until the chicken is cooked through and the prosciutto is crisp, 20 to 25 minutes.

Arugula & Tomatoes with Garlic Bread Crumbs SERVES 4

3 tablespoons **butter**
3 cloves **garlic**, grated or finely chopped
1 cup **panko bread crumbs**
1 tablespoon fresh **thyme** leaves, chopped
¼ cup grated **Parmigiano-Reggiano cheese**
A few handfuls of **baby arugula**
4 **plum tomatoes**, thinly sliced lengthwise
EVOO, for drizzling

In a small skillet, melt the butter over medium heat. Add the garlic and stir for 2 minutes. Add the panko and thyme and toast to golden. Remove from the heat and stir in the Parm.

[Make-ahead: Store in an airtight container or foil pouch at room temp.]

Arrange the arugula on a platter and top with the tomatoes. Drizzle with a little EVOO. Sprinkle the garlic bread crumbs on top.

Make-Ahead Paella-Style Casserole

Buy the seafood no more than 24 hours before you plan on serving. Quick-salting (a technique of chef George Mendez) gives the fish firmer texture. SERVES 4

7 tablespoons **butter**, softened
½ cup broken **thin spaghetti** or **orzo pasta**
1½ cups **long-grain white rice**
A generous pinch of **saffron threads**
4 cups **chicken stock**, plus more for reheating (optional)
5 tablespoons **EVOO**
Flour or **Wondra** (quick-mixing flour), for dredging
1½ teaspoons **sweet paprika** (smoked or regular)
4 boneless, skinless **chicken thighs**
Kosher salt and **pepper**
½ pound **Spanish chorizo**, casings removed, chopped
1 **onion**, chopped
3 or 4 cloves **garlic**, chopped
½ cup **dry sherry**, plus a splash
2 **red bell peppers**, roasted (see page 164), chopped
1 cup frozen **green peas**, thawed
2 tablespoons chopped fresh **thyme**
1 pound thick center-cut **cod** or **black cod fillets**
Rachael Ray Seafood Seasoning or **Old Bay seasoning**
1 pound peeled and deveined large **shrimp**
Juice of 1 **lemon**
½ cup chopped fresh **flat-leaf parsley**

In a medium saucepan, heat 2 tablespoons of the butter over medium heat. Add the pasta and toast to golden. Stir in the rice and saffron. Add 3 cups of the stock, bring to a boil, then reduce to a simmer, cover, and cook al dente, about 17 minutes. Add ½ cup water if the liquid cooks out before the rice is tender.

Meanwhile, in a Dutch oven or deep skillet, heat 3 tablespoons of the EVOO over medium-high heat. Season some flour with the paprika. Season the chicken with salt and pepper; dredge in the flour. Fry the chicken until crispy and browned, 12 to 15 minutes. Transfer the chicken to a plate lined with paper towels. When cool enough to handle, cut into thickish slices (about 6 per thigh).

[If making this dish to serve on **Cook Day**, preheat the oven to 400°F. If for later in the week, you'll preheat it on the night of.]

Add 1 tablespoon EVOO to the drippings. Add the chorizo and cook 1 to 2 minutes. Add the onion and garlic and cook 5 minutes to soften. Deglaze with a splash of sherry. Add the roasted peppers, peas, and thyme; remove from the heat.

Grease a shallow 3-quart baking dish with 2 tablespoons butter. Combine the rice, chicken, and chorizo mixture; arrange in the dish.

[Make-ahead: Let cool and refrigerate.]

[**Night of:** Return the casserole to room temp while you preheat the oven to 400°F.]

Bake until the dish is heated through, 30 to 40 minutes. Add stock (about ½ cup) if the top dries out too much.

When the casserole goes into the oven, cover the cod with about ½ cup kosher salt and let stand 10 minutes. Rinse and dry.

In a small dish, season some flour with seafood seasoning. Lightly dredge the cod in the flour. In a skillet, heat the remaining 1 tablespoon EVOO (1 turn of the pan) over medium-high heat. Add the cod and cook, turning once, until firm and opaque, 5 to 6 minutes total. Transfer to a plate. Cook the shrimp to pink, 4 to 5 minutes. Deglaze the pan with the lemon juice and ½ cup sherry. Swirl in the remaining 3 tablespoons butter, then add the parsley.

Arrange the cod and shrimp on top of the casserole. Pour the hot sherry butter on top.

Roasted Red Pepper Minestrone

Extra peppers and garlic are roasted here for use in two more dishes. SERVES 4

6 large **red bell peppers**
Garlic: 3 heads, tops cut off to expose the cloves, plus 3 or 4 extra cloves, sliced
¼ cup **EVOO**, plus more for drizzling
4 tablespoons (½ stick) **butter**, softened
¼ pound **smoky bacon** or **pancetta**, chopped
1 fresh **red Fresno chile**, seeded and finely chopped
1 **onion**, chopped
2 **carrots**, chopped
2 ribs **celery**, chopped
1 **starchy potato**, peeled and chopped
1 large fresh **bay leaf**
2 tablespoons finely chopped fresh **rosemary**
2 tablespoons fresh **thyme** leaves, finely chopped
1 tablespoon chopped fresh **oregano**
Kosher salt and **pepper**
¼ cup **tomato paste**
½ cup **white wine**
1 (15-ounce) can **red beans** or **chickpeas**, rinsed and drained
6 cups **chicken stock**
1 small bunch **lacinato kale** (also called black, Tuscan, or dinosaur kale), stemmed and chopped
Freshly grated **nutmeg**
¾ cup **small pasta** (such as ditalini or broken pasta pieces)
Crusty **Italian bread**, sliced
Grated **pecorino cheese**, for serving

Preheat the broiler.

Char the bell peppers all over under the broiler with the oven door ajar to let steam escape. Place the peppers in a bowl and cover tightly. Leave the oven on but reduce the temperature to 400°F.

Drizzle the 3 garlic heads with some EVOO. Wrap individually in foil and roast until tender and caramel color, about 40 minutes. Set aside 2 of the heads for Middle Eastern Garlic-Roasted Chicken (page 166). Squeeze the garlic out of the remaining head and mash together with the butter.

[**Make-ahead:** Cover and refrigerate.]

When the bell peppers are cool enough to handle, rub off the skins with a paper towel, then halve and seed the peppers. Set aside 2 of the peppers for the Make-Ahead Paella-Style Casserole (page 162). Puree the remaining 4 peppers in a food processor with any juices that have collected in the bowl.

In a Dutch oven, heat ¼ cup EVOO (4 turns of the pan) over medium-high heat. Add the bacon and cook until crisp. Add the chile, onion, carrots, celery, potato, extra sliced garlic cloves, bay leaf, rosemary, thyme, oregano, and salt and pepper. Cook, partially covered, until the vegetables are tender, 7 to 8 minutes. Stir in the tomato paste and cook for 1 minute. Deglaze the pan with the wine. Add the beans, stock, and pepper puree and bring to a boil. Wilt in the kale. Season lightly with a few grates of nutmeg.

[**Make-ahead:** Let cool and refrigerate or freeze.]

[**Night of:** Soften the garlic butter at room temp. Return the soup to room temp before reheating over medium heat.]

Bring the soup to a boil. Add the pasta and cook al dente (see Heads-up).

Preheat the broiler and toast the Italian bread. Spread with the garlic butter.

Serve the soup in shallow bowls topped with pecorino and a drizzle of EVOO. Serve the garlic toasts alongside.

Heads-up: If you're going to be eating all of the soup when you sit down to dinner, cook the pasta right in the soup. But if the soup will be eaten as leftovers, cook the pasta separately and add it to each bowl of soup when you serve it. That way the pasta doesn't get all bloated as the soup sits in the fridge.

Roasted Squash Chili Mac

Chili makes a great make-ahead and so does mac 'n' cheese. (Just check the freezer aisle at any grocery store!) So why not get these two great make-aheads together in one dish? This freezes really well, so might as well make two while you're up. SERVES 6

1 pound **butternut squash,** peeled and diced (see Heads-up)

EVOO, for drizzling

Kosher salt and **pepper**

Freshly grated **nutmeg**

1 pound **rigatoni** or **penne pasta**

4 tablespoons (½ stick) **butter,** plus more for greasing the baking dish

2 cloves **garlic,** pasted

1 **fresh chile** (such as red Fresno or jalapeño), finely chopped

1 tablespoon chopped fresh **oregano**

2 tablespoons **chili powder** blend (such as Gebhardt's), **ancho** (mild) **chile powder,** or **chipotle** (hot) **chile powder**

1 teaspoon ground **coriander**

1 teaspoon ground **cumin**

¼ teaspoon ground **cinnamon**

3 tablespoons **flour**

2½ cups **milk**

2 cups shredded **sharp yellow cheddar cheese**

½ cup grated **Parmigiano-Reggiano cheese**

1 (15-ounce) can **red kidney beans,** drained

1 cup shredded **pepper jack cheese** or other **hot pepper melting cheese**

Preheat the oven to 425°F.

On a baking sheet, toss the squash with a drizzle of EVOO and salt, pepper, and nutmeg. Roast until browned at the edges, 17 to 20 minutes.

[If making this to serve on **Cook Day,** leave the oven on and reduce the oven temperature to 400°F. If making this for later in the week, turn off the oven.]

Bring a large pot of water to a boil. Salt the water and cook the pasta until 2 minutes shy of al dente. Drain and return to the pot.

Meanwhile, in a saucepan, melt the 4 tablespoons butter over medium heat. Add the garlic, fresh chile, oregano, chili powder, coriander, cumin, and cinnamon and stir 2 minutes. Sprinkle with the flour and stir. Whisk in the milk and cook until thick enough to coat the back of a spoon. Add the cheddar and Parm and stir in a figure-8 motion until the cheese is melted. Add the squash, sauce, and beans to the pasta and toss well.

Lightly butter a 9 by 13-inch baking dish. Scrape in the chili-mac. Top with the pepper jack.

[**Make-ahead:** Let cool, cover with parchment paper and foil, and refrigerate.]

[**Night of:** Return the casserole to room temp while you preheat the oven to 400°F.]

Cover the casserole with foil and bake for 30 minutes. Uncover and bake until browned on top, 15 to 20 minutes.

Heads-up: Best time-saver in the supermarket produce department: peeled chunks of butternut squash.

Middle Eastern Garlic-Roasted Chicken

You can serve this as your reward on **Cook Day**, or you can refrigerate the chicken for 1 or 2 days. **Suggested side:** Naan bread or pocketless pita, heated and brushed with melted butter. SERVES 4

2 heads **roasted garlic** (see page 164)
¼ cup **EVOO**
4 tablespoons (½ stick) **butter**, softened
Grated zest and juice of 1 **lemon**
Leaves from 2 or 3 sprigs fresh **rosemary**, finely chopped
1 whole **chicken** (4 to 5 pounds), spatchcocked (see Heads-up)
Salt and **pepper**
Za'atar Spice Blend (opposite)
Green Harissa (opposite), for serving

Squeeze the roasted garlic into a small bowl. Add the EVOO, butter, lemon zest, and rosemary and mix to blend.

Loosen the skin all over the chicken, then stuff the garlic paste between the meat and skin. Season the skin with salt and pepper. Transfer to a 9 by 13-inch baking dish or small roasting pan.

[If making this to serve on **Cook Day**, let the chicken stand 1 hour, covered, in a baking dish.]

[**Make-ahead:** Cover well and store on the lowest shelf of the refrigerator; plan on baking this within 2 days.]

[**Night of:** Return the chicken to room temp while you preheat the oven.]

Preheat the oven to 325°F.

Sprinkle the chicken with two-thirds of the za'atar. Roast 1¼ hours, then increase the oven temperature to 500°F. Roast until the skin is crisp, about 15 minutes. Let the chicken rest. When cool enough to handle, cut it into serving portions.

Serve the chicken doused with lemon juice and sprinkled with the rest of the za'atar. Serve the harissa alongside.

Heads-up: Have your butcher spatchcock (spatchcocking is also called butterflying) the chicken for you. Or if you want to do it yourself, turn the chicken breast side down and use a pair of kitchen shears to cut down either side of the backbone. Discard the backbone, flip the chicken over, and press down until you hear the breastbone break.

Za'atar Spice Blend MAKES ABOUT ½ CUP

Great on chicken, beef, lamb, or eggplant and anything grilled—make extra and store for weeks. Sumac is widely available in larger markets or Middle Eastern markets, or order online at Penzey's or wholespice.com.

2 tablespoons ground **sumac**
2 tablespoons finely chopped fresh **thyme**
1 tablespoon finely chopped fresh **oregano**
2 tablespoons toasted **sesame seeds**
1 tablespoon ground **cumin**
1 teaspoon **kosher salt**
1 teaspoon coarsely ground **pepper**

Combine the sumac, thyme, oregano, sesame seeds, cumin, salt, and pepper. Store in an airtight container until ready to use.

Green Harissa MAKES ABOUT 1½ CUPS

1 cup fresh **cilantro** leaves
1 small bunch **spinach**, washed, stemmed, and chopped
2 fresh **serrano** or **jalapeño chiles**, seeded and chopped
1 large clove **garlic**, pasted
Juice of ½ **lemon**
1 teaspoon ground **cumin**
Kosher salt and **pepper**
⅓ cup **EVOO**

In a food processor, combine the cilantro, spinach leaves, chiles, garlic, lemon juice, cumin, and salt and pepper. Turn on the machine and stream in the EVOO; puree until fairly smooth. Adjust the seasonings.
  [Make-ahead: Refrigerate.]

WEEK 23

MEATLOVERS'
LANE

MEATLOVERS, LISTEN UP:
A WHOLE WEEK'S WORTH
OF MEALS WITH YOUR NAME
ALL OVER THEM.

DISH
1
BLACK
PEPPER
BEEF
PAGE 169

DISH
2
VEAL & PORK
MEATBALLS WITH
MUSHROOM
GRAVY & EGG
NOODLES
PAGE 170

DISH
3
SAUSAGE,
PUMPKIN &
ARBORIO
SOUP
PAGE 172

DISH
4
STUFFED PEPPERS
WITH BROKEN
MEATBALLS &
RICE
PAGE 173

DISH
5
ROASTED
PORK LOIN
WITH KALE &
POLENTA
PAGE 174

Black Pepper Beef

Make this meal first, as it cooks for up to 5 hours—more than enough time to get the rest of the week's meals prepared. SERVES 4 TO 6

2½ pounds **beef stew meat**, cut into 2-inch cubes
Kosher salt
Flour, for dredging
2 tablespoons **EVOO**
2 cups **beef stock**
5 or 6 cloves **garlic**, smashed
1 large fresh **bay leaf**
1½ tablespoons coarsely ground **pepper**
2 tablespoons **tomato paste**
2 cups **dry red wine**
4 **starchy potatoes** (such as russets), peeled and cubed
8 ounces **Taleggio** or **cow's milk Robiola** or other ripe soft-rind cheese, cut into cubes
A few leaves of fresh **sage**, torn
Milk or **half-and-half**
Chopped fresh **flat-leaf parsley**, for garnish

Let the meat come to room temperature and pat dry. Season with kosher salt and dredge lightly in flour, shaking off the excess.

In a large Dutch oven, heat 1 tablespoon EVOO (1 turn of the pan). Working in two batches, add the beef and brown. Transfer to a plate and add more oil for the second batch. Return all the beef cubes to the pan and add the stock and enough water to cover. Stir in the garlic and bay leaf and bring to a boil. Reduce the heat to medium-low, partially cover, and simmer for 2 hours.

Stir in the pepper, tomato paste, and wine and cook until the beef is tender enough to fall apart and the sauce is thick, 2 to 3 hours more.

[**Make-ahead:** Let cool and refrigerate.]
[**Night of:** Return the stew to room temp before reheating over medium heat, adding a splash of water to loosen it up.]

Meanwhile, cook the potatoes in boiling salted water until tender, 12 to 15 minutes. Drain and return to the hot pot. Mash the cheese and sage into the potatoes along with enough to milk to reach the desired consistency. Season with salt and pepper.

Spoon the beef and sauce into shallow bowls. Add a scoop of potatoes and garnish everything with parsley.

Veal & Pork Meatballs with Mushroom Gravy & Egg Noodles

In this recipe you roll a double batch of meatballs—half will get broken up and used in Stuffed Peppers with Broken Meatballs & Rice (page 173). SERVES 4

MEATBALLS

2 slices **white bread**, crusts trimmed
1 cup **milk** or **half-and-half**
1¼ pounds **ground veal**
1¼ pounds **ground pork**
Kosher salt and **pepper**
Freshly grated **nutmeg**
2 large **eggs**
1 cup grated **Parmigiano-Reggiano cheese**
4 cloves **garlic**, grated or pasted
A handful of fresh **flat-leaf parsley**, finely chopped
EVOO, for drizzling

MUSHROOM GRAVY

2 cups **chicken stock**
A small handful of **dried porcini mushrooms** (about ¼ cup)
1 tablespoon **EVOO**
3 tablespoons **butter**
½ pound **cremini mushrooms**, thinly sliced
1 **shallot**, finely chopped
2 cloves **garlic**, finely chopped
2 tablespoons fresh **thyme** leaves, finely chopped
Kosher salt and **pepper**
1 heaping tablespoon **flour**
½ cup **Marsala** or **dry white wine**
½ cup **heavy cream**

1 pound extra-wide **egg noodles** or **egg tagliatelle**
Finely chopped fresh **flat-leaf parsley**, to garnish

Make the meatballs: Preheat the oven to 400°F. Place wire racks over 2 baking sheets.

Soak the bread in the milk.

In a large bowl, combine the veal and pork. Squeeze the liquid from the bread and mash into small crumbs between your fingers as you add it to the meat. Season with salt, pepper, and nutmeg. Add the eggs, Parm, garlic, parsley, and a healthy drizzle of EVOO. Keep a bowl of warm water nearby for rinsing your hands. Scoop and roll into 1½-inch meatballs and place on the racks. You'll get 40 to 48 balls (20 to 24 per baking sheet). Bake until cooked through, 18 to 20 minutes. Let cool. Set aside half of the meatballs for Stuffed Peppers with Broken Meatballs & Rice (page 173).

Make the gravy: In a small saucepan, heat the stock with the dried mushrooms to soften, 10 to 15 minutes. Reserving the soaking liquid, scoop out the mushrooms and chop.

In a saucepan, heat the EVOO (1 turn of the pan) with the butter over medium to medium-high heat. Add the fresh mushrooms and cook until browned, 12 to 15 minutes. Add the shallot, garlic, thyme, salt, and pepper and stir a couple of minutes more. Add the flour and stir a minute more. Deglaze the pan with the Marsala. Add the chopped porcini and carefully pour in the soaking liquid, leaving the last few spoonfuls in the pan as grit may have settled there. Stir in the cream and cook to thicken a bit. Add the remaining meatballs.

[**Make-ahead:** Let cool and refrigerate.]

[**Night of:** Return the meatballs and gravy to room temp before reheating over medium heat.]

Bring a large pot of water to a boil. Salt the water and cook the noodles al dente. Ladle out about a cup of the starchy cooking water and add it if the gravy seems too thick. Drain the pasta.

Serve the noodles topped with the gravy and meatballs and garnished with parsley.

Stuffed Peppers with Broken Meatballs & Rice

I have a couple of interesting methods when it comes to making stuffed peppers. First of all, I can't stand it when you get a stuffed pepper and the pepper is still tough and the filling is all dried out. To guard against that, especially if I have really large peppers, I slice them lengthwise so they have lots of surface area, then I cut a small X into each pepper to act as a steam vent and precook them unfilled before I stuff them. SERVES 4 TO 6

4 large **bell peppers**
Kosher salt and **pepper**
1 tablespoon **EVOO**, plus more for drizzling
6 **plum** or small **vine-ripened tomatoes**
1 **red** or mild **yellow onion**, peeled
4 cloves **garlic**, grated or pasted
1 **fresh red chile**, finely chopped
2 tablespoons fresh **thyme** leaves, finely chopped
3 tablespoons **butter**
½ cup **orzo pasta**
1 cup **long-grain white rice**
2 cups **chicken stock**
20 to 24 small **meatballs** (from Veal & Pork Meatballs, page 170)
1¾ cups shaved or grated **Parmigiano-Reggiano cheese**

Preheat the oven to 400°F.

Halve the bell peppers lengthwise and seed. With the peppers cut side up, make a small X in the bottom of each pepper. Season with salt and pepper and drizzle with EVOO. Invert the peppers skin side up into a 9 by 13-inch baking dish. Roast until softened, about 20 minutes. Remove and let cool.

[If making this dish to serve on **Cook Day**, leave the oven on. Otherwise follow the make-ahead directions below.]

Grate the tomatoes on the large holes of the box grater into a large bowl; discard the skins. (This should yield about 2 cups.) Grate the onion, garlic, and chile into the tomatoes. Season with salt and pepper. Drizzle with EVOO and stir in the thyme.

In a medium saucepan, heat 1 tablespoon EVOO (1 turn of the pan) and the butter over medium heat. Add the orzo and toast to golden and fragrant. Stir in half the tomato sauce and the rice and stir 1 or 2 minutes. Add the stock and bring to a boil. Reduce to a simmer, cover, and cook until tender, 17 to 18 minutes.

Break up the meatballs into coarse pieces in a bowl. Add the rice and ¾ cup of the Parm and toss to combine. Flip the peppers and fill to the tops with the stuffing, then mound the remaining stuffing on top of each. Top with the remaining sauce, the remaining 1 cup Parm, and a drizzle of EVOO.

[**Make-ahead:** Let cool and refrigerate.]

[**Night of:** Return the peppers to room temp while you preheat the oven to 400°F.]

Bake the peppers until heated through and the tops are browned, about 45 minutes.

Roasted Pork Loin with Kale & Polenta

When I create the lineup for a week's worth of meals, I often imagine the fifth dish being the payoff meal, the one you get to enjoy on **Cook Day**. Of course, they're all make-aheads, but really, for all the work you've done on this day, don't you deserve to have a hot meal ready to roll when you've finished cooking? SERVES 4 (WITH LEFTOVERS)

⅓ pound **pancetta**, cut into ⅛-inch-thick slices, then finely chopped

4 cloves **garlic**, finely chopped or grated

1 tablespoon **fennel pollen** or **ground fennel**

1 rolled boneless **pork loin** roast (2½ to 3 pounds)

2 long sprigs fresh **rosemary**, broken or cut into 1½-inch pieces (8 to 10 pieces total)

Kosher salt and coarsely ground **pepper**

2 tablespoons **EVOO**, plus more for drizzling

1 cup **dry white wine**

2 cups **chicken stock**, plus 1 cup for reheating (optional)

1 cup **milk**

1 bunch **lacinato kale** (also called black, Tuscan, or dinosaur kale), stemmed

Juice of ½ **lemon**

Freshly grated **nutmeg**

1 cup quick-cooking **polenta**

2 tablespoons **butter**

1 cup grated **pecorino cheese**

Preheat the oven to 325°F.

Combine the pancetta, garlic, and fennel. Cut 18 to 20 (2-inch-deep) slits into the meat, working all over the roast. Fill the slits, alternating the pancetta mixture and the rosemary sprigs, as you work. Season the roast liberally with salt and pepper.

In a large Dutch oven, heat the 2 tablespoons EVOO (2 turns of the pan) over medium-high heat. Add the roast and brown well all over, about 5 minutes. Transfer to the oven and roast for 45 minutes. Douse with the wine and roast until the meat registers 145°F, 20 to 30 minutes more. Remove and let rest 15 minutes.

[**Make-ahead:** Let cool, cover, and refrigerate.]

[**Night of:** Return the roast to room temp while you preheat the oven to 325°F. Add 1 cup chicken stock to the Dutch oven and roast, covered, for 15 minutes. Uncover and reheat to warm through, 15 to 20 minutes more.]

Bring a large pot of water to a boil for the kale. At the same time, in a saucepan, combine 2 cups stock and the milk and bring to a low boil for the polenta.

Drop the kale into the boiling water and cook for 7 to 8 minutes. With tongs, transfer to a platter. Drizzle with EVOO and the lemon juice and season with salt, pepper, and a few grates of nutmeg.

Whisk the polenta into the stock, and keep whisking until it thickens, 2 to 3 minutes. Season with salt and pepper and stir in the butter, then the pecorino, and remove from the heat.

Transfer the pork roast to a cutting board and slice.

Serve the sliced pork with polenta and kale alongside.

WEEK 24

SOUPERSTAR SUPPERS

SOUP IS ON, PEOPLE:
5 STRAIGHT STEW AND SOUP
MEALS THAT WILL KEEP
YOU SATISFIED ALL WEEK LONG.

DISH
1
ITALIAN CHICKEN
STOUP WITH PORCINI,
PORTOBELLOS &
PEPPERS
PAGE 176

DISH
2
BBQ CHICKEN,
RED BEAN &
CORN COUNTRY
CHOWDER
PAGE 178

DISH
3
CREAMY
APPLE &
CELERY
ROOT SOUP
PAGE 179

DISH
4
BEEF STEW
SCENTED WITH
HORSERADISH
PAGE 180

DISH
5
PULLED PORK
WITH TWO-CHILE
TAMALE PIE
PAGE 182

Italian Chicken Stoup with Porcini, Portobellos & Peppers

Stoup is a term that I made up to describe a soup almost as thick as stew. This is a cacciatore that I think is the easiest way to eat and enjoy the flavors—no bones, no muss or fuss, and lots of juice. I won't turn down a bowl of the original, but I prefer this dish. SERVES 4 TO 6

1 large **red bell pepper**

3 cups **chicken stock**, homemade (page 322) or store-bought

⅓ cup **dried porcini mushrooms**

3 tablespoons **EVOO**

¼ pound **pancetta**, cut into ⅛-inch-thick slices, finely diced

2 large **portobello mushroom caps**, chopped

Leaves from 2 sprigs fresh **rosemary**, finely chopped

1 large fresh **bay leaf**

1 **onion**, finely chopped

4 cloves **garlic**, finely chopped

1 **fresh red chile**, thinly sliced

Kosher salt and **pepper**

¼ cup **tomato paste**

1 cup **dry red** or **white wine**

1 (14-ounce) can **stewed tomatoes**

4 cups shredded **Poached Chicken** (page 322); see Note

Shaved **pecorino cheese**, for garnish

Coarsely chopped fresh **flat-leaf parsley**, for garnish

Char the bell pepper all over on the stovetop over a gas flame or under the broiler with the oven door ajar to let steam escape. Place the pepper in a bowl and cover tightly. When cool enough to handle, rub off the skin with a paper towel, then halve, seed, and chop the pepper.

Meanwhile, in a saucepan, heat the stock with the dried mushrooms to soften, 10 to 15 minutes. Once tender, turn off the heat.

In a Dutch oven, heat the EVOO (3 turns of the pan) over medium-high heat. Add the pancetta and brown about 2 minutes. Add the portobellos and cook until browned and dark, 8 to 10 minutes. Add the rosemary, bay leaf, onion, garlic, chile, and salt and pepper and cook to soften the vegetables, about 10 minutes. Add the tomato paste and stir 1 minute. Deglaze with the wine. Add the porcini, then carefully pour in the stock, leaving the last few spoonfuls in the pan as grit may have settled there. Add 3 cups water, the stewed tomatoes, chicken, and roasted pepper. Bring to a low boil and simmer for 15 minutes to bring the flavors together.

[**Make-ahead:** Let cool and refrigerate.]

[**Night of:** Return the chicken to room temp before reheating over medium heat, adding water if necessary to thin.]

Serve in deep bowls and top with shaved pecorino and parsley.

Note: Make the following changes to the Basic Poached Chicken (page 322): Use 8 bone-in, skin-on chicken thighs and 2 full bone-in skin-on chicken breasts. Double the celery and onion; add 4 cloves garlic, smashed. Add 1 or 2 oregano sprigs to the herb bundle. Cook the chicken for closer to 1 hour 15 minutes. Shred the cooked chicken, making a mixture of light and dark. Divide in half: about 4 cups for this recipe and half for the BBQ Chicken, Red Bean & Corn Country Chowder (page 178).

BBQ Chicken, Red Bean & Corn Country Chowder

Make the Basic BBQ Sauce first, before you start on the chowder. SERVES 4 TO 6

1 tablespoon **EVOO**
¼ pound **smoky bacon**, chopped (optional)
5 or 6 baby **Yukon Gold potatoes**, chopped
4 **ears corn**, kernels scraped off, or 2 cups frozen **corn kernels**, thawed
1 fresh **red Fresno chile**, sliced or chopped
1 **red bell pepper**, chopped
1 **red onion**, chopped
2 or 3 ribs **celery**, chopped
4 cloves **garlic**, chopped

1 rounded tablespoon **Rachael Ray Seafood Seasoning** or **Old Bay seasoning**
3 tablespoons fresh **thyme** leaves, chopped
1 fresh **bay leaf**
1 (12-ounce) bottle **lager beer**, at room temperature
1 (15-ounce) can **red kidney beans**, drained
1 (14.5-ounce) can **fire-roasted diced tomatoes, stewed tomatoes**, or **diced tomatoes with chiles**

4 cups shredded **Poached Chicken** (see Note, page 176)
Basic BBQ Sauce (recipe follows)
4 cups **chicken stock**, homemade (page 322) or store-bought
1 **avocado**
Juice of 1 **lime**
Tortilla chips, for serving

In a soup pot, heat the EVOO (1 turn of the pan) over medium-high heat. Add the bacon (if using) and cook to crisp, 2 to 3 minutes. Add the potatoes, corn, chile, bell pepper, onion, celery, garlic, seafood seasoning, thyme, and bay leaf and stir. Cook to soften the vegetables, 8 to 10 minutes. Deglaze the pan with the beer and cook until reduced by half, 1 to 2 minutes. Add the beans, tomatoes, chicken, BBQ sauce, stock, and 2 cups water. Simmer a few minutes to combine the flavors.

[**Make-ahead:** Let cool and refrigerate.]

[**Night of:** Return the chowder to room temp before reheating gently over medium heat. Discard the bay leaf.]

Dice the avocado and dress it with lime juice.

Place diced avocado and some broken tortilla chips in each soup bowl, top with hot chowder, and serve.

Basic BBQ Sauce

1 cup good-quality **ketchup**
2 tablespoons **cider vinegar**
2 tablespoons **Worcestershire sauce**
2 tablespoons **dark brown sugar**

2 tablespoons dark amber **maple syrup**
1 teaspoon coarsely ground **pepper**
2 cloves **garlic**, finely chopped

In a small saucepan, bring all the ingredients to a low boil. Reduce the heat to low and cook to thicken, about 15 minutes.

Creamy Apple & Celery Root Soup

Serve the soup with Grilled Cheddar, Bacon & Apple–Honey Mustard Sandwiches (recipe follows). SERVES 4

3 tablespoons **EVOO**

1 large (1¼ pounds) **celery root** (celeriac), peeled and chopped

2 **parsnips**, peeled and chopped

1 **starchy potato**, peeled and chopped

1 **onion**, chopped

2 tablespoons chopped fresh **thyme**

1 fresh **bay leaf**

Kosher salt and **pepper**

2 large **Gala** or other crispy, sweet **apples**, peeled and chopped

Juice of ½ **lemon**

½ cup **Calvados** (or apple brandy) or ½ cup **sauterne** wine

4 cups **chicken stock**, homemade (page 322) or store-bought

1 cup **heavy cream** or **crème fraîche**

In a soup pot or large Dutch oven, heat the EVOO (3 turns of the pan) over medium to medium-high heat. Add the celery root, parsnips, potato, onion, thyme, bay leaf, and salt and pepper. Cook, partially covered and stirring occasionally, until softened, 10 to 12 minutes. Add the apples and lemon juice and cook 5 minutes more.

Deglaze the pan with the Calvados. Add the chicken stock and simmer over medium-low heat for 20 to 25 minutes. Discard the bay leaf and puree the soup with an immersion blender or in a food processor (in batches). If too thick, add 1 cup water. Stir in the cream.

[Make-ahead: Let cool and refrigerate.]

[Night of: Return the soup to room temp before reheating gently over medium heat, stirring occasionally.]

Serve the soup in bowls.

Grilled Cheddar, Bacon & Apple–Honey Mustard Sandwiches MAKES 4 SANDWICHES

8 tablespoons (1 stick) **butter**, softened

8 slices (½ inch thick) good-quality **white bread**

½ cup **apple butter**

⅓ cup **honey**

¼ cup **grainy Dijon mustard**

¾ pound **super-sharp white cheddar cheese**, sliced

12 slices good-quality **smoky bacon**

1 large **Gala** or other crispy, sweet **apple**, sliced

Butter one side of each slice of bread. Stir together the apple butter, honey, and mustard. With the bread buttered side down, spread all of the slices with the apple-mustard mixture. Build the sandwiches: Top 4 of the bread slices with cheese, then top with the remaining 4 slices, buttered side out.

[Make-ahead: Individually wrap and refrigerate.]

[Night of: Return sandwiches to room temp.]

Preheat the oven to 375°F.

Arrange the bacon on a slotted pan and bake until crisp, about 15 minutes. Open the sandwiches, insert the bacon and sliced apple, and reclose. Heat a griddle pan or cast-iron skillet over medium heat. Cook the sandwiches until deeply golden and crisp on both sides.

Beef Stew Scented with Horseradish

This feels like pub food to me. **Suggested side:** Pumpernickel or sourdough bread (see Heads-up). SERVES 4 TO 6

2½ pounds **stew beef**, cut into 2-inch cubes

Kosher salt and **pepper**

Flour, for dredging

4 tablespoons **EVOO** or **vegetable oil**, plus more for drizzling

2 **onions**, chopped

4 cloves **garlic**, chopped

1 fresh **bay leaf**

3 tablespoons **tomato paste**

1 (12-ounce) bottle **lager beer**, at room temperature

¼ cup **Worcestershire sauce**

3 to 4 cups **beef stock**

3 tablespoons prepared **horseradish**

2 pounds **baby Yukon Gold potatoes**, quartered

2 tablespoons **butter**

A handful of fresh **flat-leaf parsley**, chopped

1 bunch **watercress** or **upland cress**, for garnish

Pat the meat dry and season with salt and pepper. Dredge in flour, shaking off the excess.

In a large Dutch oven, heat 2 tablespoons EVOO (2 turns of the pan) over medium-high heat until hot and rippling. Add half the beef and brown, then transfer to a plate. Repeat with another 2 tablespoons EVOO and the remaining beef. Reduce the heat a bit and add another drizzle of oil if necessary, then add the onions, garlic, and bay leaf and cook to soften the onion, 7 to 8 minutes. Add the tomato paste and stir for 1 minute. Deglaze the pan with the beer and cook until reduced by half, 1 or 2 minutes. Add the Worcestershire, stock, and horseradish. Return the beef to the pan and add just enough water to surround and partially cover it. Simmer over medium-low heat until very tender, about 2 hours.

[Make-ahead: Let cool and refrigerate.]

[Night of: Return the beef to room temp before reheating gently over medium heat.]

Put the potatoes in a medium pot with water to cover and bring to a boil. Salt the water and cook to tender-firm, 10 to 12 minutes tops. Drain and return to the hot pot. Add the butter and parsley and stir to melt the butter.

Place a small pile of potatoes in the bottom of shallow bowls. Top with stew and garnish with watercress leaves.

Heads-up: If you bought the bread for this meal days before you serve the stew, don't store the bread in the refrigerator. Instead, wrap it tightly in plastic and store on the counter or in the freezer to keep it tender. Then crisp the whole loaf in a hot oven.

Pulled Pork with Two-Chile Tamale Pie

When you brown meat, you need three things: a screaming-hot pan, very dry meat, and coarse salt (which gives the meat a nice crust). SERVES 4 TO 6

8 **dried guajillo chiles**
4 cups **chicken stock**, homemade (page 322) or store-bought
2 rounded tablespoons pureed **chipotle chiles in adobe** (see Heads-up)
1 tablespoon chopped fresh **oregano** or 1 teaspoon dried

1½ teaspoons ground **coriander**
½ teaspoon ground **cinnamon**
3 tablespoons **EVOO**
3 pounds boneless **pork shoulder** (butt), patted dry
Kosher salt and **pepper**
1 large **onion**, finely chopped
4 cloves **garlic**, finely chopped
1½ cups **milk**

1½ cups fine to medium-grind **cornmeal**
1 teaspoon **fennel pollen** or **ground fennel**
3 tablespoons **butter**
1½ cups grated **sharp cheddar** or **hot pepper cheddar**

In a saucepan, combine the guajillos and 2 cups of the stock. Simmer at a low bubble until tender, about 10 minutes.

Pour the guajillos and soaking broth into a food processor. Add the chipotle puree, oregano, coriander, and cinnamon and puree until smooth.

In a large Dutch oven (preferably oval), heat 2 tablespoons EVOO (2 turns of the pan) over medium-high heat. Season the pork with salt and pepper, add to the pan, and brown all over. Transfer to a plate. Add the remaining 1 tablespoon EVOO (1 turn of the pan), the onion, and the garlic and stir to soften. Return the pork to the pan, add the chile puree, the remaining 2 cups stock, and enough water (about 4 cups) to raise the liquid level halfway up the meat. Bring to a boil, reduce to a simmer, and cook, partially covered, over medium-low heat until very tender, 2 to 2½ hours.

Remove the pork and let cool to handle. Shred the pork and return to the sauce. Bring back to a simmer and cook to thicken, about 15 minutes.

[Make-ahead: Let cool and refrigerate.]

[Night of: Return the pork to room temp before transferring to a large ovenproof skillet. Reheat gently over medium heat, stirring frequently, while you preheat the oven and make the polenta.]

Preheat the broiler to high or the oven to 500°F with a rack in the center of the oven.

In a saucepan, bring the milk to a low bubble. Separately, bring 3 cups water to a full boil. Add the cornmeal to the milk and whisk in 3 cups boiling water, the fennel, and 1½ teaspoons salt. Whisk consistently and often for 15 minutes. Remove from the heat and stir in the butter.

Top the pork with the polenta, layering it about 1 inch thick. Sprinkle with the cheddar. Bake to set and firm the top and brown, 10 to 15 minutes.

Heads-up: Buy a can of chipotle chiles in adobo. Pull the chiles out of the adobo and transfer just the sauce to a food processor. Seed the chiles, then add them to the sauce and puree. Scoop out the amount you need for the recipe and scrape the remainder into a small plastic freezer bag. Push the puree to the bottom of the bag to make a log. Store in the freezer. The next time you need some, just grate the amount you need and put the log back in the freezer.

WEEK 25

BORDER
BONANZA

A WEEKLONG FIESTA
OF MOUTHWATERING
TEX-MEX MEALS

DISH
1
GREEN
CHILE SLOPPY
JOSÉS
PAGE 184

DISH
2
MEXICAN
BRISKET 'N'
BISCUITS
PAGE 185

DISH
3
BLACK BEAN &
BEEF CHILAQUILES
WITH FRIED
EGGS
PAGE 186

DISH
4
JALAPEÑO
POPPER ORZO
MAC 'N' CHEESE
PAGE 187

DISH
5
CHICKEN
ENCHILADAS
PAGE 188

Green Chile Sloppy Josés

There's Messy Giuseppes and of course, Sloppy Josés. **Suggested side:** Refried Bean Dip (recipe follows), served with chips for dipping. SERVES 4

4 **poblano** or 6 **green New Mexican chiles**
1 fresh **jalapeño chile**
4 large **tomatillos**, husked and rinsed
3 tablespoons **honey**
Juice of 1 **lime**
Kosher salt and **pepper**

2 tablespoons **EVOO**
2 pounds **ground pork**
4 cloves **garlic**, grated or chopped
1 medium **red onion**, finely chopped
2 teaspoons ground **cumin**
2 teaspoons ground **coriander**
1 teaspoon dried **Mexican oregano**

2 tablespoons **Worcestershire sauce**
1 cup **lager beer**, at room temperature
8 soft **sandwich rolls**
1 cup shredded **Swiss cheese**
1 cup shredded **pepper jack cheese**

Preheat the broiler to high. Arrange the chiles and tomatillos on a baking sheet and place it under the broiler with the oven door ajar to let steam escape. Char the vegetables all over, turning occasionally. Place the chiles in a bowl and cover tightly. When cool enough to handle, peel the poblanos (don't bother peeling the jalapeño), seed all the chiles, and transfer to a food processor. Add the charred tomatillos, honey, and lime juice; season with salt. Puree, adding a splash of water if necessary.

In a large skillet, heat the EVOO (2 turns of the pan) over medium-high heat. Add the pork, season with salt and pepper, and cook, breaking it into crumbles as it browns. Add the garlic, onion, cumin, coriander, oregano, and Worcestershire. Deglaze the pan with the beer; stir for 1 minute. Stir in the chile-tomatillo puree and taste to adjust seasonings.

[**Make-ahead:** Let cool and refrigerate.]
[**Night of:** Return the meat mixture to room temp before reheating gently over medium heat.]
Serve sloppy sandwiches on soft rolls, topped with the shredded cheeses.

Refried Bean Dip SERVES 4

1 tablespoon **EVOO**
1 fresh **jalapeño chile**, seeded and chopped
1 small **onion**, finely chopped

2 cloves **garlic**, chopped
Kosher salt
½ teaspoon ground **cumin**
½ teaspoon ground **coriander**

½ teaspoon **cayenne pepper**
½ teaspoon **sweet paprika**
1 (15-ounce) can spicy **vegetarian refried beans**

In a medium skillet, heat the EVOO (1 turn of the pan) over medium heat. Add the jalapeño, onion, garlic, and salt and stir a few minutes to soften the onion. Add the cumin, coriander, cayenne, and paprika and stir until fragrant. Add 1 cup water and bring to a boil. Transfer to a food processor, add the beans, and puree into a smooth dip.

[**Make-ahead:** Let cool and refrigerate.]
[**Night of:** Return the bean dip to room temp.]

Mexican Brisket 'n' Biscuits

A Mexican-style brisket served up with biscuits. That's gotta be the definition of Tex-Mex! SERVES 4 TO 6

MEXI-RUB

¼ cup **kosher salt**
¼ cup packed **light brown sugar**
3 tablespoons **sweet paprika** (smoked or regular)
1 tablespoon **mustard seeds**
1 tablespoon **garlic powder**
2 teaspoons ground **cumin**
2 teaspoons ground **ginger**
2 teaspoons ground **coriander**
2 teaspoons dried **oregano**
1½ teaspoons ground **red pepper** or **cayenne pepper**
1 teaspoon ground **cinnamon**

BRISKET

5 to 6 pounds **beef brisket**, well trimmed (no more than ⅛ inch fat on top)
4 tablespoons **EVOO**
1 large or 2 medium **onions**, chopped
2 **carrots**, chopped
2 or 3 ribs **celery**, chopped
4 cloves **garlic**, chopped
Kosher salt and **pepper**
2 tablespoons pureed **chipotle chiles in adobo** (see Heads-up, page 182)
2 tablespoons **tomato paste**
1 (12-ounce) bottle **Mexican beer**, at room temperature
1 (28- or 32-ounce) can **tomato puree**
2 cups **beef stock**

1 (8-ounce) box **buttermilk biscuit mix** (I like Jiffy)
Apple-Cabbage Slaw (see QR code)

Preheat the oven to 325°F.

Make the Mexi-Rub: Combine all the ingredients. Measure out 2 tablespoons and set aside for the Black Bean & Beef Chilaquiles with Fried Eggs (page 186).

Let the brisket come to room temperature. Rub the spice blend all over the meat.

In a large Dutch oven (preferably oval), heat 3 tablespoons of the EVOO (3 turns of the pan) over medium-high to high heat. Add the meat and brown on both sides, then remove from the pan. Add the remaining 1 tablespoon EVOO (1 turn of the pan), the onions, carrots, celery, and garlic; season with salt and pepper; and stir for 5 minutes. Add the chipotle puree and tomato paste and stir for 1 minute. Deglaze the pan with the beer and stir for 1 minute more. Add the tomato puree and stock and bring to a low boil. Add the brisket and cover. Braise in the oven until very tender, 2½ to 3 hours.

Remove the brisket from the sauce. Puree the sauce with an immersion blender (or in a food processor, then return to the pan). Slice the brisket. Set about 1½ pounds of the meat aside for the chilaquiles and add the remainder back to the sauce.

[**Make-ahead:** Let cool and refrigerate.]

[**Night of:** Return the brisket to room temp before reheating gently over medium heat, stirring occasionally.]

While the brisket is reheating, bake the biscuits according to package directions.

Serve the brisket with sauce and biscuits, with slaw on the side.

Recipe for Apple-Cabbage Slaw
View a bonus Side Dish recipe.

Black Bean & Beef Chilaquiles with Fried Eggs

A hearty Tex-Mex "breakfast for dinner." SERVES 4 TO 6

10 **corn tortillas**, cut into 1-inch strips

Vegetable oil cooking spray

2 tablespoons **Mexi-Rub** (from page 185)

1 (14.5-ounce) can **fire-roasted diced tomatoes** or **diced tomatoes with green chiles**

1 (15-ounce) can **black beans**, drained

1½ pounds chopped **cooked beef brisket** (from page 185)

1½ cups shredded **pepper jack cheese**

1 cup shredded **sharp white cheddar cheese**

4 to 6 large or jumbo **organic eggs** (1 per person)

Butter, for cooking the eggs

Torn fresh **cilantro** leaves, for garnish

Thinly sliced fresh **Fresno** and **jalapeño chiles**, for garnish

Lime wedges, for garnish

Preheat the oven to 400°F. Set a cooling rack over a baking sheet.

Arrange the tortilla strips on the rack and coat with cooking spray. Sprinkle with the Mexi-Rub and bake until golden and crisp, 7 to 8 minutes.

[If making this to serve on **Cook Day**, leave the oven on. If making this for later in the week, you'll bake the casserole on the night of.]

Spread the tomatoes in the bottom of a 9 by 13-inch baking dish. Scatter the black beans over the tomatoes. Top with the tortilla strips. Layer on the chopped beef and top with the cheeses.

[**Make-ahead:** Let cool and refrigerate.]

[**Night of:** Return the casserole to room temp while you preheat the oven to 400°F.]

Bake until bubbling and browned on top, 10 to 15 minutes.

Meanwhile, in a skillet or on a griddle, cook the eggs in butter to each person's liking: sunny-side up, over easy, over hard.

Serve each portion of chilaquiles with a fried egg on top. Garnish with cilantro, sliced chiles, and a lime wedge.

Jalapeño Popper Orzo Mac 'n' Cheese

Can't do a week's worth of Tex-Mex food without a jalapeño popper. **Suggested side:** Guac Salad (recipe follows). SERVES 6

Kosher salt and **pepper**
1 pound **orzo pasta**
8 tablespoons (1 stick) **butter**
1 **onion**, finely chopped
4 cloves **garlic**, finely chopped
3 fresh **red Fresno chiles**:
   2 seeded and finely chopped;
   1 with seeds, sliced
5 fresh **jalapeño chiles**:
   4 seeded and finely chopped;
   1 with seeds, sliced
3 tablespoons **flour**
2½ cups **milk**
4 ounces **cream cheese**
2 cups shredded **sharp cheddar cheese**
2 cups **panko bread crumbs**

[If making this to serve on **Cook Day**, preheat the oven to 400°F.]

Bring a large pot of water to a boil. Salt the water and cook the orzo al dente, about 6 minutes. Drain.

In a saucepan, melt 4 tablespoons of the butter over medium heat. Add the onion, garlic, and chopped chiles. Cook to soften the onion and chiles, about 5 minutes. Sprinkle with the flour and stir. Add the milk and cook to thicken. Season the sauce with salt and pepper. Melt in the cheeses.

Combine the orzo with the sauce and place in a shallow 2 to 3-quart baking dish.

[**Make-ahead:** Let cool and refrigerate. Place the sliced Fresno chile and the sliced jalapeño chile in a plastic food storage bag and refrigerate.]

[**Night of:** Return the casserole to room temp while you preheat the oven to 400°F.]

Melt the remaining 4 tablespoons butter. Toss the panko with the melted butter.

Bake the casserole until heated through. Sprinkle the crumbs, then the sliced chiles, over the top and continue baking until browned and bubbling, 15 to 20 minutes.

Guac Salad SERVES 6

5 medium **heirloom tomatoes**, cut into thin wedges
1 small **red onion**, thinly sliced
2 almost ripe firm **avocados**, sliced
1 fresh **jalapeño chile**, finely chopped
Juice of 2 **limes**
EVOO, for liberal drizzling
Kosher salt and **pepper**
½ cup fresh **cilantro** tops, coarsely chopped

On a serving platter, combine the tomatoes, onion, avocados, and jalapeño. Drizzle with the lime juice and EVOO; season with salt and pepper. Scatter the cilantro over the top.

Chicken Enchiladas

Enchiladas are a great make-ahead. This is a good example of "The longer it sets, the better it gets." SERVES 6

RICE FILLING
3 tablespoons **butter**
⅓ cup broken **spaghetti** or **orzo pasta**
1 **tomato**
1 small to medium **onion**
2 cloves **garlic**, peeled
1 cup **long-grain white rice**
2 cups **chicken stock**
A generous pinch of **saffron threads**
Kosher salt and **pepper**

ENCHILADA SAUCE
4 **dried guajillo chiles** or **red New Mexico chiles**
2 cups **chicken stock**
1 tablespoon **EVOO** or **vegetable oil**
1 small to medium **onion**, chopped
2 cloves **garlic**, chopped
1 (29-ounce) can **tomato sauce**
1 **cinnamon stick**
1 large fresh **bay leaf**
½ cup slivered **almonds**, toasted and ground

CHICKEN FILLING
1 tablespoon **EVOO** or **vegetable oil**
1½ pounds **ground chicken**
1½ teaspoons ground **cumin**
1½ teaspoons ground **coriander**
1½ teaspoons **sweet paprika**
Kosher salt and **pepper**

12 **corn tortillas**, warmed or charred
½ pound **queso fresco**, crumbled
A handful of fresh **cilantro** leaves, coarsely chopped

Make the rice filling: In a saucepan, melt the butter. Add the pasta and cook until toasted. Grate the tomato, onion, and garlic right into the pot. Stir in the rice, stock, saffron, and salt and pepper and bring to a boil. Reduce the heat to a simmer, cover, and cook about 18 minutes. Fluff with a fork.

Make the enchilada sauce: Toast the chiles in a dry saucepan over medium-high heat until fragrant but not burned. Add the stock and bring to a simmer. Cook until softened, about 10 minutes. Transfer to a food processor and puree.

Return the saucepan to the heat and heat the EVOO (1 turn of the pan) over medium to medium-high heat. Add the onion and garlic and cook to soften, about 5 minutes. Add the tomato sauce, chile puree, cinnamon stick, and bay leaf and simmer to thicken slightly, 15 to 20 minutes. Stir in the ground almonds and turn off the heat. Discard the cinnamon stick and bay leaf.

[If making this dish to serve on **Cook Day**, preheat the oven to 400°F. If making this to serve later in the week, you'll preheat the oven on the night of.]

Make the chicken filling: In a nonstick skillet, heat the EVOO (1 turn of the pan) over medium-high heat. Add the chicken and cook, breaking it into crumbles as it browns. Season with the cumin, coriander, paprika, and salt and pepper.

Dip each tortilla in the enchilada sauce and fill with some rice and chicken; roll up. Place the enchiladas, seam side down, in a baking dish that will hold them in a single layer.

[**Make-ahead:** Let cool, cover, and refrigerate the enchiladas and remaining sauce separately.]
[**Night of:** Return the enchiladas and sauce to room temp while you preheat the oven to 400°F.]
Pour the remaining sauce over the enchiladas in an even layer. Bake to heat through, 30 to 35 minutes. Serve topped with queso fresco and cilantro.

WEEK 26

FALL IN LOVE WITH FALL

ALL OF THE AUTUMN FLAVORS
YOU LOVE—APPLES, PUMPKIN, TURKEY—
BROUGHT TOGETHER IN 5 MEALS
THAT YOUR FAMILY WILL "FALL" FOR

DISH
1
LENTIL SOUP
WITH KALE &
SAUSAGE
PAGE 191

DISH
2
PORK GOULASH
WITH APPLE &
ONION
PAGE 193

DISH
3
BEER-BRAISED
BEEF MEATBALLS
WITH HORSERADISH
SAUCE
PAGE 194

DISH
4
CHIPOTLE BBQ
TURKEY MINI MEAT
LOAVES
PAGE 195

DISH
5
PUMPKIN
LOVERS'
LASAGNA
PAGE 196

Lentil Soup with Kale & Sausage

What is more comforting when the weather starts to get chilly than a big bowl of soup? By the way, adding a small amount of potato to any soup will help prevent it from being too salty. Potatoes love salt and they tend to soak it up. SERVES 6

2 tablespoons **EVOO**, plus more for drizzling

1 pound bulk **hot or sweet Italian sausage** or links, casings removed

1 large or 2 medium **onions**, chopped

1 **carrot**, finely chopped

1 **potato**, peeled and finely diced

2 sprigs fresh **rosemary**

4 cloves **garlic**, finely chopped

2 fresh **bay leaves**

Salt and **pepper**

2 tablespoons **tomato paste**

½ cup **dry white** or **red wine**

1 bunch **lacinato kale** (also called black, Tuscan, or dinosaur kale), stemmed and chopped

Freshly grated **nutmeg**

6 cups **chicken stock**

1¼ cups **brown lentils**

Shaved **pecorino cheese**, for serving

In a soup pot, heat the EVOO (2 turns of the pan) over medium-high heat. Add the sausage and cook, breaking it into crumbles as it browns. Add the onions, carrot, potato, rosemary, garlic, bay leaves, and salt and pepper and cook to soften the vegetables, 7 to 8 minutes. Add the tomato paste and stir for 1 minute. Deglaze the pan with the wine. Add the kale and a few grates of nutmeg and let the kale start to wilt. Add the stock and 2 cups water and bring to a boil. (For a thicker soup, omit the water.) Stir in the lentils and cook at a low bubble until tender, 30 to 35 minutes.

[**Make-ahead:** Let cool and refrigerate.]

[**Night of:** Return the soup to room temp before reheating gently over medium heat.]

Remove the rosemary sprigs and bay leaves. Serve topped with a drizzle of EVOO and shaved pecorino.

Pork Goulash with Apple & Onion

You could use regular ground pork in this dish, but that will make this more like a chili than a goulash. Leftovers make great nachos over pita chips, with melted cheese and sour cream. SERVES 4 TO 6

2 tablespoons **vegetable oil** or **EVOO**

⅓ pound **smoky bacon**, chopped

2 pounds coarsely **ground pork** (from the butcher) or **hand-chopped pork shoulder**

Kosher salt and **pepper**

2 medium **apples** (such as Gala or Honeycrisp), peeled and chopped

1 large or 2 medium **onions**, finely chopped

2 fresh **red Fresno chiles**, seeded and finely chopped

2 tablespoons fresh **thyme** leaves

1 large fresh **bay leaf**

3 tablespoons **sweet paprika**

2 teaspoons ground **cumin**

2 teaspoons ground **coriander**

Juice of ½ **lemon**

½ cup cloudy **apple cider**

2 cups **chicken stock**

1 pound extra-wide **egg noodles**

2 tablespoons **butter**

2 tablespoons chopped fresh **flat-leaf parsley**

2 tablespoons chopped fresh **dill**

1 to 1½ cups shredded **sharp white cheddar cheese**

½ to ¾ cup **sour cream**

In a large Dutch oven, heat the oil over medium-high heat. Add the bacon and cook to crisp. With a slotted spoon, transfer the bacon to a plate.

Pat the pork dry with paper towels, add to the bacon drippings, and allow the meat to crust without turning. Then cook, breaking it into crumbles, and season with salt and pepper. Add the apples, onions, chiles, thyme, and bay leaf and stir to soften the onions, about 5 minutes. Add the paprika, cumin, and coriander and stir for 1 minute. Return the bacon to the pan and add the lemon juice, cider, and stock. Bring to a boil, reduce the heat to a simmer, and cook to concentrate the flavors and thicken the stew. Add a little water or stock if the goulash dries out too much, too soon.

[**Make-ahead:** Let cool and refrigerate.]

[**Night of:** Return the goulash to room temp before reheating gently over medium heat.]

Bring a large pot of water to a boil. Salt the water and cook the noodles al dente. Drain the noodles and return to the pot. Add the butter, parsley, and dill and toss.

To serve, fill bowls with noodles and a ladleful of goulash. Top with cheese and sour cream.

Beer-Braised Beef Meatballs with Horseradish Sauce

Beer? A fall ingredient? One word: Oktoberfest. **Suggested side:** Hunks of toasted pumpernickel or sourdough bread (from the loaf you need to buy to make bread crumbs for the meatballs). SERVES 4

2 slices (1 inch thick) **pumpernickel** or **sourdough bread**

1 cup **milk**

2 pounds **ground beef**

⅓ cup **Worcestershire sauce**

4 rounded tablespoons prepared **horseradish**

6 cloves **garlic**, grated or pasted

1 **egg**

½ cup fresh **flat-leaf parsley** leaves, finely chopped

Kosher salt and **pepper**

2 tablespoons **EVOO**

1 (12-ounce) bottle **amber ale** (tangy and sweeter) or **Guinness stout** (bitter), at room temperature

1 (10-ounce) can **beef consommé**

1½ cups **sour cream**

¼ cup **heavy cream**

¼ cup minced fresh **chives**

1 bunch **watercress**, stemmed, for garnish

Place the bread in a bowl with the milk to soften.

Place the beef in a large bowl. Squeeze excess liquid from the bread, then crumble it into crumbs between your fingers as you add it to the meat. Add the Worcestershire sauce, 2 tablespoons of the horseradish, the garlic, egg, parsley, and salt and pepper. Mix and roll into 2½-inch balls.

Heat a cast-iron skillet or large, wide, heavy-bottomed pan over medium-high heat. Pour the EVOO (2 turns of the pan) into the hot skillet, then add the meatballs and brown for 7 to 8 minutes. Deglaze the pan with the beer and reduce a minute. Add the consommé, cover the pan (with foil if there's no lid), and cook, shaking the pan occasionally, until the meatballs are cooked through, 12 to 15 minutes.

[Make-ahead: Let cool and refrigerate.]

Combine the sour cream, heavy cream, the remaining 2 tablespoons horseradish, the chives, and salt and pepper.

[Make-ahead: Cover and refrigerate.]

[Night of: Return the meatballs to room temp before reheating gently, covered, over medium heat. Take the sauce out of the fridge shortly before serving.]

Serve the meatballs garnished with watercress, with the sauce and hunks of toasted bread.

Chipotle BBQ Turkey Mini Meat Loaves

The chipotle BBQ sauce here is so good. You can put it on steak, on hamburgers, on chicken. **Suggested side:** Mashed Sweet Potatoes (see QR code below). SERVES 4 TO 6

EVOO, for brushing muffin tin
1½ cups seasoned **stuffing cubes**
¾ cup **chicken stock**
2 pounds **ground turkey** (light and dark meat)
1 rounded tablespoon **Rachael Ray Perfect Poultry Seasoning** or other **poultry seasoning**
2 teaspoons ground **cumin**
Kosher salt and **pepper**
8 ounces **extra-sharp yellow cheddar cheese**, finely diced
6 thin **scallions**, finely chopped
½ small **red bell pepper**, finely chopped
¼ cup finely chopped fresh **cilantro** or **flat-leaf parsley**
2 **eggs**
Chipotle BBQ Sauce (recipe below)

Preheat the oven to 375°F. Brush the cups of a muffin tin (6 jumbo or 12 medium) with EVOO.

Place the stuffing cubes in a food processor and process into crumbs. Transfer to a bowl and moisten with the stock.

Place the turkey in a bowl. Add the poultry seasoning, cumin, and salt and pepper. Add the moistened bread crumbs, cheese, scallions, bell pepper, cilantro, and eggs and mix to combine. Fill the muffin cups, mounding the meat up a bit in the center. Brush with the BBQ sauce. Place the muffin tin on a baking sheet and bake for 40 minutes.

[Make-ahead: Let cool, wrap in foil, and refrigerate or freeze.]

[Night of: Reheat the meat loaves in a 350°F oven for 30 minutes if straight from the fridge or 45 minutes from the freezer.]

Chipotle BBQ Sauce MAKES ABOUT 1¼ CUPS

1 cup good-quality **ketchup**
2 cloves **garlic**, finely chopped
2 tablespoons **Worcestershire sauce**

2 tablespoons dark amber **maple syrup**
2 tablespoons **dark brown sugar**
2 tablespoons **cider vinegar**

Coarsely ground **pepper**
2 tablespoons pureed **chipotle chiles in adobo** (see Heads-up, page 182)

In a small saucepan, combine all the ingredients. Bring to a bubble, reduce the heat to low, and simmer for 20 minutes to thicken.

Recipe for Mashed Sweet Potatoes
View a bonus Side Dish recipe.

Pumpkin Lovers' Lasagna

My favorite season: fall. My favorite fall flavor: pumpkin. One of my all-time favorite dishes: lasagna. Need I say more? SERVES 6 TO 8

Kosher salt and **pepper**

1 head **escarole**, coarsely chopped

1 head **garlic**, cloves separated, unpeeled

6 tablespoons (¾ stick) **butter**

10 to 12 leaves **sage**, torn

1 pound **butternut squash** or **sugar pumpkin**, peeled and cut into bite-size chunks

1½ cups **chicken stock**

3 tablespoons **flour**

3 cups **milk**

Freshly grated **nutmeg**

3 **eggs**

2 (15-ounce) cans **unsweetened pumpkin puree**

2 cups fresh **ricotta cheese**

2 cups grated **Parmigiano-Reggiano cheese**

1 (9-ounce) box no-boil, oven-ready **lasagna sheets**, soaked in warm water for 5 minutes

¾ pound **Italian Fontina**, **Fontina Val d'Aosta**, or **Gouda cheese**, shredded

Bring a few inches of water to a boil in a large pot. Salt the water and add the escarole. Cook for 5 minutes, drain, and reserve.

In a small saucepan, cover the garlic cloves with water and simmer for 20 minutes. Drain and cool. Squish them out of their skins and mash with a fork.

Meanwhile, in a deep, wide skillet, heat 3 tablespoons of the butter over medium heat. Stir in the sage. Add the butternut squash in one layer and stir to coat with the butter; season with salt and pepper. Add the stock and cook, stirring occasionally, until the stock is absorbed and the squash is lightly browned and tender, about 15 minutes. Turn off the heat.

[If making this to serve on **Cook Day**, preheat the oven to 375°F. If making this to serve later in the week, you'll preheat the oven on the night of.]

In another medium saucepan, heat the remaining 3 tablespoons butter over medium heat. Whisk in the flour and cook for 1 minute. Whisk in the milk and mashed garlic. Season with salt, pepper, and a few grates of nutmeg. Thicken slightly; the sauce should just very lightly coat the back of a spoon.

In a bowl, stir together 2 of the eggs and the pumpkin puree; season with salt and pepper. In another bowl, stir together the remaining 1 egg, the ricotta, and 1 cup of the Parm.

Pour about half the garlic sauce into the bottom of a 9 by 13-inch baking dish or lasagna pan and begin to build the lasagna. Layer in 3 lasagna sheets, half of the pumpkin mixture, 3 lasagna sheets, all of the ricotta mixture, the butternut squash, and escarole. Top with half the Fontina, 3 lasagna sheets, the remaining pumpkin, 4 lasagna sheets (overlapping), then the remainder of the garlic sauce, remaining Fontina, and remaining Parm.

[**Make-ahead:** Let cool and refrigerate.]

[**Night of:** Return the lasagna to room temp while you preheat the oven to 375°F.]

Bake for 45 minutes (or up to 1 hour, covered, if the lasagna is still cold). Increase the oven temperature to 400°F and bake for 15 minutes (uncover if it was covered) to brown the cheese. Let rest for 15 minutes, cut, and serve.

WEEK 27

A CHICKEN IN EVERY POT

WHO DOESN'T LOVE A GOOD OL' CHICKEN DINNER? FIVE NIGHTS OF CHICKEN DISHES EACH SO DIFFERENT YOU WON'T MIND HAVING CHICKEN ALL WEEK LONG!

DISH
1
MULLIGATAWNY WITH GREEN RAITA
PAGE 199

DISH
2
CHICKEN TETRAZZINI CASSEROLE WITH CAULIFLOWER
PAGE 200

DISH
3
TEQUILA-ORANGE BBQ CHICKEN BURRITOS
PAGE 201

DISH
4
CATALAN CHICKEN STEW
PAGE 202

DISH
5
BRAISED CHICKEN THIGHS WITH 40 CLOVES OF GARLIC
PAGE 204

Mulligatawny with Green Raita

This would be delicious with naan bread (which is made with yogurt, so the bread is a little tangy), either regular or garlic naan. To serve the naan, heat a griddle over medium-high heat. Splash some water onto the griddle and grill the naan. Then brush with melted butter. SERVES 4

MULLIGATAWNY
1 tablespoon **EVOO**
4 tablespoons (½ stick) **butter**
2 medium **onions**, chopped
4 cloves **garlic**, grated
2-inch piece fresh **ginger**, grated
1 **green apple**, peeled and
    shredded
Kosher salt and **pepper**
1 tablespoon ground **cumin**
1 tablespoon ground **coriander**
1 tablespoon ground **turmeric**
1 teaspoon **dry mustard**
3 tablespoons **flour**
6 cups **chicken stock**,
    homemade (page 322) or
    store-bought
4 cups shredded **Poached
    Chicken** (page 322); see Note

GREEN RAITA
1 cup **Greek yogurt**
1 **green apple**, peeled and
    shredded
¼ cup fresh **mint** leaves
¼ cup fresh **cilantro** leaves, plus
    more for garnish
¼ teaspoon ground **cardamom**
Juice of 1 **lime**
Salt and **pepper**

1½ cups **basmati rice**
Lime wedges, for serving

Make the mulligatawny: In a Dutch oven, heat the EVOO (1 turn of the pan) over medium-high heat. Melt the butter into the oil. Add the onions, garlic, ginger, apple, and salt and pepper. Cook until tender, 7 to 8 minutes. Add the cumin, coriander, turmeric, and dry mustard and stir in. Add the flour and stir for 1 minute. Add the stock and cook until thickened to a light sauce consistency, about 20 minutes. Stir in the chicken.

[**Make-ahead:** Let cool and refrigerate.]

Make the raita: In a food processor, combine the Greek yogurt, apple, mint, cilantro, cardamom, lime juice, and salt and pepper. Whiz to combine.

[**Make-ahead:** Refrigerate.]

[**Night of:** Return the soup to room temp before gently reheating over medium heat while you cook the rice. Get the raita out of the fridge shortly before serving time.]

Cook the rice according to package directions.

Spoon the mulligatawny into shallow bowls and top with a scoop of rice and some raita. Serve with lime wedges for squeezing. Pass any remaining raita at the table.

Note: Make the following changes to the Basic Poached Chicken (page 322): Use 4 full bone-in, skin-on chicken breasts (attached at the breastbone). Divide into 2 pots if necessary and double the flavoring ingredients so you have enough to go into each pot. Add 4 cloves garlic, smashed, to each pot.

Chicken Tetrazzini Casserole with Cauliflower

Cooking a head of cauliflower whole before attempting to cut it into florets means you don't end up with all those little crumbs of raw cauliflower all over your counter.

SERVES 4

1 small head **cauliflower**, head left whole but core cut out
Kosher salt and **pepper**
½ pound extra-wide **egg noodles** (the wider the better)
8 tablespoons (1 stick) **butter**
½ pound **mixed mushrooms** or **white mushrooms**, sliced
1 large or 2 medium **shallots**, finely chopped
4 cloves **garlic**, finely chopped
3 tablespoons **flour**
½ cup **dry sherry**
2 cups **chicken stock**
1 cup **heavy cream**
Freshly grated **nutmeg**
3 to 4 cups shredded **Poached Chicken** (see Note, page 199)
1 cup **panko bread crumbs**
1 cup grated **Parmigiano-Reggiano cheese**
¼ cup chopped fresh **flat-leaf parsley**

[If making this to serve on **Cook Day**, preheat the oven to 400°F. If making this to serve later in the week, you'll preheat the oven on the night of.]

Place the cauliflower in a pot and add 1½ cups water. Season with salt, bring to a boil, cover, and cook to just tender, 7 to 8 minutes. Drain. When cool enough to handle, cut into florets.

Bring another pot of water to a boil. Salt the water and cook the egg noodles until just shy of al dente, about 5 minutes. Drain.

Meanwhile, in a large skillet, melt 4 tablespoons of the butter over medium heat. Add the mushrooms and cook until tender and brown. Add the shallots and garlic and stir for 2 to 3 minutes. Sprinkle the flour over the pan and stir for 1 minute. Deglaze the pan with the sherry. Whisk in the stock. Bring to a boil, simmer a few minutes to thicken slightly, and stir in the cream. Season with a few grates of nutmeg and salt and pepper.

In a large bowl, combine the cauliflower, noodles, chicken, and sauce. Transfer to a shallow 3- to 4-quart baking dish.

[**Make-ahead:** Let cool and refrigerate.]

[**Night of:** Return the casserole to room temp while you preheat the oven to 400°F.]

In a medium skillet, melt the remaining 4 tablespoons butter. Add the panko and toss to combine. Remove from the heat to let cool. Toss with the Parm.

Top the casserole with the panko and bake until heated through, golden, and bubbling, 40 to 45 minutes. Garnish with the parsley.

Tequila-Orange BBQ Chicken Burritos with Cheddar, Baked Beans & Red Cabbage Slaw

I love baked beans, but I'm not happy with them just straight out of the can. I gotta doctor them, my way. SERVES 4

BBQ CHICKEN
3 or 4 **dried guajillo** or **red New Mexico chiles**, stemmed and seeded
2 cups **chicken stock**, homemade (page 322) or store-bought
1 cup good-quality **ketchup**
2 cloves **garlic**, finely chopped
2 tablespoons **dark brown sugar**
2 tablespoons dark amber **maple syrup**
2 tablespoons **cider vinegar**
2 tablespoons **Worcestershire sauce**
1 small **orange**, juiced and zest grated to get 1 tablespoon

Juice of 1 **lime**
2 shots **tequila**
4 cups shredded **Poached Chicken** (see Note, page 199)

BAKED BEANS
1 tablespoon **EVOO**
4 slices **smoky bacon**, chopped
½ **red onion**, chopped (see Heads-up)
2 cloves **garlic**, finely chopped
2 teaspoons coarsely ground **pepper**
2 (16-ounce) cans **baked beans**

¼ cup **steak sauce** (such as Lea & Perrins Thick Classic Worcestershire Sauce)

RED CABBAGE SLAW
Juice of 2 **limes**
¼ cup **cider vinegar**
½ **red onion**, peeled
⅓ cup **EVOO**
1 small **red cabbage** (1 pound), finely shredded
Salt and **pepper**

8 large **flour tortillas**
¾ pound **sharp white cheddar cheese**

Make the BBQ chicken: Toast the chiles in a dry saucepan over medium-high heat until fragrant but not burned. Add the stock and bring to a simmer. Cook until softened, about 10 minutes. Transfer to a food processor and puree.

Return the chile puree to the saucepan and add the ketchup, garlic, brown sugar, maple syrup, vinegar, Worcestershire, orange juice and zest, lime juice, and tequila. Bring to a low boil and simmer for 20 minutes. Add the chicken.

[**Make-ahead:** Let cool and refrigerate.]

Make the baked beans: In a skillet, heat the EVOO (1 turn of the pan) over medium-high heat. Add the bacon and brown. Add the onion, garlic, and pepper and cook to soften the vegetables, 3 to 4 minutes. Mix in the beans and cook to heat through. Stir in the steak sauce.

[**Make-ahead:** Let cool and refrigerate.]

[**Night of:** Return the chicken and beans to room temp before gently reheating over medium-low heat.]

Make the red cabbage slaw: In a bowl, combine the lime juice and vinegar. Grate the red onion into the bowl and whisk with the EVOO. Add the cabbage and toss; season with salt and pepper.

Char the tortillas for 30 seconds on each side. Place some chicken on the edge of a tortilla; top with cheddar, beans, and slaw; then tuck in the sides of the tortilla, wrap, and roll tightly.

Heads-up: Save the other half of the onion for grating into the red cabbage slaw.

Catalan Chicken Stew

A *picada* is a seasoning sauce typical of Catalan cooking. **Suggested side:** Warm the rest of the baguette that you need for the *picada* to mop up the stew. SERVES 4

PICADA

¼ cup raw unsalted **Marcona almonds** or **blanched almonds**

2 tablespoons **EVOO**

2 slices (½ inch thick) **baguette**

2 cloves **garlic**, grated or finely chopped

1 tablespoon **lemon** juice

A generous handful of fresh **flat-leaf parsley**

STEW

3 tablespoons **EVOO**

2 **onions**, chopped

2 **carrots**, chopped

2 or 3 ribs **celery** with leafy tops, chopped

1 **red bell pepper**, chopped

1 fresh **red Fresno** or other **chile**, finely chopped

2 to 3 tablespoons chopped fresh **thyme**

2 rounded tablespoons **sweet paprika**

A pinch of **saffron threads**

2 fresh **bay leaves**

Kosher salt and **pepper**

1 (28- or 32-ounce) can **San Marzano tomatoes** (look for DOP on the label)

4 cups **chicken stock**, homemade (page 322) or store-bought

3 to 4 cups shredded **Poached Chicken** (see Note, page 199)

1 cup pitted **Spanish green olives**, coarsely chopped

Make the *picada:* In a small dry skillet, toast the almonds. Transfer to a food processor. Pour 2 tablespoons EVOO (2 turns of the pan) into the same skillet and fry the bread slices. Chop the bread and add to the food processor. Add the garlic, a splash of water, the lemon juice, and parsley. Pulse-chop into a pesto-like consistency.

[**Make-ahead:** Refrigerate.]

Make the stew: In a Dutch oven, heat the EVOO (3 turns of the pan) over medium-high heat. Add the onions, carrots, celery, bell pepper, chile, thyme, paprika, saffron, bay leaves, and salt and pepper. Cook to soften the vegetables, 7 to 8 minutes. Add the tomatoes, breaking them up with a potato masher. Add the stock and simmer for 30 minutes. Stir in the chicken.

[**Make-ahead:** Let cool and refrigerate.]

[**Night of:** Return the stew to room temp before reheating gently over medium heat, stirring occasionally. Discard the bay leaves. Remove the *picada* from the fridge.]

Stir the *picada* and olives into the hot stew. Turn off the heat and let stand 5 minutes. Serve in shallow bowls.

Braised Chicken Thighs with 40 Cloves of Garlic

Suggested side: Ciabatta bread for mopping. SERVES 4

40 large cloves **hardneck** or **purple garlic**, unpeeled

8 large bone-in, skin-on **chicken thighs**

Kosher salt and **pepper**

2 tablespoons **EVOO**

4 tablespoons (½ stick) **butter**

1 pound **cremini mushrooms**, thinly sliced

2 tablespoons fresh **thyme** leaves, finely chopped

½ cup **Marsala wine**

3 to 4 cups **chicken stock**, homemade (page 322) or store-bought

1 small bunch **lacinato kale** (also called black, Tuscan, or dinosaur kale), stemmed and thinly sliced, or **spinach**, stemmed

Freshly grated **nutmeg**

Preheat the oven to 400°F.

In a saucepan, simmer the garlic in water to cover for 10 minutes to soften the pungency and make it easier to peel. Drain and cool, pop off the skins, and set aside.

Season the chicken with salt and pepper. In a large ovenproof skillet, heat the EVOO (2 turns of the pan). Add the chicken skin side down and brown the skin to very crisp, 7 to 8 minutes. Flip the thighs and brown the other side, 3 to 4 minutes. Transfer to a plate.

Melt the butter into the pan drippings and add the mushrooms and thyme. Cook the mushrooms to brown and very tender, 12 to 15 minutes. Deglaze the pan with the Marsala. Return the chicken to the pan and add the garlic. Add enough stock to come up and around chicken, but do not cover the skin (3 to 4 cups). Transfer the skillet to the oven and roast for 45 minutes.

[**Make-ahead:** Let cool and refrigerate.]

[**Night of:** Preheat the oven to 400°F. Remove the chicken from the sauce while you reheat the sauce on the stovetop until it comes to a bubble. Put the chicken on top and transfer to the oven to heat through and recrisp the skin. Warm a platter for 2 minutes on a low rack under the chicken pan.]

Transfer the chicken to the warm platter and loosely tent with foil. Return the skillet to the stovetop and cook to reduce the sauce until thick enough to coat a spoon. Wilt in the kale and add a few grates of nutmeg.

Serve a puddle of sauce and greens in a shallow bowl, and top with chicken.

WEEK 28

BACK TO THE GRIND

FIVE EXCITING (AND AFFORDABLE)
MEALS THAT TAKE GROUND MEAT
WAY BEYOND THE BURGER

DISH
1
ITALIAN
PORK CHILI
WITH POLENTA
PAGE 206

DISH
2
VEAL
DUMPLINGS
WITH ESCAROLE
IN BROTH
PAGE 207

DISH
3
SLOPPY JOE
'N' MACARONI
CASSEROLE
PAGE 208

DISH
4
PILGRIM
MEAT LOAF
PAGE 210

DISH
5
MOUSSAKA
PAGE 211

Italian Pork Chili with Polenta

I like the fennel that comes in sweet Italian sausage, but it's usually not in hot sausage. So I often add my own fennel seeds when I'm cooking with the hot one.

SERVES 4 TO 6

1 large **red bell pepper**
2 tablespoons **EVOO**
¼ pound **pancetta**, finely diced
½ pound bulk **hot Italian sausage** or ⅓ pound coarsely grated **Calabrese salami**
1 pound **ground pork**
1 teaspoon **fennel seeds**
1 medium **onion**, finely chopped
3 or 4 cloves **garlic**, finely chopped
Leaves from 1 sprig fresh **oregano**, finely chopped
2 tablespoons chopped fresh **thyme**
1 (for milder) or 2 (for hot) **fresh red chiles**, seeded and very finely chopped
¼ cup **tomato paste**
½ cup **dry red wine**
4 to 5 cups **chicken stock**
1 cup **milk**
1 cup quick-cooking **polenta**
2 tablespoons **butter**
1 cup grated **pecorino cheese**, plus more for serving
Salt and **pepper**
Chopped fresh **flat-leaf parsley**, for garnish

Char the pepper all over on the stovetop over a gas flame or under the broiler with the oven door ajar to vent steam. Place the pepper in a bowl and cover tightly. When cool enough to handle, rub off the skin with a paper towel, then halve, seed, and chop the pepper.

In a Dutch oven, heat the EVOO (2 turns of the pan) over medium-high heat. Add the pancetta and sausage and cook, breaking the sausage into crumbles as it browns. Add the ground pork and break it into crumbles. Add the fennel seeds, onion, garlic, oregano, thyme, chile, and roasted pepper. Cook to soften, about 5 minutes. Stir in the tomato paste and cook for 1 minute. Deglaze the pan with the wine. Add 2 to 3 cups chicken stock and simmer a few minutes to combine the flavors.

[**Make-ahead:** Let cool and refrigerate.]

[**Night of:** Return the chili to room temp before reheating gently over medium heat while you make the polenta.]

In a saucepan, combine the remaining 2 cups stock and the milk and bring to a low boil. Whisk in the polenta and keep whisking until it thickens to a thick but pourable consistency, 2 minutes. Remove from the heat and stir in the butter and 1 cup pecorino. Season with salt and pepper.

Spoon the polenta into shallow bowls and hollow out the center. Fill the center with chili and garnish with more pecorino and some parsley.

Veal Dumplings with Escarole in Broth

The veal "dumplings" are really little meatballs that get dropped into simmering broth to cook—just like dumplings. This cooking method keeps the meatballs very soft and moist. SERVES 4

2 slices good-quality **white bread**
1 cup **milk**
1¼ pounds **ground veal**
Freshly grated **nutmeg**
Kosher salt and **pepper**
10 to 12 medium fresh **sage** leaves, very thinly sliced
2 cloves **garlic**, grated or pasted
⅓ cup crumbled **Gorgonzola dolce cheese**
⅓ cup grated **Parmigiano-Reggiano cheese**
1 **egg**, lightly beaten
EVOO, for drizzling
8 cups **chicken stock**
1 head **escarole**, chopped into 2-inch pieces
⅓ of a 16-ounce bag extra-wide **egg noodles**
Grated **lemon** zest, for garnish

Soak the bread in the milk to soften.

Place the veal in a bowl and season with a little nutmeg, salt, and pepper. Add the sage, garlic, cheeses, and egg. Squeeze the liquid from the bread and crumble into fine crumbs between your fingertips as you add it to the veal. Drizzle in a little EVOO and mix well to combine. Use a 2-ounce scoop or your hands (dip them in a warm water bath as you work) to roll out the meatballs, about the size of a large walnut. Arrange on a baking sheet or large plate.

In a soup pot or Dutch oven, bring the stock and 2 to 3 cups water to a low boil. Add veal balls and cook through, 8 to 10 minutes. Wilt the escarole into the soup for the last 1 or 2 minutes of cook time.

[Make-ahead: Let cool and refrigerate.]

[**Night of:** Return the soup to room temp before reheating gently over medium heat while you cook the noodles.]

Bring a medium pot of water to a boil. Salt the water and cook the noodles al dente. Drain and add to the soup. (If you'll be saving leftovers of the soup, don't put the noodles in the soup; instead, put them in the serving bowls and ladle the soup over them. Then store any leftover noodles separately from the soup.)

Ladle the soup into bowls and garnish with a few grates of lemon zest.

Sloppy Joe 'n' Macaroni Casserole

Sloppy Joe seasoning mix is very simple to make. It's made out of ingredients that are on hand in almost everyone's pantry. Why not just make it? SERVES 4 TO 6

3 tablespoons **dark brown sugar**

3 tablespoons **Worcestershire sauce**

3 tablespoons **red wine vinegar**

1 (15-ounce) can **tomato sauce**

2 tablespoons **EVOO**

1½ pounds **ground beef** (80 to 85% lean)

Kosher salt and **pepper**

1 **onion**, finely chopped

1 **red bell pepper**, finely chopped

3 or 4 cloves **garlic**, finely chopped

1 cup **beef stock**

¾ pound **rigate** (elbow macaroni with ridges)

2 cups shredded **yellow cheddar cheese**

½ cup chopped crispy deli-style **dill pickles**

[If making this to serve on **Cook Day**, preheat the oven to 400°F. If making this to serve later in the week, you'll preheat the oven on the night of.]

Bring a large pot of water to a boil.

In a small bowl, combine the brown sugar, Worcestershire, vinegar, and tomato sauce. Set aside.

In a large skillet or Dutch oven, heat the EVOO (2 turns of the pan) over medium-high heat. Add the beef and cook, breaking it into crumbles as it browns. Season with salt and lots of pepper. Add the onion, bell pepper, and garlic and cook to soften, about 5 minutes more. Add the tomato sauce mixture and beef stock. Simmer for 5 to 10 minutes to thicken while you cook the pasta. Don't thicken it up too much, though. It should be saucier than a Sloppy Joe because it's going to cook with pasta.

Salt the boiling water and drop in the macaroni. Cook until just shy of al dente, about 5 minutes. Drain and add to the beef sauce.

Transfer the mixture to a shallow 3-quart baking dish. Top with the cheddar.

[**Make-ahead:** Let cool and refrigerate.]

[**Night of:** Return the casserole to room temp while you preheat the oven to 400°F.]

Bake until browned and bubbling, 15 to 20 minutes.

Serve straight from the casserole. Top with chopped pickles.

Pilgrim Meat Loaf

This is called a pilgrim meat loaf because it's based on a classic New England sandwich of the same name. SERVES 6

MEAT LOAF

1 tablespoon **EVOO**, plus more for drizzling

3 tablespoons **butter**

1 small **Honeycrisp** or **McIntosh apple**, peeled and chopped

2 or 3 small ribs **celery** with leafy tops, finely chopped

1 small **onion**, finely chopped

1 tablespoon fresh **thyme** leaves

Salt and **pepper**

1½ cups seasoned **corn bread** or **traditional stuffing cubes**

1 to 1½ cups **chicken stock**

⅓ cup **dried cranberries**

2 pounds **ground turkey** (light and dark meat)

1 tablespoon **Rachael Ray Perfect Poultry Seasoning** or other **poultry seasoning**

1 cup crumbled or **shredded super-sharp white cheddar cheese**

1 large **egg**

Whole berry **cranberry sauce**, homemade or store-bought, for serving

CIDER GRAVY (optional)

3 tablespoons **butter**

2 rounded tablespoons **flour**

½ cup cloudy **apple cider**

1 tablespoon **Worcestershire sauce**

2 cups **chicken** or **turkey stock**

Kosher salt and **pepper**

1 **egg** yolk (optional)

Make the meat loaf: Preheat the oven to 400°F. Line a rimmed baking sheet with parchment paper.

In a large skillet, heat the EVOO (1 turn of the pan) and butter over medium heat. When the butter melts, add the apple, celery, onion, thyme, and salt and pepper. Cook until the onion is tender, 7 to 8 minutes. Transfer to a bowl and let cool.

Process the stuffing cubes in a food processor to make crumbs, then transfer to a bowl and moisten with chicken stock.

Place the cranberries in a bowl and cover with hot water to soften. Drain.

Place the turkey in a large bowl and season with salt and pepper. Add the moistened stuffing, the apple-vegetable mixture, poultry seasoning, cranberries, cheese, and egg and combine. Form into a loaf 10 inches long and 4 inches wide on the baking sheet. Drizzle with EVOO and roast to golden, 50 to 60 minutes.

[Make-ahead: Let cool and refrigerate.]

[Night of: Return the meat loaf to room temp, then reheat in a 350°F oven. Or slice off just what you will be serving and reheat in a pan with some chicken stock.]

Meanwhile, make the cider gravy (if desired): In a saucepan, melt the butter over medium heat. Whisk in the flour and cook for 2 minutes. Whisk in the cider, Worcestershire, and stock, and season with salt and lots of pepper. Cook the sauce until thick enough to coat the back of a spoon. For a richer sauce, stir some of the hot gravy into the egg yolk to temper it. Then stir the warmed yolk back into the sauce.

Let the meat loaf stand for 10 minutes before slicing. Serve with cranberry sauce and cider gravy, if desired.

Moussaka

Moussaka is a marriage of so many of my favorite things: béchamel, eggplant, and lamb . . . all in one place. SERVES 4 TO 6

6 tablespoons **EVOO**
1½ pounds **ground lamb**
Kosher salt and **pepper**
1 **onion**, finely chopped
4 cloves **garlic**, finely chopped
1 small fresh **red Fresno chile**,
    seeded and very finely
    chopped, or 1 teaspoon
    crushed red pepper flakes
Leaves from 1 sprig fresh
    oregano, very finely chopped
¼ cup **tomato paste**
½ cup **dry red wine**
½ cup **chicken stock**
1 (28- or 32-ounce) can **chopped
    tomatoes** or **San Marzano
    tomatoes** (look for DOP on the
    label)
A few strips of **lemon** zest
1 **cinnamon stick**
1 large fresh **bay leaf**
2 medium-large **eggplants**, very
    firm and heavy
4 large or jumbo **eggs**, separated
3 cups **panko bread crumbs**
1½ teaspoons **granulated garlic**
1½ teaspoons **granulated onion**
½ cup fresh **flat-leaf parsley**
    tops, very finely chopped
1½ cups grated **kefalotiri** or
    Parmigiano-Reggiano cheese
4 tablespoons (½ stick) **butter**
3 rounded tablespoons **flour**
2 to 2½ cups **milk**
Freshly grated **nutmeg**

Preheat the oven to 400°F. Place wire racks in 2 baking sheets.

In a medium Dutch oven, heat 2 tablespoons EVOO (2 turns of the pan) over medium-high heat. Add the meat and cook, breaking it into crumbles as it browns. Season with salt and pepper. Stir in the onion, garlic, chile, and oregano and cook about 5 minutes. Stir in the tomato paste. Deglaze with the wine. Add the stock, tomatoes, lemon zest, cinnamon stick, and bay leaf and simmer for 30 minutes to thicken, stirring occasionally.

Meanwhile, trim the bulges off 2 sides of the eggplants to square them up a bit and cut lengthwise into ¼-inch-thick planks. Salt the eggplant and drain in a colander for 20 minutes.

Pat the eggplant dry. Beat the egg whites with a splash of water in a shallow bowl. Mix together the panko and ¼ cup EVOO in another bowl. Add the granulated garlic, granulated onion, parsley, and ¾ cup of the cheese and toss to blend. Dip the eggplant in the egg whites, then press into the bread crumbs. Arrange on the racks on the baking sheets. Bake to golden, 25 to 30 minutes. (Leave the oven on.)

In a saucepan, melt the butter over medium heat. Whisk in the flour and cook for 1 minute. Whisk in the milk; season with salt, pepper, and a little nutmeg. Cook until it coats the back of a spoon. Beat the egg yolks in a bowl and stir in some of the hot sauce to temper them. Whisk the warmed yolks into the sauce and turn off the heat.

Discard the bay leaf, cinnamon stick, and lemon zest from the lamb sauce. Line the bottom of a 9 by 13-inch baking dish with half of the eggplant. Top with half the lamb mixture. Repeat with the remaining eggplant and lamb sauce. Pour the béchamel over the top and sprinkle with the remaining ¾ cup cheese. Bake until browned and bubbling, 30 to 40 minutes.

[Make-ahead: Let cool, cover, and refrigerate.]

[**Night of:** Return the moussaka to room temp while you preheat the oven to 375°F. Bake, covered, to heat through, 20 to 25 minutes. Uncover, sprinkle with a little extra grated cheese, and bake to recrisp the top, 5 to 10 minutes more.]

Let the moussaka sit for at least 10 minutes before serving.

WEEK 29

DOUBLE TAKE

SOME UNEXPECTED TWISTS
(AND HIDDEN TREASURES) IN SOME
OF YOUR FAVORITE MEALS WILL
HAVE YOU DOING DOUBLE TAKES.

DISH
1
PORK TENDERLOIN
POSOLE WITH
BOTTOM-OF-THE-
BOWL NACHO
SURPRISE
PAGE 213

DISH
2
MEXICAN
CHORIZO
STRATA
PAGE 214

DISH
3
DRUNKEN
SPAGHETTI WITH
HOT SALAMI
MEAT SAUCE
PAGE 216

DISH
4
FRENCH ONION
SOUP-TOPPED
FRENCH BREAD
PIZZAS
PAGE 217

DISH
5
REUBEN-STYLE
SHEPHERD'S PIE
PAGE 218

Pork Tenderloin Posole with Bottom-of-the-Bowl Nacho Surprise

In this recipe, you'll be roasting enough chiles for two dishes: this posole and Mexican Chorizo Strata (page 214). SERVES 6

8 **New Mexico green chiles** or 6 **poblano** or **Anaheim chiles**

3 tablespoons **EVOO**

2 pounds **pork tenderloin**, cut into ½-inch cubes

Kosher salt and **pepper**

2 ribs **celery**, chopped

2 medium **onions**, chopped

4 cloves **garlic**, chopped

4 or 5 **tomatillos**, husked, rinsed, and chopped

1 tablespoon ground **cumin**

1 tablespoon ground **coriander**

1½ teaspoons dried **Mexican oregano**, lightly crushed

1 tablespoon **honey**

2 (15-ounce) cans **white** or **yellow hominy**, drained

6 cups **chicken stock**

Good-quality **tortilla chips**

2 cups shredded **asadero** or **jack cheese**

1 **avocado**, cut into small cubes

Lime **wedges**

Cilantro leaves, torn, for garnish (optional)

Char the chiles all over on the stovetop over a gas flame or under the broiler with the oven door ajar to let steam escape. Place the chiles in a bowl and cover tightly. When cool enough to handle, rub off the skins with a paper towel, then halve, seed, and chop. Set aside 3 New Mexico or 2 poblano chiles to use in Mexican Chorizo Strata (page 214).

In a large Dutch oven, heat the EVOO (3 turns of the pan) over medium to medium high heat. Add the pork, season with salt and pepper, and cook until browned and crisp at the edges. Transfer the pork to a plate. Add the celery, onions, and garlic to the pan and cook to soften, about 5 minutes. Add the tomatillos, cumin, coriander, oregano, and salt and pepper and cook 5 minutes more. Stir in the honey, hominy, stock, and chopped chiles. Transfer half the soup to a food processor and puree, then return to the pot along with the pork. Simmer at a low bubble until the pork is tender, 20 to 30 minutes.

[**Make-ahead:** Let cool and refrigerate.]

[**Night of:** Return the posole to room temp before reheating gently over medium heat, partially covered.]

Pile a few tortilla chips into the bottoms of 6 shallow soup bowls. Top with cheese, avocado, and a squeeze of lime. Top that with the posole and garnish with cilantro, if desired. Serve immediately for the best mix of textures.

Mexican Chorizo Strata

This is another of those dishes I call "breakfast for dinner." If you'd like, you can use 2 cans (4 ounces each) of chopped green chiles instead of the home-roasted chiles.

SERVES 4 TO 6

EVOO or vegetable oil, for drizzling

1 pound fresh Mexican chorizo or other spicy bulk sausage, casings removed

7 or 8 thick slices (1 inch thick) good-quality stale white or egg-based bread, cut into large cubes

3 fresh New Mexico green or 2 poblano or Anaheim chiles, roasted and chopped (from Pork Tenderloin Posole, page 213)

2 cups milk

8 tablespoons (1 stick) butter, melted and cooled to room temp

6 large eggs

1 tablespoon hot sauce

Kosher salt and pepper

2½ cups shredded sharp cheddar cheese

1 avocado

Juice of 1 lime

1 cup sour cream

Diced heirloom tomatoes, for garnish

Cilantro leaves, torn, for garnish

In a large skillet, heat a drizzle of EVOO. Add the chorizo and cook, breaking it into crumbles as it browns. Set aside.

Arrange the bread in a shallow 2- to 3-quart baking dish. Add the chorizo and gently move the bread around to get some of the chorizo down into the nooks and crannies. Arrange the chiles over the top.

In a large bowl, whisk together the milk, melted butter, eggs, hot sauce, and salt and pepper. Pour the mixture over the bread. Top with the cheddar.

[Make-ahead: Cover and refrigerate for at least overnight and up to a couple of days.]

[Night of: Return the strata to room temp while you preheat the oven.]

Preheat the oven to 325°F.

Put the strata on a baking sheet and bake until the eggs are set and the top is golden, about 1 hour.

Meanwhile, scoop the avocado into a food processor. Add the lime juice, sour cream, and salt and pepper and process to a puree.

Serve the strata topped with tomatoes, cilantro, and dollops of green sour cream.

Drunken Spaghetti with Hot Salami Meat Sauce

I love cooking with wine, and this dish is one of a few in this book where you use an entire bottle of wine to cook with. (Two other dishes I can think of are coq au vin and boeuf bourguignonne.) SERVES 4

2 tablespoons **EVOO**

⅓ pound **Calabrese salami** or good-quality **pepperoni**, casings removed, shredded on the large holes of a box grater

1 pound **ground lamb** or **beef**

Kosher salt and **pepper**

1 medium **onion**, very finely chopped

1 **carrot**, grated

4 cloves **garlic**, grated or finely chopped

Leaves from 1 or 2 sprigs fresh **rosemary**, very finely chopped

1 fresh **bay leaf**

3 tablespoons **tomato paste**

1 (750 ml) bottle plus 1 cup (save the rest for dinner) **dry red wine**

1 cup **chicken stock**

1 (28- or 32-ounce) can **San Marzano tomatoes** (look for DOP on the label)

1 pound **spaghetti**

A few **fresh basil** leaves, torn

Grated **pecorino cheese**

In a Dutch oven, heat the EVOO (2 turns of the pan) over medium-high heat. Add the salami and render some of the fat. Add the lamb and cook, breaking it into crumbles as it browns. Season with a little salt and a good amount of pepper. Add the onion, carrot, garlic, rosemary, and bay leaf and cook to soften the onion, about 5 minutes. Add the tomato paste and stir 1 minute. Deglaze the pan with 1 cup of the wine. Add the stock and tomatoes, breaking them up a bit with a potato masher, and cook for 30 minutes to thicken.

[**Make-ahead:** Let cool and refrigerate.]

[**Night of:** Return the meat sauce to room temp before reheating gently over medium heat while you cook the pasta. Discard the bay leaf.]

In a large saucepan, bring the bottle of wine plus 2 cups water to a boil. Salt the boiling liquid and cook the pasta al dente. Ladle out about a cup of the starchy cooking liquid. Drain the pasta and return it to the pot. Add the sauce and some of the starchy liquid, tossing with tongs for 1 or 2 minutes for the flavors to absorb.

Serve in shallow bowls topped with torn basil and lots of tangy pecorino.

French Onion Soup–Topped French Bread Pizzas

Pizza Night just got even better. **Suggested side:** Salad with Dijon Vinaigrette (recipe follows). SERVES 4

8 tablespoons (1 stick) **butter**
6 large **yellow onions**, very thinly sliced
1 teaspoon ground **thyme**
2 fresh **bay leaves**
Kosher salt and **pepper**
⅓ cup **dry sherry**
1 (10-ounce) can **beef consommé**
1 large (24-inch) or 2 medium (12-inch) loaves **French bread**
¾ pound ripe **Camembert cheese**, sliced
2 cups shredded **Gruyère cheese**

In a large deep skillet, melt the butter over medium heat. Add the onions, thyme, bay leaves, and salt and pepper. Cook low and slow until deeply caramel in color and very sweet, 35 to 40 minutes. Deglaze the pan with the sherry. Stir in the consommé. Cook over low heat to thicken up a bit. It should be wet but not soupy.

[**Make-ahead:** Let cool and refrigerate.]

[**Night of:** Return the soup to room temp. Discard the bay leaves. Add a splash of water to loosen and reheat gently over medium heat while you preheat the oven.]

Preheat the oven to 400°F.

Slice the loaf (or loaves) in half horizontally. If using the longer loaf, cut each of those pieces in half crosswise. You want 4 "pizza" bases. Place the bread on a baking sheet and toast in the oven. Top with the onion mixture (letting the liquid soak into the bread) and both cheeses. Return to the oven to melt and lightly brown the cheese.

Salad with Dijon Vinaigrette SERVES 4

1 tablespoon **honey** or 1 teaspoon **superfine sugar**
2 tablespoons **white wine vinegar** or **white balsamic vinegar**
2 teaspoons **lemon** juice
1 small **shallot**, grated
1 tablespoon **Dijon mustard**
⅓ cup **EVOO**
Kosher salt and **pepper**
6 to 8 cups chopped earthy or crisp **greens** (such as spinach, escarole, or romaine hearts)

In a large bowl, combine the honey, vinegar, lemon juice, and shallot and let sit for 5 to 10 minutes. Whisk in the mustard and EVOO and season with salt and pepper. Toss the greens with the dressing.

Reuben-Style Shepherd's Pie

A hearty casserole inspired by the flavors of the classic sandwich. SERVES 6

SQUASHED POTATO TOPPER
2 pounds **baby red** or **yellow
  potatoes**
Kosher salt and **pepper**
2 tablespoons **EVOO**
2 tablespoons **butter**
1 teaspoon **caraway seeds**

FILLING
2 tablespoons **EVOO**
1 pound thick-cut, good-quality
  corned beef, chopped
1 pound **ground beef sirloin**
1 **carrot**, chopped
2 or 3 small ribs **celery** with leafy
  tops, finely chopped

1 **onion**, chopped
3 or 4 cloves **garlic**, finely chopped
1 large fresh **bay leaf**
Kosher salt and **pepper**
3 tablespoons **butter**
2 rounded tablespoons **flour**
1 cup **lager beer**, at room
  temperature
1 (10-ounce) can **beef consommé**
  or 1½ cups **beef stock**
3 tablespoons **Worcestershire
  sauce**
2 tablespoons **Dijon mustard**
1 pound **sauerkraut**, rinsed and
  well drained

1½ cups shredded **Swiss cheese**
1 cup shredded or crumbled
  sharp white cheddar cheese

RUSSIAN DRESSING TOPPER
1 cup **sour cream**
⅓ cup good-quality **ketchup**
2 tablespoons **sweet pickle relish**
Few dashes of **hot sauce**
Kosher salt and **pepper**

1 small bunch **watercress**,
  chopped, for garnish

Preheat the oven to 400°F.

Make the squashed potato topper: In a large saucepan of boiling salted water, cook the potatoes until just tender, 15 to 20 minutes. In a skillet, heat the EVOO and butter over medium heat. Add the caraway seeds and toast. Drain the potatoes and toss with the caraway mixture; season with salt and pepper. Arrange the potatoes on a baking sheet; use the bottom of a glass to squish and flatten them. Roast to crispy, 25 to 30 minutes.

[If making this to serve on **Cook Day**, leave the oven on. If making this for later in the week, you'll preheat the oven on the night of.]

Meanwhile, make the filling: In a large Dutch oven, heat the EVOO (2 turns of the pan) over medium-high heat. Add the corned beef and brown. Add the ground beef and cook, breaking it into crumbles as it browns. Transfer to a plate. Cook the carrot, celery, onion, garlic, bay leaf, and salt and pepper until soft, about 5 minutes. Return the meat to the pan and set aside.

In a small saucepan, melt the butter over medium heat. Whisk in the flour and cook until light golden. Whisk in the beer, consommé, Worcestershire, and mustard; season with pepper.

Scrape the meat mixture into a shallow 3-quart casserole. Pour the sauce over the meat. Top with the sauerkraut. Combine the cheeses and sprinkle 2 cups over the sauerkraut. Top with the smashed potatoes. Sprinkle the remaining cheese over the potatoes.

[**Make-ahead:** Let cool and refrigerate.]

[**Night of:** Return the casserole to room temp while you preheat the oven to 375°F.]

Make the Russian dressing topper: In a small bowl, stir together all the ingredients.

Bake the pie until heated through and the cheese has melted. Serve with drizzled dressing and garnished with watercress.

WEEK 30

TWO FOR ONE

A WEEK'S WORTH OF SOUP AND
SAMMY-STYLE SUPPERS

DISH
1
HOT OPEN-FACED
CREAMED CHICKEN
WITH TARRAGON
OVER BUTTERED
TOAST
PAGE 221

DISH
2
COLD CHICKEN
CURRY SAMMIES WITH
TOASTED ALMONDS &
CRYSTALLIZED
GINGER
PAGE 222

DISH
3
MEDITERRANEAN
BEAN &
BACON
SOUP
PAGE 223

DISH
4
FRENCH
STEWED
CHICKEN
THIGHS
PAGE 224

DISH
5
ROMESCO
SEAFOOD
STEW
PAGE 225

Hot Open-Faced Creamed Chicken with Tarragon over Buttered Toast

This is food that I remember from when I was a little kid. My mom cooked a lot of Italian, of course (she's Sicilian), but she also cooked a lot of New England-y American food, like this. SERVES 4

3 tablespoons **butter**, plus more, softened, for toast

2 tablespoons **flour**

⅓ cup **white wine**

1½ cups **chicken stock**, homemade (page 322) or store-bought

Kosher salt and **white** or **black pepper**

¾ cup frozen **baby peas**, thawed

1 (4-ounce) jar chopped **pimientos**, drained well

½ cup **heavy cream**

Freshly grated **nutmeg**

2 to 3 tablespoons chopped fresh **tarragon**, plus more for garnish

1 rounded tablespoon **Dijon mustard**

1⅓ to 1½ pounds shredded **Poached Chicken** (page 322); see Note

4 thick slices (1 inch thick) good-quality **white bread**

In a saucepan, melt 3 tablespoons butter over medium heat. Whisk in the flour and cook for 1 minute. Whisk in the wine and cook for 1 minute. Whisk in the stock and cook until thick enough to lightly coat the back of a spoon. Season with salt and pepper. Stir in the peas, pimientos, and cream and return to a bubble. Add a pinch of nutmeg. Mix in the tarragon, Dijon mustard, and chicken.

[Make-ahead: Let cool and refrigerate.]

[Night of: Return the chicken to room temp before reheating gently, partially covered, over medium heat.]

Toast the bread and butter liberally. Cut the bread in half corner to corner. Ladle the chicken over the toast points, garnish with tarragon, and serve.

Note: Make the following changes to the Basic Poached Chicken (page 322): Use 6 bone-in, skin-on chicken breast halves or 3 full breasts attached at the breastbone. Add 4 cloves garlic, smashed. Poach the chicken for 45 minutes.

Cold Chicken Curry Sammies with Toasted Almonds & Crystallized Ginger

Suggested side: Exotic root vegetable or sweet potato chips. SERVES 4

1 cup **Greek yogurt**, **Veganaise**, or **mayo**

2 tablespoons **curry powder** (see Heads-up)

Juice of 1 **lemon**

Kosher salt and **pepper**

1 small **green apple**, peeled and finely chopped

1 **carrot**, shredded

4 **scallions**, finely chopped

1⅓ to 1½ pounds shredded **Poached Chicken** (see Note, page 221)

Butter, softened

4 **brioche lobster rolls**, split

Chopped crispy **romaine heart** or other lettuce of choice

½ to ⅔ cup **slivered almonds**, toasted, for garnish

Crystalized ginger, very thinly sliced, for garnish

Combine the Greek yogurt, curry powder, lemon juice, and salt and pepper. Add the apple, carrot, scallions, and chicken. Mix to combine and taste to adjust seasonings.

[Make-ahead: Cover and refrigerate.]

[Night of: Take the chicken salad out of the fridge.]

Butter the rolls and toast them on a hot griddle. Fill with lettuce and chicken salad. Garnish with almonds and crystallized ginger.

Heads-up: If you want to make your own curry blend, stir together 1 teaspoon each ground cumin, coriander, and turmeric, and ½ teaspoon each dry mustard and ground ginger.

Mediterranean Bean & Bacon Soup

When I buy a hard grating cheese like Parm, I always get a piece with rind on it and then I save the rind for adding to soups. It adds great flavor. SERVES 4

3 tablespoons **EVOO**, plus more for drizzling

⅓ pound **pancetta**, finely diced

2 medium **carrots**, finely diced

2 or 3 small ribs **celery**, finely diced

1 **onion**, finely diced

4 cloves **garlic**, finely chopped or grated

1 large fresh **bay leaf**

Herb bundle: sprigs of **parsley**, **sage**, **rosemary**, and **thyme**, tied together with kitchen twine

Kosher salt and **pepper**

2 tablespoons **tomato paste**

½ cup **dry white wine**

6 cups **chicken stock**, homemade (page 322) or store-bought (see Heads-up)

2 (15-ounce) cans **cannellini beans**, drained

1 small bunch **lacinato kale** (also called black, Tuscan, or dinosaur kale), stemmed and thinly shredded or finely chopped

Freshly grated **nutmeg**

Parmigiano-Reggiano cheese rind (optional)

Shaved **Parmigiano-Reggiano cheese**, for serving

In a Dutch oven or medium soup pot, heat the EVOO (3 turns of the pan) over medium-high heat. Add the pancetta and cook to crisp. Add the carrots, celery, onion, garlic, bay leaf, herb bundle, and salt and pepper. Cook until the vegetables are tender, 7 to 8 minutes. Add the tomato paste and stir for 1 minute. Deglaze the pan with the wine. Add the stock and bring to a low boil.

In a food processor, combine 1 can of the beans with a few ladles of broth from the soup and puree. Stir the puree into the soup along with the remaining whole beans. Wilt in the kale and season with a hint of nutmeg. Add the cheese rind (if using) and simmer for 15 minutes at a low bubble for the flavors to combine. Taste and adjust seasonings.

[Make-ahead: Let cool and refrigerate.]

[Night of: Return the soup to room temp before reheating gently, partially covered, over medium heat. Add a cup of water if it becomes too thick to ladle.]

Remove the cheese rind, herb bundle, and bay leaf. Serve the soup in shallow bowls, topped with shaved Parm and a drizzle of EVOO.

Heads-up: You may have to supplement the homemade stock with store-bought here.

French Stewed Chicken Thighs

Because this is a French-style dish, sort of inspired by Provençal cooking, I used picholine olives. It makes me feel fancy just to say the word *picholine,* but you could use any buttery olives (or even, shhhhh, leave them out). **Suggested side:** Baguette, sliced on an angle, toasted. SERVES 4

8 bone-in, skinless **chicken thighs**

Kosher salt and **pepper**

1 rounded teaspoon ground **thyme**

Flour, for dredging

2 tablespoons **EVOO**

4 tablespoons (½ stick) **butter**

½ pound **button mushrooms**, quartered

2 large **shallots**, finely chopped

1 **carrot**, finely chopped

½ teaspoon **sugar**

½ cup **dry white wine**

1 (28- or 32-ounce) can **crushed tomatoes**

¼ cup fresh **tarragon** leaves, chopped

⅓ cup **picholine olives**, pitted and finely chopped

Season the chicken with salt, pepper, and thyme. Dredge the chicken in the flour.

In a Dutch oven, heat the EVOO (2 turns of the pan) over medium-high heat. Add the chicken and cook until browned and crisp on the first side, 7 to 8 minutes; flip the thighs and cook until browned on the second side, 3 to 4 minutes. Transfer to a plate.

Add 2 tablespoons butter to the drippings and melt over medium heat. Add the mushrooms and lightly brown. Add the shallots and carrot and sprinkle with the sugar; season with salt and pepper. Cook a couple of minutes to soften the vegetables. Deglaze the pan with the wine. Stir in the tomatoes, tarragon, and olives and bring to a bubble. Set the chicken in the stew without submerging it and simmer, partially covered, for 30 minutes.

[Make-ahead: Let cool and refrigerate.]

[Night of: Return the chicken to room temp before reheating gently over medium heat.]

Romesco Seafood Stew

The stew base here is made ahead and refrigerated, but buy the seafood no earlier than 48 hours before you plan on serving this. SERVES 4

ROMESCO SAUCE
2 **dried pasilla** or 1 **ancho chile**, stemmed and seeded
Water or **chicken stock**, to cover
4 roasted **piquillo peppers**
1 large or 2 medium **tomatoes**, coarsely grated
2 slices (¾ to 1 inch thick) stale good-quality **white bread**, diced
¼ cup **Marcona almonds**, toasted
¼ cup blanched **hazelnuts**, toasted
2 cloves **garlic**, pasted
⅓ cup **EVOO**
1½ tablespoons **sherry vinegar**

1 tablespoon **sweet paprika** (smoked or regular)
Kosher salt and **pepper**

STEW BASE
¼ cup **EVOO**
1½ pounds small **white** or **yellow potatoes**, chopped
Kosher salt and **pepper**
2 small ribs **celery**, finely chopped
1 **onion**, finely chopped
1 large fresh **bay leaf**, finely chopped
1 bunch fresh **flat-leaf parsley**, tied with kitchen twine

1 cup **dry white wine**
2 cups **seafood** or **chicken stock**

4 thick, thick slices **ciabatta bread**
1 large clove **garlic**, halved
EVOO, for drizzling
Fine **sea salt**
24 small **mussels** or small **clams**, scrubbed or purged
¾ pound peeled, deveined medium **shrimp**
4 thick center-cut **cod fillets**
4 slices **serrano ham**
Gremolata (page 244)

Make the romesco sauce: In a dry saucepan, toast the chiles briefly. Add water to cover and bring to a low boil. Simmer until softened, about 10 minutes. Transfer to a food processor with a splash of the soaking liquid. Add the piquillos, tomatoes, bread, almonds, hazelnuts, garlic, EVOO, vinegar, paprika, and salt and pepper. Process until an almost smooth but thick sauce forms.

Make the stew base: In a Dutch oven, heat the EVOO (4 turns of the pan) over medium to medium-high heat. Add the potatoes, season with salt and pepper, and cook until lightly browned. Add the celery, onion, bay leaf, and parsley bundle and cook 5 minutes more. Deglaze the pan with the wine. Stir in the stock and the romesco sauce. Bring to a bubble and simmer until the potatoes are just tender, 5 to 10 minutes.

[Make-ahead: Let cool and refrigerate.]

[Night of: Return the stew base to room temp and bring to a low boil over medium heat.]

Preheat the oven to 375°F. Place a cooling rack on a baking sheet.

Place the ciabatta bread on the rack and toast in the oven. Rub the hot bread with the cut sides of the garlic, drizzle with a little EVOO, and sprinkle with salt. Leave the oven on.

When the stew base is at a low boil, add the mussels and shrimp, then cover and cook until the mussels open and the shrimp are firm and opaque. Discard any unopened mussels (or clams).

Meanwhile, in a large nonstick ovenproof skillet, heat a drizzle of EVOO over medium-high heat. Wrap each piece of fish in a slice of ham. Place in the pan and cook until crisp on both sides, 2 minutes each. Transfer to the oven to cook the fish through, about 5 minutes. Remove the fish from the heat.

To serve, ladle the stew into shallow bowls. Set a piece of fish in the center. Garnish with gremolata. Serve with the garlic toasts.

WEEK 31

SEASON'S SERVINGS

AROUND THE HOLIDAYS,
PEOPLE ARE ALWAYS COMING AND
GOING. AND IF YOUR FRIENDS AND FAMILY ARE LIKE
MINE, THEY'RE USUALLY HUNGRY.
SO HERE'S A WEEK'S WORTH OF MEALS
TO KEEP THE CROWDS FED . . . IN STYLE.

DISH
1
RUBY PORT–BRAISED
SHORT RIBS &
MASHED
POTATOES
PAGE 227

DISH
2
PROSCIUTTO- OR
PANCETTA-WRAPPED
PORK ROAST WITH
FENNEL & GOLDEN
RAISIN STUFFING
PAGE 228

DISH
3
PASTITSIO
WITH LAMB &
SAUSAGE
PAGE 230

DISH
4
WINTER
WHITE
COQ AU VIN
PAGE 231

DISH
5
SARTÙ
(RISOTTO
TIMBALE)
PAGE 232

Ruby Port–Braised Short Ribs & Mashed Potatoes

Whenever you're doing a braise, like this one, the first really important step is to get the meat to a nice, crusty deep brown. That adds to the flavor of the dish. **Suggested side:** Steamed green beans or a green salad. SERVES 6

12 bone-in **beef short ribs**
Kosher salt and coarsely ground **pepper**
4 to 5 tablespoons **grapeseed oil** or **vegetable oil**
2 **carrots**, chopped
2 ribs **celery** with leafy tops, chopped
2 **onions**, chopped
2 to 3 tablespoons **flour**
2 tablespoons **tomato paste**
1 (750 ml) bottle **ruby port**
4 cups **beef stock**
Herb bundle: 10 to 12 sprigs fresh **thyme**, 8 to 10 fresh **sage** leaves, 4 sprigs fresh **rosemary** (5 to 6 inches long), 2 or 3 sprigs fresh **marjoram** or **oregano**, small handful **flat-leaf parsley**, tied with kitchen twine
1 head **garlic**, halved horizontally
2½ to 3 pounds **starchy potatoes**, peeled and cubed (4 or 5 potatoes)
1 cup **heavy cream**
4 tablespoons (½ stick) **unsalted butter**
Scant ¼ teaspoon freshly grated **nutmeg**
Pomegranate seeds, for garnish (optional)
3 tablespoons chopped **flat-leaf parsley**, for garnish

Preheat the oven to 325°F.

Pat the meat dry and sprinkle liberally with salt and pepper. In a large Dutch oven, heat 2 tablespoons of the oil (2 turns of the pan) over medium-high heat. In 2 batches, add the meat and brown well on all sides. Transfer the meat to a plate.

Drain off the fat from the pot and pour in the remaining 2 to 3 tablespoons oil. Add the carrots, celery, and onions and cook to soften, 6 to 7 minutes. Stir in the flour and cook for 1 minute. Stir in the tomato paste until fragrant. Pour in the port and return the ribs to the pot. Bring to a boil, reduce the heat to a simmer, and cook until the port is reduced by half, about 30 minutes.

Stir in the stock and add the herb bundle and garlic. Return to a boil, cover, and bake in the oven until the beef is tender, about 2½ hours.

[**Make-ahead:** Let the beef and sauce cool and refrigerate.]

[**Night of:** Return the meat and sauce to room temp and reheat gently over medium heat.]

As soon as the beef comes out of the oven (or goes onto the stovetop to reheat, if this is make-ahead), place the potatoes in a large pot of salted water, bring to a boil, and cook until tender.

Transfer the beef to a platter. Strain the sauce and discard the solids. Return the sauce to the pan and skim the fat (one good way to do this is to fill a metal ladle with ice and dip the ladle into the sauce; the fat will stick to the bottom of the ladle). Return the sauce to the heat to reduce and thicken a bit. Season the sauce with salt and pepper.

Drain the potatoes and return to the cooking pot. Mash with the cream and butter and season with the nutmeg and salt and pepper.

Serve the ribs with the potatoes and top with the sauce, pomegranate seeds (if using), and the chopped parsley.

Prosciutto- or Pancetta-Wrapped Pork Roast with Fennel & Golden Raisin Stuffing

A mind-blowingly delicious meal (especially for my husband, who can eat pork at every meal), this is three porks in one: pork inside pork wrapped in pork. SERVES 6

STUFFING
⅓ cup **golden raisins**
2 tablespoons **butter**
1 tablespoon **EVOO**
3 or 4 cloves **garlic**, finely chopped
1 small **bulb fennel**, chopped, plus ¼ cup chopped **fronds**
1 **onion**, chopped
Salt and **pepper**
½ cup **dry white wine**
1 pound **ground pork**

¼ cup **pine nuts**, lightly toasted
2 tablespoons chopped fresh **thyme**

PORK ROAST
3 pounds trimmed boneless **pork loin** roast
Salt and **pepper**
⅓ pound thinly sliced (but not shaved) **prosciutto di Parma** or **pancetta**

24 **cipollini onions**
6 tablespoons **EVOO**
2 pounds small **Yukon Gold** or **white potatoes**, halved
¼ cup chopped fresh **rosemary**
3 heads **garlic**, halved horizontally
1 cup **white wine**
1 cup **chicken stock**
4 tablespoons (½ stick) **butter**

Make the stuffing: Soften the raisins in boiling water to cover.

In a skillet, melt the butter in the EVOO over medium heat. Add the garlic, chopped fennel bulb, and onion; sprinkle with salt and pepper, and cook until the vegetables soften, 12 to 15 minutes. Deglaze with the wine. Transfer to a bowl and let cool completely.

Drain and chop the raisins and add to the fennel. Add the ground pork, pine nuts, and thyme.

[If making this to serve on **Cook Day**, preheat the oven to 400°F. If making this for later in the week, you'll preheat the oven the night of.]

Make the pork roast: With one short end facing you, measure one-third down from the top of the loin; make a horizontal lengthwise cut going almost but not all the way through to the opposite side. Open the roast up like a book. Make a lengthwise cut going back in the other direction (basically a mirror image of the first cut you made), halfway down into the thicker side of the roast. Open up the pork loin; it should be butterflied into a single slab. Pound the meat to ¾ inch thick; sprinkle with salt and pepper. Spread the stuffing over the meat, leaving a 1-inch border. Roll up the pork, cover with overlapping slices of prosciutto, and tie with kitchen twine to secure.

[**Make-ahead:** Wrap the stuffed pork in plastic and store up to 2 days in the refrigerator.]

[**Night of:** Return the roast to room temp while you preheat the oven to 400°F.]

Add the cipollini to a saucepan of boiling water; cook for 3 minutes. Drain and cold-shock, then peel and trim. In a large heavy skillet, heat 2 tablespoons EVOO over medium-high heat. Brown the pork evenly all over. Toss the potatoes and onions in a roasting pan with the rosemary, garlic, the remaining ¼ cup EVOO, and some salt and pepper. Set the browned roast on top and deglaze the skillet with the wine. Pour the liquid over the pork. Roast until the internal temperature reaches 145°F, about 2 hours. Let the roast rest 30 minutes under a foil tent.

Before serving, place the roasting pan on a burner, deglaze with the stock, and stir in the fennel fronds and butter. Slice the roast, spoon the pan juices over the top, and serve with the potatoes and onions.

Pastitsio with Lamb & Sausage

SERVES 6 TO 8

BÉCHAMEL SAUCE
6 tablespoons **butter**
6 tablespoons all-purpose **flour**
4 cups **milk**
Salt and **pepper**
Freshly grated **nutmeg**
3 **egg** yolks, beaten
¾ to 1 cup grated **Parmigiano-Reggiano cheese**

SPICY MEAT SAUCE
2 tablespoons **EVOO**
1 pound **ground lamb**
½ pound bulk **hot Italian sausage** or links, casings removed
1 large fresh **bay leaf**
5 or 6 cloves **garlic**, chopped
1 **onion**, finely chopped
1 fresh **red Fresno chile**, seeded and finely chopped
3 tablespoons minced fresh **rosemary**
Salt and **pepper**
2 tablespoons **tomato paste**
2 cups **dry red wine**
2 cups **chicken** or **beef stock**
1 (28-ounce) can **San Marzano tomatoes**
1 long strip **orange** or **lemon** zest
1 **cinnamon stick**

PASTA
Salt
1½ pounds **Greek macaroni** (see Heads-up)
3 **egg** whites
½ cup grated **Parmigiano-Reggiano cheese**
EVOO, for the baking dish

Make the béchamel sauce: In a saucepan, melt the butter over medium heat. Whisk in the flour and cook for 1 minute. Whisk in the milk; season with salt and pepper and a little nutmeg. Cook the sauce until thick enough to coat the back of a spoon. Adjust the seasonings. Whisk a ladleful of sauce into the yolks to warm them; add to the sauce. Stir in the Parm and remove from the heat.

Make the spicy meat sauce: In a large Dutch oven, heat 2 tablespoons EVOO (2 turns of the pan) over medium-high heat. Add the lamb and sausage and brown well, breaking it into crumbles as it cooks. Stir in the bay leaf, garlic, onion, chile, and rosemary and sprinkle with salt and pepper. Cook until the onion softens, about 5 minutes. Stir in the tomato paste and cook until fragrant. Pour in the wine and cook to reduce by half. Add the stock and tomatoes, breaking them up with a potato masher, and reduce the heat to a simmer. Add the citrus zest and cinnamon and simmer for 30 minutes. Discard the zest, cinnamon stick, and bay leaf.

Cook the pasta: Bring a large pot of water to a boil. Salt the water and cook the pasta until 2 minutes shy of al dente. Ladle out about a cup of the starchy cooking water and add to the sauce.

Beat the egg whites until frothy and combine with the Parm. Drain the pasta and toss it with the egg whites.

[If making this to serve on **Cook Day**, preheat the oven to 350°F. If making this to serve later in the week, you'll preheat the oven on the night of.]

Grease a 9 by 13-inch baking dish with EVOO. Spoon in half the pasta; top with all the meat sauce, then the remaining pasta. Pour the béchamel on top.

[**Make-ahead:** Let cool and refrigerate or freeze.]

[**Night of:** Return the pastitsio to room temp while you preheat the oven to 350°F.]

Set the pastitsio on a baking sheet to catch any drips and bake until deeply golden on top, about 1 hour. Let stand at least 20 minutes before serving.

Heads-up: The traditional pasta for pastitsio is Greek #2 macaroni, which is long, super-fat hollow spaghetti. But if you can't find it, substitute ziti or bucatini.

Winter White Coq au Vin

I *love* coq au vin. I don't care if you make it with white or red wine, it's just a fantastic make-ahead meal. And I love wine. It was my first word: *vino*. So, heck yeah, this is one of my faves. **Suggested side:** Crusty baguette, warmed (see Heads-up). SERVES 4 TO 6

1 whole **chicken** (4 to 5 pounds), cut into 8 pieces
Salt and **pepper**
Flour, for dredging
8 tablespoons (1 stick) **butter**
EVOO, for drizzling
1 cup peeled fresh or frozen **pearl onions** (thawed and drained)
3 or 4 cloves **garlic**, sliced
2 ribs **celery** from the heart with leafy tops, finely chopped
1 baby **fennel** or ¼ small **fennel bulb**, thinly sliced
1 **leek**, thinly sliced
1 large fresh **bay leaf**
1 (750 ml) bottle **dry white wine** (such as white burgundy)
1 to 1½ cups **chicken stock**, if needed
1 cup **crème fraîche**
¼ cup **Dijon mustard**
2 to 3 tablespoons chopped fresh **tarragon**

Sprinkle the chicken with salt and pepper and dredge in flour.

In a Dutch oven, melt 2 tablespoons of the butter over medium-high heat. Working in batches, brown the chicken well. Transfer to a plate.

Add a drizzle of EVOO to the pan with the remaining 6 tablespoons butter, pearl onions, garlic, celery, fennel, and leek. Sprinkle the vegetables with salt and pepper and cook until lightly browned, 7 to 8 minutes. Stir in the bay leaf and wine, return the chicken to the pan, and cook, partially covered, at a low, rolling simmer for 30 minutes.

[**Make-ahead:** Let cool and then refrigerate.]

[**Night of:** Return to room temp. Reheat, partially covered, over low to medium-low heat.]

Transfer the chicken to a warm platter. Remove the bay leaf. Return the pan to the heat and simmer to reduce the juices (add stock if the liquid is getting too low). Stir in the crème fraîche, mustard, and tarragon.

To serve, spoon the sauce over the chicken.

Heads-up: If you're making the coq au vin as a make-ahead, keep the baguette wrapped in plastic until the night you serve the dish, then re-crisp it in the oven.

Sartù (Risotto Timbale)

You will need a 1½- to 2-quart baking mold or ovenproof bowl to prepare this Neapolitan classic, *sartù*. Traditionally this is labor-intensive, including rolling and frying mini meatballs to fill the rice dome. Here, a simple but rich meat sauce is prepared and layered with peas and mozzarella. It's impressive, to be sure, and can be prepared a few days ahead and baked the night you wish to serve. **Suggested side:** A simple salad of romaine, radicchio, and endive, tossed with balsamic vinegar and olive oil. SERVES 6

RISOTTO
2 cups **chicken stock**
A generous pinch of **saffron threads**
2 tablespoons **EVOO**
½ pound **pancetta**, finely chopped
2 cloves **garlic**, finely chopped
1 small **onion**, finely chopped
1¼ cups **arborio** or **carnaroli rice**
½ cup **dry white wine**
½ cup grated **Parmigiano-Reggiano cheese**
2 tablespoons **butter**

MEAT AND MUSHROOM FILLING
1½ cups **chicken stock**
A handful of **dried porcini mushrooms** (about 1 ounce)
3 tablespoons **butter**
1 **onion**, chopped
¼ pound **chicken livers**, trimmed and chopped
¼ teaspoon ground **thyme**
Salt and **pepper**
Splash of **dry sherry** or **Marsala**
1 tablespoon **EVOO**
¾ pound **ground beef sirloin**
⅓ to ½ pound bulk **hot** or **sweet Italian sausage** or links, casings removed

3 or 4 cloves **garlic**, chopped
2 tablespoons **tomato paste**

ASSEMBLY
¼ pound fresh **mozzarella cheese**, diced
1 cup frozen **green peas**, thawed
A handful of fresh **basil** leaves, torn
1 small **plum tomato**, seeded and diced
Butter, softened
Panko bread crumbs

Make the risotto: In a saucepan, combine the stock, 1½ cups water, and the saffron. Heat and keep warm. In another saucepan, heat the EVOO (2 turns of the pan) over medium to medium-high heat. Add the pancetta and cook to render, about 3 minutes. Stir in the garlic and onion and cook until softened, 3 to 4 minutes. Add the rice and stir for 1 minute. Pour in the wine and cook until absorbed, then begin adding the warm saffron liquid a few ladlefuls at a time, stirring frequently to develop the starches. The risotto will take exactly 18 minutes. Stir in the Parm and butter and remove from the heat.

Make the filling: In a small saucepan, heat the stock with the mushrooms to soften, 10 to 15 minutes. Reserving the soaking liquid, scoop out the mushrooms and chop.

In a large skillet, melt 2 tablespoons of the butter. Add the onion and cook to light caramel. Transfer to a plate. Melt the remaining 1 tablespoon butter, increase the heat slightly, and stir in the chicken livers. Sprinkle with the thyme and salt and pepper and brown, 3 to 4 minutes. Deglaze the pan with the sherry and transfer the mixture to a plate.

Pour the EVOO (1 turn of the pan) into the skillet. Once the oil is hot, brown the beef and sausage, breaking them into crumbles as they cook. Stir in the garlic and cook for 1 to 2 minutes. Return the onion and livers to the skillet with the tomato paste, mushrooms, and mushroom soaking liquid; leave the last few spoonfuls of liquid in the pan as grit may have settled there. Simmer over low heat to thicken and combine the flavors, about 3 minutes.

[If making this to serve on **Cook Day**, preheat the oven to 400°F. If making this for later in the week, you'll preheat the oven the night of.]

Assemble the sartù: In a small bowl, mix together the mozzarella, peas, basil, and tomato. Butter a baking mold or ovenproof bowl (I use a charlotte mold) and dust with panko. Spoon a little over half of the risotto into the mold, pressing the rice up against the sides to create a thickish wall. Spoon in the meat sauce. Create a small well in the center of the sauce and fill with the mozzarella mixture. Layer the rest of the risotto on top and smooth the surface. Dot the top with butter and an even coating of panko.

[**Make-ahead:** Let cool completely and refrigerate.]

[**Night of:** Return the mold to room temp while you preheat the oven to 400°F.]

Bake for 45 minutes. Let cool on a rack in the mold for 15 minutes. Loosen the edges with an offset spatula. Place a plate on top of the mold, invert, and serve.

WEEK 32

FIVE
FIESTA
FAVORITES

MEXICAN FOOD
LOVERS, LISTEN UP.
HERE ARE CINCO
SCRUMPTIOUS MEALS
YOU CAN MAKE IN
JUST UNO DAY.

DISH
1
CHICKEN
IN PUMPKIN
SEED SAUCE
PAGE 235

DISH
2
PORK WITH
CHILES &
ORANGE
SAUCE
PAGE 236

DISH
3
POBLANO MAC
'N' MANCHEGO
WITH CORN &
MUSHROOMS
PAGE 237

DISH
4
CHIPOTLE TURKEY
BREAST WITH
POMEGRANATE-
CRANBERRY RELISH
& POLENTA
PAGE 238

DISH
5
MEXICAN
CHORIZO &
TURKEY CHILI
PAGE 240

Chicken in Pumpkin Seed Sauce

It might seem weird to grind up pumpkin seeds and make a whole sauce out of them. But think about how many times you've used ground or chopped nuts, like pine nuts or almonds, in sauces. **Suggested side:** If you would like to serve this with a vegetable, steamed or sautéed zucchini is perfect. SERVES 4 TO 6

4 to 6 bone-in, skin-on **chicken breast** halves
Kosher salt
6 to 8 **black peppercorns**
2 fresh **bay leaves**
2 small to medium **white** or **yellow onions**: 1 quartered and 1 chopped
Herb bundle: several sprigs of fresh **cilantro, thyme**, and **marjoram** or **oregano**, tied with kitchen twine
1¼ cups raw hulled **pumpkin seeds** (pepitas)
2 or 3 leaves **romaine** or **green leaf lettuce**, torn
6 fresh **tomatillos**, husked, rinsed, and halved
2 fresh **serrano chiles** or 1 large **jalapeño**, halved and seeded
2 large cloves **garlic**, sliced
2 tablespoons **EVOO**
1 teaspoon ground **cumin**
Pinch of ground **cinnamon**
1 teaspoon **dried epazote** (optional)
Minced **red onion** and chopped **cilantro**, for garnish
Lime wedges
Charred **corn tortillas**, for serving

Place the chicken in a pot with just enough water to cover. Sprinkle with salt and add the peppercorns, bay leaves, quartered onion, and herb bundle. Bring to a low boil, then reduce the heat and poach the chicken low and slow until cooked through, 30 to 40 minutes. Remove the chicken from the broth. Strain the broth (discarding the solids) and set aside. When the chicken is cool enough to handle, discard the skin and cover the chicken to keep warm.

Wipe the pot clean and dry-toast the pumpkin seeds over medium heat until puffed and toasted, 4 to 5 minutes. Reserve ¼ cup for garnish. Puree the remaining seeds in a blender or food processor with 1 cup of the stock, the lettuce, chopped onion, tomatillos, chiles, garlic, EVOO, cumin, cinnamon, epazote (if using), and a little salt.

Combine the pumpkin seed puree with 2½ to 3 cups of the reserved chicken stock and simmer to develop flavor and thicken, 20 minutes. Adjust the seasonings.

[Make-ahead: Simmer the sauce only until not quite thick enough to serve, about 10 minutes. Return the chicken to the pot, turn off the heat, and let cool before covering and storing. Adjust the seasonings after you reheat.]

[Night of: Reheat the sauce over medium heat to thicken. Adjust the seasonings.]

Add the chicken to the sauce to heat through. Serve the chicken with lots of sauce and garnish with the reserved toasted pumpkin seeds, red onion, and cilantro. Give the whole thing a little squirt of lime. Serve with warm corn tortillas, for wrapping.

Recipe for Quick Pickled Onions
View a bonus Side Dish recipe.

Pork with Chiles & Orange Sauce

A delicious, easy, and surprisingly healthful Mexican meal. If you're going to serve this on **Cook Day**, and you want to make the Quick Pickled Onions (see QR code above), be sure to make them first, since they have to marinate for at least 2 hours. SERVES 4 TO 6

PORK
1½ pounds **pork shoulder** (pork butt)
Kosher salt
4 **guajillo chiles** (see Heads-up) or other medium-heat **dried red chiles**, stemmed and seeded
Grated zest and juice of 2 organic **oranges** or **blood oranges**
3 or 4 cloves **garlic**, grated
1 small **onion**, chopped
1 tablespoon **honey**
1 teaspoon dried **marjoram** or **Mexican oregano**
Pinch of ground **cinnamon**
Pinch of ground **cloves**
Coarsely ground **pepper**

TOPPINGS AND SIDES
1 tablespoon **butter**
1¼ cups **long-grain white rice**
2¼ cups **chicken stock** or water
Kosher salt
½ cup frozen **green peas**, thawed
2 (15-ounce) cans **black beans**
½ teaspoon ground **cumin**
Salt and **pepper**

Charred **corn tortillas**, for serving
Quick Pickled Onions (see QR code above), for serving
Cilantro leaves, torn, for garnish

Make the pork: Place the pork in a Dutch oven with just enough water to cover and sprinkle with salt. Partially cover and bring to a gentle bubble, then reduce the heat to a simmer and cook for 20 to 30 minutes.

Place the dried chiles in a small pot. Ladle in about 1½ cups of the pork cooking liquid and simmer the chiles until softened, 5 to 10 minutes. Transfer to a food processor and puree with the orange zest and juice, garlic, onion, honey, marjoram, cinnamon, cloves, some salt, and lots of pepper. Add the puree to the pork, partially cover, and simmer until the pork is nice and tender, 20 to 30 minutes.

Remove the pork and let rest until cool enough to handle, then shred or chop. Meanwhile, uncover the sauce and continue to cook to reduce (and intensify the flavors) until thickened to the desired consistency. Return the pork to the pot.

[Make-ahead: Let cool, cover, and refrigerate.]

[Night of: Return the pork and sauce to room temp before reheating, partially covered, over medium heat. If the sauce is too thick, just add a little shot of chicken stock or water.]

Keep warm over low heat until ready to serve.

For the toppings and sides: In a saucepan, melt the butter, add the rice, and stir to toast. Add the chicken stock and a sprinkle of salt. Cover, reduce the heat, and cook for 15 minutes. Stir in the peas and cook 2 to 3 minutes more. Turn off the heat, fluff with a fork, and set aside covered.

Meanwhile, season the black beans with the cumin and salt and pepper and heat.

Serve the pork and sauce with tortillas for wrapping. Garnish the pork with pickled onions and cilantro. Serve the beans and rice alongside.

Heads-up: Guajillo chiles are a mild- to medium-spice dried chile and they're interchangeable with pasilla or dried red New Mexico chiles. So if you can't find one, use either of the other two.

Poblano Mac 'n' Manchego
with Corn & Mushrooms

This is a good ol' mac 'n' cheese, but this one's got poblano chiles, Manchego cheese, corn, and nice, earthy mushrooms. It is a mac 'n' cheese to please. SERVES 4 TO 6

3 tablespoons **vegetable oil** or **EVOO**

12 ounces **mushrooms**, thinly sliced

3 **ears corn**

Salt and **pepper**

1 cup **chicken** or **vegetable stock**

2 **poblano chiles**, seeded, stemmed, and chopped

1 small **onion**, chopped

2 cloves **garlic**, chopped

1 small handful fresh **cilantro** sprigs

3 tablespoons **butter**

3 tablespoons **flour**

1 cup **milk**

2 cups shredded **Manchego cheese**

½ cup **Mexican crema**, **crème fraîche**, or **heavy cream**

1 pound **short-cut pasta** (such as ziti rigate or macaroni)

In a large skillet, heat the oil (3 turns of the pan) over medium heat. Add the mushrooms and brown, about 10 minutes. Scrape the corn kernels from the cobs (see Heads-up) and add to the mushrooms. Season with salt and pepper and cook until the corn begins to brown at the edges, 5 to 6 minutes.

Meanwhile, in a blender or food processor, combine the stock, poblanos, onion, garlic, cilantro, and salt and puree.

Melt the butter in a saucepan over medium heat. Whisk in the flour. Whisk in the milk and increase the heat a bit so the sauce comes up to a bubble and begins to thicken. Stir in the poblano puree and simmer until thickened, 20 to 25 minutes. Stir in 1 cup of the Manchego until melted. Stir in the crema.

[If making this to serve on **Cook Day**, preheat the oven to 350°F. If making this to serve later in the week, you'll preheat the oven on the night of.]

Meanwhile, bring a large pot of water to a boil for the pasta. Salt the water, add the pasta, and cook until al dente. Ladle out about a cup of the starchy cooking water.

Drain the pasta and toss with the poblano sauce and mushrooms, adding a little of the starchy water if the sauce is too thick. Pour into a 2- to 3-quart baking dish and top with the remaining 1 cup Manchego.

[**Make-ahead:** Let the pasta mixture cool, then cover and refrigerate or freeze.]

[**Night of:** Return the casserole to room temp while you preheat the oven to 350°F.]

Bake until browned and bubbling, 15 to 20 minutes, if making on **Cook Day** and the mixture is still hot, or 35 to 40 minutes if the casserole was refrigerated and is at room temperature.

Heads-up: To corral the corn kernels when I scrape the cobs, and also to catch all the corn juices, I invert a small bowl in a larger bowl and rest the end of the corncob on the small bowl as I cut off the kernels with a knife.

Chipotle Turkey Breast with Pomegranate-Cranberry Relish & Polenta

This recipe makes plenty of leftovers to be used in Mexican Chorizo & Turkey Chili (page 240). SERVES 4

2 boneless, skin-on **turkey breast** halves (about 3 pounds each)

Kosher salt and **pepper**

8 tablespoons (1 stick) **butter**, softened

2 tablespoons **honey**

2 tablespoons pureed **chipotle chiles in adobo** (see Heads-up, page 182)

1 (12-ounce) bag fresh or frozen **cranberries**

1 cup **sugar**

1 **cinnamon stick**

1 strip **orange** zest

1 **pomegranate**

1 fresh **jalapeño chile**, seeded and finely chopped

½ **red onion**, finely chopped

2 to 3 cups **chicken stock**

1 cup **milk**

1 cup quick-cooking **polenta**

1 cup shredded **Manchego cheese**

Preheat the oven to 350°F. Place a wire rack in a rimmed baking sheet.

Place the turkey on the rack. Sprinkle liberally with salt and pepper. Combine 6 tablespoons of the butter with 1 tablespoon of the honey and the chipotle puree and slather over the turkey breast. Roast the turkey for 1¼ hours. When cool enough to handle, cut off and set aside 1 pound of the turkey breast for the Mexican Chorizo & Turkey Chili (page 240).

[Make-ahead: Let the rest of the roast turkey cool to room temperature, then cover well and refrigerate.]

Meanwhile, in a saucepan, combine the cranberries, sugar, cinnamon stick, orange zest, a pinch of salt, and 1 cup water. Bring to a boil and cook until all the berries pop and the sauce thickens, about 15 minutes. Let cool and remove the cinnamon stick and orange zest. Peel the pomegranate in a bowl of water and separate and drain the seeds. Stir the pomegranate seeds, jalapeño, and onion into the sauce.

[Make-ahead: The relish can be made ahead and refrigerated.]

[Night of: Preheat the oven to 350°F. Place the turkey in a shallow baking dish with 1 cup chicken stock and cover loosely with foil. Reheat for 20 to 25 minutes, then crisp up the skin under the broiler.]

Combine 2 cups of the stock with the milk and bring to a boil. Whisk in the polenta and keep whisking until it thickens, 2 to 3 minutes. Stir in the remaining 2 tablespoons butter, the remaining 1 tablespoon honey, some salt and pepper, and the cheese.

Slice the turkey. Serve the turkey with the cranberry-pomegranate relish, chilled or at room temperature, with the polenta alongside.

Mexican Chorizo & Turkey Chili

When you've cooked all day and made enough food for the whole week, the last one you put together deserves to be an easy one, like this fan favorite. SERVES 4 TO 6

1 tablespoon **vegetable oil** or **EVOO**

1 pound fresh **Mexican chorizo**, casings removed

4 cloves **garlic**, chopped

1 **onion**, chopped

1 **red** or **green bell pepper**, chopped

1 tablespoon ground **coriander**

1 tablespoon ground **cumin**

1 (15-ounce) can **diced tomatoes**

2 to 3 cups **chicken stock**

2 tablespoons pureed **chipotle chiles in adobo** (see Heads-up, page 182)

1 tablespoon **honey**

2 tablespoons **masa harina**, **cornmeal**, or quick-cooking **polenta**

1 pound **cooked turkey breast** (from Chipotle Turkey Breast, page 238), diced

Chili-flavored tortilla chips or **Fritos**, for topping

Lime wedges, for serving

In a Dutch oven, heat the oil (1 turn of the pan) over medium-high heat. Add the chorizo, breaking it into crumbles as it browns. Add the garlic, onion, and bell pepper and cook to soften, about 5 minutes. Add the coriander and cumin. Stir in the tomatoes, stock, chipotle puree, honey, and masa harina. Simmer over low heat for 45 minutes to thicken. Stir in the turkey.

[Make-ahead: Let cool and refrigerate or freeze.]

[Night of: Return the chili to room temp before reheating over medium heat.]

Serve the chili topped with the chips, with a lime wedge alongside.

WEEK 33

COLD WEATHER COMFORTS

GRAB A BLANKET AND
GET COZY. HERE ARE 5 DISHES
THAT TASTE EVEN BETTER
WHEN IT'S COLD OUTSIDE.

DISH
1
TOUCHDOWN
CHILI
PAGE 242

DISH
2
CURRIED
SQUASH SOUP
WITH APPLE &
CHEDDAR MELTS
PAGE 243

DISH
3
OSSO BUCO
WITH GREMOLATA
PAGE 244

DISH
4
PASTA E
FAGIOLI WITH
ROASTED GARLIC
PAGE 246

DISH
5
TURKEY BREAST WITH
CREAMY GRAVY &
CRANBERRY-
POMEGRANATE
SAUCE
PAGE 247

Touchdown Chili

I make a ton of this chili, even if I'm cooking just for John and me, because it freezes beautifully. Not only is it a great make-ahead, it's a great "keep extra in the freezer" dish. SERVES 6

3 **dried ancho chiles**, stemmed and seeded

2 **dried guajillo** or **pasilla chiles**, stemmed and seeded

3 cups **beef stock**

1 tablespoon **vegetable oil** or **EVOO**

1 pound fresh **Mexican chorizo**, casings removed, or ⅓ pound center-cut **bacon**, finely chopped

1½ pounds **ground beef chuck** (ask the butcher for a coarse grind)

Kosher salt and coarsely ground **pepper**

¼ cup **Worcestershire sauce**

1 tablespoon ground **coriander**

1 tablespoon ground **cumin**

1½ teaspoons dried **Mexican oregano**

¼ teaspoon ground **cloves**

Pinch of ground **cinnamon**

4 cloves **garlic**, chopped

1 fresh **red Fresno** or **jalapeño chile**, sliced (or seeded and chopped for less heat)

1 large **onion**, chopped

12 ounces **dark lager beer** (I use Negra Modelo)

3 tablespoons **masa harina** or **cornmeal**

1 tablespoon **honey**

TOPPINGS

Cilantro leaves

Manchego or **Monterey Jack cheese**, shredded

Lime wedges

Minced raw **onions**

Hulled **pumpkin seeds** (pepitas)

Pickled jalapeño slices or chopped **giardiniera**

Sour cream

Crushed **tortilla chips** or other **chips** (such as Fritos)

Toast the ancho and guajillo chiles in a dry saucepan over medium-high heat until fragrant but not burned. Add the stock and bring to a simmer. Cook for 10 to 15 minutes to soften. Transfer to a blender and puree.

Meanwhile, in a Dutch oven, heat the oil (1 turn of the pan) over high heat. Add the chorizo and begin to render the fat. Pat the beef dry with a paper towel and sprinkle with salt and pepper. Add the beef to the chorizo with the Worcestershire. Cook, breaking up the meat as it cooks, until a nice crusty brown develops on the meat. Add the coriander, cumin, oregano, cloves, cinnamon, garlic, fresh chile, and onion and cook until the onion is soft. Deglaze the pan with the beer. Add the dried chile puree, masa harina, and honey. Reduce the heat to low and simmer to thicken and develop flavor, about 45 minutes.

[**Make-ahead:** Let cool and refrigerate.]

[**Night of:** Return to room temp and add a little water before reheating over medium heat.]

Serve with the toppings of your choice.

Curried Squash Soup
with Apple & Cheddar Melts

You can make a double batch of the soup and freeze it in plastic bags, flat. That way you can stack 'em as high as the freezer goes! It is a fabulous make-ahead. SERVES 4

CURRIED SQUASH SOUP

1 large **butternut squash** or other **orange-flesh squash**, or **pumpkin** (about 3 pounds), peeled, seeded, and sliced

EVOO

Kosher salt and **pepper**

Freshly grated **nutmeg**

2 slightly rounded tablespoons **curry powder** (see Heads-up)

3 tablespoons **butter**

3 to 4 cloves **garlic**, chopped

2 **carrots**, thinly sliced

1 **Gala** or other crisp **apple**, peeled and chopped

1 **onion**, chopped

4 cups **chicken** or **vegetable stock**

2 tablespoons **mango chutney** (I like Patak's Major Grey) or **honey**

Chopped **scallions** and **cilantro**, for garnish

APPLE AND CHEDDAR MELTS

8 slices good-quality **white bread**

Butter, softened

Mango chutney

¾ pound **super-sharp cheddar cheese**, shredded or sliced

1 **Gala** or other crisp **apple**, peeled and thinly sliced

Make the soup: Preheat the oven to 400°F.

Place the squash in a rimmed baking pan. Lightly coat the squash with EVOO. Sprinkle with salt, pepper, and a little nutmeg, and coat with the curry powder. Roast until golden on the edges and very tender, about 25 minutes. The spices will toast with the squash and fill the air with a terrific aroma.

Meanwhile, in a soup pot, heat a drizzle of EVOO over medium to medium-high heat and melt in the butter. Stir in the garlic, carrots, apple, and onion and sprinkle with salt and pepper. Cook, partially covered, until the vegetables are beginning to soften, about 10 minutes. Pour in the stock. Add the chutney or a drizzle of honey. Bring to a boil, reduce the heat to a simmer, and cook until the vegetables are soft, about 20 minutes.

Add the roasted squash and puree with an immersion blender, thinning the soup with water if necessary. (Or puree the soup in batches in a food processor or high-power blender.) Adjust the seasonings.

[**Make-ahead:** Let cool and refrigerate or freeze.]

[**Night of:** Return to room temp before reheating over medium-low heat.]

Make the apple and cheddar melts: Spread each bread slice with butter on 1 side and chutney on the other. Top half the slices on the chutney sides with the cheese and apple slices. Cover with the other bread, chutney side down. Griddle the sandwiches over medium heat until deeply golden and the cheese has melted. Cut the sandwiches in half on the diagonal.

Garnish the soup with the scallions and cilantro. Serve the cheddar melts alongside.

Heads-up: To make your own curry powder, combine 2 teaspoons ground turmeric, 1½ teaspoons each ground cumin and ground coriander, ½ teaspoon each ground mustard and ground ginger, and ¼ teaspoon each ground cinnamon and cayenne pepper.

Osso Buco with Gremolata

If you're going to be making Pasta e Fagioli with Roasted Garlic (page 246), make this with 6 veal shanks so you have the leftover veal you need. **Suggested side:** Crusty bread, split and warmed through in the oven, for mopping. SERVES 4 (WITH LEFTOVERS)

OSSO BUCO

3 tablespoons **EVOO**

6 **veal shanks**, about 2 inches thick and ¾ pound each, tied with kitchen twine

Salt and **pepper**

4 or 5 cloves **garlic**, sliced

2 or 3 small ribs **celery** with leafy tops, chopped

1 large **carrot**, chopped

1 **onion**, chopped

1 teaspoon **fennel seeds**

3 tablespoons chopped fresh **rosemary**

2 tablespoons chopped fresh **thyme**

2 tablespoons **tomato paste**

2 large fresh **bay leaves**

2 tablespoons **flour**

1 cup **dry white wine**

2 cups **chicken stock**

A healthy pinch of **saffron threads**

1 (14.5-ounce) can **diced tomatoes**

Long strip of zest and juice of 1 **orange**

1 fresh **red Fresno chile**, halved and seeded, or 1 teaspoon **crushed red pepper flakes**

GREMOLATA

Grated zest of 1 **lemon**

¼ cup fresh **flat-leaf parsley** leaves

¼ cup toasted **pistachio nuts**, chopped

Make the osso buco: Preheat the oven to 375°F.

In a large Dutch oven, heat the EVOO (3 turns of the pan) over medium-high to high heat. Sprinkle the veal with salt and pepper, add to the pot, and brown all over, turning occasionally, 12 to 15 minutes. Transfer to a large plate.

Add the garlic, celery, carrot, onion, and fennel seeds to the pot and stir 3 to 4 minutes. Add the rosemary, thyme, tomato paste, and bay leaves, sprinkle with salt and pepper, and stir 1 minute. Sprinkle the flour over the vegetables and stir 1 minute, then pour in the wine and deglaze the pot, scraping and stirring 1 minute more. Add the stock, saffron, and tomatoes. Add the orange zest and juice and the chile. Scrape down the pot and return the meat to the pot. Cover and transfer to the oven. Cook, turning the meat once about halfway through, until the meat is falling off the bone, about 2 hours.

[**Make-ahead:** Let cool and refrigerate, but first set aside 2 of the pieces to use in the Pasta e Fagioli, page 246.]

[**Night of:** Return the meat to room temp before gently reheating over medium-low heat.]

Make the gremolata: When the meat is about ready to come out of the oven (or is reheating on the stovetop if made ahead), combine the lemon zest, parsley, and pistachios and finely chop everything together.

For serving: Transfer the veal to a platter and cut off the twine. Fish the bay leaves out of the sauce and place the Dutch oven back on the stove over medium-high heat. With a potato masher, mash some of the vegetables into the sauce to help thicken it up. Whisk the sauce to combine and thicken, 4 to 5 minutes.

Serve the veal in shallow bowls, topped with the chunky sauce and gremolata.

Pasta e Fagioli with Roasted Garlic

Save the 2 extra veal shanks from Osso Buco with Gremolata (page 244) for this dish. But if you aren't making the osso buco, then you can use cooked pork. SERVES 4

2 heads **garlic**, tops cut off to expose the cloves

5 tablespoons **EVOO**, plus more for drizzling

Salt and **pepper**

¼ pound **guanciale** or **pancetta**, chopped

2 ribs **celery**, finely chopped, leaves reserved for optional garnish

1 **carrot**, finely chopped

1 **onion**, quartered lengthwise and thinly sliced

2 fresh **bay leaves**

Herb bundle: 2 sprigs fresh **rosemary** and 2 sprigs fresh **thyme**, tied with kitchen twine

2 tablespoons **tomato paste**

6 to 8 cups **chicken stock**

1 (15-ounce) can **cannellini beans**, partially drained

1 (15-ounce) can **chickpeas**, partially drained

¾ to 1 pound chopped **cooked veal** (from Osso Buco, page 244)

½ pound **mezzi rigatoni** or **penne rigate**

1 small head **escarole**, chopped

Freshly grated **nutmeg**

Grated **Parmigiano-Reggiano** or **pecorino cheese**, for serving

Minced raw **onion**, for garnish (optional)

Preheat the oven to 425°F (see Heads-up).

Drizzle the garlic with some EVOO and season with salt and pepper. Wrap in foil and roast until tender and caramel in color, 40 to 45 minutes.

Meanwhile, in a soup pot, heat the EVOO (5 turns of the pan) over medium-high heat. Add the guanciale and brown, about 3 minutes. Stir in the celery, carrot, onion, bay leaves, and herb bundle and sprinkle with salt and pepper. Cook, partially covered, stirring occasionally, until the vegetables are soft, 10 to 15 minutes. Stir in the tomato paste and cook until fragrant. Pour in the stock and bring to a boil, then reduce the heat to a simmer.

Transfer 1 cup of the soup to a blender or food processor. Squeeze the roasted garlic cloves out of their skins into the processor. Add half of the cannellini beans and chickpeas. Process until smooth, adding water if the puree is too thick to blend. Pour the puree into the soup and stir to combine, adding the remaining whole beans. Add the veal and bone.

[**Make-ahead:** The soup can be made up to this point several hours or several days ahead.]

[**Night of:** If the soup was refrigerated, let it come to room temperature.]

Fish out the bay leaves, herb bundle, and bones. Bring the soup back to a bubble. Add the pasta and cook al dente. Wilt in the escarole. Season with a few grates of nutmeg.

Top bowls of soup with cheese, an extra drizzle of EVOO, and celery leaves and minced onion (if using).

Heads-up: If you're making the osso buco, you already have the oven going, so you can throw the heads of garlic into the oven along with the osso buco. They may take a little longer to get tender.

Roasted Turkey Breast with Creamy Gravy & Cranberry-Pomegranate Sauce

Make extra garlic-herb butter and keep it in the freezer for topping any lean protein.
Suggested side: Steamed greens. SERVES 4 (WITH LEFTOVERS FOR SANDWICHES)

TURKEY BREAST

1 full boneless, skin-on **turkey breast** or 2 breast halves

2 cloves **garlic**, grated or pasted

8 tablespoons (1 stick) **butter**, softened

¼ cup finely chopped mixed **fresh herbs** (such as parsley, chives, thyme, and rosemary)

1 tablespoon **lemon** juice

Salt and **pepper**

CRANBERRY-POMEGRANATE SAUCE

1 (12-ounce) bag fresh or frozen **cranberries**

1 cup **sugar**

Pinch of **salt**

1 **cinnamon stick**

1 strip of **orange** zest

1 **pomegranate**

CREAMY GRAVY

2 tablespoons **flour**

1½ cups **chicken stock**

1 tablespoon **Worcestershire sauce**

Salt and **pepper**

⅓ cup **heavy cream**

¼ cup freshly grated **Parmigiano-Reggiano cheese**

1 cup **chicken stock** (optional, for reheating)

Roast the turkey breast: Preheat the oven to 350°F.

Place the turkey skin side up on a rack set in a rimmed baking sheet. Combine the garlic, butter, herbs, and lemon juice. Slather about 5 tablespoons of the garlic-herb butter over the turkey and sprinkle liberally with salt and pepper. Reserve the remaining butter for the gravy. Roast the turkey until the internal temperature reaches 160°F, about 45 minutes. When removed from the oven, the temperature will rise to 165° to 170°F as it sits.

[Make-ahead: Cover and refrigerate.]

Meanwhile, make the cranberry sauce: In a medium saucepan, combine the cranberries, sugar, salt, cinnamon stick, orange zest, and 1 cup water. Bring to a boil and cook until all the berries pop and the sauce thickens, about 15 minutes. Cool and remove the zest and cinnamon stick. Peel the pomegranate in a bowl of water, separating the seeds, and drain. Add the pomegranate seeds to the sauce.

[Make-ahead: Cover and refrigerate.]

[Night of: Place the turkey in a shallow baking dish with 1 cup stock and loosely cover with foil. Reheat at 350°F for 20 to 25 minutes, then crisp up the skin under the broiler.]

Make the creamy gravy: Melt the remaining garlic-herb butter in a saucepan over medium heat. Whisk in the flour, then the stock, and cook to thicken. Whisk in the Worcestershire and season with salt and pepper. Stir in the cream and Parm, and keep warm until ready to serve.

Slice the turkey and serve with the cranberry sauce and warm gravy.

WEEK 34

WINTRY MIX

FIVE MAKE-AHEAD MEALS FOR
THOSE COLD NIGHTS
WHEN YOU JUST DO NOT
FEEL LIKE COOKING

DISH
1
PORTOBELLO
MUSHROOM,
HOT & SWEET PEPPER
RAGU WITH
PAPPARDELLE
PAGE 249

DISH
2
EIGHT-SPICE
SQUASH & CHICKEN
THIGH STEW WITH
LENTIL RICE
PAGE 250

DISH
3
CREAMY
WINTER
VEGETABLE
SOUP
PAGE 252

DISH
4
JANE FOX'S
FAMOUS
TORTILLA
SOUP
PAGE 253

DISH
5
MUSHROOM &
SPINACH
BREAD-ZAGNA
PAGE 254

Portobello Mushroom, Hot & Sweet Pepper Ragu with Pappardelle

This is a really beefy-tasting vegetable-based pasta sauce. Well, vegetables plus pancetta . . . that's my kind of vegetable sauce. But you can leave the pancetta out if you want this completely meatless. SERVES 4

2 fresh **red Italian cherry peppers** or large **red Fresno chiles**

1 large or 2 medium **red bell peppers**

¼ cup **EVOO**, plus extra for drizzling

¼ pound **pancetta** or **guanciale**, cut into fat matchsticks

4 or 5 **portobello mushroom caps**, gills scraped, sliced

3 tablespoons finely chopped fresh **rosemary**

2 tablespoons thinly sliced fresh **sage**

1 tablespoon finely chopped fresh **thyme**

1½ teaspoons finely chopped fresh **marjoram** or **oregano**, or 1 teaspoon dried

4 large cloves **garlic**, sliced

1 large or 2 medium **onions**, chopped

Salt and **pepper**

2 tablespoons **tomato paste**

1½ cups **dry red wine**

1 (28- or 32-ounce) can **San Marzano tomatoes** (look for DOP on the label)

1 pound **pappardelle**

Grated **pecorino cheese**, for serving

Chopped fresh **flat-leaf parsley**, for serving

Preheat the broiler. Char the cherry peppers and bell peppers all over under the broiler with the oven door ajar to vent steam. Place the peppers in a bowl and cover tightly. When cool enough to handle, rub off the skins with a paper towel. Seed the cherry peppers and dice, and cut the bell peppers into ¼-inch cubes.

Meanwhile, in a large Dutch oven, heat the EVOO (4 turns of the pan) over medium-high heat and add the pancetta to render, 2 to 3 minutes. Stir in the mushrooms and cook until dark and tender, 12 to 15 minutes.

Add the rosemary, sage, thyme, marjoram, garlic, onions, and salt and pepper and cook for 5 minutes. Stir in the tomato paste and roasted peppers. Deglaze with the wine and cook until reduced by half, about 2 minutes. Stir in the tomatoes and break them up a bit. Simmer gently, stirring occasionally, until the tomatoes break down, about 30 minutes.

[Make-ahead: Let the ragu cool and refrigerate it.]

[Night of: Return the ragu to room temp before reheating gently over medium heat while you cook the pasta.]

Bring a large pot of water to a boil. Salt the water and cook the pappardelle al dente. Ladle out about a cup of the starchy cooking water and add to the sauce. Drain the pasta and return to the cooking pot. Add the sauce, tossing with tongs for 1 or 2 minutes for the flavors to absorb.

Serve the pasta topped with lots of grated pecorino, some parsley, and a drizzle of EVOO. Pass more cheese at the table, for topping.

Eight-Spice Squash & Chicken Thigh Stew with Lentil Rice

Dredging the chicken in flour gives a little crust to the chicken when you first put it into the pan—plus the flour helps give some "weight" to the sauce later. SERVES 4

8 bone-in, skinless **chicken thighs**

Salt and **pepper**

Flour, for dredging

3 tablespoons **butter**

2 tablespoons **EVOO**

2 tablespoons chopped fresh **ginger**

3 or 4 cloves **garlic**, chopped

2 medium or 1 large **onion**, chopped

1 **fresh red chile** (such as finger pepper or Fresno), chopped

2 rounded tablespoons **ras el hanout** (see Heads-up)

⅛ teaspoon ground **cardamom**

⅛ teaspoon ground **cinnamon**

⅛ teaspoon ground **cloves**

⅛ teaspoon freshly grated **nutmeg**

3 cups **chicken stock**

1 medium **butternut squash**, peeled and cut into 2-inch chunks

1 (28-ounce) can **diced tomatoes**

½ cup **red** or **brown lentils**

1 bunch **spinach** leaves (about 3 cups)

1 cup **long-grain rice**

1 cup **pomegranate** seeds

½ cup thinly sliced **scallions**

¼ cup fresh **cilantro** leaves

¼ cup fresh **mint** leaves

Sprinkle the chicken thighs with salt and pepper and dredge in flour. In a Dutch oven, melt 2 tablespoons of the butter into the EVOO over medium-high heat. Working in 2 batches, brown the chicken until crisp. Transfer to a plate. Add the ginger, garlic, onion, and chile to the pot and sprinkle with salt. Stir in the ras el hanout, cardamom, cinnamon, cloves, and nutmeg and cook until the vegetables are tender, 10 to 12 minutes.

Pour in 2 cups of the stock. Add the squash and tomatoes and simmer for 15 minutes. Return the chicken to the pot and simmer to cook through, 10 minutes more. Then wilt in the spinach.

[Make-ahead: Let cool and refrigerate.]

[Night of: Return the chicken to room temp and reheat over medium heat while you cook the lentils and rice.]

Bring a saucepan of salted water to a boil and cook the lentils until just tender (they should have a little bite to them): 7 to 10 minutes for red lentils, 15 minutes for brown. Drain and reserve.

Meanwhile, in a small saucepan, combine the remaining 1 cup stock and 1 tablespoon butter and ¾ cup water, and bring to a boil. Add the rice and return to a boil. Reduce the heat to a simmer, cover, and cook until tender, 16 to 18 minutes. Fluff with a fork. Add the lentils, pomegranate, scallions, cilantro, and mint and serve with the chicken.

Heads-up: If you don't have ras el hanout, you can use my recipe (page 95).

Creamy Winter Vegetable Soup

When I put together a dish like this with so many chopped vegetables, I like to work as close to the stove as possible and chop and drop the vegetables into the pan as I prep them. If you feel this puts too much pressure on you as you work, then you should absolutely prep everything in advance and have it ready to go. SERVES 6

SOUP

¼ cup **EVOO**

3 or 4 cloves **garlic**, grated

1 small **butternut squash**, peeled and cut into ½-inch cubes

2 **carrots**, thinly sliced

2 **parsnips**, thinly sliced

2 ribs **celery** with leafy tops, cut into ¼-inch dice

2 **leeks**, halved lengthwise and sliced ¼ inch thick

2 medium **starchy potatoes** (russet), peeled and cut into ½-inch cubes

1 bulb **fennel**, cut into ¼-inch dice

Salt and **pepper**

2 large fresh **bay leaves**

Herb bundle: fresh **parsley**, **sage**, **thyme**, **marjoram**, and **rosemary** sprigs, tied with kitchen twine

½ cup **dry white wine**

2 cups **chicken** or **vegetable stock**

4 tablespoons (½ stick) **butter**

¼ cup **flour**

3 cups **milk**

Freshly grated **nutmeg**

CHEESY CROUTONS

4 tablespoons (½ stick) **butter**

2 tablespoons **EVOO**

2 large cloves **garlic**, smashed

4 cups cubed stale **peasant bread**

1 cup grated **Parmigiano-Reggiano cheese**

Make the soup: In a large soup pot or Dutch oven, heat the EVOO (4 turns of the pan) over medium-high heat. Add the garlic, squash, carrots, parsnips, celery, leeks, potatoes, and fennel and sprinkle with salt and pepper. Nestle the bay leaves and herb bundle into the vegetables, partially cover, and cook until the vegetables are beginning to soften, stirring occasionally, about 10 minutes. Pour in the wine and reduce until almost dry. Add the stock, bring to a boil, and turn down to a simmer.

Meanwhile, in a medium saucepan, melt the butter over medium to medium-high heat. Whisk in the flour for 1 minute. Whisk in the milk and season with salt, pepper, and nutmeg. Cook until the sauce thickens enough to coat the back of a spoon.

Pour the sauce into the simmering soup, stir to combine, and simmer a couple of minutes more.

[**Make-ahead:** Let the soup cool and store in the refrigerator or freezer.]

Make the croutons: Preheat the oven to 350°F. In a large skillet, melt the butter into the EVOO (2 turns of the pan) over medium to medium-high heat. Stir in the garlic and cook for 1 minute. Add the bread and toast until golden, stirring occasionally. Transfer to a baking sheet and dress with the Parm. Bake to set the cheese and further dry out the croutons, 10 to 12 minutes.

[**Make-ahead:** Store the croutons in a foil pouch or airtight container at room temperature until ready to use.]

[**Night of:** Return the soup to room temp before gently reheating over medium heat.]

Remove the herb bundle and bay leaves from the soup. Serve the soup with the croutons.

Jane Fox's Famous Tortilla Soup

This recipe is from my friend Jane Fox. She's from Dallas, and they don't really have cold winters down there, but even so, her tortilla soup is great in the winter. SERVES 4

12 **corn tortillas**

All-natural **vegetable oil** or **olive oil cooking spray**

Kosher salt and **pepper**

3 to 4 tablespoons **corn oil**

2 tablespoons mild to medium-heat **chili powder** (such as ancho or a blend)

1 tablespoon ground **cumin**

2 or 3 cloves **garlic**, chopped

2 fresh **bay leaves**

1 large **onion**, chopped

A handful of fresh **cilantro** leaves, coarsely chopped, plus more for garnish

4 cups **chicken stock**

1 (14.5-ounce) can **diced tomatoes with green chiles** or 1 (14-ounce) can **diced tomatoes** mixed with 1 (4-ounce) can **chopped green chiles**

4 boneless, skinless **chicken breast** halves

2 **avocados**, diced

2 **limes**, cut into wedges

2 large fresh **jalapeño chiles**, seeded and chopped, for serving

1 small **red onion**, finely chopped, for serving

Grated **queso fresco**, for serving

Sour cream, for serving

Preheat the oven to 375°F. Slice 6 of the tortillas into 1-inch strips and arrange them on a baking sheet in a single layer. Coat with cooking spray. Bake until deeply golden, season with salt, and set aside.

[**Make-ahead:** Wrap the tortilla strips in a foil pouch and store at room temp.]

In a soup pot or large Dutch oven, heat the oil over medium-high heat. Chop the remaining 6 tortillas into 1- to 1½-inch squares and stir in the pot for 1 minute. Add the chili powder, cumin, garlic, bay leaves, onion, and some chopped cilantro, sprinkle with salt and pepper, and stir to toast the spices. Cook until the onion is translucent, 12 to 15 minutes.

Pour in the stock and tomatoes with chiles and bring to a boil. Add the chicken, reduce the heat a bit, and simmer to cook through, about 15 minutes. Remove the chicken, slice or chop the meat, and return to the soup.

[**Make-ahead:** Let the soup cool and refrigerate it.]

[**Night of:** Return the soup to room temp before reheating gently over medium heat.]

To serve, remove the bay leaves from the soup. Place some avocado at the bottom of each soup bowl and douse with a healthy squeeze of lime juice before filling the bowls with soup. At the table, top the soup with the baked tortilla strips, jalapeños, cilantro, red onion, queso fresco, and sour cream.

Mushroom & Spinach Bread-zagna

Lasagna may be the favorite comfort food of all time, but once you make bread-zagna, and you figure out how much easier your lasagna life can be, you might never look back. This will make enough to serve six grown-ups unless I'm there, then it will probably feed two—John and I could eat the whole bread-zagna by ourselves.

SERVES 6

¼ cup **EVOO**

1 pound **cremini** or **mixed mushrooms**, sliced

2 tablespoons chopped fresh **thyme**

4 cloves **garlic**, thinly sliced

1 **shallot**, finely chopped

Salt and **pepper**

¼ to ⅓ cup **Marsala** or **dry white wine**

¼ to ⅓ cup **chicken stock**

1 pound **"farm spinach,"** stemmed, washed, dried, and chopped (see Heads-up, page 37)

2 cups **half-and-half**

6 large **eggs**

Freshly grated **nutmeg**

2 tablespoons **butter** cut into small pieces, plus softened butter for the baking dish

8 slices (1 inch thick) peasant-style **white bread**

¾ pound **Fontina Val d'Aosta** or **Gruyère cheese**, shredded or thinly sliced

1½ to 2 cups freshly grated **Parmigiano-Reggiano cheese**

Preheat the oven to 350°F.

In a large skillet, heat the EVOO (4 turns of the pan) over medium-high heat. Add the mushrooms and cook until tender and dark. Stir in the thyme, garlic, shallot, and salt and pepper and cook for 1 to 2 minutes. Deglaze the pan with the Marsala and stir until almost completely evaporated. Pour in the stock, wilt in the spinach, and turn off the heat.

In a large bowl, whisk the half-and-half with the eggs, a few grates of nutmeg, and salt and pepper. Soak the bread, turning occasionally, until the liquid is absorbed.

Butter a 9 by 13-inch baking dish. Lay 4 slices of the bread on the bottom and top with the mushrooms and spinach and half of the cheeses, followed by the remaining bread and cheese. Dot the top with the 2 tablespoons butter and bake until golden, 45 minutes to 1 hour.

[**Make-ahead:** Let cool and refrigerate.]

[**Night of:** Return the bread-zagna to room temp while you preheat the oven to 325°F. Bake until heated through, about 30 minutes.]

WEEK 35

NOODLE THIS

PASTA PEOPLE, REJOICE,
BECAUSE THESE 5 RECIPES ARE
ALL ABOUT THE NOODLE.

DISH
1
PULLED
CHICKEN RAGU &
RIGATONI
PAGE 257

DISH
2
CHINESE
SPAGHETTI &
MEATBALLS
PAGE 258

DISH
3
ROASTED BUTTERNUT
BOATS STUFFED
WITH SAUSAGE,
TOASTED PASTA &
RICE
PAGE 260

DISH
4
CREAMY
CHICKEN &
NOODLES
PAGE 261

DISH
5
LASAGNA WITH
ROASTED
EGGPLANT–RICOTTA
FILLING
PAGE 262

Pulled Chicken Ragu & Rigatoni

In the first step of the recipe, you'll be poaching the chicken for this dish as well as for Creamy Chicken & Noodles (page 261). And the stock gets saved for three dishes: Creamy Chicken & Noodles, Chinese Spaghetti & Meatballs (page 258), and Roasted Butternut Boats (page 260). SERVES 4 TO 6

6 bone-in, skin-on **chicken thighs**
2 bone-in, skin-on **chicken breast** halves
2 **carrots**, coarsely chopped
2 ribs **celery**, coarsely chopped
2 **onions**: 1 quartered (root end intact), 1 chopped
2 fresh **bay leaves**
Kosher salt and **pepper**
A small handful of **dried porcini mushrooms**
¼ cup **EVOO**, plus extra for drizzling
¼ pound **pancetta** or **guanciale**, cut into thin matchsticks or chopped
4 cloves **garlic**, sliced
3 tablespoons fresh **rosemary** leaves, finely chopped
3 tablespoons **tomato paste**
1½ cups **dry white wine**
1 pound **rigatoni**
Grated **pecorino cheese**, for serving
Chopped fresh **flat-leaf parsley**, for garnish

In a medium pot, combine the chicken, carrots, celery, quartered onion, and bay leaves. Sprinkle with salt and cover with about 8 cups water. Bring to a boil, and then reduce the heat to a simmer for about 30 minutes. Transfer the chicken to a plate. Strain the stock and reserve for the other dishes. When cool enough to handle, remove the meat from the bones, discarding the skin and bones, and pull into small pieces, keeping the dark meat and breast meat separate. Set the breast meat aside for the Creamy Chicken & Noodles (page 261).

In a small saucepan, combine the dried mushrooms and 1 to 1½ cups of the stock. Bring to a simmer and cook until the mushrooms are soft, 10 to 15 minutes. Scoop out the mushrooms and set aside.

In the same pot used to cook the chicken, heat the EVOO (4 turns of the pan) over medium-high heat. Add the pancetta and cook to render, 2 to 3 minutes. Stir in the chopped onion, garlic, and rosemary. Sprinkle with salt and pepper and cook until the onion is soft, 7 to 8 minutes. Stir in the tomato paste, pour in the wine, and cook until reduced by half. Return the chicken meat to the pot with 2 cups of the stock. Reserve the remaining chicken stock for Chinese Spaghetti & Meatballs (page 258), Roasted Butternut Boats (page 260), and Creamy Chicken & Noodles.

Chop the mushrooms and add them into the ragu along with their soaking liquid, leaving the last few spoonfuls of liquid in the pan as grit may have settled there. Simmer to thicken the ragu, 20 to 30 minutes. Fish out the bay leaves.

[**Make-ahead:** Let cool and refrigerate.]

[**Night of:** Return the sauce to room temp before reheating gently over medium heat while you cook the pasta.]

Bring a large pot of water to a boil. Salt the water and cook the pasta al dente. Ladle out about a cup of the starchy cooking water and add to the ragu. Drain the pasta and return it to the cooking pot. Add the ragu and toss with tongs for 1 or 2 minutes for the flavors to absorb.

Serve the pasta topped with some pecorino, parsley, and a drizzle of EVOO.

Chinese Spaghetti & Meatballs

This is really what I would call "noodle bowls." Noodles and broth and bok choy with lots of scallion and some sweet little 5-spice meatballs. The broth here is actually the stock we got from poaching the chicken for the Pulled Chicken Ragu & Rigatoni (page 257), but you could always use store-bought stock instead. SERVES 4

12 ounces **ground pork**

1 teaspoon **Chinese 5-spice powder**

Salt and **white pepper**

2 inches fresh **ginger**: 1 inch grated, 1 inch sliced (see Heads-up)

Handful of plain dried **bread crumbs**

4 to 6 thin **scallions**: ½ minced, ½ thinly sliced

1 **egg** yolk, beaten

1 or 2 large cloves **garlic**: ½ grated, ½ sliced

Dark sesame oil, for drizzling

Vegetable oil, for drizzling

1 or 2 fresh **red Fresno chiles**, seeded and sliced

8 cups **chicken stock** (from Pulled Chicken Ragu & Rigatoni, page 257)

3 cups shredded **baby bok choy**

¼ cup **soy sauce**

8 ounces **spaghetti**

Fried onions (such as Durkee) or Chinese **chow mein noodles**, for garnish

Preheat the oven to 400°F. Place a wire rack in a rimmed baking sheet.

Place the pork in a bowl and sprinkle with the Chinese 5-spice powder, salt, and white pepper. Add the grated ginger, bread crumbs, minced scallions, egg yolk, grated garlic, and a drizzle of sesame oil. Mix together and roll into meatballs about the size of a big walnut. Drizzle with vegetable oil, place on the rack, and roast until brown and golden, 15 to 18 minutes.

In a soup pot, heat a drizzle of vegetable oil over medium to medium-high heat. Stir in the sliced ginger, sliced garlic, and chiles; add the chicken stock, 2 cups water, the bok choy, and soy sauce. Simmer until the bok choy is tender-crisp and the flavors in the broth develop. Add the meatballs.

[**Make-ahead:** Let the broth and meatballs cool, then refrigerate.]

[**Night of:** Return the broth and meatballs to room temp and reheat to a low boil while you cook the pasta.]

Bring a large pot of water to a boil. Salt the water and cook the spaghetti al dente. Drain and add to the broth.

Serve in shallow bowls, drizzled with sesame oil, the sliced scallions, and fried onions or chow mein noodles.

Heads-up: When you buy ginger to make a dish, you're going to end up with wa-a-a-y more than you need. If you throw the extra into the fridge, it'll last a few days, but eventually it'll start to shrivel up on you. Instead, try this: Just peel it, wrap it up, and pop it into the freezer. It will never dry out, and the next time you go to use it, it will grate up even more easily from frozen. It will be like "ginger snow."

Roasted Butternut Boats Stuffed with Sausage, Toasted Pasta & Rice

SERVES 4

3 tablespoons **butter**

¾ cup broken **thin spaghetti** or **orzo pasta**

3 cloves **garlic**, finely chopped

1 **onion**, finely chopped

1½ cups **long-grain white rice**

2 tablespoons thinly sliced fresh **sage**

Salt and **pepper**

½ cup **dry white wine**

3 cups **chicken stock** (from Pulled Chicken Ragu & Rigatoni, page 257) or store-bought

2 **butternut squash** (1½ to 2 pounds each), halved lengthwise and seeded

EVOO, for liberal drizzling

Freshly grated **nutmeg**

1 pound bulk **Italian sweet sausage with fennel**

1 cup grated **Parmigiano-Reggiano** or **Grana Padano cheese**

8 ounces **Fontina Val d'Aosta** or **Gruyère cheese**, shredded or grated

¼ cup **pine nuts**, toasted, for garnish

Preheat the oven to 400°F.

In a saucepan, melt the butter over medium heat. Add the pasta and toast until deep golden and nutty. Add the garlic and onion and cook until softened, about 5 minutes. Stir in the rice, coating it well, and sprinkle with the sage and salt and pepper. Pour in the wine, letting it absorb into the rice. Add the stock and bring to a boil. Reduce the heat to a simmer, cover, and cook the pilaf al dente, about 16 minutes. Remove from the heat and fluff with a fork.

Drizzle the squash with EVOO and sprinkle with salt, pepper, and a little nutmeg. Place, cut side down, on a baking sheet. Roast until the flesh is just tender, 15 to 20 minutes.

[If making this to serve on **Cook Day** or if planning to make Lasagna with Roasted Eggplant–Ricotta Filling (page 262), leave the oven on; if this is a make-ahead, you can turn the oven off.]

With a knife, score the flesh in a diamond pattern so you can scoop it out in chunks. Taking care not to break the squash "boats" and leaving a layer of flesh all around, scoop the squash into a dish.

In a skillet, heat a drizzle of EVOO over medium-high heat. Add the sausage and cook, breaking it into crumbles as it browns. Stir in the pilaf and the squash cubes. Fill the boats with the stuffing and drizzle with EVOO.

[**Make-ahead:** Let the stuffed shells cool and refrigerate.]

[**Night of:** Return the squash boats to room temp while you preheat the oven to 400°F.]

Place the boats on a baking sheet, top with the cheese, and bake until hot and browned, about 30 minutes. Garnish with the toasted pine nuts and serve hot.

Creamy Chicken & Noodles

This recipe uses the pulled chicken breast from Pulled Chicken Ragu & Rigatoni (page 257), but you can substitute rotisserie chicken, pulled or chopped, skin and bones removed. SERVES 4

3 tablespoons **butter**

2 tablespoons **EVOO**

12 ounces **white mushrooms**, sliced

2 tablespoons fresh **thyme** leaves, finely chopped

2 **leeks**, thinly sliced

1 small **carrot**, finely chopped

1 small rib **celery** with leafy top, finely chopped

Salt and **pepper**

3 tablespoons **flour**

½ cup **dry white wine**

1½ to 2 cups **chicken stock** (from Pulled Chicken Ragu & Rigatoni, page 257) or store-bought

½ cup **heavy cream**

Freshly grated **nutmeg**

2 to 3 cups pulled **poached chicken breast** (from Pulled Chicken Ragu & Rigatoni, page 257)

½ pound extra-wide **egg noodles**

2 tablespoons **Dijon mustard**

2 tablespoons chopped fresh **dill** or **tarragon**

In a large, deep skillet, melt the butter in the EVOO (2 turns of the pan) over medium to medium-high heat. Add the mushrooms and lightly brown, 10 to 12 minutes. Stir in the thyme, leeks, carrot, and celery, and sprinkle with salt and pepper. Cook, partially covered, until the vegetables soften, about 10 minutes. Sprinkle in the flour and stir for 1 minute. Stir in the wine. Add the stock and bring to a bubble. Stir in the cream, season with a few grates of nutmeg, and let the sauce thicken a bit. Add the chicken and cook to heat through.

[**Make-ahead:** Let the sauce cool and refrigerate it.]

[**Night of:** Return the sauce to room temp before reheating gently over medium heat while you cook the noodles.]

Bring a pot of water to a boil. Add salt and cook the noodles al dente.

Stir the Dijon mustard and dill into the chicken sauce. Drain the noodles and toss with the sauce.

Lasagna with Roasted Eggplant–Ricotta Filling

This lasagna is a riff on a classic Italian dish, pasta alla Norma: eggplant, tomato, and basil sauce topped with ricotta salata. I would serve this one as a reward for cooking your way through a whole week's worth of dishes. SERVES 6

4 pints **cherry tomatoes**

6 cloves **garlic**, unpeeled

4 tablespoons **EVOO**

Salt and **pepper**

2 tablespoons finely chopped fresh **thyme**

1 tablespoon fresh **oregano** or **marjoram** leaves, or 1 teaspoon dried

1 large firm **eggplant**, halved lengthwise

½ cup loosely packed fresh **basil** leaves, coarsely chopped

2 (16-ounce) containers fresh **ricotta cheese**

1 cup grated **Parmigiano-Reggiano cheese**

2 large **egg** yolks

1 (9-ounce) box no-boil **lasagna noodles**, soaked in lukewarm water for 5 minutes

3 cups shredded **mozzarella cheese**

Preheat the oven to 400°F.

Place the tomatoes and garlic on a baking sheet. Dress with 2 tablespoons of the EVOO and season with salt and pepper. Sprinkle with the thyme and oregano and toss to coat. Brush the eggplant with the remaining 2 tablespoons EVOO, sprinkle with salt and pepper, and place cut side down on another baking sheet. Place both baking sheets in the oven and roast the eggplant until soft, 30 to 40 minutes, and the tomatoes until they burst, 35 to 45 minutes.

Let the tomatoes cool slightly, and then puree them with the basil in a food processor until smooth. Squeeze the garlic cloves out of their skins into the processor and puree. Transfer the tomato sauce to a bowl.

Wipe out the processor bowl. When the eggplant has cooled, scoop the flesh into the processor. Add the ricotta, Parm, egg yolks, and some salt and pepper. Puree until smooth and season with more salt and pepper.

Spread one-third of the tomato sauce in a 9 by 13-inch baking dish. Layer 3 pasta sheets on top, followed by half of the eggplant, 3 more pasta sheets, half the remaining tomato sauce, and 1½ cups of the mozzarella. Repeat with another layer of 3 pasta sheets, then the remaining eggplant, 4 pasta sheets (overlapping), and the remaining tomato sauce. Top with the remaining mozzarella. Bake for 1 hour.

[If having this dish on **Cook Day**, let cool for 20 minutes before serving.]

[**Make-ahead:** Let the lasagna cool completely before covering and storing in the refrigerator or freezer.]

[**Night of:** Return the lasagna to room temp while you preheat the oven to 325°F. Bake, covered, for 20 to 30 minutes. Uncover and bake 10 to 15 minutes more, until bubbling.]

WEEK 36

GET SAUCY

WHAT'S THE ONE KEY TO DISHES
FROM PEERI FSS PASTA TO
BRILLIANT BARBECUE? THE SAUCE!
HERE ARE 5 SUPPERS TO
SAUCE UP YOUR WEEKNIGHTS.

DISH
1
MUSTARD & BROWN
SUGAR BBQ BEEF
SANDWICHES WITH
CELERY SLAW
PAGE 264

DISH
2
GENOVESE
RED SAUCE
PAGE 266

DISH
3
HOT & SWEET
PEPPER CURRY
SAUCE WITH
CHICKEN, LAMB,
OR BEEF
PAGE 267

DISH
4
DRUNKEN
CHICKEN
PAGE 268

DISH
5
BONNIE'S
ITALIAN STEW
PAGE 269

Mustard & Brown Sugar BBQ Beef Sandwiches with Celery Slaw

You can make the beef on the stovetop or in the oven. **MAKES ENOUGH FOR 12 SAMMIES**

BBQ BEEF
1 (3-pound) **chuck roast**
Kosher salt and lots of coarsely ground **pepper**
2 tablespoons **EVOO**, plus more for drizzling
2 **onions**, thinly sliced
4 cloves **garlic**, thinly sliced
2 (14.5-ounce) cans **stewed tomatoes**
1 cup cloudy **apple cider**
1 cup **beef stock**
1½ cups good-quality **ketchup**
½ cup **grainy Dijon mustard**
⅓ cup **Worcestershire sauce**
⅓ cup lightly packed **dark brown sugar**

CELERY SLAW
8 ribs **celery** with leafy tops, very thinly sliced on an angle
1 large **portobello mushroom cap**, gills scraped, halved, very thinly sliced
½ cup fresh **flat-leaf parsley** tops, coarsely chopped
Lemon juice
EVOO
Celery salt
Pepper

12 **hamburger** or **sandwich rolls**, split and toasted
2 cups crumbled **Stilton blue cheese** or **super-sharp white cheddar**

Make the BBQ beef: Bring the meat to room temperature. Pat dry with a paper towel and season liberally with salt and pepper. If planning on making this in the oven, preheat to 300°F.

In a large Dutch oven, heat the EVOO (2 turns of the pan) over medium heat. Add the onions and garlic, season with salt and pepper, and cook until softened, 5 to 7 minutes. Add the tomatoes, cider, stock, ketchup, mustard, Worcestershire, and brown sugar and simmer for 10 to 12 minutes. Slide in the beef and cover with the sauce. Cover the pot and simmer over low heat (or in the oven) for about 3 hours, stirring occasionally if on the stovetop. Transfer the meat to a cutting board. When cool enough to handle, cut into small pieces or shred.

Set the pot over medium to medium-high heat. Stir the sauce and cook to thicken it up. Add the beef to the sauce and stir to combine.

[Make-ahead: Let cool and refrigerate or freeze.]

[Night of: Return the beef to room temp before reheating gently over medium heat.]

Meanwhile, make the slaw: In a bowl, combine the celery, mushroom, and parsley. Dress with lemon juice and just enough EVOO to coat. Season with celery salt and pepper.

Serve the BBQ beef on the rolls, topped with the cheese and celery slaw.

Genovese Red Sauce

Your house is going to smell so good when you make this slow-cooked dish, your neighbors will invite themselves over for dinner. SERVES 4

3 tablespoons **EVOO**
¼ pound **pancetta** or **guanciale**, cut into ¼-inch cubes
¼ pound **prosciutto cotto** or **mild ham**, finely diced
1¼ pounds **ground veal**
1 large fresh **bay leaf**
1 medium **onion**, finely chopped
3 or 4 cloves **garlic**, finely chopped
Salt and **pepper**
Freshly grated **nutmeg**
¼ cup **tomato paste**
1½ cups **dry white wine**
1½ cups **milk**
1 to 2 cups **chicken stock** or water
1 pound **egg tagliatelle**
Freshly grated **Grana Padano** or **Parmigiano-Reggiano cheese**, for serving

In a Dutch oven, heat the EVOO (3 turns of the pan) over medium heat. Add the pancetta and render until it begins to crisp. Add the ham and stir 1 or 2 minutes more. Add the veal, breaking it into crumbles as it browns. Add the bay leaf, onion, and garlic; season with salt, pepper, and a few grates of nutmeg. Let cook partially covered for a few minutes, then stir in the tomato paste until fragrant. Add the wine and cook until hot. Add the milk, reduce the heat to low, and simmer gently for 3 hours, adding a little stock or water if the sauce gets too thick (up to 2 cups over the course of the cooking time).

[Make-ahead: Let cool and refrigerate or freeze.]

[Night of: Return the sauce to room temp before gently reheating over medium heat while you cook the pasta.]

Bring a large pot of water to a boil. Salt the water and cook the pasta al dente. Ladle out about a cup of the starchy cooking water and add to the sauce. Drain the pasta and return to the cooking pot. Add half of the sauce to the pasta, tossing with tongs for 1 or 2 minutes for the flavors to absorb. Top the pasta with the rest of the sauce and grated Grana Padano. Serve in shallow bowls.

Hot & Sweet Pepper Curry Sauce with Chicken, Lamb, or Beef

This is a really versatile Indian-style sauce that you can use with chicken, lamb, or beef. **Suggested sides:** Steamed basmati rice and/or grilled naan bread. SERVES 4

3 tablespoons **vegetable, grapeseed,** or **peanut oil**
1 tablespoon ground **coriander**
1 tablespoon ground **cumin** or whole cumin seed
2 teaspoons ground **turmeric**
2 **cardamom pods**, split, or ⅛ teaspoon ground **cardamom**
1-inch piece fresh **ginger**, grated
4 cloves **garlic**, thinly sliced or chopped
2 **fresh chiles** (such as red Fresnos), sliced
2 **red bell peppers**, chopped
1 **onion**, finely chopped
Salt and **pepper**
1 cup **chicken stock**
2 cups **passata** or **tomato puree**
1 (14.5 ounce) can **diced tomatoes**
½ cup **mango chutney** (I like Patak's Major Grey)
1 small **cinnamon stick**
1 large fresh **bay leaf**
1½ pounds boneless, skinless **chicken**, boneless leg of **lamb**, or **beef** sirloin cut into bite-size pieces
1 teaspoon **sweet paprika**
Juice of 2 **limes**
¾ pound "farm spinach," stemmed, washed, dried, and coarsely chopped (see Heads-up, page 37)
Greek yogurt, for serving
Cilantro leaves, for serving
Thinly sliced **scallions**, for serving

In a Dutch oven, heat the oil over medium to medium-high heat. Add the coriander, cumin, turmeric, and cardamom and stir until very fragrant, about 1 minute. Add the ginger, garlic, chiles, bell peppers, and onion and sprinkle with salt and pepper. Cook, partially covered, until softened, about 5 minutes. Add the stock, passata, diced tomatoes, chutney, cinnamon stick, and bay leaf. Partially cover and simmer over low heat for 1 hour. Remove the bay leaf and cinnamon stick.

Meanwhile, place the meat in a bowl and season with salt, pepper, and paprika. Squeeze in the lime juice and marinate the meat while the sauce cooks.

Add the meat to the sauce and simmer until tender.

[Make-ahead: Let cool and refrigerate or freeze.]

[Night of: Return the curry to room temp before reheating over medium heat.]

With the sauce at a bubble, wilt in the spinach.

Serve the curry topped with a dollop of yogurt, cilantro, and scallions.

Drunken Chicken

If you like coq au vin or boeuf bourguignonne, then you're going to love this dish.

SERVES 4 TO 6

1 full bone-in, skin-on **chicken breast**, cut into 4 pieces

4 pieces bone-in, skin-on **dark-meat chicken** (2 thighs and 2 drumsticks)

Salt and **pepper**

2 tablespoons **EVOO**

1 **carrot**, chopped

1 **onion**, chopped

2 ribs **celery** with leafy tops, chopped

4 cloves **garlic**, thinly sliced

1 fresh **bay leaf**

1 cup loosely packed chopped mixed fresh herbs: **parsley**, **sage**, **rosemary**, and **thyme**

2 tablespoons **tomato paste**

A small handful of **raisins**

3 cups **dry red wine**

¼ cup toasted **pine nuts** or sliced **almonds**

Season the chicken liberally with salt and pepper.

In a large Dutch oven, heat the EVOO (2 turns of the pan) over medium-high heat. Add the chicken and brown well on both sides. Transfer to a plate. Add the carrot, onion, celery, garlic, bay leaf, and half of the chopped herbs to the drippings, season with salt and pepper, and cook for 10 minutes, stirring frequently. Stir in the tomato paste and cook for 1 minute, until fragrant. Add the raisins and wine and bring to a bubble. Return the chicken to the pot and simmer, partially covered and turning occasionally, until the chicken is cooked through and the sauce has reduced, about 30 minutes.

[Make-ahead: Let cool and refrigerate.]

[Night of: Return the chicken to room temp before reheating gently over medium heat.]

Serve the chicken and sauce topped with the remaining herbs and the pine nuts.

Bonnie's Italian Stew

Bonnie is a woman I met in Pittsburgh. Her stew is meat and potatoes Italian style. Bonnie cooks the meatballs like dumplings, in the sauce. I brown mine in the oven first to make them more stable for a make-ahead meal—so that they won't break up as easily when you reheat them. SERVES 6

MEATBALLS

Olive oil cooking spray
2 slices (1 inch thick) good-quality **white bread**, crusts trimmed
Milk
1½ pounds **ground beef**
1 teaspoon **fennel seeds**
1 teaspoon **crushed red pepper flakes**
Salt and **pepper**
2 or 3 cloves **garlic**, grated
A generous handful of fresh **flat-leaf parsley**, finely chopped
½ cup grated **pecorino** or **Parmigiano-Reggiano cheese**
1 large **egg**
3 tablespoons **EVOO**

STEW

2 tablespoons **EVOO**, plus more for serving
2 medium **onions**, chopped
4 cloves **garlic**, thinly sliced
1 fresh **bay leaf**
Salt and **pepper**
3 tablespoons **tomato paste**
2 cups **beef stock**
2 (28- or 32-ounce) cans **San Marzano tomatoes**
A handful of **basil** leaves, torn
2 pounds small to medium **white** or **red potatoes**, cubed
¾ pound **green beans**, cut into thirds on an angle
Grated **Parmigiano-Reggiano** or **pecorino cheese**, for serving

Preheat the oven to 450°F. Coat a baking sheet with olive oil spray.

Make the meatballs: Place the bread in a shallow bowl, pour milk over it, and soak to soften.

In a bowl, combine the beef, fennel seeds, red pepper flakes, salt and pepper, garlic, parsley, cheese, egg, and EVOO (3 turns of the bowl).

Squeeze the excess milk from the bread and crumble as you add it to the meat. Gently combine the meatball mixture. Roll it into 2-inch balls. Place the meatballs on the baking sheet. Roast until browned but not fully cooked, 10 to 12 minutes.

Meanwhile, make the stew: In a large Dutch oven, heat the EVOO (2 turns of the pan) over medium heat. Add the onions, garlic, and bay leaf and season with salt and pepper. Cook, stirring occasionally, until the onions are translucent, 10 to 15 minutes.

Add the tomato paste and stir until fragrant, about 1 minute. Add the stock and tomatoes, breaking up the tomatoes with a potato masher. Add the basil, potatoes, and meatballs. Bring to a boil, reduce the heat to medium, partially cover, and cook for 10 minutes. Add the green beans and cook 7 to 8 minutes more.

[Make-ahead: Let cool and refrigerate.]

[Night of: Return the stew to room temp before reheating over medium heat, covered and stirring occasionally, or in a 325°F oven until the sauce is bubbling.]

Serve the stew in shallow bowls, topped with cheese and an extra drizzle of EVOO.

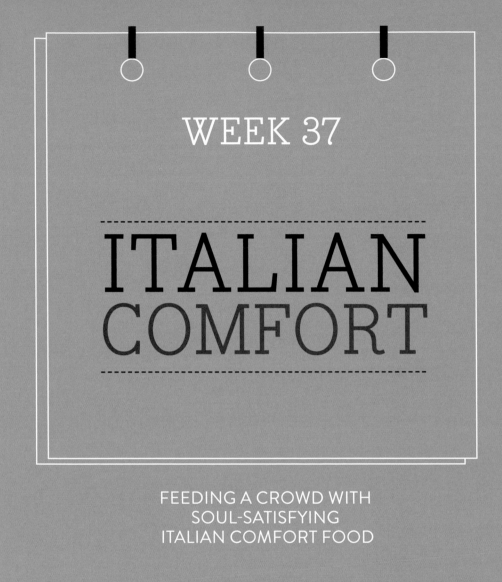

WEEK 37

ITALIAN COMFORT

FEEDING A CROWD WITH
SOUL-SATISFYING
ITALIAN COMFORT FOOD

DISH

1

CHEESY RICE
CAKE STUFFED WITH
HERBS & GREENS
PAGE 271

DISH

2

BRACIOLE &
SAUSAGES IN SUNDAY
GRAVY WITH
PEPPERS &
ONION
PAGE 272

DISH

3

PASTA SHELLS
WITH
VEAL & SWEET
SAUSAGE
PAGE 274

DISH

4

EGGPLANT &
ZUCCHINI
ROLL-UPS
PAGE 276

DISH

5

POTTED BEEF &
CELERY ROOT WITH
CELERY
GREMOLATA
PAGE 278

Cheesy Rice Cake
Stuffed with Herbs & Greens

You can serve this hot, warm, at room temperature, or chilled. It's great at any temperature. SERVES 4 TO 6 AS AN ENTRÉE OR UP TO 12 AS A STARTER OR PARTY OFFERING

4 tablespoons (½ stick) **butter**, plus more for the pan and the top of the cake
2½ cups **long-grain white rice**
4 cups **chicken stock**
1 cup grated **Grana Padano** or **Parmigiano-Reggiano cheese**
Salt and **pepper**
¼ cup **EVOO**
3 or 4 bulbs **baby fennel** or 1 bulb regular **fennel**, chopped
1 **onion**, chopped
3 or 4 cloves **garlic**, chopped
A small handful of **golden raisins** (optional)
½ cup packed chopped mixed fresh herbs: **tarragon**, **thyme**, and **parsley**
1 large bunch **Swiss chard**, stemmed and chopped
Freshly grated **nutmeg**
⅓ cup **dry white wine**
¾ cup homemade dry **bread crumbs** or **panko bread crumbs**

Preheat the oven to 375°F. Butter a 9-inch springform pan.

In a saucepan, combine the 4 tablespoons butter, the rice, stock, and 1 cup water. Bring to a boil, stir, cover, and cook until the rice is tender, 16 to 17 minutes. Stir in ¾ cup of the cheese and season with salt and pepper. Let cool.

Meanwhile, in a large skillet, heat the EVOO (4 turns of the pan) over medium to medium-high heat. Add the fennel, onion, garlic, and raisins, if using. Season with salt and pepper and cook until the onion and fennel are softened, 8 to 10 minutes. Add the herbs. Wilt in the chard and season with a little nutmeg. Deglaze the pan with the wine and cook to evaporate. When the greens have cooked down, stir. Remove from the heat and let cool.

Pile half the rice into the springform pan and press it into the bottom and up the sides. Spoon the chard mixture into the rice shell. Top with the remaining rice. Mix the bread crumbs and the remaining ¼ cup cheese. Sprinkle over the rice and dot with butter. Bake until golden, 25 to 30 minutes.

[**Make-ahead:** Let cool, cover well, and refrigerate or freeze.]

[**Night of:** Return to room temp while you preheat the oven to 350°F. Reheat, covered, until heated through, 15 to 20 minutes. Uncover and crisp the top under the broiler.]

To serve, remove the rim of the springform pan and cut the cake into wedges.

Pasta Shells with Veal & Sweet Sausage

One of the cheeses in the sauce for this dish is Fontina Val d'Aosta, one of my favorites. It's like the marriage of a nutty Swiss Gruyère and an easy-melting cheese like mozzarella. You could also make this with cannelloni instead of large pasta shells; you'll need about 12 of them. SERVES 6

2 tablespoons **EVOO**

1 pound bulk **sweet Italian sausage with fennel**, or links, casings removed

1 pound **ground veal**

About 2 tablespoons thinly sliced fresh **sage**

1 **onion**, finely chopped

2 or 3 cloves **garlic**, finely chopped

Salt and **pepper**

1 (10-ounce) package frozen **chopped spinach**, thawed and wrung dry in a kitchen towel

⅓ cup **dry white wine**

4 tablespoons (½ stick) **butter**

4 tablespoons **flour**

4 cups **milk**

Salt and **pepper**

Freshly grated **nutmeg**

2 **egg** yolks, lightly beaten

1½ cups grated **Italian Fontina cheese** (such as Fontina Val d'Aosta)

1 cup freshly grated **Parmigiano-Reggiano cheese**

18 dried large pasta **shells**

Bring a large pot of water to a boil.

In a large skillet, heat the EVOO (2 turns of the pan) over medium-high heat. Add the sausage, breaking it into crumbles as it browns. Add the veal; brown and crumble. Add the sage, onion, garlic, and salt and pepper and cook until the onion is tender. Add the spinach, pulling it into shreds, and stir to heat through. Deglaze the pan with the wine. Remove from the heat.

In a saucepan, melt the butter over medium heat. Whisk in the flour and cook 1 minute. Whisk in the milk and season with salt and pepper and a little nutmeg. Cook the sauce until thick enough to coat the back of a spoon. Taste and adjust seasonings. Stir some of the hot sauce into the egg yolks to temper them. Add the warmed egg yolks to the sauce and stir in ¾ cup of the Fontina and ½ cup of the Parm. Reduce the heat to low or cover to keep warm.

Salt the boiling water. Cook the pasta for 6 to 7 minutes until not quite al dente. Drain and let cool.

Cover the bottom of a 9 by 13-inch baking dish with one-quarter of the sauce. Fill the shells (or cannelloni) with the filling (see Heads-up). Lay the filled pasta in a single layer and cover with the remaining sauce. Top with the remaining ¾ cup Fontina and ½ cup Parm.

[**Make-ahead:** Cover well and refrigerate or freeze.]

[**Night of:** Return the dish to room temp while you preheat the oven.]

Preheat the oven to 375°F.

Bake the pasta uncovered until browned and bubbling, 30 to 40 minutes.

Heads-up: I find the easiest way to stuff cannelloni is to stand each one on end in the baking dish and just drop the stuffing into the tube with my fingertips. If any of the filling misses, it just falls into the casserole and it's no big deal. You can just scoop it up when you're serving. The same goes if you can't fit all the filling into the shells. Just put it in the baking dish, cover it with sauce, and bake.

Eggplant & Zucchini Roll-ups

This is a great vegetarian entrée to serve to a crowd when you've got meat-eaters and meat-freers all at the same table. It also makes a great side dish. SERVES 6

1 firm medium **eggplant**, ends trimmed

2 medium **zucchini**, ends trimmed

Olive oil cooking spray

Sea salt or **kosher salt** and **pepper**

2 cups **ricotta cheese**

2 **egg** yolks, lightly beaten

1½ cups grated **Parmigiano-Reggiano cheese**

1 **fresh chile** (such as red Fresno), seeded and finely chopped

4 cloves **garlic**: 2 grated or pasted, 2 chopped

Freshly grated **nutmeg**

½ cup fresh **flat-leaf parsley** tops, chopped

½ cup loosely packed fresh **mint**, finely chopped

A handful of fresh **basil** leaves, torn or shredded

3 cups **passata** or **tomato puree**

4 tablespoons (½ stick) **butter**

1 cup **panko bread crumbs**

Preheat the oven to 425°F.

Slice the eggplant and zucchini lengthwise into thin planks. Coat the eggplant and zucchini evenly on both sides with olive oil spray. Season with salt and pepper. Place on baking sheets and roast (in batches if necessary) until tender and browned, about 20 minutes. Let cool to handle.

In a bowl, combine the ricotta, egg yolks, 1 cup of the Parm, the chile, grated garlic, a little nutmeg, all but 2 tablespoons each of the parsley and mint, and salt and pepper.

Spoon the stuffing onto the eggplant and zucchini and roll up: For the zucchini, which is narrower, overlap 2 slices to make a wider roll. Do the same for any narrow eggplant slices. Arrange the rolls seam side down in a 9 by 13-inch baking dish and top with the basil. Cover evenly with the passata.

[**Make-ahead:** Cover well and refrigerate or freeze.]

Melt the butter. Add the chopped garlic and swirl a minute, remove from the heat, and toss with the panko, the remaining ½ cup Parm, and the remaining parsley and mint.

[**Make-ahead:** Store in an airtight container at room temp.]

[**Night of:** Return the roll-ups to room temp while you preheat the oven.]

Preheat the oven to 375°F.

Scatter the panko-Parm mixture over the roll-ups. Bake, uncovered, until golden and bubbling, 10 to 15 minutes.

Potted Beef & Celery Root
with Celery Gremolata

This is a humble beef stew elevated to a holiday-worthy offering. **Suggested side:** Mashed or boiled baby potatoes or crusty bread. SERVES 6

POTTED BEEF

3 pounds **beef chuck** or other **stew meat**, cut into 2-inch cubes

Kosher salt and coarsely ground **pepper**

Flour, for dredging

¼ cup **EVOO** or **vegetable oil**

2 medium **celery roots** (celeriac), peeled and cubed

2 medium **onions**, chopped

4 cloves **garlic**, smashed

3 tablespoons **tomato paste**

1½ cups **dry red wine**

¼ cup **Worcestershire sauce**

2 cups **beef stock**

Herb bundle: fresh **sage**, **bay leaf**, and **parsley** sprigs, tied together with kitchen twine

CELERY GREMOLATA

4 ribs **celery** with leafy tops, chopped

1 cup chopped fresh **flat-leaf parsley**

2 **anchovy fillets**, finely chopped (optional)

Juice of 1 **lemon**

Shaved pecorino cheese, for serving

Make the potted beef: Preheat the oven to 325°F.

Pat the meat dry and season with salt and pepper, then dredge in flour. In a large Dutch oven, heat the EVOO (4 turns of the pan) over medium-high heat. Working in batches, brown the meat all over. Transfer to a plate.

Add the celery root, onions, and garlic to the drippings and season with salt and pepper. Add the tomato paste and stir for 1 minute. Deglaze with the wine. Add the Worcestershire, stock, and herb bundle. Return the beef to the pan, cover, and cook until the beef is tender, about 2 hours.

[**Make-ahead:** Let cool and refrigerate.]

[**Night of:** Return the beef to room temp, then reheat gently over medium heat or in a 325°F oven until bubbling.]

Make the gremolata: In a small bowl, combine the celery, parsley, anchovies (if using), and lemon juice.

Serve the beef in shallow bowls with the celery gremolata and shaved pecorino on top.

WEEK 38

AMAZING GRAINS

EATING HEALTHY JUST WON'T WORK
IF THAT HEALTHY FOOD COMES
UP SHORT ON FLAVOR. HERE
ARE 5 DISHES STARRING GRAINS THAT
WILL GIVE YOU A HEAD START ON
DELICIOUS HEALTHY EATING.

DISH
1
FARRO WITH
ASPARAGUS, HAZEL-
NUTS & KALE, TOPPED
WITH ROASTED
MUSHROOMS
PAGE 280

DISH
2
QUINOA &
VEGETABLE
STUFFED
PEPPERS
PAGE 281

DISH
3
ROASTED VEGETABLE
TABBOULEH WITH
YOGURT-TAHINI
DRESSING
PAGE 282

DISH
4
MEXICAN
SLICED STEAK &
BARLEY SOUP
PAGE 284

DISH
5
BUCKWHEAT
STOUP WITH
PORCINI, BEEF &
KALE
PAGE 285

Farro with Asparagus, Hazelnuts & Kale, Topped with Roasted Mushrooms

Instead of serving the farro warm, you can serve it cold, as a salad. If the cold farro is too dry, dress with a little sherry vinegar or lemon juice and more EVOO to loosen it up. If you're serving the salad cold, you might want to roast the mushrooms the night of. SERVES 4 TO 6

Salt and **pepper**

1¼ cups **pearled farro** (I use BuonItalia)

1½ pounds mixed **fresh mushrooms** (cremini, shiitake, and hen of the woods)

6 tablespoons **EVOO**

2 tablespoons chopped fresh **thyme**

3 or 4 cloves **garlic**, finely chopped

2 **shallots**, chopped

1 bunch thin **asparagus**, thinly sliced on an angle

1 small bunch **lacinato kale** (also called black, Tuscan, or dinosaur kale), stemmed and finely chopped

1 to 2 teaspoons grated **lemon** zest

Freshly grated **nutmeg**

⅓ cup **dry sherry** or **Marsala**

½ cup chopped toasted **hazelnuts**

1 **lemon**, halved

Preheat the oven to 450°F.

Bring a pot of water to a boil. Salt the water and cook the farro to tender, about 20 minutes.

Meanwhile, prep the mushrooms: slice the cremini, stem and coarsely chop the shiitakes, and coarsely chop the hen of the woods. Spread the mushrooms on a baking sheet and toss with about ¼ cup EVOO (just enough to lightly coat), the thyme, and salt and pepper. Roast to deeply fragrant and browned, 10 to 12 minutes.

[Make-ahead: Let cool and refrigerate.]

While the mushrooms are in the oven, heat the remaining 2 tablespoons EVOO (2 turns of the pan) in a large skillet over medium-high heat. Add the garlic, shallots, and asparagus and cook to tender-crisp, 2 to 3 minutes. Wilt in the kale; season with lemon zest, salt, pepper, and nutmeg. Deglaze the pan with sherry.

Drain the farro and toss with the kale mixture.

[Make-ahead: Let cool and refrigerate.]

[Night of: Return the farro to room temp. Or to serve hot, reheat in the microwave or in a skillet. Reheat the mushrooms in a skillet to warm through.]

Sprinkle the farro with the toasted hazelnuts, a little squeeze of lemon juice, and the roasted mushrooms.

Quinoa & Vegetable Stuffed Peppers

Quinoa is like the whole-grain equivalent of couscous. Little teeny-tiny grains. They're light and bright and slightly nutty in flavor, so if you're new to eating a lot of whole grains, quinoa is a great place to start. SERVES 6

1 cup **quinoa**, rinsed

2 cups **chicken** or **vegetable stock**

6 small **bell peppers**, mixed colors, halved lengthwise (leave the stems on)

3 tablespoons **EVOO**, plus more for drizzling (or **olive oil cooking spray**)

Salt and **pepper**

1 small to medium **zucchini**, seeded and chopped

1 **red onion**, chopped

1 small firm **eggplant**, half the skin peeled (in stripes), chopped

4 cloves **garlic**, thinly sliced

1 **fresh chile** (such as red Fresno), thinly sliced, or 1 teaspoon **crushed red pepper flakes**

2 **plum tomatoes**, chopped

½ cup chopped fresh **flat-leaf parsley**

A handful of fresh **mint**, chopped

1 cup crumbled **feta** or **ricotta salata cheese**

Preheat the oven to 450°F.

In a saucepan, combine the quinoa and stock and bring to a boil. Cover, reduce the heat to a simmer, and cook until the liquid is absorbed and the grain looks translucent, 12 to 15 minutes. Fluff with a fork. You should have about 4 cups cooked quinoa.

Place the bell peppers on a baking sheet. Drizzle both sides of the pepper halves with some EVOO or coat with olive oil spray and season both sides with salt and pepper. Flip the peppers skin side up and roast until the peppers are just tender and the skins begin to char just a little at the edges, about 15 minutes. Remove from the oven and let sit until cool enough to handle.

[If making this to serve on **Cook Day**, leave the oven on, but reduce the temperature to 375°F. If making this to serve later in the week, turn the oven off; you'll bake the peppers the night of.]

Meanwhile, in a large skillet, heat the 3 tablespoons EVOO (3 turns of the pan) over medium-high heat. Add the zucchini, onion, eggplant, garlic, and chile; season with salt and pepper; and cook, partially covered, until tender, 10 to 12 minutes. Add the tomatoes, parsley, and mint. Spoon the quinoa into the skillet and mix well with the vegetables.

Flip the peppers cut side up on the baking sheet. Mound the pepper halves with the stuffing. Drizzle with a little EVOO.

[Make-ahead: Let cool and refrigerate.]

[Night of: Return the peppers to room temp while you preheat the oven to 375°F.]

Bake the peppers until hot through, 15 to 20 minutes.

Serve the pepper halves topped with lots of crumbled cheese.

Roasted Vegetable Tabbouleh with Yogurt-Tahini Dressing

This may be the most familiar of the grain dishes in this week of great grains: tabbouleh. But my version is not the typical side dish or light lunch; instead, it's a substantial supper, with a bunch of roasted vegetables added to the traditional salad base. SERVES 6

TABBOULEH
1½ cups **bulgur wheat**
1 bulb **fennel**, chopped, plus a handful of fennel fronds, chopped
1 small **zucchini**, seeded and chopped
1 small **red bell pepper**, chopped
1 small **fresh chile**, finely chopped
½ cup **EVOO**, plus more for drizzling
Salt and **pepper**
1 small to medium **butternut squash**, peeled, cut into bite-size pieces

Freshly grated **nutmeg**
Juice of 2 **lemons**
2 cloves **garlic**, grated or pasted
1 **pomegranate**
1 **red onion**, finely chopped
1 cup packed fresh **flat-leaf parsley**, chopped
⅓ cup finely chopped fresh **mint**

YOGURT-TAHINI DRESSING
¼ cup **tahini**
½ cup **Greek yogurt**
Juice of 1 **lemon**
1 clove **garlic**, grated or pasted

½ teaspoon ground **cumin**
Salt and **pepper**

FOR SERVING
6 **pita** or **naan breads**
¼ cup **pistachio nuts**, toasted
¼ cup **pine nuts**, toasted
Giardiniera (hot pickled vegetables), drained and chopped (optional)

Preheat the oven to 425°F.

Make the tabbouleh: In a heatproof bowl, pour 1½ cups boiling water over the bulgur. Cover and let cool to room temp, about 30 minutes.

Arrange the fennel, zucchini, bell pepper, and chile on a baking sheet. Drizzle with EVOO and season with salt and pepper. Arrange the butternut squash on another baking sheet. Drizzle with EVOO and season with salt, pepper, and a little nutmeg. Roast until the vegetables and squash are tender and brown at the edges, 17 to 20 minutes. Let cool.

In a large bowl, whisk together the lemon juice, ½ cup EVOO, garlic, and salt and pepper. Working in a large bowl of water, separate the pomegranate seeds and add them to the lemon dressing. Add the onion, parsley, mint, and bulgur, tossing to combine. Add the roasted vegetables and toss again.

[**Make-ahead:** Cover and refrigerate.]

Make the tahini dressing: Whisk together the tahini, ¼ cup water, yogurt, lemon juice, garlic, cumin, and salt and pepper.

[**Make-ahead:** Refrigerate.]

[**Night of:** Return the tabbouleh and dressing to room temp.]

To serve, heat a griddle pan. Douse with a splash of water, add the bread, and char 30 seconds on each side. Serve the tabbouleh topped with tahini dressing, nuts, and pickled vegetables, if using. Serve the breads on the side for stuffing or wrapping around the tabbouleh.

Mexican Sliced Steak & Barley Soup

Anytime I'm doing a make-ahead soup that has a grain (or pasta) in it, I like to keep the cooked grain separate and combine the soup and grain only at serving time. This prevents the grain from absorbing too much liquid from the soup while it sits in the refrigerator. SERVES 4 TO 6

MARINADE AND STEAK

¼ cup **EVOO**
¼ cup **Worcestershire sauce**
Juice of 1 **lime**
¼ **red onion**, minced or grated
¼ cup finely chopped fresh
   cilantro or **flat-leaf parsley**
1 **red Fresno** or **jalapeño chile**,
   seeded and finely chopped
2 large cloves **garlic**, grated
1 teaspoon dried **marjoram** or
   oregano
1 pound **skirt steak**
Kosher salt and coarsely ground
   pepper

BARLEY AND SOUP BASE

1 cup **pearl barley**
Salt and **pepper**
2 tablespoons **EVOO**, plus more
   for drizzling
4 cloves **garlic**, chopped
1 **red onion**, chopped
1 small **bell pepper**, finely
   chopped
2 ribs **celery**, finely chopped
2 **jalapeño** or **Fresno chiles**,
   seeded and chopped
2 (14-ounce) cans **stewed
   tomatoes**
A handful of fresh **cilantro** or
   parsley, chopped
4 cups **beef stock**

Lime wedges, **hot sauce**, and
   Worcestershire, for serving

Marinate the steak: Combine the EVOO, Worcestershire, lime juice (see Heads-up), onion, cilantro, chile, garlic, and marjoram in a large resealable plastic bag. Season the steak with salt and pepper and add to the bag. Squeeze out the air and seal the bag.

[Make-ahead: Refrigerate.]

Make the barley: Bring a pot of water to a boil, salt the water, and cook the barley until barely al dente, about 20 minutes. Drain and drizzle with a touch of EVOO.

[Make-ahead: Transfer to a storage container and refrigerate.]

Make the soup base: In a soup pot, heat the 2 tablespoons EVOO (2 turns of the pan) over medium-high heat. Add the garlic, onion, bell pepper, celery, and chiles. Season with salt and pepper. Cook until softened, 8 to 10 minutes. Add the tomatoes, cilantro, and stock and simmer to combine the flavors.

[Make-ahead: Let cool, cover, and refrigerate.]

[Day of: Add the lime juice to the marinating steak several hours before you intend to cook it.]

[Night of: Return the steak, barley, and soup base to room temp.]

Heat the soup base to a low boil. Add the barley and heat through.

Heat a grill pan over medium-high heat. Shake off the excess marinade and cook the steak 2 to 3 minutes per side for medium. Thinly slice on an angle.

Serve the soup in shallow bowls. Top the soup with a few slices of skirt steak. Pass lime wedges, hot sauce, and Worcestershire, for topping.

Heads-up: If you're making this dish on **Cook Day** and will be marinating the steak for only a couple of hours, add the lime juice. Otherwise, add the lime juice several hours before you will be cooking the steak.

Buckwheat Stoup with Porcini, Beef & Kale

Thicker than a soup, thinner than a stew: This is what I call a stoup. The buckwheat is cooked and stored separately from the soup base so that it doesn't get all mushy by the time you serve it. **Suggested side:** Crusty ciabatta bread, for mopping. SERVES 6

8 cups **beef stock**

A generous handful of **dried porcini mushrooms** (about 1 ounce)

Salt and **pepper**

1 cup whole-grain **kasha** (roasted buckwheat groats)

2 tablespoons **EVOO**, plus more for drizzling

¼ pound **guanciale**, **bacon**, or **pancetta**, diced

1 pound **stew beef**, cut into small cubes

2 **onions**, finely chopped

4 cloves **garlic**, chopped

2 fresh **bay leaves**

2 tablespoons **tomato paste**

2 tablespoons **Worcestershire sauce**

1 bunch **lacinato kale** (also called black, Tuscan, or dinosaur kale), stemmed and chopped

Freshly grated **nutmeg**

Shaved **pecorino cheese**, for serving

Simmer 2 cups of the stock and the mushrooms over low heat to soften, 10 to 15 minutes. Reserving the soaking liquid, scoop out the mushrooms and chop.

In a saucepan, bring 1¾ cups water to a boil. Season with salt, add the kasha, and stir. Cover, reduce the heat to a simmer, and cook until tender, 18 to 20 minutes. Drizzle with a little EVOO.

[Make-ahead: Let cool, cover, and refrigerate.]

In a soup pot or Dutch oven, heat the 2 tablespoons EVOO (2 turns of the pan). Add the guanciale and brown. Transfer to a plate. Pat the beef dry and season with salt and pepper. Add to the drippings and brown over medium-high heat. Transfer to the plate. Add the onions, garlic, and bay leaves to the drippings and cook to soften the onions, 8 to 10 minutes. Stir in the tomato paste until fragrant. Deglaze with the Worcestershire. Wilt in the kale and season with nutmeg. Add the remaining 6 cups beef stock, soaking liquid (all but the last few tablespoons, which may have grit in them), the mushrooms, beef, and guanciale. Cook, partially covered, until the beef is tender, about 1 hour.

[Make-ahead: Let cool and refrigerate.]

[Night of: Return the kasha and soup base to room temp. Reheat the soup base gently over medium-low heat. Remove the bay leaves.]

Combine the kasha with the hot soup and stir briefly over medium heat, just to heat the kasha. Serve in shallow bowls topped with shaved cheese.

WEEK 39

SOUPER-CHARGED

SOUP LOVERS, SLURP ON THIS:
5 SOUP-BASED SUPPERS.

DISH
1
GREEK
SPLIT PEA SOUP
WITH LEMON
PAGE 287

DISH
2
TOMATO SOUP WITH
ROASTED PEPPERS,
GARLIC & ONIONS
WITH GRUYÈRE
CROUTONS
PAGE 288

DISH
3
ANDOUILLE &
ROASTED SQUASH
GUMBO
PAGE 290

DISH
4
CAULIFLOWER SOUP
WITH ANCHOVY–
BREAD CRUMB
TOPPING
PAGE 291

DISH
5
SMOKY CORN
CHOWDER
PAGE 292

Greek Split Pea Soup with Lemon

I love split pea soup. Traditionally, you make it with ham or ham hock, but it is great to adapt. We're going to make it Greek style, with a lot of lemon, mint, and parsley in the soup. Then on the night of, you stir in some feta crumbles. SERVES 4 TO 6

2 tablespoons **EVOO**, plus more for drizzling

1 **onion**, chopped

4 cloves **garlic**, finely chopped

Salt and **pepper**

2 cups **green split peas**

6 to 8 cups **chicken stock**, **vegetable stock**, or a combination

Juice of 1 **lemon**

A big handful of fresh **mint** leaves (about ½ cup)

A big handful of fresh **parsley** leaves (about ½ cup)

FOR SERVING

Crumbled **Greek feta cheese**

Sweet paprika

Ground **cumin**

Pita chips, store-bought or homemade (see Heads-up)

In a soup pot, heat the EVOO over medium heat. Add the onion and garlic, season with salt and pepper, and cook until tender, 8 to 10 minutes.

Add the split peas and 6 cups stock and bring to a boil. Reduce the heat to a simmer and cook until just tender, about 20 minutes. If the peas start to get too dry, add 1 to 2 cups more stock.

Transfer half of the soup to a food processor or blender. Add the lemon juice, mint, and parsley and puree until smooth. Return to the soup pot. Season with salt and pepper.

[**Make-ahead:** Let cool and refrigerate.]

[**Night of:** Return the soup to room temp, then reheat gently over medium heat.]

Serve the soup topped with a generous amount of crumbled feta (for stirring in). Sprinkle with a hint of paprika and a pinch of cumin. Serve the pita chips alongside.

Heads-up: To make homemade pita chips, preheat the oven to 350°F. Cut 2 pita breads into 8 wedges each. Place a rack over a baking sheet. Coat both sides of the wedges with olive oil cooking spray. Season with salt and oregano. Bake until toasted and crisp.

If making ahead, store at room temp in an airtight container.

Tomato Soup with Roasted Peppers, Garlic & Onions with Gruyère Croutons

Not your mother's tomato soup. This one has the deep flavors of roasted peppers, garlic, and onions. SERVES 4

SOUP
2 **onions**, cut into wedges with the root end attached
Olive oil spray
2 tablespoons fresh **thyme** leaves
Salt and **pepper**
2 heads **garlic**, tops cut off to expose the cloves
EVOO, for liberal drizzling
2 large **red bell peppers**
1 (28- or 32-ounce) can **fire-roasted diced tomatoes**
2 cups **chicken stock**
2 cups **passata** or **tomato puree**
1½ teaspoons dried **herbes de Provence**
A few leaves of fresh **basil**, torn

CROUTONS
Butter, softened
4 slices **white bread**
¼ pound **Gruyère cheese**, thinly sliced

Preheat the oven to 425°F.

Make the soup: Place the onions on a baking sheet and coat lightly with olive oil spray. Sprinkle with the thyme and season liberally with salt and pepper. Drizzle the garlic with EVOO and season with salt and pepper. Wrap the garlic in foil. Roast the onions until tender and golden, 30 minutes, turning once, and the garlic until very tender, about 40 minutes. Let cool.

Char the peppers all over on the stovetop over a gas flame or under the broiler with the oven door ajar to vent steam. Place the peppers in a bowl and cover tightly. When cool enough to handle, rub off the skins with a paper towel, then halve and seed the peppers and coarsely chop.

Squeeze the garlic cloves from one of the heads of garlic into a food processor. Add half each of the onions, peppers, tomatoes, and chicken stock and puree until fairly smooth. Transfer to a soup pot. Repeat with the remaining garlic, onions, peppers, tomatoes, and stock. Add the passata, herbes de Provence, and basil and simmer the soup for about 20 minutes to thicken a little and combine the flavors. Adjust the salt and pepper.

[**Make-ahead:** Let cool and refrigerate.]

[**Night of:** Return the soup to room temp and reheat gently over medium heat.]

Make the croutons: Heat a grill pan over medium heat. Butter all the bread slices on one side. Make 2 sandwiches with the cheese, leaving the buttered sides facing out. Grill the sandwiches until golden and crisp on both side. Dice into bite-size squares.

Serve the soup in shallow bowls. Top with a few grilled cheese croutons.

Andouille & Roasted Squash Gumbo

A gumbo is definitely what I call a stoup: thicker than a soup, thinner than a stew. I wrote this recipe for my father, who's from Louisiana. **Suggested sides:** In my family, gumbo is served with a little scoop of cooked rice up on top. But if I'm making it just for myself, I just serve it simply with the sliced scallions on top. SERVES 4

1 **butternut squash** or small **pumpkin** (about 1½ pounds), peeled and cut into bite-size pieces

Olive oil cooking spray

Salt and coarsely ground **pepper**

Freshly grated **nutmeg**

⅓ cup **vegetable oil**, plus more for drizzling

1 pound **andouille sausage**, coarsely chopped

⅓ cup **flour**

1 teaspoon **sweet paprika** (smoked or regular)

1 **green bell pepper**, chopped

1 **onion**, chopped

2 or 3 ribs **celery** with leafy tops, chopped

½ pound fresh **okra** trimmed and sliced, or ½ (16-ounce) bag frozen sliced okra, thawed (optional)

4 cloves **garlic**, thinly sliced

1 **fresh chile**, thinly sliced

2 tablespoons fresh **thyme**, finely chopped

1 large fresh **bay leaf**

1 (12-ounce) bottle **larger beer**

2 cups **chicken stock**

2 (14-ounce) cans **stewed tomatoes**

Hot sauce

Sliced **scallions**, for garnish

Preheat the oven to 400°F.

Place the squash on a baking sheet and coat with olive oil spray. Season with salt, pepper, and nutmeg. Roast until tender and browned at the edges, 20 to 25 minutes.

Heat a soup pot over medium-high heat. Add a drizzle of oil and the andouille and cook to brown. Transfer to a plate. Pour ⅓ cup oil into the pan, then stir in the flour, paprika, and ground pepper. Cook, stirring, for 20 minutes, until the roux is brown and very fragrant. Add the bell pepper, onion, and celery; season with salt and pepper and cook to soften, about 5 minutes. Add the fresh okra (if using), the garlic, chile, thyme, and bay leaf and stir a few minutes more. Add the beer, stock, and tomatoes. Season with hot sauce to taste and simmer to thicken, 20 to 30 minutes.

[If making this to serve on **Cook Day**, you can cook the longer time to get it to the thickness you like; but if this is for make-ahead, then cook the shorter time, as the gumbo will thicken up more on the reheat.]

Add the andouille and roasted squash (and the frozen okra, if using) to the gumbo and stir to combine.

[**Make-ahead:** Let cool and refrigerate.]

[**Night of:** Return the gumbo to room temp and reheat gently over medium heat.]

Serve the gumbo in shallow bowls, topped with scallions.

Cauliflower Soup with Anchovy–Bread Crumb Topping

This soup is topped with one of my favorite ingredients in the whole world: toasted bread crumbs with anchovy, Parm, and black pepper. I love them so much that some of my friends actually gave me a T-shirt that said, "I love anchovy bread crumbs."

SERVES 4

SOUP

2 tablespoons **EVOO**

2 tablespoons **butter**

1 **onion**, chopped

Leaves from 2 sprigs **rosemary**, finely chopped

4 cloves **garlic**, finely chopped or grated

Salt and **pepper**

½ cup **dry white wine**

3 cups **chicken stock**

1 large head **cauliflower**, left whole but core removed (see Heads-up)

1 large (1 pound) **starchy potato**, peeled and chopped

2 cups whole **milk**

Freshly grated **nutmeg**

A couple of pinches of **cayenne pepper** or **ground red pepper**

TOPPING

⅓ cup **EVOO**

6 to 8 **anchovy fillets**

4 cloves **garlic**, finely chopped

Coarsely ground **pepper**

1 cup homemade dry **bread crumbs** or **panko bread crumbs**

½ cup fresh **flat-leaf parsley**, finely chopped

⅓ cup grated **Parmigiano-Reggiano cheese**

Make the soup: In a soup pot, heat the EVOO (2 turns of the pan) over medium to medium-high heat. Melt in the butter. Add the onion, rosemary, and garlic and season with salt and pepper. Cook, partially covered, to soften the onion, about 10 minutes. Add the wine, about ½ cup of the stock, and the cauliflower. Cover and steam the cauliflower until very tender, about 15 minutes.

Uncover and break up the cauliflower with a potato masher. Add the potato, milk, the remaining 2½ cups stock, a little nutmeg, and cayenne to taste. Bring to a boil and cook until the potato is tender, about 10 minutes. Puree the soup with an immersion blender. Simmer over low heat to thicken to the desired consistency. Adjust the seasonings.

[**Make-ahead:** Let cool and refrigerate.]

Make the topping: In a large skillet, heat the EVOO over medium heat. Add the anchovies, cover the pan with a splatter screen or lid, and shake until the anchovies begin to break up. Reduce the heat a bit, uncover, and stir until the anchovies melt. Reduce the heat more, add the garlic and pepper, and stir for 1 to 2 minutes. Stir in the bread crumbs and cook until deeply fragrant and well toasted. Remove from the heat and let cool completely. Combine the garlic crumbs with the parsley and Parm.

[**Make-ahead:** Store in an airtight container or foil pouch.]

[**Night of:** Return the soup to room temp, then reheat gently over medium heat.]

Serve the soup in shallow bowls topped with the bread crumbs.

Heads-up: Just trim off the big leaves at the base of the cauliflower, then use a sharp knife to get out as much of the core as you can without letting the cauliflower fall into florets.

Smoky Corn Chowder

If you're making a corn chowder or soup, throw the cobs in there. They give some sweetness and add a thickening agent as well. SERVES 4

2 tablespoons EVOO
¼ pound lean center-cut **smoky bacon**, chopped
2 medium **onions**, chopped
1 **fresh chile** (such as red Fresno), seeded and chopped
4 cloves **garlic**, finely chopped
6 large **ears corn**, kernels scraped from the cobs, cobs reserved
Salt and **pepper**
1 tablespoon **smoked sweet paprika**
2 tablespoons fresh **thyme**, finely chopped
2 fresh **bay leaves**
1 large (1-pound) **starchy potato**, peeled and diced
4 cups **chicken stock**
2 tablespoons **butter**, softened
Juice of 1 **lime**
Hot sauce

FOR SERVING
Sour cream or **crème fraîche**
Chopped **cilantro** or **parsley**
Sliced **scallions**
Crumbled **queso fresco** or shredded **cheddar** or **pepper jack cheese**

In a soup pot, heat the EVOO (2 turns of the pan) over medium-high heat. Add the bacon and cook until browned and crisp. Transfer to paper towels with a slotted spoon.

[**Make-ahead:** Store the bacon bits in an airtight container in the refrigerator.]

Add the onions, chile, and garlic to the drippings and cook to soften, stirring occasionally, 8 to 10 minutes. Add the corn kernels and season with salt and pepper. Stir in the paprika and thyme, then add the bay leaves, corncobs, potato, and stock (add a little water if the liquid does not cover the corn). Cook the soup, partially covered, for 20 to 30 minutes.

Discard the cobs and bay leaves. Puree the soup with an immersion blender until the corn is creamed but still a bit chunky. Stir in the butter and lime juice. Season with hot sauce to taste.

[**Make-ahead:** Let cool and refrigerate.]

[**Night of:** Return the chowder to room temp, then reheat gently over medium heat. Put the bacon on a paper towel and briefly zap in the microwave to warm.]

Serve the chowder topped with a little sour cream (for stirring in) and a sprinkle of cilantro, the bacon bits, scallions, and cheese.

WEEK 40

TRICKS & TREATS

A HALLOWEEN MENU
SURE TO SATISFY GHOULS,
GHOSTS, AND GOBLINS ALIKE

DISH
1
RATATOUILLE-
STUFFED JACK-O'-
PEPPERS
PAGE 294

DISH
2
BLOODY MARY SOUP
WITH PUMPERNICKEL
GRILLED CHEESE
CROUTONS
PAGE 295

DISH
3
PUMPKIN,
PENNE &
CABBAGE
PAGE 297

DISH
4
GARLICKY
BEEF
PAGE 298

DISH
5
HALLOWEEN
GROUND MEAT
GHOUL-ASH
PAGE 299

Ratatouille-Stuffed Jack-o'-Peppers

If you're trying to get your kids to eat more vegetables, making the food cute or cool always helps. In this case, it's both. When you're shopping for the peppers, pick the squarest ones you can find, for better plate presentation. SERVES 6

½ cup **EVOO**

2 tablespoons **butter**

4 cloves **garlic**, minced

1 cup homemade dry **bread crumbs** or **panko bread crumbs**

½ cup grated **Parmigiano-Reggiano cheese**

¼ cup finely chopped fresh **flat-leaf parsley**

7 medium **red** and **orange bell peppers**

Salt and **pepper**

Olive oil cooking spray

1 medium **eggplant**, half the skin peeled (in stripes), cut into ½-inch cubes

1 medium **zucchini**, cut into ½-inch cubes

1 medium **onion**, chopped

1 small **fresh red chile**, finely chopped, or ½ teaspoon **crushed red pepper flakes**

2 tablespoons fresh **thyme** leaves

3 **plum** or **small vine-ripened tomatoes**, chopped

2 cups **passata** or **tomato puree**

Preheat the oven to 450°F.

In a large skillet, heat ¼ cup EVOO (4 turns of the pan) and the butter. When the butter foams, add the garlic and stir for 1 minute. Stir in the bread crumbs to soak in the oil and butter. Cook until light golden, toasted, and fragrant. Remove from the heat and let cool. Stir in the Parm and parsley.

Chop one of the bell peppers and set aside. Trim the tops off the remaining 6 bell peppers about ½ inch down from the top. Scoop out the seeds and, using a small, sharp paring knife, cut out a jack-o'-lantern face on one of the sides. Set the peppers upright; if a pepper is very unstable, trim the bottom to make it stand. Season the peppers on the inside with salt and pepper. Invert the peppers onto a baking sheet and place the tops alongside. Coat the peppers with a little cooking spray. Bake until tender-crisp and a bit charred at the edges, 10 to 12 minutes. Let cool.

Meanwhile, salt the eggplant and drain in a colander or on paper towels.

In a large deep skillet, heat the remaining ¼ cup EVOO (4 turns of the pan) over medium to medium-high heat. Add the chopped bell pepper, eggplant, zucchini, onion, chile, and thyme and season with salt and pepper. Cook the vegetables, partially covered and stirring occasionally, until tender, 12 to 15 minutes. Add the tomatoes, stir another minute, and remove from the heat.

Combine the bread crumbs with the vegetables and adjust the seasonings. Pour the passata into an oven-to-table baking dish that will hold all 6 peppers snugly. Stuff the peppers, overstuffing a bit, and set the tops in place. Set the peppers in the baking dish as you fill them.

[If making this dish to serve on **Cook Day,** you can serve the peppers right away.]

[**Make-ahead:** Let cool, cover, and refrigerate.]

[**Night of:** Return the peppers to room temp while you preheat the oven to 400°F. Bake until hot through, 30 to 35 minutes.]

Bloody Mary Soup with Pumpernickel Grilled Cheese Croutons

Appropriate for Halloween, this is everyone's favorite tomato soup spiced up with typical Bloody Mary seasonings: Worcestershire, hot sauce, celery salt, horseradish, and (yes) vodka. SERVES 4 TO 6

2 tablespoons **EVOO**
2 **onions**, chopped
6 cloves **garlic**, chopped
3 ribs **celery**, chopped
1 tablespoon grated **lemon** zest
2 tablespoons fresh **thyme** leaves
Celery salt
Coarsely ground **pepper**
½ cup **vodka**
2 cups **beef stock**
2 cups **Spicy Hot V8 vegetable juice**
2 tablespoons **Worcestershire sauce**
¼ cup **prepared horseradish**
1 (28- or 32-ounce) can **fire-roasted whole** or **diced tomatoes**
Frank's RedHot hot sauce
Butter, softened
8 slices **pumpernickel bread**
8 deli slices **yellow cheddar cheese**
Juice of ½ **lemon**
¼ cup finely chopped fresh **flat-leaf parsley**

In a soup pot or large Dutch oven, heat the EVOO (2 turns of the pan) over medium-high heat. Add the onions, garlic, celery, lemon zest, and thyme. Season with celery salt and pepper. Cook until the vegetables are tender, 8 to 10 minutes. Deglaze the pan with the vodka. Add the stock, V8, Worcestershire, horseradish, and tomatoes (break up the whole tomatoes with a potato masher). Add hot sauce to taste, starting with 1 tablespoon and going up from there if you want. (My family likes things really spicy and we use ¼ cup!) Bring the soup to a boil, then reduce to a simmer and cook for 30 minutes to thicken and combine flavors.

[**Make-ahead:** Let cool and refrigerate.]

[**Night of:** Return the soup to room temp before reheating gently over medium heat.]

Heat a large skillet or griddle over medium heat. Spread all 8 slices of the bread on one side with softened butter. Build 4 cheese sandwiches with buttered sides facing out. Grill the sandwiches until the cheese has melted and the bread is deeply crispy. Using a serrated knife, cut each sandwich into 9 croutons.

Stir the lemon juice into the hot soup just before serving. Ladle the soup into shallow bowls, sprinkle with parsley, and top with the croutons.

Pumpkin, Penne & Cabbage

Here is an earthy, delicious, and really healthy dish loosely based on a traditional Italian dish called *pizzoccheri*, which is buckwheat pasta with cabbage and potatoes. In this version, I'm using pumpkin instead of potatoes, because you can't have a week's worth of Halloween food without doing something with pumpkin! SERVES 4 TO 6

1 small **sugar pumpkin** or 1 medium **butternut squash**, peeled and cut into bite-size pieces
Olive oil cooking spray
Salt and **pepper**
Freshly grated **nutmeg**
A fat pinch of **saffron threads**
2 cups **chicken stock**
1 pound **cabbage**, cored and thickly sliced
6 tablespoons (¾ stick) **butter**
18 to 20 fresh **sage** leaves
1 pound **buckwheat**, **farro**, or **whole wheat penne**
1 cup grated **Parmigiano-Reggiano cheese**, plus more for topping

Preheat the oven to 400°F.

Arrange the pumpkin on a baking sheet and lightly coat with olive oil spray. Season with salt, pepper, and a little nutmeg. Roast to tender and brown at the edges, about 20 minutes.

[If making this to serve on **Cook Day**, leave the oven on, but reduce the temperature to 375°F. If making this to serve later in the week, you'll preheat the oven the night of.]

Meanwhile, in a large saucepan, combine the saffron, stock, and cabbage. Bring to a low boil, reduce the heat to a simmer, cover, and cook until very tender, about 20 minutes.

Bring a large pot of water to a boil.

In a medium skillet, melt the butter over medium heat. Add the sage and fry to crisp. Transfer the leaves to paper towels to drain, then crumble. Return the pan to the heat and cook the butter to lightly brown.

Salt the boiling water and cook the pasta al dente. Drain the pasta and add it to the cabbage. Add the squash, browned butter, and fried sage and toss to combine. Transfer to a 10 by 14-inch casserole. Top with the Parm.

[Make-ahead: Let cool, cover, and refrigerate.]

[Night of: Return the casserole to room temp while you preheat the oven to 375°F.]

Bake, loosely covered with foil, until heated through. Uncover, top with a little Parm, and broil to crisp at the edges.

Garlicky Beef

Vampires hate this recipe. **Suggested side:** Crusty bread for mopping. SERVES 4 TO 6

2½ pounds **beef chuck**, cubed for stew

Kosher salt and coarsely ground **pepper**

2 tablespoons **EVOO** or **vegetable oil**

2 tablespoons **butter**

1 head **garlic**, cloves smashed and peeled

1 pound **red** or **yellow pearl onions**, peeled (see Heads-up)

2 tablespoons **tomato paste**

½ cup **dry red** or **white wine**

2 cups **beef stock**

2 (14.5-ounce) cans **stewed tomatoes**

Chopped fresh **flat-leaf parsley**, for garnish

Preheat the oven to 325°F.

Pat the meat dry and season liberally with salt and pepper. In a Dutch oven, heat the EVOO (2 turns of the pan) over medium-high heat. Working in batches, brown the meat evenly all over, then transfer to a plate. Reduce the heat to medium and melt in the butter. Add the garlic and onions, season with salt and pepper, and stir for a few minutes to lightly brown. Stir in the tomato paste and cook for 1 minute. Deglaze the pan with the wine. Add the stock and tomatoes. Return the beef to the pan, cover, and bake until tender, 2 to 2½ hours.

[Make-ahead: Let cool and refrigerate.]

[Night of: Return the beef to room temp before reheating gently over medium heat, stirring frequently, or in a 325°F oven.]

Serve garnished with parsley.

Heads-up: You can often find fresh pearl onions around holiday time, but if you can't, you can thaw a 16-ounce bag of frozen onions. If you're starting with fresh, you have to peel them. Bring a pot of water to a boil. Add the onions and boil for 3 to 4 minutes, then drain and cool. Holding them with the root end facing away from you, pinch the ends of the pearl onions and they should pop right out of their skins.

You can't have Halloween without candy, so here you go!

Recipe for Chile-Cinnamon Brittle with Mixed Nuts

View a bonus Treat recipe.

Halloween Ground Meat Ghoul-ash

I like to use the long, pointed bell peppers (sometimes called field peppers) for this instead of small, squarish bell peppers. SERVES 6

2 **red bell peppers**
2 tablespoons **EVOO**
2 pounds **ground lamb** or **beef**
Salt and **pepper**
2 tablespoons **sweet paprika**
2 teaspoons **hot paprika, ground red pepper,** or **chili powder** blend
2 tablespoons fresh **rosemary,** finely chopped
1 tablespoon chopped fresh **marjoram,** or 1 teaspoon dried
1 **onion,** finely chopped
3 or 4 cloves **garlic,** finely chopped
2 tablespoons **tomato paste**
1 cup **passata** or **tomato puree**
2 cups **chicken** or **beef stock**
3 tablespoons **Worcestershire sauce**
1 pound extra-wide **egg noodles**
3 tablespoons **butter,** diced
½ cup chopped fresh **flat-leaf parsley**
Crème fraîche, for garnish

Char the peppers all over on the stovetop over a gas flame or under the broiler with the oven door ajar to vent steam. Place the peppers in a bowl and cover tightly. When cool enough to handle, rub off the skin with a paper towel, then halve, seed, and chop the peppers.

Heat a large Dutch oven or deep skillet over medium-high heat. Add the EVOO (2 turns of the pan). Pat the meat dry and add to the pan, breaking it into crumbles as it browns. Season with salt and pepper. Add the sweet paprika, hot paprika, rosemary, and marjoram and stir well. Add the onion and garlic and cook, partially covered, until the onion is tender, 7 to 8 minutes. Stir in the tomato paste and cook for 1 minute, until fragrant. Add the passata, stock, Worcestershire, and roasted peppers and simmer a couple of minutes to thicken.

[Make-ahead: Let cool and refrigerate.]

[Night of: Return the goulash to room temp before reheating gently over medium heat, stirring frequently.]

Bring a large pot of water to a boil. Salt the water and cook the noodles al dente. Ladle out about ⅓ cup of the starchy cooking water. Drain the noodles and return to the pot. Add the butter, parsley, and salt to taste, tossing with tongs for 1 or 2 minutes for the butter to melt. Add some of the starchy water if the noodles begin to stick together.

Serve the goulash in shallow bowls on a nest of noodles. Top with a dollop of crème fraîche.

WEEK 41

GAME ON!

WHEN WATCHING A GAME WITH FRIENDS,
YOU GOTTA GO BIG WITH THE FOOD OR GO HOME.
BUT EVEN IF YOU'RE NOT A BIG SPORTS FAN,
IT'S GOOD TO HAVE AN ARSENAL OF TAILGATING
DISHES OR POTLUCK RECIPES ON HAND—HEARTY FOOD
THAT TRAVELS WELL, BECAUSE IT'S JUST THE
EASIEST FOOD TO ENTERTAIN WITH.

DISH
1
CINCINNATI
SPAGHETTI
PAGE 301

DISH
2
PORK &
BROCCOLI RABE
CIABATTA SUBS WITH
GREMOLATA
PAGE 303

DISH
3
BUFFALO TURKEY
SLOPPY JOES WITH
BLUE CHEESE
RANCH DRESSING
PAGE 304

DISH
4
BRISKET BOWLS
WITH GREEN RICE
PAGE 305

DISH
5
BACON
BURGER
MAC 'N' CHEESE
PAGE 306

Cincinnati Spaghetti

I love Cincinnati spaghetti. And you don't have to be a Bengals fan to dig it. I mean, what's not to love? It has two of my favorite things in one bowl: pasta and spicy chili!

SERVES 6 TO 8

2 tablespoons **EVOO**

2 or 3 slices **smoky bacon**, finely chopped

1½ pounds **ground beef chuck** (fattier) or **sirloin** (leaner)

1 **onion**, finely chopped

4 or 5 large cloves **garlic**, finely chopped

3 fresh **jalapeño chiles**, seeded and finely chopped

Salt and **pepper**

2 tablespoons **ancho chile powder** or **chili powder blend** (I like Gebhardt's)

1 tablespoon **unsweetened cocoa powder**

1 tablespoon **smoked sweet paprika**

1 teaspoon ground **allspice**

½ teaspoon ground **cinnamon**

A healthy pinch of ground **cloves**

1½ teaspoons dried **oregano**, lightly crushed

3 tablespoons **Worcestershire sauce**

2 tablespoons **tomato paste**

2 cups **beef stock**

1 (15-ounce) can **tomato sauce**

1 (28-ounce) can **fire-roasted crushed** or **diced tomatoes**

1 (15-ounce) can **red kidney beans**, drained

1½ pounds **bucatini** or **spaghetti**

TOPPINGS BAR

Finely chopped **white**, **red**, or **green onions**

Shredded **cheddar cheese**

Grated **pecorino** or **Parmigiano-Reggiano cheese**

Pickled **jalapeño** slices

Chopped **cilantro** or **parsley**

In a large Dutch oven or soup pot, heat the EVOO (2 turns of the pan) over medium-high heat. Add the bacon and cook until crisp. Add the beef and cook, breaking it into crumbles as it browns. Add the onion, garlic, and fresh chiles. Season with salt and pepper. Add the chile powder, cocoa, paprika, allspice, cinnamon, cloves, oregano, and Worcestershire. Cook until the onion is tender, about 10 minutes. Add the tomato paste and stir for a minute, until fragrant. Add the stock, tomato sauce, tomatoes, and beans and bring to a bubble. Reduce the heat and simmer, partially covered, for 45 minutes.

[**Make-ahead:** Let cool and refrigerate.]

[**Night of:** Return the sauce to room temp before reheating gently over medium heat, stirring frequently. Add a splash of water or stock if the sauce is too thick.]

Bring a large pot of water to a boil. Salt the water and cook the pasta al dente. Ladle out 1 cup of the starchy cooking water and add to the sauce. Drain the pasta and return it to the pot. Add about two-thirds of the sauce, tossing with tongs for 1 or 2 minutes for the flavors to absorb. Transfer the pasta to a large serving platter and top with the remaining sauce. Set up the toppings in front of the platter.

Pork & Broccoli Rabe
Ciabatta Subs with Gremolata

There are two different make-ahead strategies possible with this dish. Option 1: You can prep the pork and trim the broccoli rabe ahead but not cook them until the night of. Option 2: You can cook the pork and rabe ahead and reheat on the night of (you'll need some chicken stock for the reheating). SERVES 10

1 (5-pound) boneless skin-on (see Heads-up) **pork shoulder** (butt)
8 to 10 cloves **garlic**, finely chopped
2 teaspoons **fennel seeds**
1½ teaspoons **crushed red pepper flakes**
Kosher salt and coarsely ground **pepper**
3 to 4 tablespoons **rosemary** leaves, chopped
1 small **onion**, peeled
1 teaspoon **baking soda** (optional)
EVOO, for drizzling
Chicken stock, for reheating (optional)
2 bunches **broccoli rabe**, trimmed into 5- to 6-inch stalks

10 **ciabatta rolls**, 6 to 8 inches long, split
EVOO, for drizzling
Lemon juice
Gremolata (page 244)

Butterfly the pork by cutting the meat across but not all the way through and opening it up like a book. If it's uneven, pound it out a little. Season the pork evenly across the surface with the garlic, fennel seeds, red pepper flakes, salt, pepper, and rosemary. Grate the onion over the meat, using the large holes on a box grater or with a wide-tooth Microplane, and spread it around. Roll the pork with the skin outside and tie with kitchen string to secure.

[**Make-ahead option #1:** Cover and refrigerate the pork.]

[**Night of option #1:** Let the pork return to room temp while you preheat the oven.]

Preheat the oven to 350°F.

Rub the pork skin with a little baking soda to make it extra-crispy. Drizzle with a little EVOO and season with salt and pepper.

Place the pork on a rack set over a baking sheet. Cover the pork with a loose foil tent and roast until the center reads 145°F on a meat thermometer, 2 to 3 hours. Remove the foil and broil to crisp the skin, 15 to 20 minutes. Let the pork rest before slicing.

[**Make-ahead option #2:** Let cool, then cover and refrigerate the sliced, roasted pork.]

[**Night of option #2:** Return the pork to room temp before reheating gently in chicken stock over medium heat.]

Meanwhile, bring a few inches of water to a boil in a deep skillet. Salt the water, add the broccoli rabe, and boil to cook out its bitterness, 5 to 7 minutes. Drain well.

Toast the rolls and drizzle with EVOO. Arrange 3 or 4 slices of pork on each roll and squirt with lemon juice. Top with gremolata and the broccoli rabe and set the tops in place.

Heads-up: Most pork shoulder comes with the skin off. Ask the butcher to give you a roast with the skin still on. And while you're at it, ask him to butterfly it, too.

Buffalo Turkey Sloppy Joes
with Blue Cheese Ranch Dressing

Butter and hot sauce are the two principal flavors in Buffalo wings. That's what the wings are tossed in when they come out of the fryer. So here, we're making a much leaner dish, starting with ground turkey breast, which is 99% fat free.

MAKES 12 SANDWICHES

SLOPPY JOES
3 tablespoons **butter**
2 pounds **ground turkey breast**
Celery salt
Pepper
2 **carrots**, finely chopped, plus 2 or 3 carrots cut into sticks for garnish
2 or 3 ribs **celery**, finely chopped, plus a few ribs cut into sticks for garnish
1 **onion**, finely chopped
4 cloves **garlic**, finely chopped

2 tablespoons fresh **thyme** leaves
1 cup **beer** or **chicken stock**
2 tablespoons **cider vinegar**
2 tablespoons **Worcestershire sauce**
1 (15-ounce) can **tomato sauce**
¼ to ½ cup **Frank's RedHot hot sauce**, to taste

BLUE CHEESE RANCH
1 cup **sour cream**
2 tablespoons **lemon** juice or **cider vinegar**

1 large clove **garlic**, grated
¼ cup chopped mixed fresh herbs: **dill**, **chives**, and **parsley**
1 cup crumbled **blue cheese**
⅓ to ½ cup **buttermilk**
Salt and **pepper**

12 **brioche hamburger rolls**

TOPPINGS
Chopped **dill pickles**
Chopped raw **onion** or **scallions**

Make the Sloppy Joe mixture: In a large skillet, melt the butter over medium-high heat. When the butter foams, add the turkey, breaking it into crumbles as it browns. Season with celery salt and pepper. Add the chopped carrots, chopped celery, onion, garlic, and thyme and cook, partially covered, to soften, 12 to 15 minutes. Deglaze the pan with the beer. Add the vinegar, Worcestershire sauce, tomato sauce, and hot sauce and simmer to thicken.

[**Make-ahead:** Let cool and refrigerate.]

[**Night of:** Return the meat mixture to room temp before reheating gently over medium heat.]

Make the blue cheese ranch: Whisk together the sour cream, lemon juice, garlic, herbs, and blue cheese. Whisk in buttermilk to get the consistency you like. Season with salt and pepper.

Serve the meat mixture on rolls topped with pickles, onions, and a dollop of dressing. Garnish the plates with the carrot and celery sticks and serve additional dressing for dipping.

Brisket Bowls with Green Rice

This is an Asian-style brisket with ginger, tamari, and mirin. Brisket is a great make-ahead meal because you get so much out of it. The house smells great while it cooks, and then "the longer it sets, the better it gets," because it's braised. And the leftovers? I am telling you, there's nothing better than a brisket hash topped with an over-easy egg. SERVES 6 TO 8

1 (5-pound) **beef brisket**, trimmed well (no more than ⅛ inch fat on top)

Salt and **pepper**

4 tablespoons **EVOO** or **vegetable oil**

1 large or 2 medium **onions**, chopped

2 **carrots**, chopped

2 or 3 ribs **celery**, chopped

4 cloves **garlic**, chopped

1-inch piece fresh **ginger**, grated

2 **fresh red chiles** (such as red Fresno or Thai), seeded and chopped

2 tablespoons **tomato paste**

2 tablespoons **mirin**

2 tablespoons **rice vinegar**

½ cup **tamari**

3 cups **beef stock**

GREEN RICE

2¾ cups **chicken stock**

2 tablespoons **butter**

1½ cups **basmati rice**

Salt

½ cup packed fresh **cilantro**

1 cup packed **baby spinach**

Grated zest and juice of 1 **lime**

FOR SERVING

Dark sesame oil

loasted **sesame seeds**

Sriracha or other **hot sauce**

Preheat the oven to 325°F.

Bring the beef to room temp and pat dry. Season with salt and pepper. In a large Dutch oven, heat 3 tablespoons EVOO (3 turns of the pan) over medium-high to high heat. Add the meat and brown on both sides. Remove. Add the remaining 1 tablespoon EVOO (1 turn of the pan) and the onions, carrots, celery, garlic, ginger, and chiles. Season with pepper, stir, partially cover, and let the vegetables sweat for 8 to 10 minutes. Add the tomato paste and stir for 1 minute, until fragrant. Deglaze the pan with the mirin, vinegar, and tamari. Add the stock. Add the brisket, cover, and bake until very tender, 2½ to 3 hours.

Remove the brisket from the sauce. When cool enough to handle, slice the brisket and return it to the sauce.

[**Make-ahead:** Let cool and refrigerate.]

[**Night of:** Return the brisket to room temp before reheating gently over medium heat, stirring occasionally.]

Make the green rice: In a saucepan, bring the stock and butter to a boil. Add the rice and stir; season with salt. Reduce to a simmer, cover, and cook for 15 minutes.

Meanwhile, in a food processor, finely pulse-chop the cilantro, spinach, lime zest, and lime juice.

After the rice has cooked 15 minutes, stir in the cilantro-spinach mixture. Cover and cook until the rice is tender, about 3 minutes more. Fluff with a fork.

To serve, fill bowls with rice and make a well in the center. Fill with beef. Top with a drizzle of sesame oil, some sesame seeds, and a few drops of sriracha.

Bacon Burger Mac 'n' Cheese

When I think of "guy food," I go to the all-star list of comfort foods, and right up there at the top are bacon cheeseburgers and mac 'n' cheese. So here's the dish you would get if those two dishes got together and had a kid. SERVES 8 TO 10

1 tablespoon **EVOO**
¾ pound (about 12 slices) **smoky bacon**, chopped
1½ pounds **ground beef sirloin**
Kosher salt and coarsely ground **pepper**
1 **onion**, finely chopped
3 tablespoons **Worcestershire sauce**
½ cup **beef stock**
1½ pounds **cavatappi pasta**
6 tablespoons (¾ stick) **butter**
5 tablespoons **flour**
3 cups **milk**
4 cups shredded **yellow cheddar cheese**
⅓ cup **yellow mustard**, plus more for garnish (I like French's or Plochman's)
⅓ cup **ketchup**, plus more for garnish
2 tablespoons **pickle relish**, plus more for garnish
"Burger toppings": chopped **iceberg lettuce**, diced **tomatoes**, chopped **onion**, **bread-and-butter pickle** chips

Bring a large pot of water to a boil.

In a Dutch oven or deep skillet, heat the EVOO (1 turn of the pan) over medium-high heat. Add the bacon and cook to crisp. Transfer with a slotted spoon to paper towels. Pour out all but a thin layer of bacon drippings from the pan. Add the beef, breaking it into crumbles as it browns but leaving a few larger pieces. Season with salt and pepper. Add the onion and cook to tender. Add the Worcestershire and stock and reduce the heat to low.

Salt the boiling water and cook the pasta about 2 minutes shy of al dente.

Meanwhile, in a saucepan, melt the butter over medium heat. Whisk in the flour and cook for 1 minute. Whisk in the milk and season with salt and pepper. Cook the sauce until thick enough to coat the back of a spoon. Stir in the cheddar. When the cheese has melted into the sauce, stir in the mustard, ketchup, and relish.

Drain the pasta and return to the pot. Add the beef and the cheese sauce. Scrape into a large, deep baking dish.

[**Make-ahead:** Let cool, cover, and refrigerate. Store the bacon in an airtight container at room temp.]

[**Night of:** Return the casserole to room temp while you preheat the oven.]

Preheat the oven to 375°F. Bake until browned and bubbling on top and golden at the edges, 45 to 50 minutes.

Crumble the bacon bits on top and serve with the other "burger toppings."

WEEK 42

COUNT YOUR CHICKENS

A CHICKEN IN EVERY POT?
TWO IS EVEN BETTER. USE POACHED
CHICKEN AS THE BUILDING BLOCK
FOR MOST OF THE WEEK'S MEALS.

DISH
1
CHICKEN &
MUSHROOMS WITH
RIGATONI
PAGE 308

DISH
2
SAGE DERBY
MAC 'N' CHEESE
WITH HAM
PAGE 309

DISH
3
ADIRONDACK
BACON BBQ
CHICKEN, APPLES
& ONIONS
PAGE 310

DISH
4
CHICKEN &
CHORIZO SPANISH
ENCHILADAS
PAGE 312

DISH
5
PICK-A-PEPPER
PASTA
PAGE 313

Chicken & Mushrooms with Rigatoni

If you love chicken Marsala and order it in restaurants, you're going to love this dish. It's got all those same flavors, and it's a great make-ahead. SERVES 4

2 tablespoons **EVOO**

2 tablespoons **butter**

1 pound **cremini** or **button mushrooms**, sliced

2 **shallots**, finely chopped

3 or 4 cloves **garlic**, finely chopped

Leaves from a few sprigs each fresh **sage** and **thyme**, finely chopped

Salt and **pepper**

2 tablespoons **tomato paste**

⅓ cup **Marsala** or **dry sherry**

1 cup **chicken stock**, homemade (page 322) or store-bought

2 cups **passata** or **tomato puree**

½ cup **heavy cream**

2 cups shredded **Poached Chicken** (page 322); see Note

1 pound **rigatoni**

Grated **Parmigiano-Reggiano cheese**

In a large, deep skillet, heat the EVOO (2 turns of the pan) over medium-high heat. Melt the butter into the oil. Add the mushrooms and brown well. Add the shallots, garlic, herbs, and salt and pepper. Cook 2 to 3 minutes more. Add the tomato paste and stir for 1 minute. Deglaze the pan with the Marsala. Stir in the stock, passata, and cream. Add the chicken and simmer over low heat to thicken. Adjust the seasonings.

[Make-ahead: Let cool and refrigerate.]

[Night of: Return the chicken mixture to room temp before reheating gently, partially covered, over medium heat.]

Bring a large pot of water to a boil. Salt the water and cook the pasta al dente. Ladle out about a cup of the starchy cooking water. Drain the pasta and return it to the pot. Add the sauce and some of the starchy water if the sauce seems dry or tight, tossing with tongs for 1 or 2 minutes for the flavors to absorb.

Serve topped with Parm.

Note: Make these changes to the Basic Poached Chicken (page 322): Use 2 whole chickens (4 to 5 pounds each) and 2 large pots. Double all the flavoring ingredients so you have enough to go into each pot. Add sage to the herb bundles. Add 4 cloves garlic, smashed, to each pot.

Sage Derby Mac 'n' Cheese with Ham

Sage Derby cheese is a green-veined sage-scented cheese from Derbyshire in England. Derbies are mild cousins of cheddars. SERVES 6

Salt and **pepper**
1 pound **cavatappi, penne rigate,** or **ridged elbow macaroni**
4 tablespoons (½ stick) **butter**
2 cloves **garlic**, chopped or grated
2 **shallots**, finely chopped
¼ cup **flour**
3 cups **milk**
Freshly grated **nutmeg**
2½ cups grated **Sage Derby cheese** (¾ pound) or **cheddar cheese** mixed with a small handful of thinly sliced fresh **sage** leaves
¾ pound **baked** or **boiled ham**, chopped
1 (9- or 10-ounce) box frozen **chopped spinach**, thawed and wrung dry in a kitchen towel
½ cup grated **Parmigiano-Reggiano cheese**

[If making this to serve on **Cook Day**, preheat the oven to 400°F. If making this to serve later in the week, you'll preheat the oven the night of.]

Bring a large pot of water to a boil. Salt the water and cook the pasta just shy of al dente, 5 to 6 minutes.

Meanwhile, melt the butter in a deep skillet over medium to medium-high heat. When it foams, add the garlic and shallots. Sprinkle in the flour and cook for 1 minute. Whisk in the milk and season with salt, pepper, and a little nutmeg. Cook the sauce until thick enough to coat the back of a spoon. Melt in the Sage Derby. Add the ham and spinach, pulling them into shreds as you add.

Drain the pasta and return to the pot. Add the ham and spinach sauce and toss to combine. Transfer to a shallow 2- to 3-quart baking dish. Top with the Parm.

[Make-ahead: Let cool and refrigerate.]

[**Night of**: Return the casserole to room temp while you preheat the oven to 400°F.]

Bake the casserole until browned and bubbling, 35 to 45 minutes.

Adirondack Bacon BBQ
Chicken, Apples & Onions

It's Sandwich Night! If you buy the rolls on **Cook Day** but won't be having the sandwiches until later in the week, keep the bread in a plastic bag and throw it into a warm oven on the night of to bring it back to life. SERVES 6

EVOO, for drizzling
¼ pound good-quality **smoky bacon**, cut crosswise into ½-inch slices
1 **yellow onion**, finely chopped
2 cloves **garlic**, finely chopped
1 cup good-quality **ketchup**
1 cup **chicken stock**, homemade (page 322) or store-bought
¼ cup dark amber **maple syrup**
¼ cup **grainy Dijon mustard**
3 tablespoons **Worcestershire sauce**
2 tablespoons **cider vinegar**
Salt and coarsely ground **pepper**
2 tablespoons **butter**
2 **apples**, such as Golden Delicious, Gala, or Honeycrisp, sliced
1 large **red onion**, quartered and thinly sliced
Freshly grated **nutmeg**
3 cups pulled **Poached Chicken** (see Note, page 308)
Hard rolls (poppy or plain), split
Grated **white sharp cheddar cheese**, for topping
Sliced **bread-and-butter** or **dill pickles**, for topping

In a saucepan, heat a drizzle of EVOO over medium-high heat. Add the bacon and cook to crisp. Add the yellow onion and garlic and stir for 3 minutes to soften. Add the ketchup, stock, maple syrup, mustard, Worcestershire, vinegar, and pepper. Stir and simmer to thicken, about 20 minutes.

In a large skillet, heat a drizzle of EVOO over medium-high heat. Melt in the butter. Add the apples, red onion, a few grates of nutmeg, and salt and pepper. Cook to tender-crisp, 5 to 6 minutes. Stir the BBQ sauce and chicken into the apples and onions.

[Make-ahead: Let cool and refrigerate.]

[Night of: Return the chicken mixture to room temp before reheating gently over medium heat.]

Serve the BBQ chicken on rolls topped with cheese and pickles.

Chicken & Chorizo Spanish Enchiladas

I love enchiladas, and I love Spanish flavors. So why not mix them up? Here I'm using Spanish-style chorizo instead of Mexican, and lots of the other flavors you find in Spanish cooking, like paprika, olives, and Manchego cheese. SERVES 4 TO 6

2 tablespoons **EVOO**, plus more for drizzling

¾ pound **Spanish chorizo**, casings removed, diced

1 large **Spanish onion**, chopped

4 cloves **garlic**, chopped

2 fresh **jalapeño** or **red Fresno chiles**, seeded and chopped

1 fresh **bay leaf**

Salt and **pepper**

1 (28- or 32-ounce) can **fire-roasted tomatoes**, diced, crushed, or whole

1 cup **passata, tomato puree,** or **tomato sauce**

1½ teaspoons **sweet paprika**

A pinch of ground **cinnamon**

1 cup **chicken stock**, homemade (page 322) or store-bought

2 cups pulled or chopped **Poached Chicken** (see Note, page 308)

2 cups shredded **Manchego cheese**

1 cup shredded **pepper jack cheese**

½ cup chopped **pimiento-stuffed Spanish olives**

½ cup fresh **flat-leaf parsley** leaves, finely chopped

8 (8-inch) **flour tortillas**

[If making this to serve on **Cook Day**, preheat the oven to 400°F. If making this to serve later in the week, you'll preheat the oven on the night of.]

In a large skillet, heat a drizzle of EVOO over medium-high heat. Add the chorizo and brown. With a slotted spoon, transfer the chorizo to paper towels to drain and cool. Pour off the grease from the skillet but reserve the drippings at the bottom.

Add 2 tablespoons EVOO (2 turns of the pan) to the drippings. Add the onion, garlic, chiles, bay leaf, and salt and pepper. Cook to soften, 6 to 7 minutes. Add the tomatoes, passata, paprika, cinnamon, and stock. Bring to a simmer and cook about 15 minutes to thicken.

Pour one-third to one-half of the sauce into a shallow 2- to 3-quart baking dish. In a bowl, combine the chorizo, chicken, 1 cup of the Manchego, ½ cup of the pepper jack, the olives, and parsley.

Char the tortillas in a dry pan or over the flame on gas burners. Divide the filling among the tortillas and roll up. Arrange the enchiladas in the casserole seam side down. Cover with the remaining sauce, 1 cup Manchego, and ½ cup pepper jack.

[Make-ahead: Let cool and refrigerate.]

[Night of: Return the enchiladas to room temp while you preheat the oven to 400°F.]

Bake the enchiladas until browned and bubbling, 35 to 45 minutes.

Pick-a-Pepper Pasta

Mild peppers—like field peppers or bell peppers—like to hang out with cubanelles or Italian frying peppers. And they love to hang out with little hot peppers. So let's get 'em all in there. The real secret to this sauce, though, is the pickled Italian cherry peppers. SERVES 4 TO 6

2 tablespoons **EVOO**
¼ pound **guanciale, speck, pancetta**, or **bacon**, cut into ¼-inch cubes
1 **red onion**, chopped
1 **red bell pepper**, chopped
1 **cubanelle pepper**, chopped
1 **red Fresno chile**, seeded and chopped
3 or 4 cloves **garlic**, chopped or sliced
3 tablespoons chopped **pickled hot Italian cherry peppers**, plus 2 tablespoons of the juice from the jar
1 (28- or 32-ounce) can **San Marzano tomatoes** (look for DOP on the label)
2 cups **passata, tomato puree**, or **tomato sauce**
A few leaves of fresh **basil**, torn
A handful of fresh **flat-leaf parsley**, chopped
Salt and **pepper**
1 pound **bucatini pasta**
2 tablespoons **butter**
Grated pecorino cheese, for serving

In a deep skillet or Dutch oven, heat the EVOO (2 turns of the pan) over medium-high heat. Add the guanciale and cook until lightly crisp. Add the onion, bell and cubanelle peppers, chile, and garlic and cook until tender, 7 to 8 minutes. Add the pickled cherry peppers. Deglaze the pan with the juice from the jar—hold your head back or you'll really clean out your sinuses. Add the tomatoes and crush them up a bit, then stir in the passata and basil. Simmer for 30 minutes or so to thicken. Add the parsley and season with salt and pepper to taste.

[Make-ahead: Let cool and refrigerate.]

[Night of: Return the sauce to room temp before reheating gently over medium heat.]

Bring a large pot of water to a boil. Salt the boiling water and cook the pasta al dente. Ladle out about a cup of the starchy cooking water. Drain the pasta and toss with the butter and half the sauce, adding some of the starchy water if it's too thick. Serve the pasta in shallow bowls topped with the remaining sauce and some pecorino.

WEEK 43

THANKSGIVING BEFORE & AFTER

DISHES TO FEED A CROWD IN THE DAYS LEADING UP TO THANKSGIVING; DISHES THAT DOUBLE AS DINNERS OR SIDES FOR THE BIG DAY ITSELF; AND OF COURSE WHAT TO DO WITH SOME OF THOSE LEFTOVERS

DISH
1
CARROT, SWEET POTATO & SQUASH SOUP
PAGE 315

DISH
2
BACON & BRUSSELS SPROUTS MAC 'N' CHEESE
PAGE 316

DISH
3
BBQ TURKEY OR CHICKEN GUMBO
PAGE 318

DISH
4
ROAST TURKEY, FENNEL & ONIONS WITH BUTTERED EGG NOODLES
PAGE 319

DISH
5
TURKEY, MUSHROOM & CORN MEXICAN CASSEROLE
PAGE 320

Carrot, Sweet Potato & Squash Soup

This soup is a delicious meal or Thanksgiving starter or a clever use-up for leftovers of any of the three main ingredients after the holiday. SERVES 4 TO 6 AS AN ENTRÉE OR 8 TO 10 AS A STARTER

2 tablespoons **EVOO**
2 tablespoons **butter**
1-inch piece fresh **ginger**, finely chopped or grated
2 cloves **garlic**, chopped
2 **onions**, chopped
1 crisp **apple**, peeled and chopped
1 teaspoon ground **cumin**
1 teaspoon ground **coriander**
1 teaspoon **sweet paprika**
A pinch of ground **cinnamon**
Freshly grated **nutmeg**
Salt and **pepper**

1 to 2 tablespoons pureed **chipotle chiles in adobo** (see Heads-up, page 182)
4 cups **chicken stock**, plus more if needed
1 pound **carrots**, peeled and sliced
2 large **sweet potatoes**, peeled and chopped
1½ pounds **pumpkin, kabocha,** or **butternut squash**, peeled and chopped
1 tablespoon **honey**

1 tablespoon **lemon** or **orange** juice

GARNISHES
Browned crumbled **Mexican chorizo**
Finely chopped **red onions** or **scallions**
Toasted **pumpkin seeds**
Crème fraîche
Shredded **smoked cheddar** or **smoked Gouda cheese**
Chopped **parsley** or **cilantro**

In a soup pot, heat the EVOO (2 turns of the pan) over medium-high heat. Melt in the butter. Add the ginger, garlic, onions, apple, cumin, coriander, paprika, cinnamon, a few grates of nutmeg, and salt and pepper. Stir in the chipotle puree. Cook, partially covered, to soften, about 5 minutes. Add the stock, carrots, sweet potatoes, pumpkin, and honey and cook, partially covered, until very tender, about 30 minutes. Puree with an immersion blender or in batches in a food processor.

[**Make-ahead:** Let cool and refrigerate.]

[**Night of:** Return the soup to room temp before reheating gently over medium heat. Add 1 cup of stock or water to loosen the soup enough to reheat.]

Just before serving, add a little citrus juice for a pop. Serve in shallow bowls or cups, topped with garnishes of your choice.

Bacon & Brussels Sprouts Mac 'n' Cheese

Around Thanksgiving time, you can usually find brussels sprouts on the stalk. You'll need 1 large stalk for this. SERVES 6 AS AN ENTRÉE OR 10 TO 12 AS A STARTER OR SIDE

2 pints **brussels sprouts** (on the larger side)
Salt and **pepper**
⅓ pound center-cut **bacon** or **pancetta**, chopped
3 tablespoons **butter**
1 **onion**, chopped
3 or 4 cloves **garlic**, chopped
3 tablespoons **flour**
½ cup **dry white wine**
1 cup **chicken stock**
3 cups **milk**
Freshly grated **nutmeg**
1 cup shredded **sharp white cheddar cheese**
1 cup shredded **Gruyère cheese**
1 cup grated **Parmigiano-Reggiano cheese**
1 pound **cavatappi** or **penne pasta**

[If making this to serve on **Cook Day**, preheat the oven to 375°F. If making this to serve later in the week, you'll preheat the oven on the night of.]

With the tip of a sharp paring knife, dig out the core of the brussels sprouts and separate the leaves. Bring a large pot of water to a boil. Salt the water, add the brussels sprouts leaves, and cook to tender-crisp, about 2 minutes. With a slotted spoon, scoop out the leaves and spread on a kitchen towel to drain and cool. Add more water to fill the pot back up for cooking the pasta; return to a boil.

Heat a deep skillet over medium heat. Brown the bacon. With a slotted spoon, transfer the bacon to paper towels to drain. Pour most of the bacon grease out of the pan. Return it to the heat and melt in the butter. Add the onion and garlic, season with salt and pepper, and cook to soften, about 5 minutes. Sprinkle with the flour and cook for 1 minute. Whisk in the wine. Whisk in the stock and milk and season with salt and pepper and a little nutmeg. Cook the sauce until thick enough to coat the back of a spoon. Add two-thirds of the cheeses and stir in a figure-8 until melted. Reduce the heat to low.

Add the pasta to the boiling water and cook just shy of al dente, 5 to 6 minutes. Drain the pasta; toss with the brussels sprouts, bacon, and cheese sauce. Pour into a shallow 3-quart baking dish and top with the remaining cheese.

[**Make-ahead:** Let cool and refrigerate.]

[**Night of:** Return the casserole to room temp while you preheat the oven to 375°F.]

Bake the casserole, loosely covered, for 30 minutes. Uncover and bake until browned and bubbling, 10 to 15 minutes.

BBQ Turkey or Chicken Gumbo

This is a great use-up for leftover Thanksgiving turkey (see Heads-up), but you could also use rotisserie chicken meat, pulled from the bone. Gumbo is traditionally served with rice, so if you'd prefer, cook up some rice to serve with this instead of the oyster crackers. SERVES 4 TO 6

2 tablespoons **EVOO** or
   vegetable oil

3 tablespoons **butter**

3 or 4 ribs **celery**, chopped

1 large **green bell pepper**,
   chopped

1 large or 2 medium **onions**,
   chopped

3 or 4 cloves **garlic**, finely
   chopped

1 large fresh **bay leaf**

2 tablespoons fresh **thyme**
   leaves, finely chopped

Salt and **pepper**

3 tablespoons **flour**

2 shots **bourbon**

2 cups **chicken stock**

1 (15-ounce) can **tomato sauce**

2 tablespoons **light brown sugar**

2 tablespoons **cider vinegar**

3 to 4 tablespoons
   Worcestershire sauce

3 to 4 tablespoons **Frank's
   RedHot hot sauce**

1 to 1½ pounds cooked **turkey**
   or **chicken**, white and dark
   meat, chopped or pulled (see
   Heads-up)

1 (16-ounce) bag frozen sliced
   okra, thawed (optional)

Oyster crackers, for serving

Thinly sliced **scallions**, for serving

In a large pot or Dutch oven, heat the EVOO (2 turns of the pan) over medium to medium-high heat. Melt in the butter. Add the celery, bell pepper, onions, garlic, bay leaf, thyme, and salt and pepper. Cook, partially covered, to tender, about 15 minutes. Sprinkle in the flour and stir a couple of minutes. Add the bourbon, then the stock. Reduce the heat a bit and cook to thicken. Stir together the tomato sauce, brown sugar, vinegar, Worcestershire sauce, and hot sauce. Pour into the gumbo. Stir in the turkey and okra (if using) and simmer to thicken.

[**Make-ahead:** Let cool and refrigerate.]

[**Night of:** Return the gumbo to room temp before reheating gently over medium heat.]

Serve in shallow bowls. Top each serving with oyster crackers and scallions.

Heads-up: If you're making any of these dishes sometime other than post-Thanksgiving—meaning that you don't have leftover roast turkey on hand—do this: Preheat the oven to 325°F. Rub the skin of one or more turkey breast halves (depending on how much meat you need) with butter or oil, season with salt and pepper, and roast until the internal temperature reaches 165°F, 1 hour for boneless, 1 to 1½ hours for bone-in.

Roast Turkey, Fennel & Onions with Buttered Egg Noodles

In the first step, you caramelize some onion and fennel. If you stopped right there and didn't continue, you would have the basis for fabulous crostini. Just put the caramelized vegetables on little toast rounds, and maybe sprinkle on a little Gorgonzola dolce (though that would definitely be gilding the lily). SERVES 4 TO 6

2 tablespoons **EVOO**

4 tablespoons (½ stick) **butter**

2 large **onions**, quartered and thinly sliced

2 bulbs **fennel**, quartered and thinly sliced

3 or 4 cloves **garlic**, thinly sliced

2 tablespoons fresh **thyme** leaves, finely chopped

Salt and **pepper**

2 rounded tablespoons **flour**

½ cup **dry white wine**

2 cups **chicken stock**

1 to 1½ pounds **roast turkey breast** (see Heads-up, page 318), cut into bite-size pieces

1 pound extra-wide **egg noodles**

¼ cup finely chopped fresh **flat-leaf parsley**

A handful of grated **Parmigiano-Reggiano cheese**

½ cup **heavy cream**

Toasted **pine nuts**, for garnish

In a deep skillet, heat the EVOO (2 turns of the pan) over medium heat. Melt in 2 tablespoons of the butter. Add the onions, fennel, garlic, thyme, and salt and pepper. Cook, stirring frequently, until very soft and light golden, about 20 minutes.

Sprinkle the flour over the vegetables and stir a minute. Whisk in the wine. Stir in the stock and cook to thicken. Stir in the turkey.

[**Make-ahead:** Let cool and refrigerate.]

[**Night of:** Return the turkey mixture to room temp before reheating gently over medium heat.]

Bring a large pot of water to a boil. Salt the water and cook the noodles al dente. Drain and return to the pot. Add the remaining 2 tablespoons butter, the parsley, Parm, and salt and pepper.

Meanwhile, stir the cream into the turkey mixture and cook to thicken. Adjust the seasonings.

Serve the turkey on a bed of egg noodles, garnished with pine nuts.

Turkey, Mushroom & Corn Mexican Casserole

A serrated knife is the most efficient way to cut through a dense, layered casserole like this. For a beefier flavor, use cremini instead of button mushrooms. SERVES 4 TO 6

SAUCE
3 medium **poblano chiles**, stemmed, seeded, and chopped

1 cup **turkey** or **chicken stock**

1 small **onion**, chopped

2 cloves **garlic**, chopped

A small handful of fresh **cilantro** leaves, plus more for garnish

Salt and **pepper**

4 tablespoons (½ stick) **butter**

2 tablespoons **flour**

1 cup **milk**

½ cup **heavy cream** or **Mexican crema**

CASSEROLE
2 tablespoons **EVOO**

3 tablespoons **butter**

¾ pound **button mushrooms**, sliced

2 cups **corn** kernels, fresh (from 4 ears) or thawed frozen

2 **shallots** or 1 small **red onion**, chopped

4 to 5 cups chopped **roast turkey** meat (see Heads-up, page 318)

1 cup **turkey** or **chicken stock**

6 (8-inch) **flour tortillas**

2½ cups shredded **Monterey Jack** or **cheddar cheese**

[If making this to serve on **Cook Day**, preheat the oven to 400°F. If making this to serve later in the week, you'll preheat the oven on the night of.]

Make the sauce: In a blender or food processor, puree the poblanos, stock, onion, garlic, cilantro, and salt and pepper. In a saucepan, melt 3 tablespoons of the butter over medium heat. Whisk in the flour and cook a minute. Whisk in the milk and cream and increase the heat a bit. Add the poblano puree and simmer to thicken and cook the sauce, 20 to 25 minutes.

Prepare the casserole: In a large skillet, heat the EVOO (2 turns of the pan) over medium-high heat. Melt in the remaining 1 tablespoon butter. Add the mushrooms and cook until well browned, about 10 minutes. Add the corn and shallots and cook 5 minutes more to lightly brown the corn and soften the shallots. Add the turkey and stock and heat through.

Char the tortillas in a dry skillet or over a flame of a gas burner.

Spread half the turkey mixture in the bottom of a shallow 2- to 3-quart baking dish. Top with half the sauce, 3 tortillas (overlapping), and half the cheese. Top with the rest of the turkey mixture. Add another layer of tortillas, the remainder of the sauce, and the remainder of the cheese.

[**Make-ahead:** Let cool and refrigerate.]

[**Night of:** Return the casserole to room temp while you preheat the oven to 400°F.]

Bake until hot through, browned, and bubbling, 20 to 25 minutes. Let it sit for 10 to 15 minutes before serving.

FOUNDATION RECIPES

BASIC POACHED CHICKEN
PARMIGIANO-HERB STOCK
ROASTED TOMATOES
PULLED PORK

Getting ready for your *Week in a Day*
Rachael shares timing and
organizational tips for getting the
most out of *Week in a Day*.

Basic Poached Chicken

Many, many of the dishes in this book use cooked chicken that you poach yourself. Not only is this easy on the budget, but the real bang for the buck comes when you end up with a flavorful broth and don't always have to rely on stock in a box. This recipe is a template for all the poached chicken called for in the book. The quantity of chicken changes from recipe to recipe, and sometimes the amount of cooking time and the herbs change, but this is the basic recipe.

1 whole **chicken** (4 to 5 pounds)

1 large **onion**, quartered with root end attached

2 **carrots**, quartered

2 ribs **celery**, quartered

1 **lemon**, sliced

2 fresh **bay leaves**

Herb bundle: 2 or 3 sprigs each fresh **parsley**, **rosemary**, and **thyme** tied with kitchen twine

A few black **peppercorns**

Salt

Place the chicken in a large pot and add the onion, carrots, celery, lemon, bay leaves, herb bundle, and peppercorns. Season well with salt. Cover with water (ideally 3 to 4 quarts) and bring to a boil. Reduce the heat to a simmer and poach the chicken for 1 hour. Transfer the chicken to a cutting board, and when cool enough to handle, discard the skin and bones and pull the meat into bite-size shreds. Strain the stock and reserve.

Parmigiano-Herb Stock

Always save the rinds of hard grating cheeses for making cool stocks like this. Just throw the rinds into the freezer and hold on to them until you need them. Or throw a piece of rind into any soup you're making. Makes about 3 quarts.

1 large rind from a hunk of **Parmigiano-Reggiano cheese** or a few small pieces of rind (perhaps saved up?)

Herb bundle: several sprigs each fresh **thyme**, **parsley**, and **rosemary**, tied together with kitchen twine

1 **onion**, quartered, with root end attached

2 ribs **celery**, sliced on an angle

2 **carrots**, sliced on an angle

Zest of 1 **lemon**, pulled off in long strips with a vegetable peeler

2 fresh **bay leaves**

4 cups **chicken stock**

In a soup pot or large Dutch oven, combine all the ingredients and 3 quarts (12 cups) water and bring to a bubble. Reduce the heat to a simmer and cook for at least 1 hour. Strain the stock before using or storing it.

Roasted Tomatoes

24 vine-ripened **tomatoes** or large **plum tomatoes**, halved

4 cloves **garlic**, smashed

EVOO, for liberal drizzling

Salt and **pepper**

Preheat the oven to 500°F.

Arrange the tomatoes on 2 baking sheets in a single layer. Scatter the garlic among the tomatoes, drizzle with EVOO to coat, and season with salt and pepper. Roast the tomatoes until the skins split and begin to char, about 30 minutes. Let the tomatoes cool until cool enough to handle, then peel. Store the tomatoes and garlic separately.

Pulled Pork

4 pounds boneless **pork shoulder** (butt)

Kosher salt and **pepper**

2 tablespoons **vegetable oil**

1 **onion**, cut into thin wedges, root end intact

1 large **carrot**, sliced on an angle

2 or 3 small ribs **celery** from the heart with leafy tops, sliced on an angle

1 small bulb **fennel**, sliced

4 large cloves **garlic**, sliced

2 tablespoons fresh **thyme** leaves, chopped

2 fresh **bay leaves**

1½ cups **dry white wine**

4 cups **chicken stock**

Preheat the oven to 350°F.

Pat the pork dry and season generously with salt and pepper. In a large Dutch oven or heavy-bottomed pot, heat the oil over medium-high heat. Add the pork and brown well on all sides. Transfer the pork to a plate. Reduce the heat to medium. Add the onion, carrot, celery, fennel, garlic, thyme, bay leaves, and salt and pepper. Cook to soften the vegetables, about 10 minutes. Deglaze the pan with the wine. Stir in the stock, slide the pork back into the pot (the stock should come two-thirds of the way up the meat), and bring to a low boil. Cover the pot, place in the oven, and cook until the meat is tender and falls apart when pulled at with a fork, 2 to 2½ hours, turning the meat halfway through cooking.

Transfer the pork to a platter. When cool enough to handle, pull apart with 2 forks. Divide the meat into two equal portions, one for the Red Pork Posole (page 93) and one for the Pappardelle with Pulled Pork (page 98). Strain the braising liquid and add to the pork for the pasta dish.

1

GROCERY
BAG

3

MEALS

THE GROCERY BAG ❶

- ☐ 4 (8-OUNCE) SIRLOIN OR FLAT IRON STEAKS, ABOUT 1 INCH THICK
- ☐ 4 (6-OUNCE) BONELESS, SKINLESS CHICKEN BREAST HALVES
- ☐ 10 LARGE SHALLOTS
- ☐ 4 LARGE STARCHY (RUSSET) POTATOES
- ☐ 1 BUNCH LACINATO KALE (AKA BLACK, TUSCAN, OR DINOSAUR KALE)
- ☐ 1 BUNCH FLAT-LEAF PARSLEY
- ☐ 1 BUNCH FRESH ROSEMARY
- ☐ 1 BUNCH FRESH THYME
- ☐ 2 LEMONS
- ☐ 1 (3-OUNCE) JAR CAPERS
- ☐ 1 (750 ML) BOTTLE WHITE WINE
- ☐ 1 (750 ML) BOTTLE RED WINE

OPTIONAL SIDES
- ☐ 1-POUND LOAF TUSCAN-STYLE BREAD
- ☐ 1 PINT CHERRY TOMATOES
- ☐ 1 (5-OUNCE) BAG BABY ARUGULA

IN THE PANTRY
- ☐ BUTTER
- ☐ PECORINO OR PARMIGIANO-REGGIANO CHEESE
- ☐ GARLIC
- ☐ SPAGHETTI
- ☐ FLOUR
- ☐ BALSAMIC VINEGAR
- ☐ EVOO

Chicken Piccata

Suggested side: Crusty Tuscan-style bread, warmed. SERVES 4

4 boneless, skinless **chicken breast** halves (6 ounces each)
Salt and **pepper**
Flour, for dredging
4 to 5 tablespoons **EVOO**
4 tablespoons (½ stick) **butter**
2 **lemons**: 1 thinly sliced, 1 for juicing
4 cloves **garlic**, finely chopped
3 tablespoons **capers**, rinsed and drained
½ cup **dry white wine**
¼ cup fresh **flat-leaf parsley** tops, finely chopped

Split and butterfly the chicken: Starting on a fat side of the chicken breast, cut horizontally across the breast but not all the way through. Open it up like a book. Pound the chicken to ⅛ to ¼ inch thick.

Preheat the oven to 250°F and place a serving platter or large plate in the oven to warm as it preheats.

Heat a large skillet over medium to medium-high heat. Season the chicken with salt and pepper and dredge in flour, shaking off the excess. Pour 1 or 2 tablespoons EVOO (1 or 2 turns of the pan) into the preheated pan. Working in batches, brown the chicken lightly on each side, adding more EVOO as necessary. Transfer to the warmed platter, cover with foil, and keep warm while you make the lemon-butter sauce.

Melt the butter into the drippings. Add the lemon slices and lightly brown. Add the garlic and stir for 1 minute. Add the capers. Deglaze the pan with the wine. Add the juice of the other lemon and the parsley. Slide the chicken back into the pan and coat with the sauce. To serve, return the chicken to the platter and drizzle with the pan sauce.

1 Grocery Bag, 3 Meals: List #1
Scan to view the shopping list for Grocery Bag #1 on your mobile device.

10-Shallot Spaghetti with Kale

SERVES 4

2 tablespoons **EVOO**
4 tablespoons (½ stick) **butter**, cut into small pieces
10 large **shallots**, halved lengthwise and thinly sliced crosswise
4 cloves **garlic**, thinly sliced
2 tablespoons fresh **thyme** leaves, chopped
Salt and **pepper**
1 pound **spaghetti**, preferably farro or whole wheat
1 bunch **lacinato kale** (also called black, Tuscan, or dinosaur kale), stemmed and thinly sliced
½ cup grated **pecorino** or **Parmigiano-Reggiano cheese**
¼ to ½ cup chopped fresh **flat-leaf parsley**

Bring a large pot of water to a boil.

In a large skillet, heat the EVOO (2 turns of the pan) over medium heat. Melt the butter into the oil. Add the shallots, garlic, and thyme; season with salt and pepper. Cook, stirring frequently, until light caramel color, 15 to 20 minutes.

Salt the boiling water and cook the pasta al dente; add the kale for the last 4 minutes of cook time. Ladle out about a cup of the starchy cooking water and add to the shallot sauce. Drain the pasta and return it to the pot. Add the sauce, tossing with tongs for 1 or 2 minutes for the flavors to absorb. Adjust the salt and pepper and toss in a couple of handfuls of cheese and parsley.

Drunken Steaks with Peppery Oven Fries

Suggested side: A simple arugula and tomato salad: halved cherry tomatoes and baby arugula, dressed with EVOO, salt, and pepper. SERVES 4

½ cup **dry red wine**
2 tablespoons **balsamic vinegar**
4 cloves **garlic**, smashed
3 tablespoons fresh **rosemary** leaves, chopped
4 (8-ounce) **sirloin** or **flat iron steaks**, about 1 inch thick
Kosher salt and coarsely ground **pepper**
4 large **starchy potatoes** (russet), cut lengthwise into ¾-inch wedges
5 tablespoons **EVOO**
2 tablespoons chopped fresh **thyme**

In a large food storage bag, combine the wine, vinegar, garlic, and rosemary. Season the steaks with salt and pepper and add to the marinade. Refrigerate the steaks overnight.

Preheat the oven to 375°F.

Soak the potatoes in salted water in a large bowl for a few minutes. Drain and pat dry. Toss the potatoes with 3 tablespoons EVOO and the thyme; season with salt and lots of pepper and toss again. Spread out on a baking sheet and bake for 20 minutes. Remove from the oven and let cool to room temp. Leave the oven on and increase the temperature to 450°F.

Return the potatoes to the oven and roast until deeply golden and crispy, about 15 minutes.

Heat a cast-iron or ovenproof skillet over medium-high heat. Pat the steaks dry and coat evenly with 2 tablespoons EVOO. Place the steaks in the preheated pan and brown on each side, then pop into the oven to cook to medium, about 5 minutes. Let rest before serving.

1 GROCERY BAG

3 MEALS

THE GROCERY BAG ②

- ☐ ⅓ POUND SLAB BACON
- ☐ 2 POUNDS GROUND SIRLOIN OR CHUCK
- ☐ 1 POUND HOT ITALIAN SAUSAGE OR FRESH MEXICAN CHORIZO
- ☐ 8 BONE-IN, SKIN-ON CHICKEN THIGHS
- ☐ ½ POUND GORGONZOLA CHEESE
- ☐ 4 LARGE ONIONS
- ☐ 2 FRYING OR BELL PEPPERS (RED OR GREEN)
- ☐ 2 FRESH RED FRESNOS OR JALAPEÑOS
- ☐ BABY ARUGULA (A COUPLE OF HANDFULS) OR 1 BUNCH WATERCRESS
- ☐ 1 BUNCH FLAT-LEAF PARSLEY
- ☐ 1 BUNCH FRESH ROSEMARY
- ☐ 2 (28- OR 32-OUNCE) CANS SAN MARZANO TOMATOES WITH BASIL
- ☐ 1 POUND ZITI RIGATE
- ☐ 4 KAISER ROLLS
- ☐ 1 (750 ML) BOTTLE WHITE WINE
- ☐ 1 (750 ML) BOTTLE RED WINE

OPTIONAL SIDE
- ☐ 4 PORTUGUESE OR CIABATTA ROLLS

IN THE PANTRY

- ☐ PECORINO OR PARM CHEESE
- ☐ GARLIC
- ☐ BEEF STOCK AND CHICKEN STOCK
- ☐ EVOO
- ☐ SWEET PAPRIKA (SMOKED OR REGULAR)

MEAL 1

Bacon Burgers with Caramelized Onions & Gorgonzola

For the burger rolls, you can also use onion, sesame, or poppy seed. SERVES 4

EVOO, for drizzling and coating
⅓ pound good-quality **slab bacon**, chopped
3 large **onions**, thinly sliced
Salt and **pepper**
Splash of **white wine**
1½ pounds **ground sirloin** or **chuck**, at room temperature
2 tablespoons minced fresh **rosemary**
4 **burger rolls**, split and toasted
½ pound **Gorgonzola cheese**, crumbled
A few handfuls of **arugula** or **watercress**

Heat a large skillet over medium-high heat. Drizzle in EVOO. Cook the bacon until almost crispy. Transfer to a plate and let cool.

Stir the onions into the drippings, season with pepper, reduce the heat to medium-low, and cook until caramel color, about 30 minutes. Season the onions with salt and deglaze the pan with a little wine. Transfer to a bowl and cover to keep warm.

Meanwhile, combine the beef, cooled bacon, the rosemary, and salt and pepper. Score the mixture into 4 equal portions and form them into patties slightly thinner at the center than at the edges for even cooking and to ensure a flat surface (burgers plump as they cook). Coat the burgers with EVOO.

Return the skillet to the burner and increase the heat to medium-high. Add the burgers and cook, flipping once, for 8 minutes for medium-rare (adjust the timing for more well-done burgers).

Place the burgers on the toasted rolls and top with the caramelized onions, Gorgonzola crumbles, and spicy greens.

1 Grocery Bag, 3 Meals: List #2
Scan to view the shopping list for Grocery Bag #2 on your mobile device.

MEAL 2

Spicy Ziti with Sausage

SERVES 4

2 tablespoons **EVOO**
½ pound **ground beef sirloin** or **chuck**
Salt and **pepper**
½ pound **hot Italian sausage** or fresh **Mexican chorizo**, casings removed
3 tablespoons fresh **rosemary** leaves, chopped
4 cloves **garlic**, chopped
½ cup **dry red** or **white wine**
2 (28- or 32-ounce) cans **San Marzano tomatoes** (look for DOP on the label)
1 cup **beef** or **veal stock**
1 pound **ziti rigate**
1 cup grated **pecorino** or **Parmigiano-Reggiano cheese**

In a large Dutch oven, heat the EVOO (2 turns of the pan) over medium-high heat. Add the beef and season with salt and pepper. Add the sausage and cook, breaking it into crumbles as it browns. Add the rosemary and garlic and stir a couple of minutes. Deglaze the pan with the wine. Add the tomatoes and stock and simmer for 30 minutes.

Bring a large pot of water to a boil. Salt the water and cook the pasta al dente. Ladle out about a cup of the starchy cooking water and add to the sauce. Drain the pasta and return it to the pot. Add the sauce, tossing with tongs for 1 or 2 minutes for the flavors to absorb.

Serve with cheese.

MEAL 3

Skillet Chicken with Hot & Sweet Peppers

Suggested side: Warmed Portuguese rolls or ciabatta rolls for mopping.
SERVES 4

1 tablespoon **EVOO**
½ pound **hot Italian sausage** or fresh **Mexican chorizo**, casings removed
8 bone-in, skin-on **chicken thighs**
1 tablespoon **sweet paprika** (smoked or regular)
Salt and **pepper**
1 large **onion**, chopped
2 **fresh chiles** (red Fresno or jalapeño), sliced
2 **frying** or **bell peppers** (red or green), chopped
4 cloves **garlic**, sliced
½ cup **dry white wine** or **sherry**
1 cup **chicken stock**
½ cup chopped fresh **flat-leaf parsley**

In a cast-iron or other heavy-bottomed skillet, heat the EVOO (1 turn of the pan) over medium-high heat. Add the sausage and cook, breaking it into crumbles as it browns. Transfer to a plate.

Season the chicken with the paprika and salt and pepper. Add the chicken to the drippings and brown on both sides, about 8 minutes. Transfer the chicken to the plate.

Cook the onion, chiles, frying peppers, and garlic with salt and pepper until softened, 8 to 10 minutes. Deglaze the pan with the wine. Add the stock and slide the chicken and sausage back into the pan. Loosely cover with foil and simmer until the chicken is cooked through, 12 to 15 minutes.

Serve topped with the parsley.

1 GROCERY BAG

3 MEALS

THE GROCERY BAG ❸

- ☐ 1¼ POUNDS FLANK STEAK
- ☐ 8 BONELESS, SKINLESS CHICKEN THIGHS
- ☐ 1¼ POUNDS MEDIUM SHRIMP, PEELED AND DEVEINED
- ☐ 8 OUNCES CRÈME FRAÎCHE
- ☐ 1 CUP WHOLE-MILK GREEK YOGURT
- ☐ ONIONS, 1 SMALL AND 2 LARGE
- ☐ 2 LARGE STARCHY (RUSSET) POTATOES
- ☐ 1 POBLANO CHILE
- ☐ 1 BUNCH CILANTRO
- ☐ 2 INCHES FRESH GINGER
- ☐ 1 LIME
- ☐ 12 OUNCES FROZEN SHELLED EDAMAME
- ☐ 1 (1-POUND) BAG YELLOW SPLIT PEAS
- ☐ 12 OUNCES SOBA NOODLES
- ☐ 1 POUND LINGUINE
- ☐ 1 BOTTLE (ANY SIZE) SRIRACHA SAUCE
- ☐ 1 JAR CUMIN SEEDS

OPTIONAL SIDE
- ☐ GARLIC NAAN BREAD

IN THE PANTRY

- ☐ BUTTER
- ☐ GARLIC
- ☐ FLOUR
- ☐ HONEY
- ☐ TAMARI OR SOY SAUCE
- ☐ STOCK, CHICKEN AND BEEF
- ☐ CANOLA OIL OR OTHER HIGH-TEMP OIL
- ☐ EVOO
- ☐ CURRY POWDER

MEAL 1

Poblano Cream Linguine with Shrimp

SERVES 4

6 tablespoons (¾ stick) **butter**
1 small **onion**, finely chopped
4 cloves **garlic**, finely chopped
1 **poblano chile**, seeded and finely chopped
3 tablespoons **flour**
1½ cups **chicken stock**
½ cup **crème fraîche** or **Mexican crema**
Salt and **pepper**
1 pound **linguine**
1¼ pounds medium **shrimp**, peeled and deveined
Cilantro leaves, for garnish

Bring a large pot of water to a boil.

In a saucepan, melt 4 tablespoons of the butter over medium to medium-high heat. Add the onion, garlic, and chile and cook until softened, 7 to 8 minutes. Sprinkle with the flour and stir for about a minute. Whisk in the stock, bring to a bubble, and simmer for 5 minutes to thicken slightly.

Meanwhile, in a small saucepan, heat the crème fraîche over medium heat. Add the crème fraîche to the sauce and whisk to combine. Transfer the sauce to a food processor or blender and puree until very smooth. Return the sauce to low heat and season with salt.

Salt the boiling water and cook the linguine al dente. Before draining, ladle out about a cup of the starchy cooking water.

In a large skillet, melt the remaining 2 tablespoons butter over medium-high heat. Add the shrimp and cook to firm and pink; season with salt and pepper. Deglaze the skillet with the starchy water. Add the shrimp and deglazing liquid to the cream sauce.

Drain the linguine and return it to the pot. Add the sauce, tossing with tongs for 1 or 2 minutes for the flavors to absorb. Adjust the seasonings and serve in shallow bowls. Garnish with cilantro leaves.

MEAL 2

Creamy Chicken Curry with Potatoes & Split Peas

Suggested side: Garlic naan bread, grilled according to package directions. SERVES 4

2 tablespoons **EVOO**
1 large **onion**, chopped
1-inch piece fresh **ginger**, grated
4 cloves **garlic**, sliced
1 teaspoon **cumin seeds**
Salt and **pepper**
2 rounded tablespoons **curry powder**
4 cups **chicken stock**
2 large **starchy potatoes** (russet), peeled and cut into 1½- to 2-inch chunks
1 cup **yellow split peas**
8 boneless, skinless **chicken thighs**
1 **lime**, halved
1 cup whole-milk **Greek yogurt**
Chopped fresh **cilantro**, for serving

In a Dutch oven, heat the EVOO (2 turns of the pan) over medium-high heat. Add the onion, ginger, garlic, cumin seeds, and salt and pepper. Sweat the onion a few minutes. Add the curry powder and stir for 1 or 2 minutes. Add the stock and bring to a boil, then reduce the heat to a simmer. Add the potatoes, split peas, and chicken. Cover and simmer until the chicken is cooked through and the peas are tender, 1 to 1¼ hours.

Pull the chicken out of the pan. Shred the meat with 2 forks and add it back to the curry. Squeeze in the lime juice and stir in the yogurt. Adjust the seasonings. Serve sprinkled with cilantro.

MEAL 3

Hot & Sweet Sliced Steak Noodle Bowls

To make the meat easier to slice, put it in the freezer for about 15 minutes to firm up. SERVES 4

3 tablespoons **canola oil** or other high-temperature oil
1¼ pounds **flank steak**, thinly sliced (against the grain)
Salt and **pepper**
1 large **onion**, thinly sliced
1-inch piece fresh **ginger**, grated
4 cloves **garlic**, thinly sliced
⅓ cup **tamari** or **soy sauce**
¼ cup **sriracha sauce**
3 tablespoons **honey**
1 cup **beef stock**
12 ounces **soba noodles** or 1 pound **whole-grain spaghetti**
1½ cups frozen shelled **edamame**, thawed
Chopped fresh **cilantro**, for serving

Bring a large pot of water to a boil.

In a large skillet, heat the oil over high heat. Add the beef and season with pepper. Stir-fry a minute or so to get some color on it. Add the onion, ginger, and garlic and stir-fry until the onion is softened, 2 to 3 minutes. Add the tamari, sriracha, honey, and stock.

Meanwhile, salt the boiling water and cook the noodles al dente.

Drain the noodles and add to the beef along with the edamame. Toss to combine and heat through. Serve sprinkled with cilantro.

1 Grocery Bag, 3 Meals: List #3
Scan to view the shopping list for Grocery Bag #3 on your mobile device.

1 GROCERY BAG
3 MEALS

THE GROCERY BAG 4

- [ ] 8 (4- TO 5-OUNCE) LAMB RIB CHOPS (¾ INCH THICK)
- [ ] 8 BONE-IN, SKIN-ON CHICKEN THIGHS
- [ ] 1 PINT HALF-AND-HALF
- [ ] ONIONS, 2 MEDIUM AND 1 LARGE
- [ ] 2 WHOLE HEADS GARLIC
- [ ] 2 POUNDS STARCHY POTATOES (RUSSET)
- [ ] 1 HEAD CAULIFLOWER
- [ ] 1 LARGE HEAD ESCAROLE
- [ ] 2 BUNCHES FLAT-LEAF SPINACH
- [ ] 1 BUNCH FRESH ROSEMARY
- [ ] 1 BUNCH FRESH THYME
- [ ] FRESH BAY LEAVES
- [ ] 1 LEMON
- [ ] 1 (1-POUND) BAG DRIED CHICKPEAS
- [ ] 1 (1-POUND) BAG DRIED CANNELLINI BEANS
- [ ] 1 JAR PREPARED HORSERADISH
- [ ] 1 (750 ML) BOTTLE MARSALA OR 1 (500 ML) BOTTLE DRY SHERRY
- [ ] 1 (750 ML BOTTLE) BOTTLE DRY WHITE WINE

OPTIONAL SIDE
- [ ] 1 LOAF GOOD CRUSTY BREAD

IN THE PANTRY

- [ ] PARMIGIANO-REGGIANO CHEESE
- [ ] CHICKEN STOCK
- [ ] EVOO
- [ ] NUTMEG

MEAL 1

Braised Chicken Thighs with Escarole & White Beans

Suggested side: Nice, crusty bread for mopping, warmed in the oven and torn into pieces (not sliced). SERVES 4

1 rounded cup **dried cannellini beans**
2 **onions**: 1 halved, 1 chopped
1 fresh **bay leaf**
Salt and pepper
3 tablespoons **EVOO**
8 bone-in, skin-on **chicken thighs**
4 cloves **garlic**, sliced
2 tablespoons fresh **rosemary** leaves, chopped
1 **lemon**, zest grated to get 2 teaspoons, and halved
1 large head **escarole**, coarsely chopped
Freshly grated **nutmeg**
4 cups **chicken stock**

In a saucepan, cover the beans with water by 2 inches. Bring to a boil, turn off the heat, cover, and let stand for 1 hour.

Drain the beans and place in a 4- to 5-quart pot. Cover with water by about 2 inches. Add the halved onion and bay leaf and bring to a simmer. Salt the water and cook the beans at a low boil until tender, 30 to 35 minutes. Drain the beans, discarding the onion and bay leaf.

In a large deep skillet or Dutch oven, heat the EVOO (3 turns of the pan) over medium-high heat. Season the chicken with salt and pepper. Cook until the skin is crispy and browned, about 8 minutes, turning once. Transfer to a plate.

Reduce the heat under the pan to medium and add the chopped onion, garlic, rosemary, and lemon zest. Cook until softened, stirring often, 8 to 10 minutes. Wilt the escarole into the pan, seasoning with a few grates of nutmeg. Add the beans and chicken stock.

Nestle the chicken into the greens and beans and braise at a low simmer until the chicken is cooked through but still juicy, 15 to 18 minutes.

Squeeze in a little lemon juice. Serve the chicken, escarole, beans, and broth in shallow bowls.

MEAL 2

Chickpea Soup with Roasted Cauliflower

SERVES 4

1½ cups **dried chickpeas**
1 head **garlic**, top cut off to expose the cloves
3 tablespoons **EVOO**, plus more for drizzling
Salt and **pepper**
1 head **cauliflower**, florets sliced about 1 inch thick
½ cup grated **Parmigiano-Reggiano cheese**
1 large **onion**, chopped
1 tablespoon fresh **thyme** leaves, chopped
2 sprigs fresh **rosemary**
1 fresh **bay leaf**
1 cup **dry white wine**
4 cups **chicken stock**

Place the chickpeas in a bowl and cover with boiling water. Let stand for 1 hour. Drain.

Preheat the oven to 425°F.

Meanwhile, drizzle the garlic with EVOO; season with salt and pepper. Wrap in foil. Drizzle the cauliflower with EVOO and toss to coat; season with salt and pepper. Arrange the cauliflower and garlic packet on a nonstick baking sheet. Roast, turning the cauliflower once, until the garlic is soft and the cauliflower tender, about 40 minutes. Remove the garlic and let cool. Sprinkle the Parm over the cauliflower and roast 5 to 7 minutes longer to brown the cheese. Set aside and keep warm.

In a soup pot, heat the EVOO over medium to medium-high heat. Add the onion, thyme, rosemary, bay leaf, and salt and pepper and cook, stirring, until softened, about 10 minutes. Stir in the wine and cook until reduced to about ¼ cup. Squeeze the garlic out of its skins into the pot. Add the chickpeas, stock, and 2 cups water and bring to a simmer. Cover and simmer until the chickpeas are tender, 1½ to 2 hours.

Remove the rosemary stems and bay leaf. Use an immersion blender to puree, or puree in small batches in a food processor. Adjust the seasonings.

Serve the soup in shallow bowls topped with roasted cheesy cauliflower.

MEAL 3

Lamb Chops with Horseradish Mash & Wilted Spinach

SERVES 4

2 pounds **starchy potatoes** (russet), peeled and cut into 1-inch pieces
Salt and **pepper**
⅔ cup **half-and-half**
2 rounded tablespoons **prepared horseradish**
½ cup grated **Parmigiano-Reggiano cheese**
8 (4- to 5-ounce) **lamb rib chops** (¾ inch thick), at room temperature
2 tablespoons **EVOO**, plus more for drizzling
2 sprigs fresh **rosemary**
½ cup **Marsala** or **dry sherry**
1 clove **garlic**, smashed
2 bunches **flat-leaf spinach**, stems trimmed, washed and dried
Freshly grated **nutmeg**

Place the potatoes in a pot with water to cover. Bring to a boil, salt the water, and cook until tender, about 15 minutes. Drain and return to the pot. Mash the potatoes with the half-and-half, horseradish, and Parm. Season with salt. Cover to keep warm.

Heat a cast-iron or other heavy skillet over medium-high heat. Season the chops with salt and pepper and drizzle with EVOO. Place the chops in the pan and top with the rosemary. Cook the chops, flipping once (place the rosemary under the chops), about 8 minutes for medium-rare. Deglaze the pan with the Marsala. Remove from the heat.

Meanwhile, in a second large skillet, heat the 2 tablespoons EVOO (2 turns of the pan) and the garlic over medium heat, swirling the garlic for 1 or 2 minutes. Wilt in the spinach and season with salt, pepper, and a few grates of nutmeg.

Serve the chops on or alongside the spinach and potatoes. Spoon the pan juices over the chops.

 1 Grocery Bag, 3 Meals: List #4
Scan to view the shopping list for Grocery Bag #4 on your mobile device.

1 GROCERY BAG
3 MEALS

THE GROCERY BAG 5

- ☐ 1½ POUNDS ITALIAN SAUSAGE (SWEET OR HOT)
- ☐ 2 POUNDS MUSSELS
- ☐ 1 DOZEN LARGE EGGS
- ☐ 1 (8-OUNCE) CONTAINER SOUR CREAM
- ☐ ½-POUND BRICK GOUDA, GRUYÈRE, OR FONTINA CHEESE
- ☐ 2 ONIONS
- ☐ 4 LARGE LEEKS
- ☐ 1 LARGE STARCHY POTATO (RUSSET)
- ☐ 1 LARGE BULB FENNEL
- ☐ 2 CARROTS
- ☐ 1 SMALL HEAD CELERY
- ☐ 1 PINT CHERRY TOMATOES
- ☐ 1 BUNCH LACINATO KALE (AKA TUSCAN, DINOSAUR, OR BLACK KALE)
- ☐ 1 BUNCH FRESH THYME
- ☐ 1 BUNCH FRESH ROSEMARY
- ☐ 1 (1-POUND) BAG BROWN LENTILS

OPTIONAL SIDES

- ☐ 2 BUNCHES ARUGULA
- ☐ 2 LEMONS
- ☐ 1 LOAF CRUSTY BREAD

IN THE PANTRY

- ☐ GARLIC
- ☐ TOMATO PASTE
- ☐ CHICKEN STOCK
- ☐ EVOO
- ☐ CRUSHED RED PEPPER FLAKES

MEAL 1

Mussels with Fennel & Garlic

Suggested side: Good crusty bread, warmed in the oven and torn, for mopping up the juices. SERVES 4

3 tablespoons **EVOO**
½ pound **Italian sausage** (sweet or hot), casings removed
1 large bulb **fennel**, chopped (reserve a few fronds)
1 **onion**, chopped
2 or 3 small ribs **celery**, chopped
2 tablespoons chopped fresh **thyme**
1 teaspoon **crushed red pepper flakes**
6 cloves **garlic**, sliced
Salt and **pepper**
½ pint **cherry tomatoes**, halved
2 cups **chicken stock**
2 pounds **mussels**, scrubbed

In a large deep lidded skillet or soup pot, heat the EVOO (3 turns of the pan) over medium-high heat. Add the sausage and cook, breaking it into crumbles as it browns. Transfer to a plate.

Add the fennel, onion, celery, thyme, red pepper flakes, garlic, and salt and pepper to the drippings. Reduce the heat to medium, partially cover, and cook, stirring occasionally, until the fennel and onion are soft, 10 to 12 minutes. Stir in the tomatoes. Deglaze the pan with the chicken stock.

Add the sausage and mussels. Cover the pan and increase the heat to medium-high. Cook until all the mussels open, 5 to 7 minutes. (Discard any unopened shells.)

Serve the mussels and sauce in shallow bowls. Garnish with fennel fronds.

1 Grocery Bag, 3 Meals: List #5
Scan to view the shopping list for Grocery Bag #5 on your mobile device.

Lentil Soup with Sausage & Kale

SERVES 4

2 tablespoons **EVOO**
1 pound **Italian sausage** (sweet or hot), casings removed
2 **carrots**, chopped
2 or 3 ribs **celery**, chopped
1 **onion**, chopped
4 cloves **garlic**, chopped
1 sprig fresh **thyme**
1 sprig fresh **rosemary**
Salt and **pepper**
1 large **starchy potato** (russet), peeled and chopped
3 tablespoons **tomato paste**
6 cups **chicken stock**
1 rounded cup **brown lentils**
1 bunch **lacinato kale** (also called black, Tuscan, or dinosaur kale), stemmed and shredded or chopped

In a soup pot, heat the EVOO (2 turns of the pan) over medium-high heat. Add the sausage and cook, breaking it into crumbles as it browns. Transfer to a plate.

Add the carrots, celery, onion, garlic, herb sprigs, and salt and pepper to the drippings. Partially cover and cook for 5 minutes, stirring occasionally. Stir in the potato and cook 5 minutes more. Stir in the tomato paste and cook until fragrant, about 1 minute. Add the stock, 2 cups water, the sausage, and lentils. Bring the soup to a boil, then reduce to a low rolling simmer and cook until the lentils are tender, about 40 minutes.

Remove the herb sprigs. Wilt in the kale. Taste to adjust the seasonings.

Sour Cream & Leek Frittata

Suggested side: Arugula salad of 6 cups arugula and ½ pint halved cherry tomatoes (use the other half of the tomatoes from the Mussels with Fennel & Garlic, page 334) tossed with lemon juice, EVOO, salt, and pepper. SERVES 4

¼ cup **EVOO**
4 large **leeks**, trimmed, halved lengthwise, sliced 1 inch thick
2 cloves **garlic**, thinly sliced
2 tablespoons chopped fresh **thyme** leaves
Salt and **pepper**
12 large **eggs**
¾ cup **sour cream**
Salt and **pepper**
1½ cups shredded **Gouda**, **Gruyère**, or **Fontina cheese**

Preheat the oven to 375°F.

In a 10-inch ovenproof skillet, heat the EVOO (4 turns of the pan) over medium heat. Add the leeks and garlic. Season with the thyme and salt and pepper. Stir until the leeks are tender, 7 to 10 minutes.

Whisk together the eggs and sour cream. Season with salt and pepper. Stir in three-fourths of the cheese.

Pour the eggs over the leeks and stir to combine. Cook until the eggs are set around the edges, 5 to 6 minutes. Transfer to the oven and bake for 15 minutes. Top with the remaining cheese and bake until the frittata is cooked through, 15 to 20 minutes.

Cut the frittata into wedges to serve (with the arugula salad alongside, if having).

1 GROCERY BAG 3 MEALS

THE GROCERY BAG 6

- ☐ ½ POUND SLAB BACON
- ☐ 4 BONELESS, SKINLESS CHICKEN BREAST HALVES
- ☐ 1½ POUNDS SKINLESS SALMON FILLETS
- ☐ 4 SHALLOTS
- ☐ 2 POUNDS BABY POTATOES
- ☐ WATERCRESS OR LETTUCE
- ☐ 1 BUNCH EACH FLAT-LEAF PARSLEY, DILL, FRESH CHIVES, THYME
- ☐ 2 LEMONS
- ☐ 1 (8-OUNCE) CONTAINER SOUR CREAM
- ☐ ½ DOZEN LARGE EGGS
- ☐ 1 POUND SAUERKRAUT
- ☐ 3 CUPS ARTICHOKE HEARTS
- ☐ 10 OUNCES FROZEN GREEN PEAS
- ☐ 2 (6-OUNCE) CANS ITALIAN TUNA
- ☐ 1 JAR PREPARED HORSERADISH
- ☐ 1 CONTAINER CARAWAY SEEDS
- ☐ 4 BRIOCHE OR OTHER BURGER BUNS
- ☐ 1 (750 ML) BOTTLE DRY VERMOUTH OR DRY WHITE WINE

IN THE PANTRY

- ☐ BUTTER
- ☐ PARMIGIANO-REGGIANO CHEESE
- ☐ GARLIC
- ☐ SPAGHETTI
- ☐ PANKO BREAD CRUMBS
- ☐ DIJON MUSTARD
- ☐ WORCESTERSHIRE SAUCE
- ☐ EVOO
- ☐ CRUSHED RED PEPPER FLAKES

MEAL 1

Spaghetti with Tuna & Artichokes

SERVES 4

BREAD CRUMBS
4 tablespoons (½ stick) **butter**
1 clove **garlic**, smashed
¾ cup **panko bread crumbs**
Grated zest of 1 **lemon**
1 teaspoon **crushed red pepper flakes**
3 tablespoons chopped fresh **flat-leaf parsley**
½ cup grated **Parmigiano-Reggiano cheese**

PASTA
2 tablespoons **EVOO**
2 tablespoons **butter**
3 **shallots**, chopped
4 cloves **garlic**, chopped
2 (6-ounce) cans Italian **tuna** or American line-caught tuna, drained and flaked
3 cups **artichoke hearts**, sliced lengthwise
2 tablespoons chopped fresh **thyme** leaves
Salt and **pepper**
1 cup **dry vermouth** or **white wine**
1 pound **spaghetti**
Juice of 1 **lemon**

Make the bread crumbs: In a medium skillet, melt the butter over medium to medium-high heat. Add the garlic and swirl for 1 or 2 minutes. Discard the garlic and stir in the panko, lemon zest, and red pepper flakes. Toast until deeply golden and fragrant. Let cool; toss with the parsley and Parm.

Make the pasta: Bring a pot of water to a boil.

In a large skillet, heat the EVOO over medium-high heat. Melt in the butter. Add the shallots and garlic and stir for 3 minutes. Add the tuna and stir to heat through. Add the artichokes; season with the thyme, salt, and pepper. Swirl in the vermouth. Reduce the heat to low.

Salt the boiling water and cook the pasta al dente. Ladle out about a cup of the starchy cooking water and add to the sauce along with the lemon juice. Drain the pasta and return it to the pot. Add the sauce, tossing with tongs for 1 or 2 minutes. Adjust the seasonings.

Serve the pasta topped with the bread crumbs.

MEAL 2

German Roast Chicken & Potatoes with Sauerkraut

SERVES 4

EVOO, for drizzling
½ pound **slab bacon**, chopped
2 pounds **baby potatoes**, halved
Salt and **pepper**
1 cup frozen **green peas**
3 tablespoons **butter**
1 clove **garlic**, smashed
1½ teaspoons **caraway seeds**
1 cup **panko bread crumbs**
3 tablespoons chopped fresh **dill**
3 tablespoons chopped fresh **flat-leaf parsley**
4 boneless, skinless **chicken breast** halves
½ cup **Dijon mustard** (regular or grainy)
1 pound **sauerkraut**, rinsed and drained

Preheat the oven to 425°F. Be sure there are 2 racks in the oven because the potatoes and chicken roast at the same time.

In a large skillet, heat a drizzle of EVOO over medium-high heat. Add the bacon and cook to light brown but not fully crisp, about 10 minutes. Add the potatoes and toss to mix. Season lightly with salt and a whole lot of pepper. Arrange the potatoes on a baking sheet and roast to golden brown, 30 to 35 minutes. Add the peas to the potatoes for the last 5 minutes of cook time.

When the potatoes go in the oven, in a medium skillet, melt the butter over medium to medium-high heat. Add the garlic and swirl 1 or 2 minutes. Discard the garlic, add the caraway seeds, swirl for a minute, then stir in the panko. Let cool, then combine with the dill and parsley.

Arrange the chicken on a nonstick or parchment paper–lined baking sheet. Dress the chicken with EVOO, salt, and pepper. Spread 2 tablespoons of the mustard across each chicken breast and then press the herbed panko onto the chicken. Roast until cooked through and golden, 20 to 25 minutes.

Warm the sauerkraut in a small saucepan.

Serve the chicken on a bed of warm sauerkraut with the potatoes and peas alongside.

MEAL 3

Salmon Burgers with Horseradish Cream

SERVES 4

1½ pounds skinless **salmon fillets**, coarsely chunked
1 **shallot**, coarsely chopped
1 clove **garlic**, grated or pasted
2 tablespoons **Dijon mustard** (regular or grainy)
2 teaspoons **Worcestershire sauce**
2 large **eggs**
½ cup **panko bread crumbs**
3 tablespoons chopped fresh **dill**
3 tablespoons chopped fresh **flat-leaf parsley**
Salt and **pepper**
1 tablespoon **EVOO**
½ **lemon**
1 cup **sour cream**
3 tablespoons **prepared horseradish**
3 tablespoons finely chopped fresh **chives**
4 **brioche** or other **burger buns**, split and lightly toasted
Watercress or **lettuce**

In a food processor, combine the salmon, shallot, garlic, mustard, Worcestershire, eggs, panko, dill, parsley, and salt and pepper. Pulse-chop to combine. Form into 4 large patties.

In a large nonstick skillet, heat the EVOO (1 turn of the pan) over medium-high heat. Add the patties and cook, flipping once, 6 to 8 minutes for barely pink centers, 2 minutes more for fully cooked burgers. Squeeze the lemon juice over the burgers.

Meanwhile, stir together the sour cream, horseradish, and chives and season with salt and pepper.

Serve the burgers on toasted rolls with watercress and lots of sauce.

1 Grocery Bag, 3 Meals: List #6
Scan to view the shopping list for Grocery Bag #6 on your mobile device.

1 GROCERY BAG 3 MEALS

THE GROCERY BAG 7

- ☐ 8 (4- TO 5-OUNCE) LAMB RIB CHOPS, ¾ INCH THICK
- ☐ 8 BONE-IN, SKIN-ON CHICKEN THIGHS
- ☐ 4 (6-OUNCE) RED SNAPPER FILLETS
- ☐ ½ DOZEN LARGE ORGANIC EGGS (OPTIONAL; SEE CAESAR BREAD SALAD & CHICKEN THIGHS, PAGE 339)
- ☐ 2 ONIONS
- ☐ 2 BUNCHES LACINATO KALE (AKA TUSCAN, DINOSAUR, OR BLACK KALE)
- ☐ 1 BUNCH FLAT-LEAF PARSLEY
- ☐ 1 BUNCH FRESH ROSEMARY
- ☐ 2 PINTS CHERRY TOMATOES
- ☐ 4 LEMONS
- ☐ 1 TUBE ANCHOVY PASTE
- ☐ 1 (3-OUNCE) JAR CAPERS
- ☐ 1 (1-POUND) BAG DRIED WHITE BEANS
- ☐ 8 OUNCES PEARLED FARRO
- ☐ ⅓ CUP OIL-CURED OR KALAMATA OLIVES (FROM THE SALAD BAR OR DELI COUNTER)
- ☐ 1 LARGE LOAF CIABATTA OR PEASANT BREAD
- ☐ 1 (750 ML) BOTTLE DRY VERMOUTH OR WHITE WINE

IN THE PANTRY

- ☐ GARLIC
- ☐ PECORINO-ROMANO CHEESE
- ☐ DIJON MUSTARD
- ☐ EVOO
- ☐ CRUSHED RED PEPPER FLAKES

MEAL 1

Lemony Lamb Chops with Farro, Kale & White Beans

SERVES 4

½ cup **dried white beans**
1 **onion**, halved
2 cloves **garlic**, smashed
2 sprigs fresh **rosemary**
Salt and **pepper**
1 cup **pearled farro**
2 cups loosely packed stemmed, chopped **lacinato kale** (also called Tuscan, black, or dinosaur kale)
¼ cup **EVOO**, plus more for coating
8 (4- to 5-ounce) **lamb rib chops** (¾ inch thick)
1 **lemon**, halved

Place the beans in a bowl and cover with boiling water. Let stand for 1 hour.

Drain the beans, place in a large pot, and cover with about 1½ inches water. Add the onion halves, garlic, and rosemary. Bring to a boil, salt the water, then reduce the heat to a low rolling simmer and cook until tender, 30 to 35 minutes.

Discard the rosemary stems (the leaves will have fallen off into the beans) and onion. Drain the beans, transfer to a bowl, and cover to keep warm.

Meanwhile, in a saucepan of boiling salted water, cook the farro until tender, 20 to 25 minutes. Add the kale for the last 2 to 3 minutes of cook time. Drain the farro and kale and add to the beans. Stir in the EVOO and season with salt and pepper.

Preheat the broiler with the rack in the upper third of the oven. Coat the lamb chops with EVOO and season with salt and pepper. Broil the lamb chops, flipping once, for about 8 minutes for pink centers.

Squeeze the lemon juice over the lamb. Serve with the farro, kale, and beans alongside.

1 Grocery Bag, 3 Meals: List #7
(Page 338) Scan to view the shopping list for Grocery Bag #7 on your mobile device.

Caesar Bread Salad & Chicken Thighs

When you buy the bread for this recipe (and for the Red Snapper Livornese), keep it wrapped in plastic until you're ready to use it. SERVES 4.

2 cloves **garlic**, pasted or grated
Juice of 2 **lemons**
1 **egg** yolk, lightly beaten (optional)
2 teaspoons **Dijon mustard**
1 rounded teaspoon **anchovy paste**
Salt and **pepper**
⅓ cup plus 2 tablespoons **EVOO**
A couple of handfuls of grated **Pecorino Romano cheese**
4 cups diced or torn **ciabatta** or **peasant bread**
6 cups stemmed, coarsely chopped **lacinato kale** (also called black, Tuscan, or dinosaur kale)
8 bone-in, skin-on **chicken thighs**

Preheat the oven to 350°F.

In a large bowl, whisk together the garlic, lemon juice, egg yolk (if using), mustard, anchovy paste, lots of pepper, ⅓ cup of the EVOO, and the cheese.

Spread the bread on a baking sheet and bake until nutty and fragrant and medium brown, 8 to 10 minutes. Add to the dressing. (Leave the oven on for the chicken.)

Meanwhile, bring a large pot of water to a boil. Salt the water, add the kale, and cook until the kale is bright green, 4 to 5 minutes. Drain well and add to the salad. Toss the salad and let stand to soften the bread. Keep warm.

In a large ovenproof skillet, heat the remaining 2 tablespoons EVOO (2 turns of the pan) over medium-high heat. Season the chicken on both sides with salt and pepper. Place in the skillet skin side down and cook without turning until deeply browned and crispy, 4 to 5 minutes. Flip and brown the second side for 2 minutes. Transfer to the oven and bake until cooked through, 10 to 12 minutes.

Serve the warm salad with 2 crispy thighs per person on top.

Red Snapper Livornese

SERVES 4

4 tablespoons **EVOO**, plus more for drizzling
1 **onion**, chopped
4 cloves **garlic**: 3 thinly sliced, 1 halved
1 teaspoon **crushed red pepper flakes**
3 tablespoons **capers**, drained
⅓ cup **oil-cured** or **kalamata olives**, pitted and chopped
2 pints **cherry tomatoes**
½ cup fresh **flat-leaf parsley** tops, chopped
Salt and **pepper**
4 slices **ciabatta** or **peasant bread**
4 **red snapper fillets** (about 6 ounces each)
⅓ cup **dry vermouth** or **white wine**
1 **lemon**, halved

In a skillet with a tight-fitting lid, heat 2 tablespoons EVOO (2 turns of the pan) over medium to medium-high heat. Add the onion, sliced garlic, and red pepper flakes; cook until the onion softens, 5 to 6 minutes. Stir in the capers, olives, and tomatoes. Cover and cook until the tomatoes burst, shaking the pan occasionally, about 20 minutes. Stir in the parsley and season with salt and pepper.

Meanwhile, preheat the broiler to high. Spread the bread on a baking sheet and char under the broiler on both sides. Rub the toasts with the garlic halves and drizzle with a little EVOO.

With a small, sharp knife, make a few slits through the skin side of the fish fillets but without cutting into the flesh. In a large skillet, heat 2 tablespoons EVOO (2 turns of the pan) over medium-high heat. Season the fish with salt and pepper. Place in the pan skin side down and cook until the skin is crisp, 4 to 5 minutes. Turn the fillets and cook on the second side until the flesh is firm and opaque, about 3 minutes. Deglaze the pan with vermouth. Squeeze the lemon juice over the fish.

Transfer the fish to plates or shallow bowls with the garlic toasts. Stir the tomato sauce into the fish drippings, then spoon over the fish and toasts and serve.

1 GROCERY BAG
3 MEALS

THE GROCERY BAG 8

- ☐ 1½ POUNDS SKIRT STEAK
- ☐ 1½ POUNDS GROUND TURKEY
- ☐ 4 (6-OUNCE) BONELESS, SKINLESS CHICKEN BREAST HALVES
- ☐ 4 SLICES (THIN BUT NOT SHAVED) SPECK OR PROSCIUTTO DI PARMA
- ☐ 1 PINT HALF-AND-HALF
- ☐ 1 POUND FRESH MOZZARELLA CHEESE (PLAIN OR SMOKED)
- ☐ 1 ONION
- ☐ 3 SHALLOTS
- ☐ 1 CARROT
- ☐ 6 VINE-RIPENED TOMATOES
- ☐ 1 LARGE BUNCH FLAT-LEAF PARSLEY
- ☐ 1 BUNCH EACH FRESH BASIL, ROSEMARY, THYME
- ☐ 1 (6- TO 8-OUNCE) JAR WATER-PACKED PIQUILLO PEPPERS
- ☐ ½ CUP SLIVERED ALMONDS
- ☐ 1 POUND ZITI RIGATE
- ☐ 1 (500 ML) BOTTLE DRY SHERRY
- ☐ 1 (750 ML) BOTTLE DRY WHITE WINE

IN THE PANTRY

- ☐ BUTTER
- ☐ PARMIGIANO-REGGIANO CHEESE
- ☐ GARLIC
- ☐ TOMATO PASTE
- ☐ FLOUR
- ☐ SHERRY VINEGAR OR WINE VINEGAR
- ☐ CHICKEN STOCK
- ☐ EVOO

Spanish Sliced Skirt Steak with Piquillo Cream & Tomato Salad

SERVES 4

2 tablespoons **butter**
3 **shallots**: 2 finely chopped, 1 very thinly sliced
4 cloves **garlic**, finely chopped or grated
Salt and **pepper**
1 (6- to 8-ounce) jar water-packed **piquillo peppers**, drained and chopped
2 tablespoons **flour**
⅓ cup **dry sherry**
½ cup **chicken stock**
1 cup **half-and-half**
1½ pounds **skirt steak**, at room temperature
3 tablespoons **EVOO**, plus more for drizzling
4 **vine-ripened tomatoes**, seeded and sliced
1 cup loosely packed fresh **flat-leaf parsley** leaves
1 tablespoon **sherry vinegar** or **wine vinegar** (red or white)
½ cup slivered **almonds**, toasted

In a small skillet, melt the butter over medium heat. Add the chopped shallots, garlic, and salt and pepper and cook until tender, 3 to 5 minutes. Add the piquillo peppers and sprinkle with the flour. Stir for 1 or 2 minutes. Whisk in the sherry, stock, and half-and-half. Bring to a bubble, then puree until smooth in a blender or food processor. Return the sauce to the heat and simmer for 5 to 10 minutes to thicken slightly.

Preheat a grill or grill pan to medium-high heat.

Cut the steak into 4 portions and drizzle with EVOO. Season with salt and pepper.

In a salad bowl, combine the tomatoes, sliced shallot, parsley, vinegar, and 3 tablespoons EVOO. Season with salt and pepper. Add the almonds and toss.

Grill the steaks for 6 to 7 minutes for medium (pink in the center). Let the steaks rest a couple of minutes, then very thinly slice on an angle, against the grain.

To serve, pour some piquillo cream onto each of 4 plates, set a steak into it, and top with the salad.

MEAL 2

Turkey Ragu Baked Ziti

SERVES 4 TO 6

2 tablespoons **EVOO**
1½ pounds **ground turkey**
1 **carrot**, grated or finely chopped
1 **onion**, finely chopped
4 cloves **garlic**, finely chopped or grated
3 tablespoons fresh **rosemary** leaves, finely chopped
Salt and **pepper**
¼ cup **tomato paste**
½ cup **dry white wine**
2 cups **chicken stock**
1 cup **half-and-half**
1 pound **ziti rigate** or other **short-cut pasta**
½ pound **mozzarella cheese** (plain or smoked),
   diced or shredded
1 cup grated **Parmigiano-Reggiano cheese**
½ cup chopped fresh **flat-leaf parsley**

In a Dutch oven, heat the EVOO (2 turns of the pan) over medium-high heat. Add the turkey and cook, breaking it into crumbles as it browns (a potato masher does a good job here). Add the carrot, onion, garlic, rosemary, and salt and pepper. Partially cover and cook, stirring frequently, until the onion is softened, 5 to 7 minutes. Stir in the tomato paste and cook for 1 minute, until fragrant. Deglaze the pan with the wine. Add the stock and half-and-half. Simmer for 30 minutes at a low bubble.

Preheat the oven to 375°F.

Bring a large pot of water to a boil. Salt the water and cook the pasta until 2 minutes shy of al dente. Ladle out about a cup of the starchy cooking water and add to the sauce. Drain the pasta and toss it with the sauce. Transfer to a 9 by 13-inch baking dish. Top with the mozzarella, Parm, and parsley. Bake until bubbling and browned, 20 to 25 minutes.

MEAL 3

Chicken with Ham, Mozzarella & Broiled Tomatoes

SERVES 4

4 (6-ounce) boneless, skinless **chicken breast**
   halves
Salt and **pepper**
2 tablespoons **EVOO**
2 tablespoons **butter**
1 large clove **garlic**, smashed
1 tablespoon chopped fresh **thyme** leaves
4 slices (½ inch thick) **mozzarella cheese** (plain
   or smoked)
4 slices (thin but not shaved) **speck** or **prosciutto
   di Parma**
8 slices **vine-ripened tomato**
½ cup freshly grated **Parmigiano-Reggiano cheese**
A few leaves of fresh **basil**, torn, for garnish

Preheat the oven to 400°F.

Season the chicken with salt and pepper.

In a large skillet, heat 1 tablespoon EVOO (1 turn of the pan) over medium to medium-high heat. Melt the butter into the oil; add the garlic and swirl around until fragrant. Add the chicken and lightly brown, 2 to 3 minutes per side. Transfer to a plate. Discard the garlic.

Sprinkle the thyme over the chicken and top each breast with a slice of mozzarella, then wrap with speck. Arrange the chicken on a baking sheet and drizzle with the remaining 1 tablespoon EVOO to lightly coat.

Bake until the chicken is cooked through, about 20 minutes. Remove from the oven. Turn on the broiler. Arrange the tomato slices on a baking sheet and cover with Parm. Broil to golden, 3 minutes or so.

To serve, arrange 2 slices tomato on top of each chicken breast and garnish with torn basil.

1 Grocery Bag, 3 Meals: List #8
Scan to view the shopping list for Grocery Bag #8 on your mobile device.

ACKNOWLEDGMENTS

Thank you to Food Network and to the crew of *Week in a Day*. To Andrew "Kappy" Kaplan. To Judith Curr, president and publisher of the Atria Publishing Group, and her fantastic team: my editor, Johanna Castillo; Sybil Pincus; Dana Sloan; and to every person involved with this project. To Jill Armus, for designing the cover and interior. Special thanks to my family of good eaters who continue to test these books by way of stomach first.

INDEX

(Page numbers in *italic* refer to photographs.)

A

Adirondack Bacon BBQ Chicken, Apples & Onion, 310, *311*
almond(s):
  Picada, 202
  Romesco Sauce, 225
  Toasted Bread Crumbs, 149
ancho chile(s):
  Chipotle Turkey Chili, 122
  Savory & Sweet Pork Stew with, 139
anchovy(ies):
  Bagna Cauda, 151
  Bread Crumb Topping, 291
Andouille & Roasted Squash Gumbo, 290
apple(s):
  Adirondack Bacon BBQ Chicken, Onion &, 310, *311*
  & Celery Root Soup, Creamy, 179
  & Cheddar Melts, 243
  Chutney, Spicy, 117
  Cider Gravy, 210
  Honey Mustard, 179
  Pork Goulash with Onion &, *192*, 193
  Smoky Chicken & Cider, 96
Arborio, Sausage & Pumpkin Soup, 172
Argentine Chili, 16
Arrabbiata, Deconstructed, 134, *135*
artichoke(s):
  Roasted Chicken Dinner with Potatoes &, on a Bed of Crispy Kale, 157
  Spaghetti with Tuna &, 336
  & Spinach Baked Whole-Grain Pasta, 52
Arugula & Tomatoes with Garlic Bread Crumbs, 161
Asian-style dishes:
  Beef & Broccoli, 137
  Brisket Bowls with Green Rice, 305

Chinese Spaghetti & Meatballs, 258, *259*
  Hot & Sweet Sliced Steak Noodle Bowls, 331
  Thai Ribs & Drumsticks, *154*, 154–55
asparagus:
  Farro with Hazelnuts, Kale &, Topped with Roasted Mushrooms, 280
  & Pistachio Pesto Pasta, 143
avocados:
  Chunky Guacamole, 28, *29*
  Guac Salad, 187
  Jane Fox's Famous Tortilla Soup, 253

B

bacon:
  BBQ Chicken, Apples & Onion, Adirondack, 310, *311*
  Bean &, Soup, Mediterranean, 223
  & Brussels Sprouts Mac 'n' Cheese, 316, *317*
  Burger Mac 'n' Cheese, 306
  Burgers with Caramelized Onions & Gorgonzola, 328
  Cheddar & Apple–Honey Mustard Sandwiches, Grilled, 179
  & Eggs Chilaquiles, Tex-Mex, *124*, 125
Bagna Cauda, Garden-Style Straw & Hay Pasta with, *150*, 151
Baked Bean(s), 201
  & Cowboy Chili Pot, 97
Balsamic BBQ Sauce, 38
Barbecued Beef Sandwiches, Italian, 38
Barley & Sliced Steak Soup, Mexican, 284
Basil and Parsley Pesto, 134

BBQ:
  Bacon Chicken, Apples & Onion, Adirondack, 310, *311*
  Buffalo Pulled Chicken with Blue Cheese Corn Bread Topper, 102, *103*
  Chicken, Red Bean & Corn Country Chowder, 178
  Chipotle Turkey Mini Meat Loaves, 195
  Mustard & Brown Sugar Beef Sandwiches with Celery Slaw, 264, *265*
  Tequila-Orange, Chicken Burritos with Cheddar, Baked Beans & Red Cabbage Slaw, 102
  Turkey or Chicken Gumbo, 318
BBQ sauces:
  Balsamic, 38
  Basic, 178
  Chipotle, 195
bean(s):
  & Bacon Soup, Mediterranean, 223
  Baked, 201
  Baked, & Chili Pot, Cowboy, 97
  & Knocks Supreme, 58
  Pasta e Fagioli with Roasted Garlic, 246
  Red, BBQ Chicken & Corn Country Chowder, 178
  Refried, Dip, 184
  refried, in Nacho-Topped Chili Pot, 84
  3-Bean Minestrone, Hearty & Healthy, 64
  White, Farro, Kale &, 338
  see also black bean(s); cannellini beans; chickpea(s)
Béchamel Sauce, 230
beef:
  Argentine Chili, 16

Bacon Burger Mac 'n' Cheese, 306
Bacon Burgers with Caramelized
    Onions & Gorgonzola, 328
Barbecued, Sandwiches, Italian, 38
& Black Bean Chilaquiles with Fried
    Eggs, 186
Black Pepper, 169
Bolognese, Double-Batch Classic,
    108
Bonnie's Italian Stew, 269
Braciole, Spinach-Stuffed, in Sunday
    Sauce with Pappardelle, 48–50, 49
Braciole & Sausages in Sunday
    Gravy with Peppers & Onion,
    272–73
Braised, Grandpa's, 115
Brisket Bowls with Green Rice, 305
Brisket 'n' Biscuits, Mexican, 185
& Broccoli, 137
Buckwheat Stoup with Porcini, Kale
    &, 285
Cincinnati Spaghetti, 301
Cowboy Chili & Baked Bean Pot, 97
Drunken Spaghetti with Hot Salami
    Meat Sauce, 216
Garlicky, 298
Halloween Ground Meat Ghoul-ash,
    299
Hot & Sweet Pepper Curry Sauce
    with, 267
Italian Pot Roast, 34, 35
Meatballs, Beer-Braised, with Horse-
    radish Sauce, 194
Mustard & Brown Sugar BBQ, Sand-
    wiches with Celery Slaw, 264, 265
Nacho-Topped Chili Pot, 84
& Pork Polpette, Minestra with, 83
& Pork Tamale Pie, 129
Potted, & Celery Root with Celery
    Gremolata, 278
Reuben-Style Shepherd's Pie, 218
Sartù (Risotto Timbale), 232–33, 233
Sloppy Joe 'n' Macaroni Casserole,
    208, 209
Spanish Sliced Skirt Steak with
    Piquillo Cream & Tomato Salad, 340
Spicy Ziti with Sausage, 329
Stew Scented with Horseradish, 180,
    181
On Top of Ol' Smoky, All Covered

with Cheese: Spaghetti & Meat
    balls, 62
Touchdown Chili, 242
see also short rib(s); steak
beer-braised:
    Beef Meatballs with Horseradish
        Sauce, 194
    Chicken Thighs, 109
biscuit(s):
    Drop, Chicken Potpie, 12
    Mexican Brisket 'n,' 185
black bean(s):
    & Beef Chilaquiles with Fried Eggs,
        186
    Meaty Meatless Chili, 53
    Tex-Mex Bacon & Eggs Chilaquiles,
        124, 125
Black Pepper Beef, 169
Bloody Mary Soup with Pumpernickel
    Grilled Cheese Croutons, 295
blue cheese:
    Corn Bread Topper, Buffalo BBQ
        Pulled Chicken with, 102, 103
    Ranch Dressing, 304
bocconcini, in Hot & Sweet Caprese
    Salad, 38
Bolognese:
    Double-Batch Classic, 108
    Lamb Ragu, 106
    Portobello & Spinach, 89
braciole:
    & Sausages in Sunday Gravy with
        Peppers & Onion, 272–73
    Spinach-Stuffed, in Sunday Sauce
        with Pappardelle, 48–50, 49
bread:
    Mexican Chorizo Strata, 214, 215
    Salad, Caesar, & Chicken Thighs,
        339
    see also Croutons
Bread Crumb(s), 336
    Anchovy Topping, 291
    Garlic, Arugula & Tomatoes with,
        161
    Toasted Almond, 149
Bread-zagna, Mushroom & Spinach,
    254, 255
"breakfast for dinner":
    Black Bean & Beef Chilaquiles with
        Fried Eggs, 186

Mexican Chorizo Strata, 214, 215
brisket:
    'n' Biscuits, Mexican, 185
    Bowls with Green Rice, 305
broccoli (rabe):
    Beef &, 137
    & Pork Ciabatta Subs with Gremo-
        lata, 302, 303
    & Sausage Stoup, 22
Broccoli & Cauliflower Gratin Mac 'n'
    Cheese, 42
Broth, Veal Dumplings with Escarole
    in, 207
Brussels Sprouts & Bacon Mac 'n'
    Cheese, 316, 317
Buckwheat Stoup with Porcini, Beef &
    Kale, 285
Buffalo:
    BBQ Pulled Chicken with Blue
        Cheese Corn Bread Topper, 102,
        103
    Turkey Sloppy Joes with Blue Cheese
        Ranch Dressing, 304
burger(s):
    Bacon, Mac 'n' Cheese, 306
    Bacon, with Caramelized Onions &
        Gorgonzola, 328
    Salmon, with Horseradish Cream,
        337
Burritos, Tequila-Orange BBQ Chicken,
    with Cheddar, Baked Beans & Red
    Cabbage Slaw, 102
buttermilk biscuit mix:
    Drop Biscuit Chicken Potpie, 12
    Mexican Brisket 'n' Biscuits, 185
    Vegetable & Dumpling Soup, 60, 61
butternut squash:
    Creamy Winter Vegetable Soup, 252
    Eight-Spice Squash & Chicken
        Thigh Stew with Lentil Rice, 250,
        251
    Pumpkin Lovers' Lasagna, 196, 197
    Roasted, Boats Stuffed with Sausage,
        Toasted Pasta & Rice, 260
    Roasted Squash Chili Mac, 165
    Roasted Vegetable Tabbouleh with
        Yogurt-Tahini Dressing, 282, 283
    Sausage, Pumpkin & Arborio Soup,
        172
    see also squash (winter)

C

cabbage:
    Pumpkin, Penne &, *296*, 297
    Red, Slaw, 201
Cacciatore, Portobello-Porcini, 19
Caesar:
    Bread Salad & Chicken Thighs, 339
    Croutons, 142
    Grilled Chicken Mac, 126
Calabrese Chicken One-Pot, 76
Camembert cheese, in French Onion
    Soup–Topped French Bread Pizzas,
    217
cannellini beans:
    Braised Chicken Thighs with Esca-
      role & White Beans, 332
    Escarole Soup with Caesar Croutons,
      142
    Hearty & Healthy 3-Bean Mine-
      strone, 64
    Mediterranean Bean & Bacon Soup,
      223
    Pasta e Fagioli with Roasted Garlic,
      246
Caprese Salad, Hot & Sweet, 38
carrot(s):
    Creamy Winter Vegetable Soup, 252
    Roasted Root Vegetable Soup with
      Grilled Cheese Croutons, 127
    Soup, Ginger-Soy, 44, *45*
    Spring Chicken with Peas &, 147
    Sweet Potato & Squash Soup, 315
    Vegetable & Dumpling Soup, 60, *61*
casseroles:
    Baked Ziti with Spinach & Veal, 59
    Black Bean & Beef Chilaquiles with
      Fried Eggs, 186
    Buffalo BBQ Pulled Chicken with
      Blue Cheese Corn Bread Topper,
      102, *103*
    Cauliflower Mac 'n' Cheese, 82
    Chicken Tetrazzini, with Cauliflower,
      200
    Green Pastitsio, 91
    Grilled Chicken Caesar Mac, 126
    Moussaka, 211
    Paella-Style, 162, *163*
    Parsnip, Potato & Spinach, with
      Roasted Mushrooms, 43
    Pastitsio with Lamb & Sausage, 230

Reuben-Style Shepherd's Pie, 218
Rice Pilaf & Chorizo, 23
Roast Chicken Enchiladas Suizas
    Stacked, 20, *21*
Roasted Squash Chili Mac, 165
Sloppy Joe 'n' Macaroni, 208, *209*
Spinach & Artichoke Baked Whole-
    Grain Pasta, 52
Tex-Mex Bacon & Eggs Chilaquiles,
    124, 125
Turkey, Mushroom & Corn Mexican,
    320
Turkey Ragu Baked Ziti, 341
Catalan Chicken Stew, 202, *203*
cauliflower:
    & Broccoli Gratin Mac 'n' Cheese, 42
    Chicken Tetrazzini Casserole with,
      200
    Mac 'n' Cheese, 82
    Roasted, Chickpea Soup with, 333
    Soup with Anchovy–Bread Crumb
      Topping, 291
Ceci Sauce with Penne, 120, *121*
celery:
    Gremolata, 278
    Slaw, 264, *265*
celery root:
    & Apple Soup, Creamy, 179
    Potted Beef &, with Celery Gremo-
      lata, 278
    Roasted Root Vegetable Soup with
      Grilled Cheese Croutons, 127
chard:
    Cheesy Rice Cake Stuffed with Herbs
      & Greens, 271
    Hearty & Healthy 3-Bean Mine-
      strone, 64
    Sautéed, 117
cheddar cheese:
    & Apple Melts, 243
    Bacon & Apple–Honey Mustard
      Sandwiches, Grilled, 179
    Bacon & Brussels Sprouts Mac 'n'
      Cheese, 316, *317*
    Bacon Burger Mac 'n' Cheese, 306
    Beef & Pork Tamale Pie, 129
    Black Bean & Beef Chilaquiles with
      Fried Eggs, 186
    Broccoli & Cauliflower Gratin Mac 'n'
      Cheese, 42

Cauliflower & Broccoli Gratin Mac 'n'
    Cheese, 42
Chipotle BBQ Turkey Mini Meat
    Loaves, 195
Crab Cake Mac 'n' Cheese, 4
Grilled Cheese Croutons, 127
hot pepper, in Tex-Mex Bacon &
    Eggs Chilaquiles, *124*, 125
Mexican Chorizo Strata, 214, *215*
Nacho-Topped Chili Pot, 84
Pilgrim Meat Loaf, 210
Pumpernickel Grilled Cheese Crou-
    tons, 295
Sloppy Joe 'n' Macaroni Casserole,
    208, *209*
Tequila-Orange BBQ Chicken
    Burritos with Baked Beans, Red
    Cabbage Slaw &, 102
Turkey, Mushroom & Corn Mexican
    Casserole, 320
cheese(y):
    Croutons, 252
    Croutons, Grilled, 127
    Polenta, 77
    Rice Cake Stuffed with Herbs &
      Greens, 271
    see also mac 'n' cheese; *specific*
    cheeses
chicken:
    Bacon BBQ, Apples & Onion,
      Adirondack, 310, *311*
    BBQ, Gumbo, 318
    BBQ, Red Bean & Corn Country
      Chowder, 178
    Braised, with Mushrooms, *118*, 119
    Breasts, Easy-Brine, with Sicilian
      Glaze, 159
    Buffalo BBQ Pulled, with Blue
      Cheese Corn Bread Topper, 102,
      103
    & Chorizo Spanish Enchiladas, 312
    & Cider, Smoky, 96
    Curry, Creamy, with Potatoes & Split
      Peas, 331
    Curry Sammies, Cold, with Toasted
      Almonds & Crystallized Ginger, 222
    Drunken, 268
    Enchiladas, 188, *189*
    German Roast, & Potatoes with
      Sauerkraut, 337

Golden Lemon-Olive, with Pine Nut
  Couscous, 14, *15*
Grilled, Caesar Mac, 126
with Ham, Mozzarella & Broiled
  Tomatoes, 341
Hot & Sweet Pepper Curry Sauce
  with, 267
Hot Open-Faced Creamed, with
  Tarragon over Buttered Toast, *220,
  221*
Middle Eastern Garlic-Roasted,
  166–67
Moroccan Meat Loaf with Lemon-
  Honey Gravy, 5
Mulligatawny with Green Raita, 199
& Mushroom Creamy One-Pot with
  Potpie Toppers, 79
& Mushrooms with Rigatoni, 308
& Noodles, Creamy, 261
Noodle Soup, Souped-up Traditional,
  100
One-Pot, Calabrese, 76
Paella Style Casserole, 162, *163*
Piccata, 326
Poached, Basic, 322
Potpie, Drop Biscuit, 12
Pulled, Ragu & Rigatoni, 257
in Pumpkin Seed Sauce, 235
& Rice Soup, Spanish, 51
Roast, Dinner with Roasted Garlic, 18
Roast, Enchiladas Suizas Stacked
  Casserole, 20, *21*
Roasted, Dinner with Potatoes &
  Artichokes on a Bed of Crispy
  Kale, 157
Salsa-Marinated, with Mexican Rice,
  140, 141
Skillet, with Hot & Sweet Peppers,
  329
Smoky Spanish Hunter's, 65
Spring, with Carrots & Peas, 147
Stew, Catalan, 202, *203*
Stoup, Italian, with Porcini, Portobel-
  los & Peppers, 176, *177*
Stuffed, Saltimbocca, 161
Tequila-Orange BBQ, Burritos with
  Cheddar, Baked Beans & Red
  Cabbage Slaw, 102
Tetrazzini Casserole with Cauli-
  flower, 200

Thai Ribs & Drumsticks, *154*,
  154–55
Thigh & Squash Stew, Eight-Spice,
  with Lentil Rice, 250, *251*
Thighs, Beer-Braised, 109
Thighs, Braised, with 40 Cloves of
  Garlic, 204
Thighs, Braised, with Escarole &
  White Beans, 332
Thighs, Caesar Bread Salad &
  Chicken, 339
Thighs, Chipotle, 28, *29*
Thighs, French Stewed, 224
Tortilla Soup, Jane Fox's Famous,
  253
Turmeric & Cumin, with Oranges,
  Olives & Chickpea Couscous, 136
Vindaloo of, 144, *145*
Winter White Coq au Vin, 231
chicken livers:
  Double-Batch Classic Bolognese, 108
  Sartù (Risotto Timbale), 232–33,
    233
chickpea(s):
  Ceci Sauce with Penne, 120, *121*
  Couscous, 136
  Hearty & Healthy 3-Bean Mine-
    strone, 64
  Moroccan Meatballs with Egg,
    94–95, *95*
  Pasta e Fagioli with Roasted Garlic,
    246
  Roasted Red Pepper Minestrone,
    164
  Soup with Roasted Cauliflower, 333
chilaquiles:
  Bacon & Eggs, Tex-Mex, *124*, 125
  Black Bean & Beef, with Fried Eggs,
    186
chile(s):
  Ancho, Savory & Sweet Pork Stew
    with, 139
  Ancho-Chipotle Turkey Chili, 122
  Green, Sloppy Josés, 184
  Jalapeño Popper Orzo Mac 'n'
    Cheese, 187
  Paste, 134
  Pickled Red Onions &, 93
  Piquillo Cream, 340
  Pork with Orange Sauce &, 236

Pulled Pork with Two-Chile Tamale
  Pie, 182
roasting, 213
see also chipotle; poblano
chili:
  Ancho-Chipotle Turkey, 122
  Argentine, 16
  & Baked Bean Pot, Cowboy, 97
  Cincinnati Spaghetti, 301
  Mac, Roasted Squash, 165
  Meaty Meatless, 53
  Mexican Chorizo & Turkey, 240
  Nacho-Topped, 84
  Pork, Italian, with Polenta, 206
  Pork & Poblano Green, 77
  Touchdown, 242
Chili Sauce, Sweet & Sour, 155
Chimichurri, 16
Chinese Spaghetti & Meatballs, 258,
  259
chipotle:
  Ancho Turkey Chili, 122
  BBQ Sauce, 195
  BBQ Turkey Mini Meat Loaves, 195
  Chicken Thighs, 28, *29*
  Turkey Breast with Pomegran-
    ate-Cranberry Relish & Polenta,
    238, *239*
chorizo:
  & Chicken Spanish Enchiladas, 312
  Paella-Style Casserole, 162, *163*
  & Rice Pilaf Casserole, 23
  Strata, Mexican, 214, *215*
  Touchdown Chili, 242
chowder(s):
  BBQ Chicken, Red Bean & Corn
    Country, 178
  Clam & Corn, Spicy, with Croutons, 148
  Corn, Smoky, 292
  Corn & Crab, Potpies, 73
Chutney, Spicy Apple, 117
Ciabatta Subs, Pork & Broccoli Rabe,
  with Gremolata, *302*, 303
cider:
  Gravy, 210
  Smoky Chicken &, 96
Cincinnati Spaghetti, 301
clam(s):
  & Corn Chowder, Spicy, with Crou-
    tons, 148

clam(s) (*cont.*):

Romesco Seafood Stew, 225

Sauce, Linguine with, 56, *57*

cod:

Paella-Style Casserole, 162, *163*

Romesco Seafood Stew, 225

condiments:

Apple–Honey Mustard, 179

Celery Gremolata, 278

Fresh Seafood Seasoning Paste, 56

Green Harissa, 167

Green Raita, 199

Gremolata, 244

Pickled Red Onions & Chiles, 93

Pomegranate-Cranberry Relish, 238, *239*

Spicy Apple Chutney, 117

see also spice blends

Coq au Vin, Winter White, 231

corn:

BBQ Chicken & Red Bean Country Chowder, 178

Chowder, Smoky, 292

& Clam Chowder, Spicy, with Croutons, 148

& Crab Chowder Potpies, 73

Poblano Mac 'n' Manchego with Mushrooms &, 237

Turkey & Mushroom Mexican Casserole, 320

see also hominy

Corn Bread Blue Cheese Topper, Buffalo BBQ Pulled Chicken with, 102, *103*

corned beef, in Reuben-Style Shepherd's Pie, 218

cornmeal, *see* polenta

couscous:

Chickpea, 136

Pine Nut, 14, 15

Zucchini, 5

Cowboy Chili & Baked Bean Pot, 97

crab:

Cake Mac 'n' Cheese, 4

& Corn Chowder Potpies, 73

cranberry:

Pomegranate Relish, 238, *239*

Pomegranate Sauce, 247

Croutons, 148

Caesar, 142

Cheesy, 252

Garlic, 6

Grilled Cheese, 127

Gruyère, 288, *289*

Pumpernickel Grilled Cheese, 295

curry(ied):

Chicken, Creamy, with Potatoes & Split Peas, 331

Cold Chicken, Sammies with Toasted Almonds & Crystallized Ginger, 222

Eggplant & Squash, 104, *105*

Lentil Soup, Fleuri's, 37

Sauce, Hot & Sweet Pepper, with Chicken, Lamb, or Beef, 267

Spice Blend, Hot, 144

Squash Soup, 243

D

Deconstructed Arrabbiata, 134, *135*

Dijon Vinaigrette, 217

dips:

Bagna Cauda, 151

Refried Bean, 184

dressings:

Blue Cheese Ranch, 304

Dijon Vinaigrette, 217

Russian, 218

Yogurt-Tahini, 282

Drop Biscuit Chicken Potpie, 12

Drunken Chicken, 268

Drunken Spaghetti with Hot Salami Meat Sauce, 216

Drunken Steaks with Peppery Oven Fries, 327

dumpling(s):

Veal, with Escarole in Broth, 207

& Vegetable Soup, 60, *61*

E

edamame, in Hot & Sweet Sliced Steak Noodle Bowls, 331

egg(s):

& Bacon Chilaquiles, Tex-Mex, *124*, 125

Fried, Black Bean & Beef Chilaquiles with, 186

Ginger-Soy Carrot Soup, 44, *45*

Mexican Chorizo Strata, 214, *215*

Moroccan Meatballs with, 94–95, *95*

Poached, Ratatouille with Garlic Croutons &, 6, *7*

Sour Cream & Leek Frittata, 335

eggplant:

Moussaka, 211

Parm Stacks, 70

Quinoa & Vegetable Stuffed Peppers, 281

Ratatouille-Stuffed Jack-o'-Peppers, 294

Ratatouille with Poached Eggs & Garlic Croutons, 6, *7*

Roasted, Ricotta Filling, Lasagna with, 262

Roasted Pepper &, Marinara, 128

& Squash Curry, 104, *105*

Stuffed, with Veal & Spinach, 36

Stuffed Peppers with Lamb &, 31

& Zucchini Roll-ups, 276, *277*

Eight-Spice Squash & Chicken Thigh Stew with Lentil Rice, 250, *251*

enchilada(s):

Chicken, 188, *189*

Chicken & Chorizo, Spanish, 312

Sauce, 188

Suizas Stacked Casserole, Roast Chicken, 20, *21*

escarole:

Braised Chicken Thighs with White Beans &, 332

Hearty & Healthy 3-Bean Minestrone, 64

Minestra with Beef & Pork Polpette, 83

Pasta e Fagioli with Roasted Garlic, 246

Peas & Potato Soup with Tarragon Pesto, 30

Pumpkin Lovers' Lasagna, 196, *197*

Soup with Caesar Croutons, 142

Veal Dumplings with, in Broth, 207

F

farro:

with Asparagus, Hazelnuts & Kale, Topped with Roasted Mushrooms, 280

Kale & White Beans, 338

fennel:

Cheesy Rice Cake Stuffed with Herbs & Greens, 271

Creamy Winter Vegetable Soup, 252

& Golden Raisin Stuffing, 228

Mussels with Garlic &, 334

Roasted Vegetable Tabbouleh with Yogurt-Tahini Dressing, 282, *283*

Roast Turkey & Onions with Buttered Egg Noodles, 319

Vegetable & Dumpling Soup, 60, *61*

feta cheese, in Green Pastitsio, 91

fish:

Red Snapper Livornese, 339

Salmon Burgers with Horseradish Cream, 337

Spaghetti with Artichokes & Tuna, 336

Supper, Portuguese, 26, *27*

see seafood

Fontina cheese, in Pasta Shells with Veal & Sweet Sausage, 274, *275*

Fra Diavolo Sauce, Cherry Tomato, with Seafood & Pasta, 156

French-style dishes:

Onion Soup–Topped French Bread Pizzas, 217

Onion Soup with Porcini, 13

Stewed Chicken Thighs, 224

Winter White Coq au Vin, 231

Fries, Peppery Oven, 327

Frittata, Sour Cream & Leek, 335

G

Garden-Style Straw & Hay Pasta with Bagna Cauda, *150*, 151

garlic(ky):

Bagna Cauda, 151

Beef, 298

Braised Chicken Thighs with 40 Cloves of, 204

Bread Crumbs, 161

Croutons, 6

Roasted, 127

Roasted, Pasta e Fagioli with, 246

Roasted, & Roasted Tomato Puttanesca, 113

-Roasted Chicken, Middle Eastern, 166–67

Gazpacho, Yellow Tomato, with Toasted Almond Bread Crumbs, 149

Genovese Red Sauce, 266

German Roast Chicken & Potatoes with Sauerkraut, 337

ginger:

Crystallized, Cold Chicken Curry Sammies with Toasted Almonds &, 222

Soy Carrot Soup, 44, *45*

Gnocchi, Turkey & Creamy Mushroom-Tomato "Gravy" with, 46

goulash:

Halloween Ground Meat Ghoul-ash, 299

Pork, with Apple & Onion, *192*, 193

gravy:

Cider, 210

Creamy, 247

Maple-Worcestershire, 40

Mushroom, 170

Greek-style dishes:

Green Pastitsio, 91

Moussaka, 211

Pastitsio with Lamb & Sausage, 230

Split Pea Soup with Lemon, 287

green beans, in Hearty & Healthy 3-Bean Minestrone, 64

Green Chile Sloppy Josés, 184

Green Harissa, 167

Green Pastitsio, 91

Green Raita, 199

Green Rice, 305

Gremolata, 244

Celery, 278

grilled cheese:

Cheddar, Bacon & Apple–Honey Mustard Sandwiches, 179

Croutons, 127

Croutons, Pumpernickel, 295

Gruyère (cheese):

Bacon & Brussels Sprouts Mac 'n' Cheese, 316, *317*

Cauliflower & Broccoli Gratin Mac 'n' Cheese, 42

Crab Cake Mac 'n' Cheese, 4

Croutons, 288, *289*

French Onion Soup–Topped French Bread Pizzas, 217

French Onion Soup with Porcini, 13

Parsnip, Potato & Spinach Casserole with Roasted Mushrooms, 43

Guacamole, Chunky, 28, *29*

Guac Salad, 187

gumbo:

Andouille & Roasted Squash, 290

BBQ Turkey or Chicken, 318

H

Halloween Ground Meat Ghoul-ash, 299

ham:

Chicken with Mozzarella, Broiled Tomatoes &, 341

Sage Derby Mac 'n' Cheese with, 309

Harissa, Green, 167

hazelnuts:

Farro with Asparagus, Kale &, Topped with Roasted Mushrooms, 280

Romesco Sauce, 225

Herb-Parmigiano Stock, 323

Hoagies, Minute Steak, with Homemade Steak Sauce, *74*, 75

hominy:

Pork Tenderloin Posole with Bottom-of-the-Bowl Nacho Surprise, 213

Red Pork Posole, 93

Honey-Apple Mustard, 179

horseradish:

Beef Stew Scented with, 180, *181*

Cream, 337

Mash, 333

Sauce, 194

Hot Curry Spice Blend, 144

Hungarian-style dishes:

Halloween Ground Meat Ghoul-ash, 299

Pork Goulash with Apple & Onion, *192*, 193

Veal or Lamb Paprikash, *132*, 133

I

Indian-style dishes:

Mulligatawny with Green Raita, 199

Vindaloo of Chicken, 144, *145*

see also curry(ied)

Italian-style dishes:

Barbecued Beef Sandwiches, 38

Braciole & Sausages in Sunday Gravy with Peppers & Onion, 272–73

Calabrese Chicken One-Pot, 76

Italian-style dishes (*cont.*):

Cheesy Rice Cake Stuffed with Herbs & Greens, 271

Chicken Stoup with Porcini, Portobellos & Peppers, 176, *177*

Easy-Brine Chicken Breasts with Sicilian Glaze, 159

Eggplant Parm Stacks, 70

Eggplant & Zucchini Roll-ups, 276, *277*

Escarole Soup with Caesar Croutons, 142

Hearty & Healthy 3-Bean Minestrone, 64

Hot & Sweet Caprese Salad, 38

Minestra with Beef & Pork Polpette, 83

Osso Buco with Gremolata, 244, *245*

Pasta e Fagioli with Roasted Garlic, 246

Pork Chili with Polenta, 206

Pork Ragu, 8

Pot Roast, 34, *35*

Potted Beef & Celery Root with Celery Gremolata, 278

Red Snapper Livornese, 339

Risotto-Stuffed Peppers & Zucchini, 152

Roasted Red Pepper Minestrone, 164

Sartù (Risotto Timbale), 232–33, *233*

Sausage, Pepper & Onion One-Pot, *80*, 81

Southern Italian–Style Short Ribs, 131

Spinach-Stuffed Braciole in Sunday Sauce with Pappardelle, 48–50, *49*

Stew, Bonnie's, 269

Stuffed Chicken Saltimbocca, 161

see also Bolognese; lasagna; pasta; pesto; ragu

J

Jalapeño Popper Orzo Mac 'n' Cheese, 187

K

kale:

Buckwheat Stoup with Porcini, Beef &, 285

Caesar Bread Salad & Chicken Thighs, 339

Crispy, Roasted Chicken Dinner with Potatoes & Artichokes on a Bed of, 157

Farro & White Beans, 338

Farro with Asparagus, Hazelnuts &, Topped with Roasted Mushrooms, 280

Lentil Soup with Sausage &, 191, 335

Mediterranean Bean & Bacon Soup, 223

Roasted Red Pepper Minestrone, 164

Roast Pork Loin with Polenta &, 174

Sausage & Lentil Soup, 112

10-Shallot Spaghetti with, 327

Knocks & Beans Supreme, 58

L

lamb:

Chops, Lemony, with Farro, Kale & White Beans, 338

Chops with Horseradish Mash & Wilted Spinach, 333

Drunken Spaghetti with Hot Salami Meat Sauce, 216

Halloween Ground Meat Ghoul-ash, 299

Hot & Sweet Pepper Curry Sauce with, 267

Moroccan Meatballs with Egg, 94–95, *95*

Moroccan Meat Loaf with Lemon-Honey Gravy, 5

Moussaka, 211

Paprikash, *132*, 133

Pastitsio with Sausage &, 230

Ragu, Lazy Lasagna with Spinach, Ricotta &, 106

& Rice Stuffed Peppers, 110, *111*

Slow-Roasted Parchment-Wrapped Leg of, wtih Garlic & Herbs, 25

Stuffed Peppers with Eggplant &, 31

lasagna:

with Lamb Ragu, Spinach & Ricotta, Lazy, 106

Pumpkin Lovers', 196, *197*

with Roasted Eggplant–Ricotta Filling, 262

Leek & Sour Cream Frittata, 335

lemon(y):

Lamb Chops with Farro, Kale & White Beans, 338

Olive Chicken, Golden, with Pine Nut Couscous, 14, *15*

lentil:

Rice, 250, *251*

Sausage & Kale Soup, 112

Soup, Curry, Fleuri's, 37

Soup with Kale & Sausage, 191

Soup with Sausage & Kale, 335

Stoup with Mushrooms, 158

linguine:

with Clam Sauce, 56, *57*

Poblano Cream, with Shrimp, 330

Whole Wheat, Portobello Cream Sauce with, 33

Louisiana-Style Shrimp, 10, *11*

M

Macaroni, Sloppy Joe 'n,' Casserole, 208, *209*

mac 'n' cheese:

Bacon & Brussels Sprouts, 316, *317*

Bacon Burger, 306

Broccoli & Cauliflower Gratin, 42

Cauliflower, 82

Crab Cake, 4

Grilled Chicken Caesar, 126

Jalapeño Popper Orzo, 187

Poblano Mac 'n' Manchego with Corn & Mushrooms, 237

Roasted Squash Chili, 165

Sage Derby, with Ham, 309

Manchego (cheese):

Cheesy Polenta, 77

Chicken & Chorizo Spanish Enchiladas, 312

Poblano Mac 'n,' with Corn & Mushrooms, 237

Rice Pilaf & Chorizo Casserole, 23

Maple-Worcestershire Gravy, 40

marinara:

Roasted Pepper & Eggplant, 128

Spicy Roasted-Tomato, 66

meatballs:

Beef, Beer-Braised, with Horseradish Sauce, 194

Beef & Pork Polpette, Minestra with, 83

Bonnie's Italian Stew, 269

Broken, Stuffed Peppers with Rice &, 173
Moroccan, with Egg, 94–95, *95*
Spaghetti &, Chinese, 258, *259*
On Top of Ol' Smoky, All Covered with Cheese: Spaghetti &, 62
Veal Dumplings with Escarole in Broth, 207
Veal & Pork, with Mushroom Gravy & Egg Noodles, 170, *171*
meat loaves:
    Chipotle BBQ Turkey Mini, 195
    Moroccan, with Lemon-Honey Gravy, 5
    Pilgrim, 210
    Turkey Stuffing, 88
Meat Sauce, Spicy, 230
Meaty Meatless Chili, 53
Mediterranean Bean & Bacon Soup, 223
Mexican-style dishes:
    Beef & Pork Tamale Pie, 129
    Braised Pork Tacos, 2, *3*
    Brisket 'n' Biscuits, 185
    Chicken in Pumpkin Seed Sauce, 235
    Chipotle Chicken Thighs, 28, *29*
    Chipotle Turkey Breast with Pomegranate-Cranberry Relish & Polenta, 238, *239*
    Chorizo & Turkey Chili, 240
    Chorizo Strata, 214, *215*
    Chunky Guacamole, 28, *29*
    Pesto with Whole-Grain Pasta, 68, *69*
    Poblano Mac 'n' Manchego with Corn & Mushrooms, 237
    Pork Tenderloin Posole with Bottom-of-the-Bowl Nacho Surprise, 213
    Pork with Chiles and Orange Sauce, 236
    Pulled Pork with Two-Chile Tamale Pie, 182
    Red Pork Posole, 93
    Roast Chicken Enchiladas Suizas Stacked Casserole, 20, *21*
    Salsa-Marinated Chicken with Mexican Rice, *140*, 141
    Savory & Sweet Pork Stew with Ancho Chiles, 139
    Sliced Steak & Barley Soup, 284

Tequila-Orange BBQ Chicken Burritos with Cheddar, Baked Beans & Red Cabbage Slaw, 102
Turkey, Mushroom & Corn Casserole, 320
see also chili; Tex-Mex–style dishes
Mexi-Rub, 185
Middle Eastern–style dishes:
    Garlic-Roasted Chicken, 166–67
    Roasted Vegetable Tabbouleh with Yogurt-Tahini Dressing, 282, *283*
    Za'atar Spice Blend, 167
Minestra with Beef & Pork Polpette, 83
minestrone:
    Roasted Red Pepper, 164
    3-Bean, Hearty & Healthy, 64
Mint & Shallot Sauce, 25
Minute Steak Hoagies with Homemade Steak Sauce, *74*, 75
Monterey Jack cheese:
    Braised Pork Tacos, 2, *3*
    Nacho-Topped Chili Pot, 84
    Roast Chicken Enchiladas Suizas Stacked Casserole, 20, *21*
    Turkey, Mushroom & Corn Mexican Casserole, 320
Moroccan-style dishes:
    Golden Lemon-Olive Chicken with Pine Nut Couscous, 14, *15*
    Meatballs with Egg, 94–95, *95*
    Meat Loaf with Lemon-Honey Gravy, 5
    Ras el Hanout (Head of the Shop) Spice Blend, 95
    Turmeric & Cumin Chicken with Oranges, Olives & Chickpea Couscous, 136
Moussaka, 211
mozzarella cheese:
    bocconcini, in Hot & Sweet Caprese Salad, 38
    Chicken with Ham, Broiled Tomatoes &, 341
    Eggplant Parm Stacks, 70
    Lasagna with Roasted Eggplant–Ricotta Filling, 262
Mulligatawny with Green Raita, 199
mushroom(s):
    Braised Chicken with, *118*, 119
    & Chicken Creamy One-Pot with Potpie Toppers, 79

& Chicken with Rigatoni, 308
Gravy, Veal & Pork Meatballs with Egg Noodles &, 170, *171*
Lentil Stoup with, 158
Poblano Mac 'n' Manchego with Corn &, 237
Roasted, Farro with Asparagus, Hazelnuts & Kale Topped with, 280
Roasted, Parsnip, Potato & Spinach Casserole with, 43
Sausage & 3-Pepper Open-Faced Sandwiches with Provolone, 54
Smoky Spanish Hunter's Chicken, 65
& Spinach Bread-zagna, 254, *255*
Tomato Turkey "Gravy" with Gnocchi, 46
Turkey & Corn Mexican Casserole, 320
see also porcini; portobello(s)
mussels:
    with Fennel & Garlic, 334
    Romesco Seafood Stew, 225
mustard:
    Apple Honey, 179
    & Brown Sugar BBQ Beef Sandwiches with Celery Slaw, 264, *265*

N

nacho:
    Surprise, Bottom-of-the-Bowl, Pork Tenderloin Posole with, 213
    -Topped Chili Pot, 84
noodle(s):
    Bowls, Hot & Sweet Sliced Steak, 331
    Chicken, Soup, Souped-up Traditional, 100
    Chicken Tetrazzini Casserole with Cauliflower, 200
    Creamy Chicken &, 261
    Egg, Buttered, Roast Turkey, Fennel & Onions with, 319
    Egg, Veal & Pork Meatballs with Mushroom Gravy &, 170, *171*
    Veal Dumplings with Escarole in Broth, 207
North African–style dishes:
    Green Harissa, 167
    Ras el Hanout (Head of the Shop) Spice Blend, 95

North African–style dishes (*cont.*): *see also* Moroccan-style dishes

O

olive(s):
Lemon Chicken, Golden, with Pine Nut Couscous, 14, *15*
Turmeric & Cumin Chicken with Oranges, Chickpea Couscous &, 136
one-pots, *see* stews and one-pots
onion(s):
Adirondack Bacon BBQ Chicken, Apple &, 310, *311*
Peppers &, 272–73
Pork Goulash with Apple &, *192*, 193
Red, Pickled Chiles &, 93
Roast Turkey & Fennel with Buttered Egg Noodles, 319
Sausage & Pepper One-Pot, *80*, 81
Soup, French, –Topped French Bread Pizzas, 217
Soup with Porcini, French, 13
On Top of Ol' Smoky, All Covered with Cheese: Spaghetti & Meatballs, 62
Open-Faced Sausage, 3-Pepper & Mushroom Sandwiches with Provolone, 54
orange(s):
Sauce, Pork with Chiles &, 236
Tequila BBQ Chicken Burritos with Cheddar, Baked Beans & Red Cabbage Slaw, 102
Turmeric & Cumin Chicken with Olives, Chickpea Couscous &, 136
orzo:
Mac 'n' Cheese, Jalapeño Popper, 187
Roasted Butternut Boats Stuffed with Sausage, Toasted Pasta & Rice, 260
Osso Buco with Gremolata, 244, *245*

P

Paella-Style Casserole, 162, *163*
Pancetta-Wrapped Pork Roast with Fennel & Golden Raisin Stuffing, 228
pappardelle:
Drunken, Short Rib Ragu with, 90
Portobello Mushroom, Hot & Sweet Pepper Ragu with, 249
with Pulled Pork, 98

Spinach-Stuffed Braciole in Sunday Sauce with, 48–50, *49*
Paprikash, Veal or Lamb, *132*, 133
Parmigiano-Reggiano cheese:
Cauliflower & Broccoli Gratin Mac 'n' Cheese, 42
Cheesy Croutons, 252
Eggplant Parm Stacks, 70
Green Pastitsio, 91
Herb Stock, 323
Parsnip, Potato & Spinach Casserole with Roasted Mushrooms, 43
Parsley and Basil Pesto, 134
parsnip(s):
Creamy Winter Vegetable Soup, 252
Potato & Spinach Casserole with Roasted Mushrooms, 43
Roasted Root Vegetable Soup with Grilled Cheese Croutons, 127
Vegetable & Dumpling Soup, 60, *61*
pasta:
Asparagus & Pistachio Pesto, 143
Bolognese, Double-Batch Classic, 108
Ceci Sauce with Penne, 120, *121*
Cherry Tomato Fra Diavolo Sauce with Seafood &, 156
Chicken & Mushrooms with Rigatoni, 308
Chinese Spaghetti & Meatballs, 258, *259*
Cincinnati Spaghetti, 301
Deconstructed Arrabbiata, 134, *135*
Drunken Spaghetti with Hot Salami Meat Sauce, 216
e Fagioli with Roasted Garlic, 246
Garden-Style Straw & Hay, with Bagna Cauda, *150*, 151
Green Pastitsio, 91
Linguine with Clam Sauce, 56, *57*
Pappardelle with Pulled Pork, 98
Pastitsio with Lamb & Sausage, 230
Pick-a-Pepper, 313
Poblano Cream Linguine with Shrimp, 330
Pork Ragu with, 8
Portobello & Spinach Bolognese, 89
Portobello Cream Sauce with Whole Wheat Linguine, 33
Portobello Mushroom, Hot & Sweet

Pepper Ragu with Pappardelle, 249
Portobello-Porcini Cacciatore, 19
Pulled Chicken Ragu & Rigatoni, 257
Pumpkin, Penne & Cabbage, *296*, 297
Roasted Pepper & Eggplant Marinara, 128
Roasted Tomato & Roasted Garlic Puttanesca, 113
10-Shallot Spaghetti with Kale, 327
Shells with Veal & Sweet Sausage, 274, *275*
Short Rib Ragu with Drunken Pappardelle, 90
Sloppy Joe 'n' Macaroni Casserole, 208, *209*
Spaghetti with Tuna & Artichokes, 336
Spicy Ziti with Sausage, 329
Spinach-Stuffed Braciole in Sunday Sauce with Pappardelle, 48–50, *49*
Toasted, Roasted Butternut Boats Stuffed with Sausage, Rice &, 260
On Top of Ol' Smoky, All Covered with Cheese: Spaghetti & Meatballs, 62
Turkey & Creamy Mushroom-Tomato "Gravy" with Gnocchi, 46
Turkey Ragu Baked Ziti, 341
Whole-Grain, Mexican-Style Pesto with, 68, *69*
Whole-Grain, Spinach & Artichoke Baked, 52
Ziti with Spinach & Veal, Baked, 59
see also lasagna; mac 'n' cheese
pastitsio:
Green, 91
with Lamb & Sausage, 230
pea(s):
& Potato Soup with Tarragon Pesto, 30
Split, Creamy Chicken Curry with Potatoes &, 331
Split, Soup with Lemon, Greek, 287
Spring Chicken with Carrots &, 147
Vegetable & Dumpling Soup, 60, *61*
pecorino cheese, in Grilled Chicken Caesar Mac, 126

penne:
  Ceci Sauce with, 120, *121*
  Pumpkin & Cabbage, *296, 297*
pepper(s):
  Hot & Sweet, Curry Sauce with
    Chicken, Lamb, or Beef, 267
  Hot & Sweet, Portobello Mushroom
    Ragu with Pappardelle, 249
  Hot & Sweet, Skillet Chicken with,
    329
  Italian Chicken Stoup with Porcini,
    Portobellos &, 176, *177*
  Lamb & Rice Stuffed, 110, *111*
  & Onion, 272–73
  Pick-a-Pepper Pasta, 313
  Quinoa & Vegetable Stuffed, 281
  Ratatouille-Stuffed Jack-o'-Peppers,
    294
  Ratatouille with Poached Eggs &
    Garlic Croutons, 6, *7*
  Red, Roasted, Minestrone, 164
  Risotto-Stuffed Zucchini and, 152
  Roasted, & Eggplant Marinara, 128
  Roasted, Tomato Soup with Garlic,
    Onions &, with Gruyère Croutons,
    288, *289*
  Roasted Vegetable Tabbouleh with
    Yogurt-Tahini Dressing, *282, 283*
  Sausage, 3-Pepper & Mushroom
    Open-Faced Sandwiches with
    Provolone, 54
  Sausage & Onion One-Pot, *80, 81*
  stuffed, guarding against under-
    cooked peppers, 173
  Stuffed, with Broken Meatballs &
    Rice, 173
  Stuffed, with Lamb & Eggplant, 31
  Zucchini & Potato Soup, Spicy, 101
pepper jack cheese:
  Black Bean & Beef Chilaquiles with
    Fried Eggs, 186
  Chicken & Chorizo Spanish Enchila-
    das, 312
  Green Chile Sloppy Josés, 184
  Tex Mex Bacon & Eggs Chilaquiles,
    124, 125
Peppery Oven Fries, 327
pesto:
  Asparagus & Pistachio, 143
  Mexican-Style, 68

Parsley and Basil, 134
  Tarragon, 30
Picada, 202
Pick-a-Pepper Pasta, 313
Pickled Red Onions & Chiles, 93
pies (savory):
  Reuben-Style Shepherd's, 218
  see also potpie(s); tamale pies
Pilaf, Rice, & Chorizo Casserole, 23
Pilgrim Meat Loaf, 210
Pine Nut Couscous, 14, *15*
Piquillo Cream, 340
Pistachio & Asparagus Pesto Pasta, 143
Pizzas, French Bread, French Onion
  Soup–Topped, 217
poblano:
  Cream Linguine with Shrimp, 330
  Mac 'n' Manchego with Corn &
    Mushrooms, 237
  & Pork Green Chili Pot, 77
polenta (cornmeal):
  Beef & Pork Tamale Pie, 129
  Cheesy, 77
  Italian Pork Chili with, 206
  Pork Ragu with, 8
  Pulled Pork with Two-Chile Tamale
    Pie, 182
  Roast Pork Loin with Kale &, 174
  Smoky Spanish Hunter's Chicken,
    65
Polpette, Beef & Pork, Minestra with,
  83
pomegranate:
  Cranberry Relish, 238, *239*
  Cranberry Sauce, 247
porcini:
  Buckwheat Stoup with Beef, Kale
    &, 285
  French Onion Soup with, 13
  Italian Chicken Stoup with Portobel-
    los, Peppers &, 176, *177*
  Portobello Cacciatore, 19
  Risotto Timbale (Sartù), 232–33,
    233
pork:
  & Beef Polpette, Minestra with, 83
  & Beef Tamale Pie, 129
  & Broccoli Rabe Ciabatta Subs with
    Gremolata, *302, 303*
  with Chiles & Orange Sauce, 236

Chili, Italian, with Polenta, 206
Chinese Spaghetti & Meatballs, 258,
  259
Goulash with Apple & Onion, *192,*
  193
Green Chile Sloppy Josés, 184
Loin, Roasted, with Kale & Polenta,
  174
Moroccan Meatballs with Egg,
  94–95, *95*
& Poblano Green Chili Pot, 77
Posole, Red, 93
Pulled, 324
Pulled, Pappardelle with, 98
Pulled, with Two-Chile Tamale Pie,
  182
Ragu, 8
Roast, All-Day, 116
Roast, Prosciutto- or Pancetta-
  Wrapped, with Fennel & Golden
  Raisin Stuffing, 228
Roast Potatoes &, 72
Stew with Ancho Chiles, Savory &
  Sweet, 189
Stuffed Peppers with Broken Meat-
  balls & Rice, 173
Tacos, Braised, 2, *3*
Tenderloin Posole with Bottom-of-
  the-Bowl Nacho Surprise, 213
Thai Ribs & Drumsticks, *154,*
  154–55
On Top of Ol' Smoky, All Covered
  with Cheese: Spaghetti & Meat-
  balls, 62
& Veal Meatballs with Mushroom
  Gravy & Egg Noodles, 170, *171*
portobello(s):
  Celery Slaw, 264, *265*
  Cream Sauce with Whole Wheat
    Linguine, 33
  Hot & Sweet Pepper Ragu with
    Pappardelle, 249
  Italian Chicken Stoup with Porcini,
    Peppers &, 176, *177*
  Meaty Meatless Chili, 53
  Open-Faced Sausage, 3-Pepper
    & Mushroom Sandwiches with
    Provolone, 54
  Porcini Cacciatore, 19
  & Spinach Bolognese, 89

Portuguese Fish Supper, 26, *27*
posole:
    Pork Tenderloin, with Bottom-of-the-
      Bowl Nacho Surprise, 213
    Red Pork, 93
potato(es):
    Bonnie's Italian Stew, 269
    Creamy Winter Vegetable Soup,
      252
    German Roast Chicken &, with
      Sauerkraut, 337
    Horseradish Mash, 333
    Mashed, 227
    Parsnip & Spinach Casserole with
      Roasted Mushrooms, 43
    & Peas Soup with Tarragon Pesto, 30
    Peppery Oven Fries, 327
    Reuben-Style Shepherd's Pie, 218
    Roasted Chicken Dinner with
      Artichokes &, on a Bed of Crispy
      Kale, 157
    Roast Pork &, 72
    Vegetable & Dumpling Soup, 60, *61*
    Zucchini & Pepper Soup, Spicy, 101
potpie(s):
    Corn & Crab Chowder, 73
    Drop Biscuit Chicken, 12
    Toppers, Creamy Chicken & Mush-
      room One-Pot with, 79
Pot Roast, Italian, 34, *35*
Potted Beef & Celery Root with Celery
    Gremolata, 278
prosciutto:
    Stuffed Chicken Saltimbocca, 161
    -Wrapped Pork Roast with Fennel &
      Golden Raisin Stuffing, 228
Provolone, Open-Faced Sausage,
    3-Pepper & Mushroom Sandwiches
    with, 54
puff pastry:
    Corn & Crab Chowder Potpies, 73
    Creamy Chicken & Mushroom One-
      Pot with Potpie Toppers, 79
pulled chicken:
    Buffalo BBQ, with Blue Cheese Corn
      Bread Topper, 102, *103*
    Ragu & Rigatoni, 257
Pulled Pork, 324
    Pappardelle with, 98
    with Two-Chile Tamale Pie, 182

Pumpernickel Grilled Cheese Croutons,
    295
pumpkin:
    Lovers' Lasagna, 196, *197*
    Penne & Cabbage, *296*, 297
    Sausage & Arborio Soup, 172
    see also squash (winter)
Pumpkin Seed Sauce, Chicken in, 235
Puttanesca, Roasted Tomato & Roasted
    Garlic, 113

Q

queso fresco, in Braised Pork Tacos, 2, *3*
Quinoa & Vegetable Stuffed Peppers,
    281

R

ragu:
    Lamb, 106
    Pork, 8
    Portobello Mushroom, Hot & Sweet
      Pepper, 249
    Pulled Chicken, 257
    Short Rib, 90
    Turkey, 341
Raisin, Golden, & Fennel Stuffing, 228
Raita, Green, 199
Ranch Dressing, Blue Cheese, 304
Ras el Hanout (Head of the Shop) Spice
    Blend, 95
ratatouille:
    with Poached Eggs & Garlic Crou-
      tons, 6, *7*
    -Stuffed Jack-o'-Peppers, 294
Red Cabbage Slaw, 201
Red Pork Posole, 93
Red Sauce, Genovese, 266
Red Snapper Livornese, 339
red wine:
    Drunken Chicken, 268
    Drunken Spaghetti with Hot Salami
      Meat Sauce, 216
    Ruby Port–Braised Short Ribs &
      Mashed Potatoes, 227
    Short Rib Ragu with Drunken Pap-
      pardelle, 90
    Sicilian Glaze, 159
    Zinfully Delicious Short Ribs, 86, *87*
Refried Bean Dip, 184
Reuben-Style Shepherd's Pie, 218

ribs:
    Thai Drumsticks &, *154*, 154–55
    see also short rib(s)
rice:
    Arborio, Sausage & Pumpkin Soup,
      172
    Cake, Cheesy, Stuffed with Herbs &
      Greens, 271
    Chicken &, Soup, Spanish, 51
    Chicken Enchiladas, 188, *189*
    Green, 305
    & Lamb Stuffed Peppers, 110, *111*
    Lentil, 250, *251*
    Mexican, *140*, 141
    Paella-Style Casserole, 162, *163*
    Pilaf & Chorizo Casserole, 23
    Risotto-Stuffed Peppers & Zucchini,
      152
    Risotto Timbale (Sartù), 232–33,
      233
    Roasted Butternut Boats Stuffed with
      Sausage, Toasted Pasta &, 260
    Stuffed Peppers with Broken Meat-
      balls &, 173
ricotta (cheese):
    Eggplant & Zucchini Roll-ups, 276,
      277
    Lazy Lasagna with Lamb Ragu,
      Spinach &, 106
    Roasted Eggplant Filling, Lasagna
      with, 262
    Stuffed Chicken Saltimbocca, 161
rigatoni:
    Chicken & Mushrooms with, 308
    Pulled Chicken Ragu &, 257
risotto:
    -Stuffed Peppers & Zucchini, 152
    Timbale (Sartù), 232–33, *233*
roast(ed):
    Chicken Dinner with Potatoes &
      Artichokes on a Bed of Crispy
      Kale, 157
    Chicken Dinner with Roasted Garlic,
      18
    Chicken & Potatoes with Sauerkraut,
      German, 337
    Pork, All-Day, 116
    Pork, Prosciutto- or Pancetta-
      Wrapped, with Fennel & Golden
      Raisin Stuffing, 228

Pork & Potatoes, 72
Pork Loin with Kale & Polenta, 174
Turkey Breast, Brined, 40, *41*
Turkey Breast with Creamy Gravy &
    Cranberry-Pomegranate Sauce, 247
Romesco Seafood Stew, 225
Root Vegetable, Roasted, Soup with
    Grilled Cheese Croutons, 127
Ruby Port–Braised Short Ribs &
    Mashed Potatoes, 227
Russian Dressing, 218

S
Sage Derby Mac 'n' Cheese with Ham,
    309
salads:
    Caesar Bread, & Chicken Thighs,
        339
    Caprese, Hot & Sweet, 38
    Celery Slaw, 264, *265*
    with Dijon Vinaigrette, 217
    Guac, 187
    Red Cabbage Slaw, 201
Salami Meat Sauce, Hot, Drunken
    Spaghetti with, 216
Salmon Burgers with Horseradish
    Cream, 337
Salsa-Marinated Chicken with Mexican
    Rice, *140*, 141
Saltimbocca, Stuffed Chicken, 161
sandwiches:
    Adirondack Bacon BBQ Chicken,
        Apples & Onion, 310, *311*
    Apple & Cheddar Melts, 243
    Buffalo Turkey Sloppy Joes with Blue
        Cheese Ranch Dressing, 304
    Cold Chicken Curry Sammies with
        Toasted Almonds & Crystallized
        Ginger, 222
    Green Chile Sloppy Josés, 184
    Grilled Cheddar, Bacon & Apple–
        Honey Mustard, 179
    Hot Open-Faced Creamed Chicken
        with Tarragon over Buttered Toast,
        220, 221
    Italian Barbecued Beef, 38
    Minute Steak Hoagies with Home-
        made Steak Sauce, *74*, 75
    Mustard & Brown Sugar BBQ Beef,
        with Celery Slaw, 264, *265*

Open-Faced Sausage, 3-Pepper &
    Mushroom, with Provolone, 54
Pork & Broccoli Rabe Ciabatta Subs
    with Gremolata, *302*, 303
Sartù (Risotto Timbale), 232–33,
    233
sauces:
    Béchamel, 230
    Cherry Tomato Fra Diavolo, 156
    Chili, Sweet & Sour, 155
    Chimichurri, 16
    Cranberry-Pomegranate, 247
    Enchilada, 188
    Horseradish, 194
    Horseradish Cream, 337
    Hot & Sweet Pepper Curry, 267
    Mint & Shallot, 25
    Picada, 202
    Piquillo Cream, 340
    Red, Genovese, 266
    Romesco, 225
    Steak, Homemade, 75
    Tomato, 134
    see also BBQ sauces; Bolognese;
        marinara; pesto; ragu
sauerkraut:
    German Roast Chicken & Potatoes
        with, 337
    Reuben-Style Shepherd's Pie, 218
sausage(s):
    Andouille & Roasted Squash Gumbo,
        290
    & Braciole in Sunday Gravy with
        Peppers & Onion, 272–73
    & Broccoli Rabe Stoup, 22
    Italian Pork Chili with Polenta, 206
    Kale & Lentil Soup, 112
    Knocks & Beans Supreme, 58
    Lentil Soup with Kale &, 191, 335
    Pastitsio with Lamb &, 230
    Pepper & Onion One-Pot, *80*, 81
    Pumpkin & Arborio Soup, 172
    Roasted Butternut Boats Stuffed with
        Toasted Pasta, Rice &, 260
    Sartù (Risotto Timbale), 232–33,
        233
    Spicy Ziti with, 329
    Sunday Sauce, 48–50
    Sweet, Pasta Shells with Veal &,
        274, *275*

3-Pepper & Mushroom Open-Faced
    Sandwiches with Provolone, 54
see also chorizo
seafood:
    Cherry Tomato Fra Diavolo Sauce
        with Pasta &, 156
    Clam Sauce, Linguine with, 56, *57*
    Crab & Corn Chowder Potpies, 73
    Mussels with Fennel & Garlic, 334
    Seasoning Paste, Fresh, 56
    Stew, Romesco, 225
    see also fish; shrimp
shallot(s):
    & Mint Sauce, 25
    10-Shallot Spaghetti with Kale,
        327
Shepherd's Pie, Reuben-Style, 218
short rib(s):
    Beef & Broccoli, 137
    Ragu with Drunken Pappardelle, 90
    Ruby Port–Braised, & Mashed
        Potatoes, 227
    Southern Italian–Style, 131
    Zinfully Delicious, 86, *87*
shrimp:
    Louisiana-Style, 10, *11*
    Paella-Style Casserole, 162, *163*
    Poblano Cream Linguine with, 330
    Romesco Seafood Stew, 225
Sicilian Glaze, Easy-Brine Chicken
    Breasts with, 159
sides:
    Arugula & Tomatoes with Garlic
        Bread Crumbs, 161
    Bacon & Brussels Sprouts Mac 'n'
        Cheese, 316, *317*
    Baked Beans, 201
    Broccoli & Cauliflower Gratin Mac 'n'
        Cheese, 42
    Chard, Sautéed, 117
    Chickpea Couscous, 136
    Farro, Kale & White Beans, 338
    Fries, Peppery Oven, 327
    Horseradish Mash, 333
    Lentil Rice, 250, *251*
    Parsnip, Potato & Spinach Casserole
        with Roasted Mushrooms, 43
    Peppers & Onion, 272–73
    Pine Nut Couscous, 14, *15*
    Polenta, Cheesy, 77

sides (*cont.*):
  Pomegranate-Cranberry Relish, 238, *239*
  Potatoes, Mashed, 227
  Red Cabbage Slaw, 201
  Rice, Green, 305
  Rice, Mexican, *140*, 141
  Spinach, Wilted, 333
  Sweet Potatoes, Mashed Citrus, 117
  Zucchini Couscous, 5
Skillet Chicken with Hot & Sweet Peppers, 329
slaws:
  Celery, 264, *265*
  Red Cabbage, 201
Sloppy Joe(s):
  Buffalo Turkey, with Blue Cheese Ranch Dressing, 304
  'n' Macaroni Casserole, 208, *209*
Sloppy Josés, Green Chile, 184
Smoky Chicken & Cider, 96
Smoky Corn Chowder, 292
Smoky Spanish Hunter's Chicken, 65
soups:
  Apple & Celery Root, Creamy, 179
  Bean & Bacon, Mediterranean, 223
  Bloody Mary, with Pumpernickel Grilled Cheese Croutons, 295
  Carrot, Sweet Potato & Squash, 315
  Cauliflower, with Anchovy–Bread Crumb Topping, 291
  Chicken & Mushroom One-Pot, Creamy, 79
  Chicken & Rice, Spanish, 51
  Chicken Noodle, Souped-up Traditional, 100
  Chickpea, with Roasted Cauliflower, 333
  Escarole, with Caesar Croutons, 142
  Ginger-Soy Carrot, 44, *45*
  Lentil, Curry, Fleuri's, 37
  Lentil, with Kale & Sausage, 191
  Lentil, with Sausage & Kale, 335
  Minestra with Beef & Pork Polpette, 83
  Minestrone, Hearty & Healthy 3-Bean, 64
  Minestrone, Roasted Red Pepper, 164
  Mulligatawny with Green Raita, 199
  Onion, French, French Bread Pizzas Topped with, 217

Onion, French, with Porcini, 13
Pasta e Fagioli with Roasted Garlic, 246
Peas & Potato, with Tarragon Pesto, 30
Root Vegetable, Roasted, with Grilled Cheese Croutons, 127
Sausage, Kale & Lentil, 112
Sausage, Pumpkin & Arborio, 172
Split Pea, with Lemon, Greek, 287
Squash, Curried, 243
Steak, Sliced, & Barley, Mexican, 284
Tomato, with Roasted Peppers, Garlic & Onions with Gruyère Croutons, 288, *289*
Tortilla, Jane Fox's Famous, 253
Vegetable & Dumpling, 60, *61*
Winter Vegetable, Creamy, 252
Yellow Tomato Gazpacho with Toasted Almond Bread Crumbs, 149
Zucchini, Pepper & Potato, Spicy, 101
  see also chowder(s); stoups
Sour Cream & Leek Frittata, 335
Southern Italian–Style Short Ribs, 131
Soy-Ginger Carrot Soup, 44, *45*
spaghetti:
  Cincinnati, 301
  Drunken, with Hot Salami Meat Sauce, 216
  & Meatballs, Chinese, 258, *259*
  & Meatballs: On Top of Ol' Smoky, All Covered with Cheese, 62
  10-Shallot, with Kale, 327
  with Tuna & Artichokes, 336
Spaghetti Squash, Spicy Roasted-Tomato Marinara with, 66, *67*
Spanish-style dishes:
  Catalan Chicken Stew, 202, *203*
  Chicken & Chorizo Enchiladas, 312
  Chicken & Rice Soup, 51
  Paella-Style Casserole, 162, *163*
  Picada, 202
  Romesco Seafood Stew, 225
  Sliced Skirt Steak with Piquillo Cream & Tomato Salad, 340
  Smoky Hunter's Chicken, 65
  Yellow Tomato Gazpacho with

Toasted Almond Bread Crumbs, 149
spice blends:
  Hot Curry, 144
  Mexi-Rub, 185
  Ras el Hanout (Head of the Shop), 95
  Za'atar, 167
spinach:
  & Artichoke Baked Whole-Grain Pasta, 52
  Baked Ziti with Veal &, 59
  Curry Lentil Soup, Fleuri's, 37
  Green Harissa, 167
  Lazy Lasagna with Lamb Ragu, Ricotta &, 106
  & Mushroom Bread-zagna, 254, *255*
  Parsnip & Potato Casserole with Roasted Mushrooms, 43
  pasta, in Garden-Style Straw & Hay Pasta with Bagna Cauda, *150*, 151
  & Portobello Bolognese, 89
  -Stuffed Braciole in Sunday Sauce with Pappardelle, 48–50, *49*
  Stuffed Eggplant with Veal &, 36
  Wilted, 333
split pea(s):
  Creamy Chicken Curry with Potatoes &, 331
  Soup with Lemon, Greek, 287
Spring Chicken with Carrots & Peas, 147
squash (winter):
  Carrot & Sweet Potato Soup, 315
  & Eggplant Curry, 104, *105*
  Roasted, & Andouille Gumbo, 290
  Soup, Curried, 243
  Spaghetti, Spicy Roasted-Tomato Marinara with, 66, *67*
  see also butternut squash; pumpkin
steak:
  Drunken, with Peppery Oven Fries, 327
  Hot & Sweet Sliced, Noodle Bowls, 331
  Minute, Hoagies with Homemade Steak Sauce, *74*, 75
  Skirt, Spanish Sliced, with Piquillo Cream & Tomato Salad, 340
  Sliced, & Barley Soup, Mexican, 284
Steak Sauce, Homemade, 75

stews and one-pots:
Andouille & Roasted Squash Gumbo, 290
BBQ Turkey or Chicken Gumbo, 318
Beef Stew Scented with Horseradish, 180, *181*
Black Pepper Beef, 169
Bonnie's Italian Stew, 269
Calabrese Chicken One-Pot, 76
Catalan Chicken Stew, 202, *203*
Creamy Chicken & Mushroom One-Pot with Potpie Toppers, 79
Eggplant & Squash Curry, 104, *105*
Eight-Spice Squash & Chicken Thigh Stew with Lentil Rice, 250, *251*
French Stewed Chicken Thighs, 224
Halloween Ground Meat Ghoul-ash, 299
Moroccan Meatballs with Egg, 94–95, *95*
Pork Goulash with Apple & Onion, *192*, 193
Portuguese Fish Supper, 26, *27*
Potted Beef & Celery Root with Celery Gremolata, 278
Red Pork Posole, 93
Romesco Seafood Stew, 225
Sausage, Pepper & Onion One-Pot, *80*, 81
Savory & Sweet Pork Stew with Ancho Chiles, 139
Skillet Chicken with Hot & Sweet Peppers, 329
Smoky Chicken & Cider, 96
Spring Chicken with Carrots & Peas, 147
Veal or Lamb Paprikash, *132*, 133
Vindaloo of Chicken, 144, *145*
see also casseroles; chili; mac 'n' cheese; potpie(s); stoups; tamale pies
Stock, Parmigiano-Herb, 323
stoups:
Buckwheat, with Porcini, Beef & Kale, 285
Chicken, Italian, with Porcini, Portobellos & Peppers, 176, *177*
Lentil, with Mushrooms, 158
Sausage & Broccoli Rabe, 22
Strata, Mexican Chorizo, 214, *215*

stuffing:
Fennel & Golden Raisin, 228
Turkey, Meat Loaves, 88
Subs, Pork & Broccoli Rabe Ciabatta, with Gremolata, *302*, 303
Sunday sauce or gravy:
Braciole & Sausages in, with Peppers & Onion, 272–73
Spinach-Stuffed Braciole in, with Pappardelle, 48–50, *49*
Sweet & Sour Chili Sauce, 155
sweet potato(es):
Carrot & Squash Soup, 315
Mashed Citrus, 117
Roasted Root Vegetable Soup with Grilled Cheese Croutons, 127
Swiss chard, see *chard*
Swiss cheese:
Crab Cake Mac 'n' Cheese, 4
Green Chile Sloppy Josés, 184
Reuben-Style Shepherd's Pie, 218
Roast Chicken Enchiladas Suizas Stacked Casserole, 20, *21*
see also Gruyère cheese

T

Tabbouleh, Roasted Vegetable, with Yogurt Tahini Dressing, 282, *283*
Tacos, Braised Pork, 2, *3*
Tahini-Yogurt Dressing, 282
tamale pies:
Beef & Pork, 129
Pulled Pork with Two-Chile, 182
Tarragon Pesto, 30
Tequila-Orange BBQ Chicken Burritos with Cheddar, Baked Beans & Red Cabbage Slaw, 102
Tetrazzini, Chicken, Casserole with Cauliflower, 200
Tex-Mex–style dishes:
Bacon & Eggs Chilaquiles, *124*, 125
Black Bean & Beef Chilaquiles with Fried Eggs, 186
Chicken Enchiladas, 188, *189*
Green Chile Sloppy Josés, 184
Jalapeño Popper Orzo Mac 'n' Cheese, 187
Mexican Brisket 'n' Biscuits, 185
see also Mexican-style dishes
Thai Ribs & Drumsticks, *154*, 154–55

3-Bean Minestrone, Hearty & Healthy, 64
Timbale, Risotto (Sartù), 232–33, *233*
tomato(es):
& Arugula with Garlic Bread Crumbs, 161
Bloody Mary Soup with Pumpernickel Grilled Cheese Croutons, 295
Broiled, Chicken with Ham, Mozzarella &, 341
Cherry, Fra Diavolo Sauce with Seafood & Pasta, 156
cherry, halving quickly, 156
Guac Salad, 187
Moroccan Meatballs with Egg, 94–95, *95*
Mushroom Turkey "Gravy" with Gnocchi, 46
Ratatouille with Poached Eggs & Garlic Croutons, 6, *7*
Roasted, 323
Roasted, & Roasted Garlic Puttanesca, 113
Roasted, Marinara, Spicy, with Spaghetti Squash, 66, *67*
Roasted Pepper & Eggplant Marinara, 128
Sauce, 134
Soup with Roasted Peppers, Garlic & Onions with Gruyère Croutons, 288, *289*
Sunday Sauce, 48–50
Yellow, Gazpacho with Toasted Almond Bread Crumbs, 149
tortilla(s):
Black Bean & Beef Chilaquiles with Fried Eggs, 186
Braised Pork Tacos, 2, *3*
Chicken & Chorizo Spanish Enchiladas, 312
Chicken Enchiladas, 188, *189*
chips, in Nacho Topped Chili Pot, 84
chips, in Pork Tenderloin Posole with Bottom-of-the-Bowl Nacho Surprise, 213
Roast Chicken Enchiladas Suizas Stacked Casserole, 20, *21*
Soup, Jane Fox's Famous, 253

tortilla(s) (cont.):
 Tequila-Orange BBQ Chicken Burritos with Cheddar, Baked Beans & Red Cabbage Slaw, 102
 Tex-Mex Bacon & Eggs Chilaquiles, *124*, 125
 Turkey, Mushroom & Corn Mexican Casserole, 320
Touchdown Chili, 242
Tuna, Spaghetti with Artichokes &, 336
turkey:
 Ancho-Chipotle Chile, 122
 BBQ, Gumbo, 318
 Breast, Chipotle, with Pomegranate-Cranberry Relish & Polenta, 238, *239*
 Breast, Roasted, with Creamy Gravy & Cranberry-Pomegranate Sauce, 247
 Breast, Roasted Brined, 40, *41*
 Buffalo, Sloppy Joes with Blue Cheese Ranch Dressing, 304
 & Creamy Mushroom-Tomato "Gravy" with Gnocchi, 46
 & Mexican Chorizo Chili, 240
 Mini Meat Loaves, Chipotle BBQ, 195
 Mushroom & Corn Mexican Casserole, 320
 Pilgrim Meat Loaf, 210
 Ragu Baked Ziti, 341
 Roast, Fennel & Onions with Buttered Egg Noodles, 319
 Stuffing Meat Loaves, 88
Turmeric & Cumin Chicken with Oranges, Olives & Chickpea Couscous, 136

V
veal:
 Baked Ziti with Spinach &, 59

Double-Batch Classic Bolognese, 108
Dumplings with Escarole in Broth, 207
Genovese Red Sauce, 266
Osso Buco with Gremolata, 244, *245*
Paprikash, *132*, 133
Pasta e Fagioli with Roasted Garlic, 246
Pasta Shells with Sweet Sausage &, 274, *275*
& Pork Meatballs with Mushroom Gravy & Egg Noodles, 170, *171*
Spinach-Stuffed Braciole in Sunday Sauce with Pappardelle, 48–50, *49*
Stuffed Eggplant with Spinach &, 36
Stuffed Peppers with Broken Meatballs & Rice, 173
vegetable(s):
 & Dumpling Soup, 60, *61*
 Roasted, Tabbouleh with Yogurt-Tahini Dressing, 282, *283*
 Root, Roasted, Soup with Grilled Cheese Croutons, 127
 Winter, Soup, Creamy, 252
 see also sides; *specific vegetables*
V8 vegetable juice, in Bloody Mary Soup with Pumpernickel Grilled Cheese Croutons, 295
Vinaigrette, Dijon, 217
Vindaloo of Chicken, 144, *145*

W
white beans:
 Farro, Kale &, 338
 see also cannellini beans
white wine:
 Genovese Red Sauce, 266
 Winter White Coq au Vin, 231

whole wheat or whole-grain pasta:
 Ceci Sauce with Penne, 120, *121*
 Grilled Chicken Caesar Mac, 126
 Mexican-Style Pesto with, 68, *69*
 Portobello Cream Sauce with Linguine, 33
 Portobello & Spinach Bolognese, 89
 Spinach & Artichoke Baked, 52
wine, *see* red wine; white wine
Winter Vegetable Soup, Creamy, 252
Winter White Coq au Vin, 231
Worcestershire-Maple Gravy, 40

Y
Yellow Tomato Gazpacho with Toasted Almond Bread Crumbs, 149
yogurt:
 Green Raita, 199
 Tahini Dressing, 282

Z
Za'atar Spice Blend, 167
Zinfully Delicious Short Ribs, 86, *87*
ziti:
 Spicy, with Sausage, 329
 Turkey Ragu Baked, 341
zucchini:
 Couscous, 5
 & Eggplant Roll-ups, 276, *277*
 Moroccan Meatballs with Egg, 94–95, *95*
 Pepper & Potato Soup, Spicy, 101
 Quinoa & Vegetable Stuffed Peppers, 281
 Ratatouille-Stuffed Jack-o'-Peppers, 294
 Ratatouille with Poached Eggs & Garlic Croutons, 6, *7*
 Risotto-Stuffed Peppers and, 152
 Roasted Vegetable Tabbouleh with Yogurt-Tahini Dressing, 282, *283*

Scan here for even more
Week in a Day recipes!